Simon Stone

A Silent-Speech Interface using Electro-Optical Stomatography

TUDpress

Studientexte zur Sprachkommunikation
Hg. von Rüdiger Hoffmann
ISSN 0940-6832
Bd. 102

Simon Stone

A Silent-Speech Interface using Electro-Optical Stomatography

TUDpress
2021

Supplemental Materials can be downloaded using the following code

Bibliografische Information der Deutschen Nationalbibliothek
Die Deutsche Nationalbibliothek verzeichnet diese Publikation in der Deutschen Nationalbibliografie; detaillierte bibliografische Daten sind im Internet über http://dnb.d-nb.de abrufbar.

Bibliographic information published by the Deutsche Nationalbibliothek
The Deutsche Nationalbibliothek lists this publication in the Deutsche Nationalbibliografie; detailed bibliographic data are available in the Internet at http://dnb.d-nb.de.

ISBN 978-3-95908-457-4

D-01309 Dresden
Tel.: +49 351 4721463
http://www.tudpress.de

TUDpress ist ein Imprint von Thelem

Gesetzt von den Herausgebern.
Printed in Germany.

Technische Universität Dresden

A Silent-Speech Interface using Electro-Optical Stomatography

Dipl.-Ing.

Simon Stone

Von der Fakultät Elektrotechnik und Informationstechnik der Technischen Universität Dresden

zur Erlangung des akademischen Grades

Doktoringenieur

(Dr.-Ing.)

genehmigte Dissertation

Vorsitzender:	Prof. Dr.-Ing. habil. Hagen Malberg (TU Dresden)
1. Gutachter:	Prof. Dr.-Ing. Peter Birkholz (TU Dresden)
2. Gutachter:	Prof. Dr. rer. nat. habil. Gerhard Weber (TU Dresden)
3. Gutachter:	Prof. Pascal Perrier, PhD (Université Grenoble Alpes/Grenoble INP)

Tag der Einreichung: 22.10.2020
Tag der Verteidigung: 27.09.2021

Statement of authorship

I hereby certify that I have authored this document entitled *A Silent-Speech Interface using Electro-Optical Stomatography* independently and without undue assistance from third parties. No other than the resources and references indicated in this document have been used. I have marked both literal and accordingly adopted quotations as such. During the preparation of this document I was only supported by the following persons:

Prof. Dr.-Ing. Peter Birkholz

Additional persons were not involved in the intellectual preparation of the present document. I am aware that violations of this declaration may lead to subsequent withdrawal of the academic degree.

Dresden, 22nd October 2020

Simon Stone

Faculty of Electrical and Computer Engineering Institute of Acoustics and Speech Communication

Chair of Speech Technology and Cognitive Systems

Abstract

Speech technology is a major and growing industry that enriches the lives of technologically-minded people in a number of ways. Many potential users are, however, excluded: Namely, all speakers who cannot easily or even at all produce speech. Silent-Speech Interfaces offer a way to communicate with a machine by a convenient speech recognition interface without the need for acoustic speech. They also can potentially provide a full replacement voice by synthesizing the intended utterances that are only silently articulated by the user. To that end, the speech movements need to be captured and mapped to either text or acoustic speech. This dissertation proposes a new Silent-Speech Interface based on a newly developed measurement technology called Electro-Optical Stomatography and a novel parametric vocal tract model to facilitate real-time speech synthesis based on the measured data. The hardware was used to conduct command word recognition studies reaching state-of-the-art intra- and inter-individual performance. Furthermore, a study on using the hardware to control the vocal tract model in a direct articulation-to-speech synthesis loop was also completed. While the intelligibility of synthesized vowels was high, the intelligibility of consonants and connected speech was quite poor. Promising ways to improve the system are discussed in the outlook.

Zusammenfassung

Sprachtechnologie ist eine große und wachsende Industrie, die das Leben von technologieinteressierten Nutzern auf zahlreichen Wegen bereichert. Viele potenzielle Nutzer werden jedoch ausgeschlossen: Nämlich alle Sprecher, die nur schwer oder sogar gar nicht Sprache produzieren können. Silent-Speech Interfaces bieten einen Weg, mit Maschinen durch ein bequemes sprachgesteuertes Interface zu kommunizieren ohne dafür akustische Sprache zu benötigen. Sie können außerdem prinzipiell eine Ersatzstimme stellen, indem sie die intendierten Äußerungen, die der Nutzer nur still artikuliert, künstlich synthetisieren. Diese Dissertation stellt ein neues Silent-Speech Interface vor, das auf einem neu entwickelten Messsystem namens Elektro-Optischer Stomatografie und einem neuartigen parametrischen Vokaltraktmodell basiert, das die Echtzeitsynthese von Sprache basierend auf den gemessenen Daten ermöglicht. Mit der Hardware wurden Studien zur Einzelworterkennung durchgeführt, die den Stand der Technik in der intra- und inter-individuellen Genauigkeit erreichten und übertrafen. Darüber hinaus wurde eine Studie abgeschlossen, in der die Hardware zur Steuerung des Vokaltraktmodells in einer direkten Artikulation-zu-Sprache-Synthese verwendet wurde. Während die Verständlichkeit der Synthese von Vokalen sehr hoch eingeschätzt wurde, ist die Verständlichkeit von Konsonanten und kontinuierlicher Sprache sehr schlecht. Vielversprechende Möglichkeiten zur Verbesserung des Systems werden im Ausblick diskutiert.

Contents

Statement of authorship iii

Abstract v

List of Figures vii

List of Tables xi

Acronyms xiii

1. Introduction 1
- 1.1. The concept of a Silent-Speech Interface 4
- 1.2. Structure of this work 4

2. Fundamentals of phonetics 7
- 2.1. Components of the human speech production system 7
- 2.2. Vowel sounds 9
- 2.3. Consonantal sounds 10
- 2.4. Acoustic properties of speech sounds 15
- 2.5. Coarticulation 18
- 2.6. Phonotactics 19
- 2.7. Summary and implications for the design of a Silent-Speech Interface (SSI) 21

3. Articulatory data acquisition techniques in Silent-Speech Interfaces 25
- 3.1. Introduction 25
- 3.2. Scope of the literature review 27
- 3.3. Video Recordings 27
- 3.4. Ultrasonography 30
- 3.5. Electromyography 34
- 3.6. Permanent-Magnetic Articulography 41
- 3.7. Electromagnetic Articulography 44
- 3.8. Radio waves 47
- 3.9. Palatography 49
- 3.10. Conclusion and Discussion 52

4. Electro-Optical Stomatography 55
- 4.1. Contact sensors 55
- 4.2. Optical distance sensors 57
- 4.3. Lip sensor 81

4.4. Sensor Unit . . . 84
4.5. Control Unit . . . 89
4.6. Software . . . 93

5. Articulation-to-Text **99**
5.1. Introduction . . . 99
5.2. Command word recognition pilot study . . . 99
5.3. Command word recognition small-scale study . . . 102

6. Articulation-to-Speech **109**
6.1. Introduction . . . 109
6.2. Articulatory synthesis . . . 109
6.3. The six point vocal tract model . . . 113
6.4. Objective evaluation of the vocal tract model . . . 116
6.5. Perceptual evaluation of the vocal tract model . . . 120
6.6. Direct synthesis using EOS to control the vocal tract model . . . 125
6.7. Pitch and voicing . . . 132

7. Summary and outlook **145**
7.1. Summary of the contributions . . . 145
7.2. Outlook . . . 146

A. Overview of the International Phonetic Alphabet **151**

B. Mathematical proofs and derivations **153**
B.1. Combinatoric calculations illustrating the reduction of possible syllables using phonotactics . . . 153
B.2. Signal Averaging . . . 155
B.3. Effect of the contact sensor area on the conductance . . . 155
B.4. Calculation of the forward current for the OP280V diode . . . 155

C. Schematics and layouts **157**
C.1. Schematics of the control unit. . . . 158
C.2. Layout of the control unit . . . 163
C.3. Bill of materials of the control unit . . . 164
C.4. Schematics of the sensor unit . . . 165
C.5. Layout of the sensor unit . . . 166
C.6. Bill of materials of the sensor unit . . . 167

D. Sensor unit assembly **169**

E. Firmware flow and data protocol **177**

F. Palate file format **181**

G. Supplemental material regarding the vocal tract model **183**

H. Articulation-to-Speech: Optimal hyperparameters **189**

Bibliography **191**

List of Figures

1.1. Size of the speech recognition market worldwide from 2015 to 2024 2
1.2. General framework of a Silent-Speech Interface 5

2.1. Schematic view of the human vocal tract and places of articulation 9
2.2. Articulatory and acoustic vowel spaces 11
2.3. Example articulations of [m], [n], and [ŋ] 12
2.4. Example articulations of [p|b], [t|d], and [g|k] 12
2.5. Example articulations of [f|v], [s|z], [ʃ|ʒ], [ç|ʝ], and [x|ʁ] 13
2.6. Example articulations of [w], [ɹ], and [j] 14
2.7. Example articulation of [l] 15
2.8. Excitation spectrum (source), vocal tract transfer function (filter), and spectrum of the signal at the lips 16
2.9. Spectrograms of /a/, /i/, and /u/ 16
2.10. Example spectrograms of voiced versus voiceless minimal pairs 17
2.11. Voice Onset Time (VOT) of voiced and unvoiced stops 18

3.1. Example codebook of binary mouth images 28
3.2. The Lip Reading in the Wild corpus 29
3.3. Example sonogram of the tongue 31
3.4. The head and ultrasound transducer support system 31
3.5. The Ouisper system 32
3.6. Typical action potential 34
3.7. Intramuscular versus Surface EMG 36
3.8. Sugie & Tsunoda's state transition diagram 37
3.9. Sensor setups in sEMG-based SSI 40
3.10. PMA setups 42
3.11. A subject using an EMA system 45
3.12. Setups for HF-based SSIs 48
3.13. Comparison of various EPG-palates 50
3.14. Distribution of the research topics covered by EPG studies 51

4.1. Components of the proposed EOS system 56
4.2. Simplified equivalent circuit of the contact sensor measurement 56
4.3. Contact sensor arrangement 57
4.4. Principle of optical distance sensing 58
4.5. Optical sensor components 59
4.6. Circuitry surrounding the optical components 59
4.7. Basic tongue distance spacer configuration 60

4.8. Reflectors used in the spacer study . . . 61
4.9. Reference setup in the spacer study . . . 62
4.10. Setup of the spacer comparison study . . . 62
4.11. Sampled characteristics using four spacer configurations . . . 63
4.12. Sensor characteristics for different detector gains . . . 64
4.13. Effect of the gap between emitter and receiver on the distance sensing function . . . 64
4.14. Characteristic of the OP280V VCSEL diode at different forward currents . . . 66
4.15. Fit and evaluation of the analytic distance sensing function . . . 67
4.16. Fit and evaluation of the regression-based, piece-wise distance sensing function . . . 69
4.17. Vowel tongue shapes from optical distance sensor data using regression-based calibration . . . 71
4.18. Principal geometry of the optical distance measurement setup . . . 72
4.19. Photo of the tongue's radiance when reflecting a light dot . . . 74
4.20. Brightness profiles of a light spot on the tongue . . . 74
4.21. Geometry of *in-vivo* measurements translated to a model scene . . . 76
4.22. Simulated irradiance versus measured sensor output at three different detector positions and different reflector distances . . . 77
4.23. Normalized irradiance, impulse response and radiance of the tongue surface for three reflector angles . . . 77
4.24. Simulated irradiance versus measured sensor output at three different detector positions and different reflector angles . . . 78
4.25. Ratio of the irradiance at the posterior detector E_{D_p} to the irradiance at the anterior detector E_{D_a}. . . . 79
4.26. Ratio of measured to true distances using model data . . . 79
4.27. Ratio of measured to true distances using subject data . . . 80
4.28. Vowel tongue shapes from optical distance sensor data using angle-corrected calibration . . . 81
4.29. Examples for the lip sensor output using the single detector design . . . 82
4.30. Schematic description of the ambiguity inherent to the single detector design . . . 82
4.31. Schematic description of the single-source, dual-detector design . . . 83
4.32. Schematic description of the dual-source, dual-detector design . . . 84
4.33. Palate dimensions measured in a large-scale study . . . 86
4.34. Circuit boards carrying the sensors . . . 88
4.35. Thermoformed base plate of the sensor unit . . . 89
4.36. Assembled sensor units . . . 90
4.37. Filter response of the reference voltage output filter for the contact sensor measurements . . . 92
4.38. Timing of a single complete sensor unit scan . . . 94
4.39. Graphical User Interface of the EOS Workbench . . . 95
4.40. Screenshots of the Vocal Tract Visualization Tool . . . 96
4.41. The tongue-controlled Biofeedback Game . . . 97
4.42. GUI of Second Voice PC . . . 98

5.1. SSI tab of the EOS Workbench . . . 100
5.2. Confusion matrix of the ATT pilot study results . . . 102
5.3. Example manual segmentation of a word . . . 103
5.4. Matrix representation of the contact sensor layout . . . 104
5.5. Comparison of the lip sensor setup of two subjects . . . 107
5.6. Effect of the different lip sensor axes . . . 108

6.1. An example area function created with the six point model . . . 115
6.2. Effect of the exponents in the six point model . . . 115
6.3. Virtual targets in the six point model . . . 116

6.4. Workflow to obtain the reference area functions 117
6.5. Objective comparison of the six point model using the full parameter set versus the reduced set 118
6.6. Reference and model area functions of vowels and consonants using the full configuration 119
6.7. Example of a time-varying area function 122
6.8. Confusion matrix vowels 123
6.9. Confusion matrix consonants 124
6.10. Low-dimensional projections of the high-dimensional training data in the ATS study . 131
6.11. Example f_0 contour generated with the Fujisaki intonation model 135
6.12. Graphical user interface of the Wearable Intonation Generator 136
6.13. Naturalness scores from the WIG usability study 138
6.14. Example f_0 contours from the WIG usability study 139
6.15. Histogram of the pitch values included in the analyzed subset of the `mngu0` dataset . . 141
6.16. Voiced/unvoiced/silence classification score in percent of correctly classified frames . 142
6.17. RMSE of predicted f_0 contour with respect to the reference f_0 143
6.18. Average naturalness rating in the listening test of the resynthesized utterances using the orignal, predicted, and flattened f_0 contours. 143

7.1. Step response of the contact sensor input filter 146

A.1. IPA Chart 151

C.1. Connections to and from the ATSAM3S4B microcontroller. 158
C.2. Incoming and outgoing board connections (Joint Test Action Group (JTAG) for debugging, universal asynchronous receiver-transmitter (UART) for communication with the computer software, and a custom connector to connect the sensor unit) and optical sensor detector circuitry. 159
C.3. Supply voltage generation. 160
C.4. Analog contact sensor circuitry: Reference voltage generation, incoming contact sensor signal registration, and analog filtering. 161
C.5. Incoming and outgoing board connections: JTAG for debugging, UART for communication with the computer software, and a custom connector to connect the sensor unit. 162
C.6. Layout of the control unit for a double-sided printed circuit board (PCB). 163
C.7. Schematics of the sensor unit. 165
C.8. Layout of the sensor unit for a double-sided flexible printed circuit board (PCB). The area around the connector socket should be stiffened with a thicker polyamide layer. 166

D.1. Instructions given in SecondVoice_SensorBoard_glueAreas.pdf regarding the order of glueing the flexible PCB to the base plate 175

E.1. Program flow of the firmware 178

G.1. Reference and model area functions of vowels and consonants using the reduced configuration 185

List of Tables

2.1. Consonant sequences occurring within German syllables . . . 21
2.2. Examples of English and German vowels and consonants . . . 23

3.1. Properties of several Electropalatography (EPG) systems . . . 50

4.1. Tongue distance spacer configurations . . . 60
4.2. Comparison of the measured sensor values using different spacers . . . 63
4.3. Pearson correlation coefficient of the two detectors in the single-source, dual-detector lip sensor design . . . 83

5.1. List of the words used in the ATT studies . . . 100
5.2. Hyperparameter settings of the BLSTM networks used in the small-scale recognition study . . . 105
5.3. Intra-speaker recognition accuracy on the numbers corpus . . . 106
5.4. Intra-speaker recognition accuracy on the frequent words corpus . . . 106
5.5. Inter-speaker recognition accuracy on the numbers corpus . . . 107
5.6. Inter-speaker recognition accuracy on the frequent words corpus . . . 108

6.1. Eliminated degrees of freedom of the six point model . . . 116
6.2. Formant frequencies of the modeled vocal tract transfer functions . . . 120
6.3. List of the sentences used in the ATS study . . . 127
6.4. Hyperparameters in the ATS study . . . 129
6.5. Subject-dependent cross-validation results using the optimal hyperparameters for each model . . . 130
6.6. Comparison of three intonation models commonly used in speech synthesis . . . 134
6.7. List of German test sentences used in the WIG usability study . . . 136
6.8. Timing and number of attempts from the WIG usability study . . . 137
6.9. Optimal hyperparameters for the silence/voiced/unvoiced classifiers . . . 142
6.10. Optimal hyperparameters for the f_0 regression. The optimal learning rate (LR) was the same for every number of hidden layers of the Deep Neural Network (DNN). . . . 142

E.1. Deprecated frame format of the data sent from the control unit to the computer . . . 177
E.2. Control parameter frame format . . . 177
E.3. Frame format of the data sent from the control unit to the computer . . . 179

G.1. Parameter values for the geometrically fitted full configuration of the six point model 183
G.2. Parameter values for the geometrically fitted reduced configuration of the six point model . . . 184

G.3. Parameter values for the perceptually optimized full configuration of the six point model . . . 186
G.4. Parameter values for the perceptually optimized reduced configuration of the six point model . . . 187
G.5. Formant frequencies of the perceptually optimized modeled vocal tract transfer functions . . . 188

H.1. Optimal hyperparameters for subject 1 . . . 189
H.2. Optimal hyperparameters for subject 2 . . . 190
H.3. Optimal hyperparameters for subject 3 . . . 190
H.4. Optimal hyperparameters for subject 4 . . . 190

Acronyms

AC Alternating Current

ADC Analog-to-Digital Converter

ASR Automatic Speech Recognition

ATS Articulation-to-Speech

ATT Articulation-to-Text

BCI Brain-Computer Interface

BLSTM Bidirectional Long Short-Term Memory

C consonant

CNN Convolutional Neural Network

CV consonant-vowel

DAC Digital-to-Analog Converter

DMA Direct Memory Access

DNN Deep Neural Network

DOF Degree Of Freedom

DTW Dynamic Time Warping

ECoG Electrocorticography

EEG Electroencephalography

EMA Electromagnetic Articulography

EMC Electromagnetic Compatibility

EMG Electromyography

EOS Electro-Optical Stomatography

EPG Electropalatography

fMRI functional Magnetic Resonance Imaging

fNIRS functional Near-Infrared Spectroscopy

FSM finite state machine

GPR Gaussian Process Regression

GUI Graphical User Interface

HF High-Frequency Radio Waves

HMM Hidden Markov Model

IC Intergrated Circuit

IPA International Phonetic Association

IPA International Phonetic Alphabet

KRR Kernel Ridge Regression

LED Light Emitting Diode

LPC Linear Predictive Coding

LSTM Long Short-Term Memory

MCU Microcontroller Unit

MEG Magnetoencephalography

MLP Multi-Layer Perceptron

MRI Magnetic Resonance Imaging

OPG Optopalatography

PCB printed circuit board

PDF probability density function

PMA Permanent-Magnetic Articulography

RMSE Root-Mean-Square Error

RNN Recurrent Neural Network

SAMPA Speech Assessment Methods Phonetic Alphabet

SD standard deviation

sEMG Surface Electromyography

SNR Signal-to-Noise Ratio

SPI Serial Peripheral Interface

SSI Silent-Speech Interface

SVM Support Vector Machine

TAM Target Approximation Model

TTS Text-to-Speech

UART universal asynchronous receiver-transmitter

US Ultrasonography

V vowel

VAD Voice Activity Detection

VCSEL vertical-cavity surface-emitting laser

VOT Voice Onset Time

WIG Wearable Intonation Generator

1. Introduction

Listen to the silence. It has so much to say.

(Rumi)

The ability to produce, perceive, and understand speech is arguably the most important human skill. As part of humanity's on-going efforts to create machines ever more similar to itself, attempts to develop a technology to mimic the human speech processing capability were only a matter of time.

In the 20th century, the field of Automatic Speech Recognition (ASR) summarized these attempts and grew into its own scientific discipline. The earliest recognized speech recognition system was "Audrey", introduced in [1], that came out of the legendary Bell Laboratories in 1952 (for more information on that institutions stunning portfolio of inventions and discoveries, see [2]). This groundbreaking, fully analog system was able to recognize the spoken digits from 0 to 9 with a reported accuracy of 97 to 99 %. In the following two decades, some first successes were achieved: William C. Dersch's "Shoebox" system, for example, was presented at the 1962 World's Fair in Seattle [3]. Shoebox extended Audrey's vocabulary by six command words (including "plus", "minus" and "total") to perform simple arithmetic operations entirely based on spoken input. The scientific community, however, also saw some concepts emerge that would stay central to the research efforts in the field of ASR. The "Phonetic Typewriter" [4], a phoneme recognizer developed at the Kyoto University, already tackled the difficult task of continuous speech recognition (as opposed to the isolated command word recognition task other systems of the time focused on). At the University College London, Denes [5] imposed phonotactic constraints by allowing only certain phoneme sequences and thus introduced statistical syntax as another tool to the community. The pace quickened after Vintsyuk [6] proposed dynamic programming to help with the difficult non-linear time alignment of a reference and a sample utterance. This technique was most prominently featured in the Viterbi algorithm [7], which became the de-facto standard for time-alignment (or Dynamic Time Warping (DTW)) more than ten years later, after it crossed over into speech research from the field of information theory, popularized by [8].

Since then, the performance and availability of computer systems rapidly increased and alongside these developments, numerous breakthroughs in ASR research were achieved: Hidden Markov Models and stochastic language models greatly improved the performance of continuous speech recognition systems in the 1980s (e.g., [9, 10]), the vocabularies of the systems grew quickly in the 90s, when statistical learning entered the field, and moved beyond the task of *recognition* towards truly *understanding* speech and even entering a dialog with the user in the 2000s. For a more detailed look at the history of speech recognition, see the review by Juang [11] (which was also the basis of this short introduction) or, for an even more in-depth retrospective, the book by Pieraccini [12].

Today, ASR systems are ubiquitous, used not only as dictation systems on office computers but also in cars, service hotlines, televisions, smart speakers, and many more. We even have voice-enabled personal assistants on smartphones (e.g., Apple's *Siri*, Google's *Google Now*, or Amazon's *Alexa*) that attempt to engage with the user in a way that is supposed to mimic a human interlocutor. The market for speech technology is enormous and still booming (see Figure 1.1).

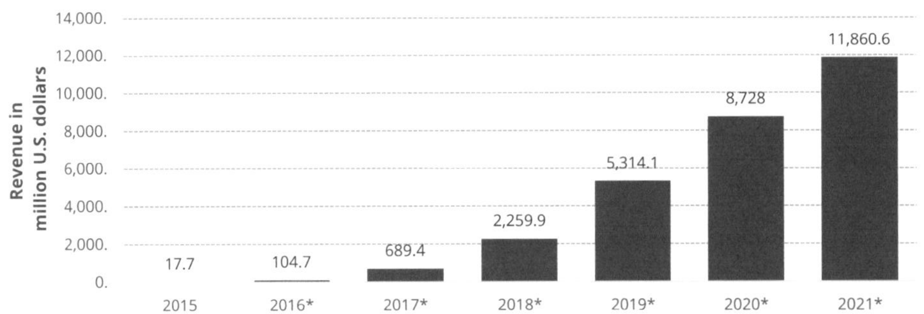

Figure 1.1.: Size of the speech recognition market worldwide from 2015 to 2024. The asterisk (*) denotes projected years. Data according to [13].

However, there is one major problem with the current-day ASR systems: it excludes a significant part of the population. Some people cannot talk to machines, either because of the circumstances (e.g., the loud and noisy environment of a jet plane, the obstructions caused by the breathing masks of fire fighters or divers) or because of physical limitations (e.g., the elderly, laryngectomized cancer patients or intensive care patients with a tracheostoma). Especially the latter demographic is completely shunned by the global innovation drivers in the sector of consumer speech technology (i.e., Google, Amazon, and Apple), despite the fact that they together make up a sizable chunk of the market: According to projections by the United Nations[1], the median age in Germany will be 49 years by the year 2019. While future generations of elderly will be used to the convenience and productivity of speech technology, the physical effort to produce speech makes it inreasingly difficult with age to continue using consumer devices in the same way they used to. But why is it even necessary to talk to the machine? Why does sound need to travel through the air to the machine's microphone, only to be decoded into the actual signal of interest: the speech sound identities (and subsequently the linguistic and semantic content of the speech sound sequence)?

While this is of course merely a matter of convenience and quality-of-life, laryngectomized people have far more pressing concerns regarding speech technology. Given that this demographic is not just of substantial size (five-year prevalence of 488 900 wordwide[2]), but also growing steadily (177 422 new cases worldwide in 2018[3]). In Germany in the year 2018 alone, more than 4800 patients have suffered loss or severe impairment of their voice due to a complete or partial laryngectomy[4].

A few therapies and prostheses are commonly used to rehabilitate the patients' ability in clinical practice, but all of them have their individual drawbacks. There are currently three major kinds of techniques in use [14]: the electrolarynx, esophageal speech (more of a replacement voice than a prostheses), and the so-called tracheoesophageal speech.

The electrolarynx [15] is a hand-held device that is usually pressed against the skin roughly at the height of the (now removed) vocal cords. The device then sends vibrations (usually at a fixed frequency) through the neck into the pharynx, where these vibrations turn into sound pressure

[1] https://population.un.org/wpp/

[2] https://de.statista.com/statistik/daten/studie/1095977/umfrage/zahl-der-weltweiten-krebsfaelle-nach-krebsart/ [In German]

[3] https://de.statista.com/statistik/daten/studie/286545/umfrage/zahl-der-krebsneuerkrankungen-weltweit/ [In German]

[4] Fallpauschalenbezogene Krankenhausstatistik (DRG-Statistik): Operationen und Prozeduren der vollstationären Patientinnen und und Patienten in Krankenhäusern. Online: www.gbe-bund.de[In German]

waves and excite the vocal tract (for more on the speech production process see chapter 2). In the roughly 100 years since the introduction of the first such device in the late 1920s, this basic principle has remained the same and very little improvements of the sound quality and variation of the fundamental frequency have been made [15], with very few notable exceptions (e.g., [16]). Electrolaryngeal speech can be described as robotic, artificial, difficult to understand, and generally unnatural sounding (for an example, please visit `https://www.youtube.com/watch?v=Kmk46U2yjow` [Last visited on September 9, 2020]. Still, it is a widely used technique, probably because it requires very little training (at least in its most basic form).

Esophageal speech avoids any kind of technology, because it re-purposes existing mucosa flaps at the upper end of the esophagus as a *pseudoglottis*: By swallowing air and then expelling it through the esophagus, these flaps can be excited to oscillate, similar to the way that air from the trachea excites the actual vocal folds in a non-laryngectomized speaker (see section 2.1). This manner of speaking is difficult to learn and, even when mastered, usually has a distinct "belching" sound quality to it (visit `https://www.youtube.com/watch?v=UTLg-2N4hyw` for an example of a very capable esophageal speaker [Last visited on September 9, 2020]). Esophageal speech is therefore also sometimes called ructus voice (ructus from Latin *ructare* - belch). Futhermore, many speakers never learn to properly communicate in this way. Exact numbers are unreliable here because these statistics are usually not recorded, but the voice prostheses manufacturer Atos Medical claims that only 20 % of those who try to learn esophageal speech actually succeed [5].

Finally, today's preferred method to rehabilitate laryngectomized patients is tracheoesophageal speech using an artificial valve [14]. These valves are placed into a fistula, a surgically made connection, between the trachea and the esophagus. If not speaking, the valve blocks airflow into the esophagus and air is exhaled from the lungs through the tracheostoma, a hole in the patient's neck[6]. When the patient wants to speak, they can cover the tracheostoma and exhale, thus creating a positive pressure on the valve and forcing it open. The air then escapes into the pharynx, where it is used to excite a pseudoglottis, similar to esophageal speech. In contrast to that, however, the fact that the air does not need to be swallowed and is instead simply exhaled, makes it much more convenient and easier to speak in this way. The resulting high success rate (95 % in long-term users [14]) has helped this technique, which is also called a *voice prostheses*, claim its place as the state-of-the-art in voice rehabilitation after total laryngectomy. But it is not without substantial disadvantages: Laryngectomized patients are often elderly patients and as such have the same difficulties as non-laryngectomized speakers regarding the effort of speech production. The surgery to create the fistula is also not without risks and can result in harmful punctuations of the trachea and/or esophagus. But the main disadvantage of this method is the dependency of the patients on constant clinical and surgical care, because the valves must be regularly checked and replaced to avoid clogging, inflammations, scarring, and other complications. This greatly limits the patients' mobility and self-determined living and may even result in health hazards if patients' miss their checkup appointments.

The state of the art in speech prostheses therefore raises some questions: If it is so difficult to create a new *internal* voice source, why not try to create an *external* voice? So instead of bringing the excitation source *into* the vocal tract, take the articulation *out* of the vocal tract and produce the speech extra-orally?

Producing speech with technology has always fascinated researchers and records of attempts to build speech producing machines go back to the 18th century and the days of Christian Gottlieb Kratzenstein [17], who built a set of acoustic resonators that produced vowel sounds, and Wolfgang Von Kempelen [18], who developed a machine that was even capable to produce short utterances (for more details and examples of historic speech analysis and synthesis systems and devices see [19]). In the second half of the 20th century, three major branches of synthesis systems emerged: articulatory synthesizers (e.g., the Kelly-Lochbaum model [20]) that simulate the

[5] `https://www.atosmedical.us/support/esophageal-speech/` [Last visit: September 9, 2020]

[6] The tracheostoma is not made specifically for this voice prosthesis, but is necessary for all laryngectomized patients because the larynx also protects the trachea from contamination by food or saliva. When the larynx is removed, the connection between the trachea and the pharynx therefore needs to be blocked and the tracheostoma is made to create an airway for breathing.

propagation of sound waves through the human vocal tract for speech production, formant synthesizers (e.g., Klatt's well-known Klattalk system [21]) that use the source-filter model of speech production ([22,23]), and systems based on concatenation of very short pre-recorded speech segments (e.g., [24]). Today, artificial neural networks working in the cloud directly map written letters to acoustic waveforms in end-to-end systems (e.g, WaveNet [25] and Tacotron [26]) and allow high-quality speech synthesis in portable, miniature devices (as long as they have a fast and stable connection to the internet).

So with a long history of speech synthesis research and a wide range of systems available, connecting a voice-less (or voice-impaired) user to such a system in some way seems like an obvious way of restoring their ability to communicate. Especially since the users described above usually retain their ability to still *articulate* speech, i.e. silently mouthing the intended words, this leads to the fundamental ideas underlying a technology called Silent-Speech Interfaces: What if we could (a) remove the acoustic stage from a speech recognition system and use the speech *movements* as the input, or (b) use the speech movements to control some kind of technological speech generator?

This dissertation presents the development of one incarnation of such a Silent-Speech Interface, using a newly developed measurement technique to capture the speech movements, state-of-the-art algorithms for a silent speech recognition system, and a novel vocal tract model to generate speech based on the measured movements.

1.1. The concept of a Silent-Speech Interface

A Silent-Speech Interface (SSI) is a technologically enabled channel of communication between a human and a machine that uses speech to encode the information but does not require any audible, acoustic speech. There are two basic paradigms for SSIs: Articulation-to-Text (ATT) and Articulation-to-Speech (ATS). An ATS system can also incorporate an ATT frontend, which translates the articulatory data to text as an intermediary representation that is then used with a standard Text-to-Speech (TTS) system to generate speech. These systems can possibly exploit text-based linguistic models to regularize the mapping from articulation to speech, but are limited to the pre-defined vocabulary and thus the language they were trained with. An ATS system without a textual intermediary cannot use text-level linguistic models but can, in theory, generate all speech (and even non-speech) sounds by learning the direct mapping from articulation. Such systems are therefore also called *direct* ATS systems.

The general framework of an SSI consists of three components: an articulatory data acquisition frontend using some kind of sensor technology, a recognition (in ATT systems) or parametric synthesis (in ATS systems) backend, and a mapping between the articulatory data and the vocabulary (ATT) or the parameters of the synthesis (ATS) (see Figure 1.2). Due to the unstandardized interfaces between the components, research around SSIs usually involves the entire pipeline, with each research group setting up their own framework. Some efforts have been made to uncouple research into each component, e.g., by publishing datasets of articulatory data for the specific purpose of allowing other researchers to focus on the mapping. But because of the heterogeneous input modalities across the various technologies, no unified framework or defined interfaces between components have been established in the field, making every SSI a stand-alone solution, which usually needs to be developed "from scratch" every time.

1.2. Structure of this work

To understand the requirements and challenges of SSI development, an at least basic understanding of the speech production processes is necessary. Chapter 2 therefore introduces the fundamentals of phonetics to the reader, limited to and focused on everything directly related to the subjects of this dissertation. As described in section 1.1, developing the synthesis or recognition backend of an SSI usually goes hand in hand with the development of the articulatory data acqui-

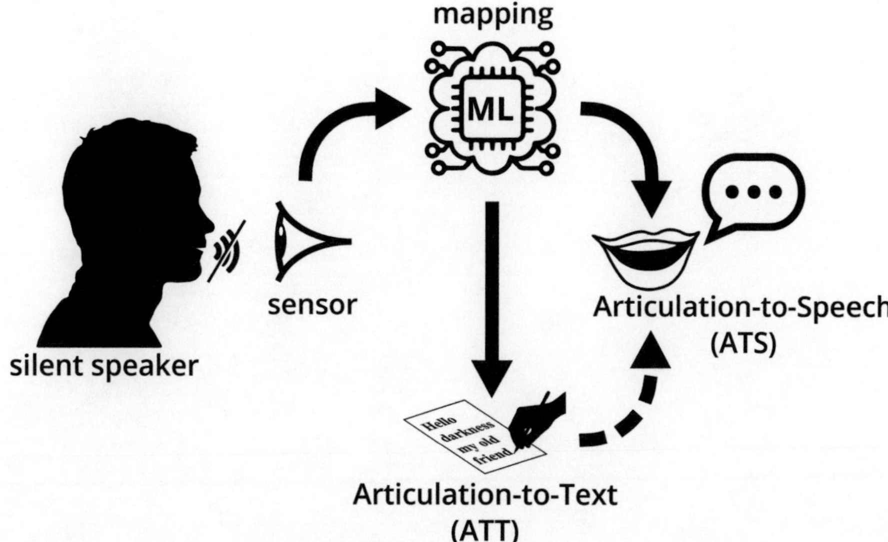

Figure 1.2.: General framework of a Silent-Speech Interface. In the ATT paradigm, the mapping is from the sensor data to a word label (classification). In the ATS paradigm, the mapping is from the sensor data to a set of synthesis parameters. By using a regular TTS synthesizer, an ATT system can be extended to an ATS system.

sition frontend. The literature review in chapter 3 therefore covers the state-of-the-art and the history of both algorithms and measurement technologies in the field of SSI research. After this overview, a newly developed articulometric technology called Electro-Optical Stomatography (EOS) is presented in chapter 4 that aims to overcome the shortcomings and limitations of the previously existing techniques. In chapter 5, EOS is used to develop and evaluate two command word recognition systems in an ATT paradigm. Chapter 6 presents a study on using EOS in an ATS system. To that end, a newly developed vocal tract model well-suited for real-time articulatory speech synthesis is also presented therein. Two additional experiments on the generation of pitch and voicing information in an ATS system close out the chapter. Finally, chapter 7 summarizes the findings and contributions of this dissertation and presents an outlook on future work towards a fully-developed SSI based on EOS.

2. Fundamentals of phonetics

In order to understand the requirements and challenges of articulatory measurements, it is important to understand how humans produce speech and how speech is structured from an articulatory perspective. The field of phonetics, or more specifically articulatory phonetics, concerns itself with the systematic analysis and description of exactly these characteristics of speech, has a long and rich tradition, and is an ongoing, fertile field of research. Within the scope of this dissertation, only the fundamentals of speech production are of immediate interest. To that end, I will discuss the *speech organs* involved in the process (section 2.1), provide a basic breakdown of the various *sounds* making up speech (section 2.2 and section 2.3), take a brief look at the *acoustic properties* of speech sounds (section 2.4), and introduce a somewhat advanced concept called *coarticulation*, which goes beyond the basics of phonetics but has an immediate bearing on Silent-Speech Interface (SSI)-related matters (section 2.5). Finally, the summary of these concepts in section 2.7 further focuses on the presented aspects of speech and articulation most relevant in the context of SSIs. The information presented in this chapter is based on [27], except where stated otherwise. The languages of the world are a very diverse domain and it is not helpful (nor even possible) to describe the entire state of the art in phonetics in the context of this dissertation. Instead, only the sounds most relevant to English and German are the major focus of this chapter because of the global importance of the former and the latter's use in the experiments of this dissertation. Even within these two languages, there are numerous dialectal variants and accents that not only use the same sounds in a different way but also use entirely different sounds. To avoid confusion, the terms English and German are regarded as synonomous with General American English and Standard German, respectively. All schematic articulations in this chapter are reproduced from [28] and slightly modified for clarity.

2.1. Components of the human speech production system

Speech sounds are produced by the time-varying interplay of three functional components (see Figure 2.1): initiation of the airflow from the lungs, modulation of this airflow (phonation) to generate an acoustic excitation, and a "tube" formed by the upper airways and shaped by body parts called articulators that functions as a resonator and/or an aerodynamic tube system (similar to the body of a trumpet or trombone). The airflow from the lungs, funneled through the trachea, passes through the larynx (also known as the "voice box"). Inside the larynx, small pieces of layered soft tissue are stretched across the trachea. When at rest, they form a V-shape pointing towards the front. These *vocal folds* (also sometimes imprecisely called vocal cords) typically have a length of 1.75 cm to 2.5 cm in males and 1.25 cm to 1.75 cm in females [29] and the area between them is called the *glottis*. The vocal folds are kept wide apart (abducted) in a neutral state so that airflow can pass unhindered through the open glottis in both directions during breathing. The muscles that are part of the vocal folds can also completely shut them (keeping them adducted), which happens, e.g., in the initial phase of coughing to build up pressure below the vocal folds. During speech, the vocal folds are slightly less abducted for some sounds and are narrowed for others (see section 2.2 and section 2.3). If the vocal folds are narrowed below a certain critical distance while air is flowing through the gap in between, they start to vibrate and thus produce a complex, wideband sound (similar to a vibrating reed in a woodwind instrument's mouthpiece). This flow-induced oscillation is a complex and multi-faceted process and its analysis and modeling is subject of ongoing research [30, 31]. For the purposes of this overview, it shall suffice to say that due to the airflow from the lungs the pressure below the narrowly constricted (or even closed) glottis builds up until the pressure differential across the vocal folds becomes too large and they are blown open again. The rapid airflow through the glottis resumes and, thanks to the Bernoulli effect, the vocal folds are drawn back together by the created suction, and another cycle of sub-glottal pressure rise, opening burst, and closing suction begins. This oscillation continues as long as the airflow from the lungs is kept up (and sufficiently fast for the Bernoulli effect to occur) and the distance between the vocal folds is small enough. This vibration is called the *voiced excitation* of the vocal tract (i.e., the system of cavities above the glottis consisting of the *pharynx*, the *nasal cavity*, and the *mouth*). Conversely, if the vocal folds do not oscillate but air still flows through the glottis, it is called the *voiceless excitation*. A mixed excitation, where only some part of the vocal folds oscillates and/or the glottis is permanently open to some extent, is also not just possible but actually quite common. However, since only the simplified binary voicing is used to group speech sounds, mixed excitation, the various voice qualities, and other idiosyncracies of the glottal excitation shall not be discussed here and the reader is instead directed to [29] for further research. Similarly, other types of flow than the egressive pulmonic airstream (exhaled air from the lungs), e.g., those occurring in the ejectives or clicks of African languages, are ignored for the purposes of this dissertation.

The (voiced or voiceless) excitation signal is modified by the vocal tract before it results in speech sounds. This modification depends on the geometry of the vocal tract, which can be shaped by means of the *articulators*. Articulators are a set of body parts and anatomical landmarks, which in combination can create the speech sounds of all languages from the two basic excitation signals. There are two basic kinds of articulators: active articulators that can be (voluntarily or involuntarily) moved by the speaker (the vocal folds, the larynx, the tongue, the soft palate, the lower jaw, and the lips), and the passive articulators, which usually remain still in Western languages (the pharynx wall, the hard palate, the alveolar ridge, and the upper teeth). Based on the shape created by the articulators, the vocal tract acts in two different but not necessarily mutually exclusive ways: If the vocal tract is mostly open, i.e. there are no narrow constrictions and it is essentially a tube through which air can flow, it functions as an acoustic resonator with a distinct set of resonance frequencies that is defined by the geometrical shape of the complex tube. If there are one or more narrow constrictions (e.g., less than 20 mm^2) anywhere in the vocal tract, they can cause aerodynamic turbulences downstream that create noisy sound sources. Speech sounds, especially in running speech, are usually created through a combination of these two cases, although they are often grouped by the dominant of the two conditions of *open* versus *constricted* or even closed vocal tract. Sounds produced with an open vocal tract are called *vowel* sounds, while sounds produced with a constricted or closed vocal tract are called *consonants*. Besides this distinction, vowels and consonants can also be grouped into two subsets called *sonorants* (which are produced with a non-turbulent airflow in the vocal tract) and *obstruents* (which are produced with some sort of turbulence-causing obstruction of the airflow). Before we can discuss speech sounds, we need an unambiguous way of transcribing them. The orthographic spelling conventions of different languages make it difficult to map letters to sounds in a general, language-independent way. And even within a language, the same letter is used for very different sounds: for example the letter *i* denotes very different sounds in the English pronoun *I* and in the preposition *in*. Sometimes there are also more sounds in a language than are actually used to discriminate words and thus the letters of the alphabet may not be enough. Therefore, the International Phonetic Association (IPA) developed an alphabet that uses unique symbols to denote each sound. This International Phonetic Alphabet (IPA), which is unfortunately going by the same acronym as its inventor, contains not only symbols for the general sounds (a *broad tran-*

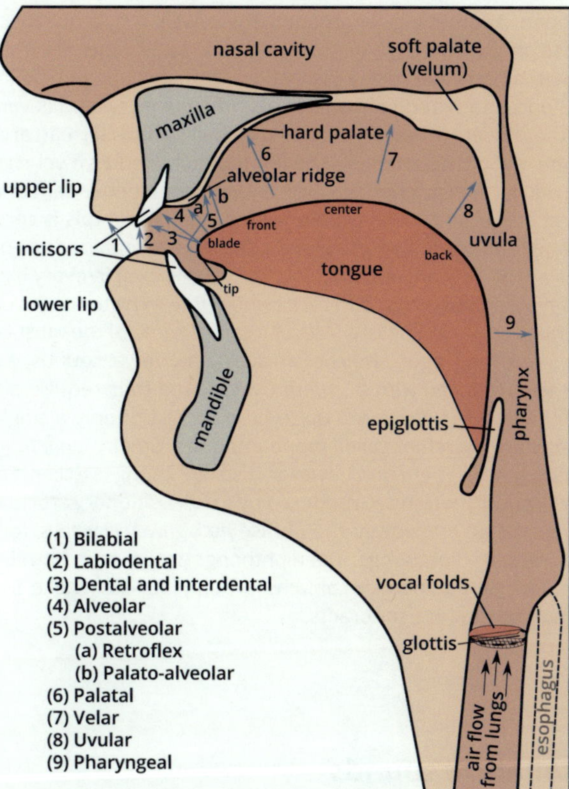

Figure 2.1.: Schematic view of the human vocal tract and places of articulation (adapted and expanded from [27]).

scription), but also provides diacritics to mark the exact pronunciation variations and minute details of phonation and articulation (a *narrow transcription*). The broad transcription is also called *phonemic*, because it only identifies the *phonemes* used to make up a word. Phonemes are the sounds used to discriminate meaning in a language and are the smallest units that cannot be swapped for a different one in a word without changing its meaning. Phonemic transcriptions are usually enclosed in forward slashes /·/. Narrow transcriptions are also called *phonetic* because they transcribe words at the level of the *phones*. Phones are any and all discernible speech sounds, regardless of their importance regarding the meaning of words. Phonetic transcriptions use square brackets [·]. The slashes-versus-brackets convention is not generally adhered to, however, especially in more technical-leaning works. A comprehensive chart with all symbols in the alphabet can be found in Appendix A.

2.2. Vowel sounds

Vowel sounds (Latin vocalis meaning "voiced") are produced with a mostly open vocal tract and a voiced excitation (except when whispering, when they may be produced with a voiceless excitation). They are usually entirely characterized by only three articulatory parameters: the degree of lip rounding or spreading, and the tongue position along the high/low and front/back axes. From the perspective of the airflow, a high tongue position means a more closed vocal tract, while a low tongue position means a more open vocal tract. Therefore, the high/low dimension is also often called closed/open. Another way of grouping the vowels is by a quality called *tension*, where tense vowels are those produced with larger muscular effort and generally longer durations than lax vowels. This is, however, a rather vague distinction, since it is not well-defined what constitutes large effort, and the duration criterion is often fluid. The vowel system is very distinctive for any given language and the subsets of vowels occurring in English and German are shown in the summary in Table 2.2a at the end of this chapter. The IPA has compiled a vowel chart (see Figure 2.2a) based on the tongue and lip characteristics, which is language-independent and should in theory be able to assign a location for any vowel from any language. While this is certainly true with regards to the relative configurations of the articulators, the acoustic realizations of these "canonical" vowels can vary drastically across languages and not all vowels exist in every language. In some cases, the same sound is transcribed with a different symbol due to historic conventions (e.g., the sound /ɐ/ is often transcribed as /ʌ/ in English). Articulations of some of the most common vowels are shown in Figure 2.2c. Some languages also contain additional vowel sounds, e.g., the nasalized vowels in French, which are produced with a lowered velum and thus require another articulatory dimension. Lastly, all the vowels discussed up to here consist of only a single, quasi-static articulatory configuration and are therefore called monophthongs (Greek *monóphthongos* from mónos "single" and phthóngos "sound"). There are, however, also diphthongs (Greek *diphthongos* from di "double" and phthóngos "sound"), which are produced by a non-stationary articulation. where the beginning vowel glides towards an end vowel: the phrase *no highway cowboys*, for example, contains five of these gliding vowels, or diphthongs. The diphthongs occurring in both English and German are [a͜ɪ] and [a͜ʊ], while German additionally contains [ɔ͜ʏ] and English instead uses [ɔ͜ɪ] and additionally [eɪ] and [oʊ]. All vowel sounds are sonorants.

2.3. Consonantal sounds

Consonants (Latin consonans from con meaning "with" and sonare meaning "to sound") are sounds that are produced with an obstruction somewhere in the vocal tract (although confusingly, not all consonants are also obstruents). They are classified by the place and manner of this obstruction. The obstruction is formed when an articulator moves towards a *place of articulation*. A consonantal sound can therefore be specified by naming these two components. A "labio-dental" sound, for example, is a sound where the lower lip (Latin *labium*) as the articulator moves towards the teeth (Latin *dens*) to form the obstruction (see the numbered arrows in Figure 2.1). To differentiate further between sounds formed at the same place of articulation with the same articulators, the so-called *manner of articulation* describes the way the sound is articulated at that place in categorical terms. There are a total of seven manners of articulation [35], although some sources use six (e.g., [27], see section 2.3). Three of these categorize the degree of the obstruction: A *stop* is a sound including a complete closure as the obstruction (e.g., [p] in *peace*), a *fricative* has a narrow constriction instead (e.g., [f] in *fleece*), and an *approximant* has a slightly wider constriction (making the sound vowel-like, e.g., [w] in *wheeze*). In addition to these, other manners of articulation used to describe consonantal sounds are *trill* (caused by an airflow-induced vibration of the articulator, e.g., [r] in Spanish *perro*), *tap* (which is essentially a very brief stop, e.g., [ɾ] in *latter*), *lateral* (in which the airflow is directed through a lateral canal formed by the tongue, e.g., [l] in *fall*), and *nasal* (which is produced with a lowered velum, e.g., [m] in *home*). Since consonants can be produced using either a voiced or voiceless excitation (see section 2.1), a fully qualified consonant name consists of three components: (1) excitation mode, (2) articulator and place of articulation, and (3) manner of articulation. The consonant chart in Appendix A uses this terminology to describe the consonantal sounds of most languages. The subsets occuring in English and German, which are most relevant for this dissertation, are summerized with examples at the end of this chapter in Table 2.2b. The following subsections discuss the manners of articulation mentioned above in greater detail.

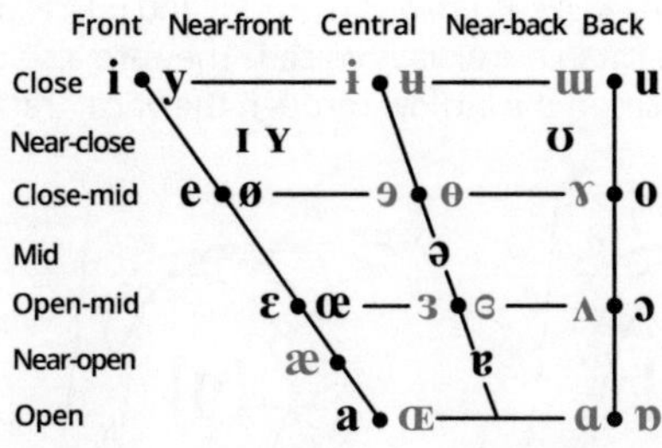

(a) Vowel chart according to the International Phonetic Association [32]. Adjacent symbols indicate a minimal pair, where both sounds are produced with the same tongue position, but the sound on the left is produced with retracted lips (as if smiling) and the sound on the right is produced with rounded lips (as if pursing your lips). Only the solid black (monophthong) vowels appear in non-dialectal German, which was the language used in all experiments conducted for this dissertation.

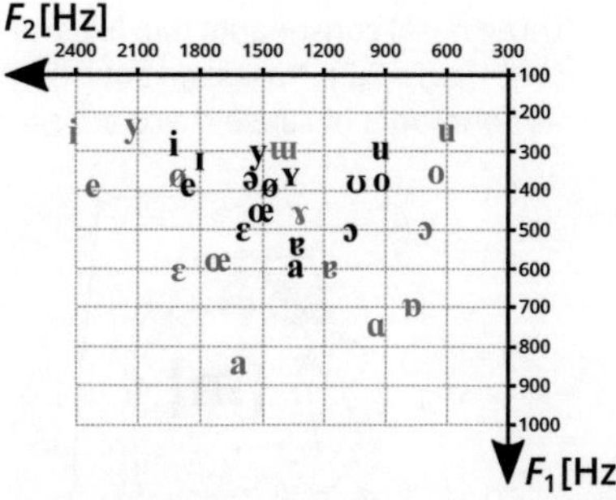

(b) Formant map of General American English (gray, [33]) and German (black, [34]) vowels. The German vowels are more numerous and acoustically more densely bunched, although the relative ordering is similar to the English ones.

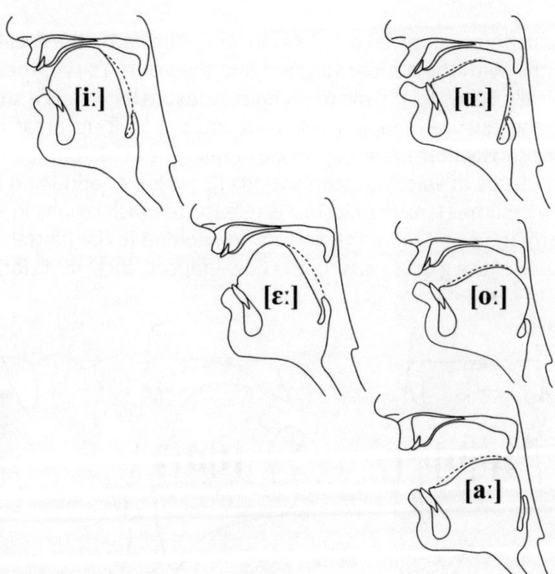

(c) Example vowel articulations. The dashed lines are the contours of the side of the tongue.

Figure 2.2.: Articulatory and acoustic vowel spaces. While the relative order of the vowels is very similar in both spaces, the distances between the sounds are very different.

Nasals

A nasal sound is articulated with a lowered velum and thus an open velo-pharyngeal port, which is the opening between the nasal cavity and the pharynx. Theoretically, many sounds can be nasalized in this way (e.g., the French nasalized vowels [ɔ̃] in *b<u>on</u>jour*), but in English and German, only the three nasal consonants [m], [n], and [ŋ] exist as the nasalized versions of [b], [d] and [g], respectively (see Figure 2.3). Nasalized sounds in English and German are always voiced. They are also counted as sonorants because there are no major turbulences in the airflow through the vocal tract.

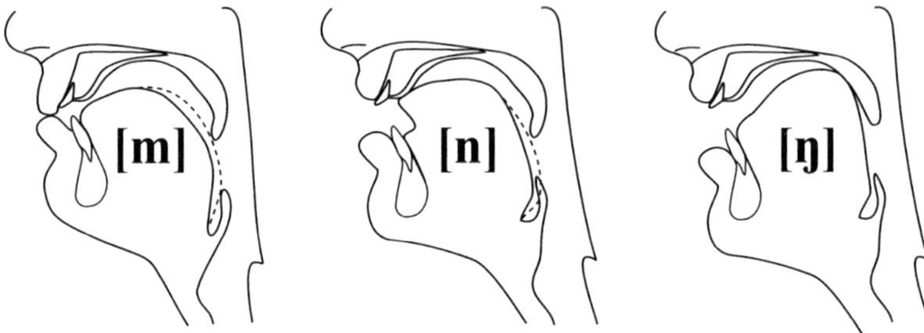

Figure 2.3.: Example articulations of the three English and German nasal consonants [m], [n], and [ŋ]. Note the lowered velum and thus open velo-pharyngeal port, which causes the airflow to continue despite the closed oral cavity. The dashed lines are the contours of the side of the tongue.

Stops

During the articulation of stops, a complete closure is formed in the vocal tract that stops the airflow (hence the name). With the airflow stopped and the velum raised, the pressure in the oral cavity rises. After typically 50 ms to 150 ms of complete closure (and thus a short period of silence in the speech signal), the closure is rapidly released and the built-up pressure discharges in a sudden burst sound (see subsection 2.4.3), e.g., in *pie* or *buy*. The vocal folds can be either abducted (glottis is open), which results in voiceless stop sounds ([p, t, k]), or adducted so that they start vibrating once the airflow resumes (i.e., the closure is released), which results in voiced stops ([b, d, g]. Both English and German use all six of these stops in addition to the glottal stop [ʔ], which is a sudden, deliberate closure of the glottis causing the flow-induced vocal fold vibration to stop.

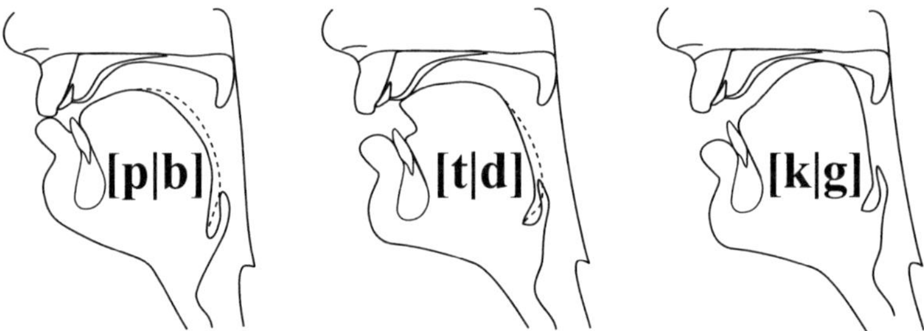

Figure 2.4.: Example articulations of the three English and German stops [p|b], [t|d], and [g|k]. The supra-glottal articulatory configuration is the same for each voiced-voiceless pair. The dashed lines are the contours of the side of the tongue.

Some sources (e.g., [27]) include nasals such as [m] and [n] in this category, since they are very similarly articulated and also include a closure in the oral cavity (see Figure 2.3). However, these sounds do not exhibit the closure release dynamics that are characteristic for stop sounds and they belong to the subset of sonorant sounds, whereas stop sounds are obstruents. Therefore, for the purposes of this dissertation, I will adhere to the commonly used system that includes nasals as their own manner of articulation.

Fricatives

Fricative sounds are produced by very close approximation of two articulators, which creates a narrow constriction that causes the airflow to become turbulent. The result is a hissing or whistling sound as in, e.g., the words *freeze* or *seize*. Fricatives can be voiced or voiceless. The fricatives [f|v], [s|z], and [ʃ|ʒ], as well as the glottal fricative [h] occur in both German and English. In addition to these, English also contains a dental fricative [θ|ð], and German contains the voiceless palatal fricative [ç] and the voiceless velar fricative [x]. The voiced palatal fricative [ʝ] is also sometimes described as the palatal approximant [j] [36]. The voiced velar fricative is [ɣ]. However, in this work, I will transcribe the voiced counterpart of [x] by the symbol [ʁ], which actually stands for the voiced velar fricative or the velar approximant in narrow transcription. The so-called /r/-like (or *rhotic*) sounds are a complicated subgroup of consonants that have various (sometimes context-dependent) realizations in many languages. For the purposes of this dissertation, this broad transcription (as phonetically imprecise as it may be) is adopted because it represents the way the [ʁ] was produced in the synthesis experiments (see chapter 6). All fricatives are obstruent consonants.

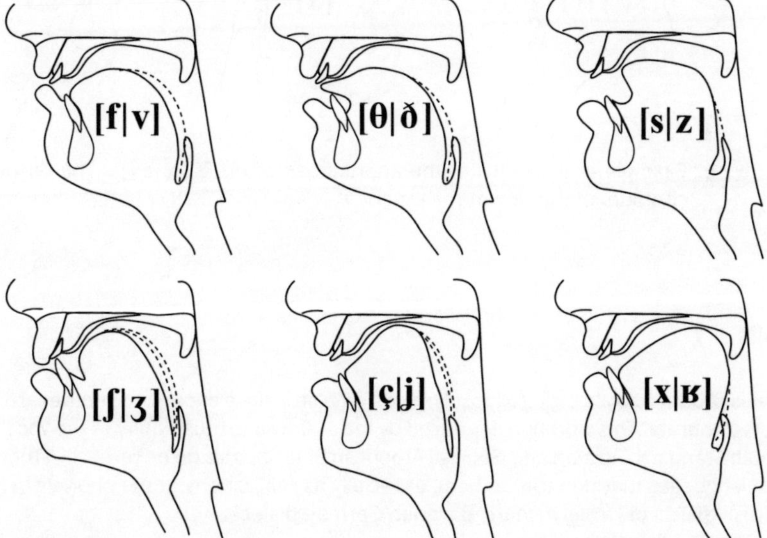

Figure 2.5.: Example articulations of the fricatives [f|v], [s|z], [ʃ|ʒ], [ç|ʝ], and [x|ʁ]. The supra-glottal articulatory configuration is the same for each voiced-voiceless pair. The dashed lines are the contours of the side of the tongue.

Affricates

When the release of a stop is extended in duration and strongly frictional, this phase can be perceived as a separate fricative sound. When this segment is notably different from the two sounds being produced "separately", this compound sound is called an *affricate* (or affricative) [35]. In English, there are only the two affricates [t͡ʃ] (as in *watch*) and [d͡ʒ] (as in *jungle*), while in German the affricates [p͡f] (as in *Pflaume*) and [t͡s] (as in *Katze*) occur as well. When observing the two phases of the affricate separately, they appear to be identical to the constituent stop and fricative. The phonetic difference lies solely in the time dynamics due to the slower release of the stop. A contrastive example in English are the phrases *why choose* [waɪ t͡ʃuːz] and *white shoes* [waɪt ʃuːz], and in German the words *Mattscheibe* [ˈmat͜ʃaɪbə] und *Matschhose* [ˈmat͡ʃˌhoːzə]. Just like fricatives, affricates are obstruent consonants.

Approximants

When the approximation of the two articulators is too close to be a clear vowel, but not close enough to cause a strongly turbulent airflow, the resulting sound is called an approximant. The palatal approximant [j] occurs in both English (*year*) and German (*Jahr*), while English additionally contains the labio-velar approximant [w] (as in *what*) and the alveolar (or post-alveolar) approximant [ɹ] (as in *read*). In English and German, only voiced approximants exist. The palatal approximant [j] and the palatal fricative [ʝ] are often difficult to distinguish. For the purposes of this dissertation, they are treated as the same sound and thus the voiced palatal fricative is transcribed as [j] for simplicity's sake. Approximants are sonorant consonants.

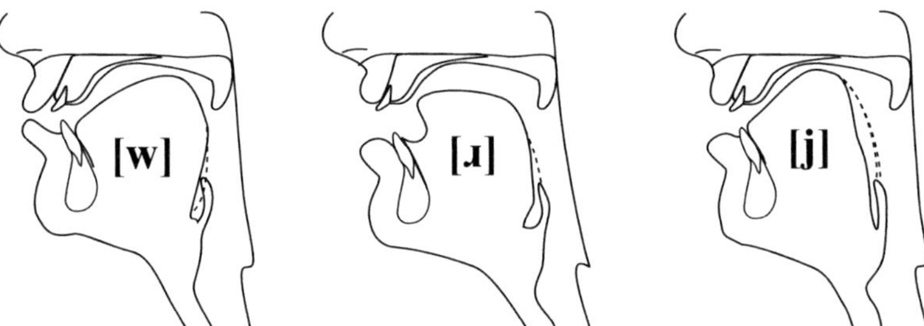

Figure 2.6.: Example articulations of the approximants [w], [ɹ], and [j]. The dashed lines are the contours of the side of the tongue.

Trills

A trill is produced by bringing a loosely-held articulator close enough to another articulator so that it starts to vibrate. This vibration is induced by the airflow and thus similar to the vocal folds' vibration. In both Standard German and General American English, trills do not exist, but there are dialects in both languages that do include them, especially as realizations of the phonem /r/ as in *rye* in the Scottish dialect or *richtig* in many Bavarian German dialects.

Taps

Taps are a single tap of a loosely-held articulator against a second articulator and thus are essentially very quickly articulated stops. In English, the middle sound in *letter* is often realized in this way but there are no taps in German. Taps are obstruents.

Laterals

A lateral sound is produced by closing the vocal tract along the mid-line, but leaving one or two openings on the side (*laterally*), where the airflow can still continue. In English and German, this is only the case for the sonorant sound [l] as in, e.g., *love* or *Liebe*. There is no voiceless lateral consonant in English or German.

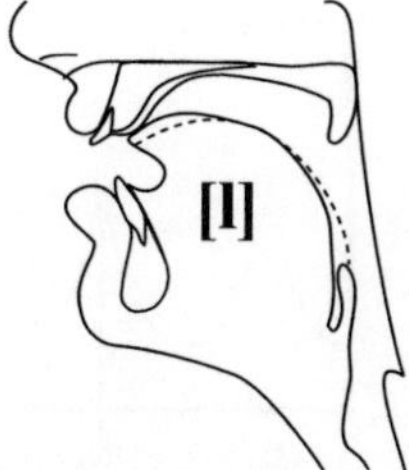

Figure 2.7.: Example articulation of the lateral [l]. Note the lowered side(s) of the tongue (indicated by the dashed line), which forms a narrow lateral canal for the air to flow through.

2.4. Acoustic properties of speech sounds

Most of this chapter deals with the articulation of speech sounds (articulatory phonetics), but a brief excourse into the acoustic properties of speech sounds (acoustic phonetics) will also be helpful to discuss certain aspects of the articulatory synthesis in chapter 6. The symbolic notation used throughout this work is according to [37], while the concepts and relationships presented are according to [29] and [23]. Speech acoustics can be deconstructed into two components: a harmonic component, which is caused by a vibrating sound source (usually the vocal folds) and shaped by the vocal tract acting as an acoustic resonator, and a noisy component, which is caused by aerodynamic, turbulent sources in the vocal tract "tube". Both components will be discussed separately here but always occur together in different compositions in natural speech.

2.4.1. Vocal tract resonances and formants

As mentioned in section 2.1, a (mostly) open vocal tract acts as an acoustic resonator that is excited by the airflow pulses injected through the oscillating glottis (voiced excitation). These *resonance frequencies* f_{Ri} (where i is the index of the resonance ordered from low frequencies to high frequencies) of the resonator are determined by its geometric configuration, i.e., the tongue position and lip rounding. These resonances shape the acoustic spectrum of the glottal excitation signal and lead to local maxima of the energy in the spectrum of the radiated speech called *formants*, which are usually identified by their center frequencies F_i. However, the maxima measured in speech spectra are not necessarily identical to the resonance frequencies f_{Ri} due to the interaction of the vocal tract frequency response with the harmonic excitation structure. The latter are the maxima of the continuous frequency transfer function of the vocal tract that is independent of the excitation signal. But since the excitation signal is a (continuous) periodic signal, it has a discrete spectrum containing spectral lines at the fundamental frequency f_0 of the vocal fold oscillation and all integer multiples thereof (the *harmonics*). Under the assumption that an open vocal tract is a linear acoustic system and thus does not add any frequency components to the input signal, each formant frequency F_i can only be one of the discrete signal components already present in the excitation signal (see Figure 2.8). Formant extraction methods may correctly estimate the envelope of the spectral signal, but the most frequently used methods based on Linear Predictive Coding (LPC) are still prone to errors due to influences of the glottal time dynamics [38, 39]. Formants are most frequently used to describe vowel sounds, which have very distinct, individual formant structures (see the example spectrograms shown in Figure 2.9). In fact, when analyzing the first two formants F_1 and F_2 of different vowels, a pattern emerges (see Figure 2.2b) that is very similar to the vowel chart shown in Figure 2.2a. Note that despite the apparent correlation between the acoustic property F_1 and the articulatory property of tongue height or vocal tract openness, and between F_2 and the tongue frontness/backness, these relationships should not be considered to be one-to-one mappings since other degrees of freedom of the vocal tract (e.g. the lip protrusion) may also affect the formants (as in /i/ versus /y/). Nevertheless, the perceptual relevance of the first two formants and the diffi-

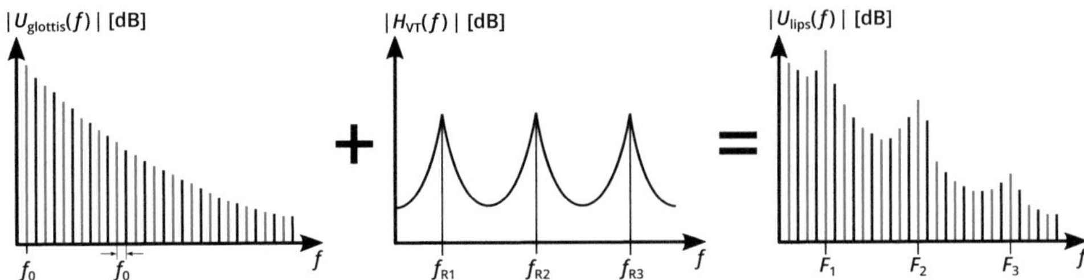

Figure 2.8.: Excitation spectrum (source), vocal tract transfer function (filter), and spectrum of the signal at the lips. For low f_0 (black and gray lines), the high density of harmonics means that the difference between the formant frequencies F_i and the resonance frequencies f_{Ri} may become smaller. When f_0 is high (only black lines), however, the harmonic structure becomes more sparse and f_{Ri} and F_i diverge more strongly.

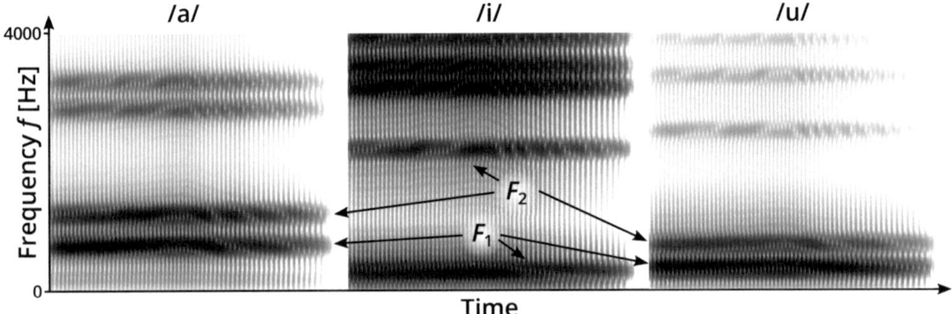

Figure 2.9.: Spectrograms of (synthetic) realizations of the corner vowels /a/, /i/, and /u/. The formants F_i show up as dark, high energy bands and their absolute and relative positions are major acoustic distinctive features of the sound identity.

culty to precisely measure higher-order formants led to the common convention of defining vowel sounds by their first two formant frequencies (see Figure 2.2b).

While formants are the result of the resonances of the main tube of the vocal tract (the pharynx and oral cavity), other side branches (e.g., the nasal cavity during nasalized articulations) impact the final transfer behavior, too. These side cavities add resonances but also absorb energy from the sound wave in the vocal tract in a frequency-selective way and thus introduce attenuations at certain frequencies defined by their geometric dimensions called *antiresonances*, consequently creating *antiformants* in the speech signal.

Although mostly used to describe vowel sounds, formants are a result of a voiced excitation of the vocal tract in a specific configuration. Therefore, any sound with a voiced excitation exhibits a formant structure, including consonants (as shown by the examples in Figure 2.10). However, the relationship between the observable maxima in spectra of non-vowel sounds and the resonances of the vocal tract is much more entangled due to the complex interactions of the (supraglottal) sound sources and the vocal tract. Therefore, consonants are generally discerned by a different property (the side cavities for nasals and laterals, the temporal pattern for stops, or the noise components for fricatives) and thus usually not described in terms of their formants.

2.4.2. Noise sources in the vocal tract

Whenever the airflow in the vocal tract becomes turbulent, a new additional sound source is created that adds a noisy component to the speech signal. This noise can be very subtle and have little impact on the perceived sound identity (e.g., during breathy phonation), it can be a distinctive feature to distinguish between sounds (e.g., in voiced/voiceless pairs of consonants like [v] and [f]), or unwanted and/or pathological as in hoarse voices. The characteristics of these noise sources depend on the exact configuration of the turbulence-causing constriction (cross-sectional area, circumference, involved articulators) and on the position within the vocal tract or, more specifically the tube systems up- and downstream from the constriction. Examples for different noise characteristics are given in Figure 2.10.

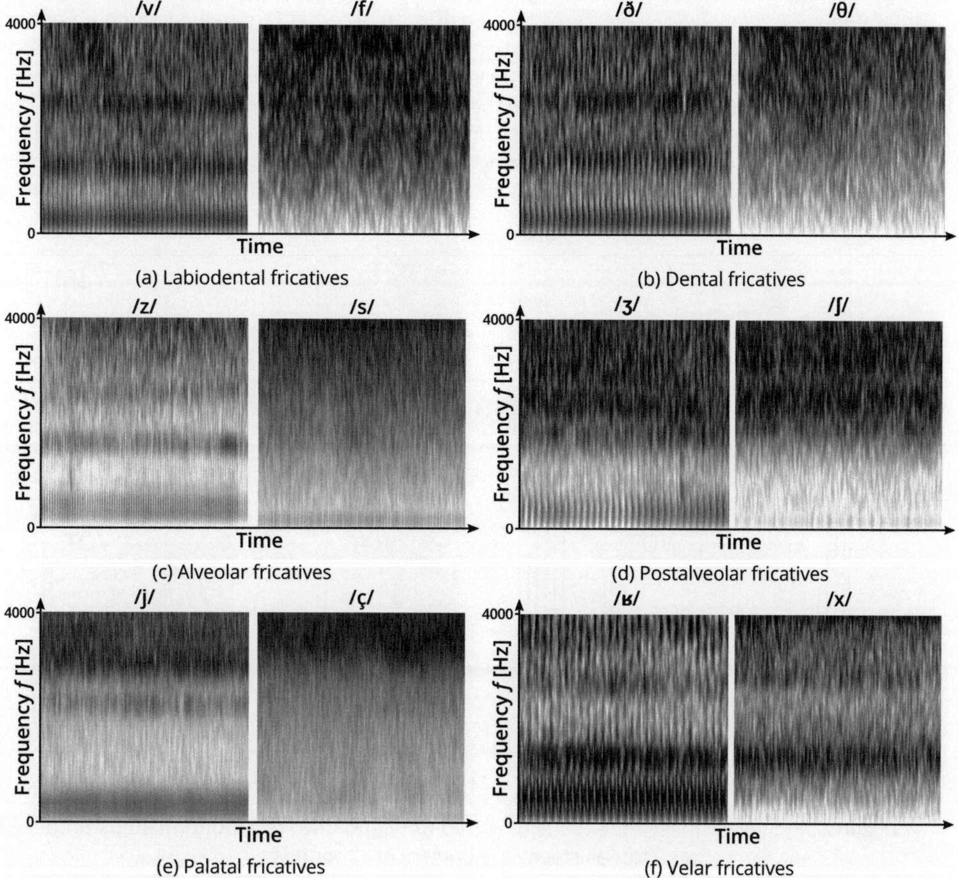

Figure 2.10.: Example spectrograms of voiced (left) versus voiceless (right) minimal pairs. In the voiced examples, formants can still be recognized as they stand out from the noise floor. In the voiceless examples, the signals apparently consist entirely of shaped noise with no harmonic structure.

2.4.3. Time dynamics

Some sounds are mostly defined by the static vocal tract shape (like vowels and fricatives) and thus have fairly static acoustic properties, while others are very distinctly defined by their temporal pattern and therefore have more pronounced time dynamics. The flow-induced vibration of the primary articulator in trills, for example, causes a secondary oscillation in the time domain, which is superimposed on the periodicity caused by the (higher) fundamental frequency of the vocal folds vibration. Stops, however, have an even more complex temporal acoustic structure, reflecting the two articulatory stages (closure, release) by five acoustic stages: When the vocal tract is *closed*, there is very little acoustic signal (stage 0). Instead, the pressure in front of (upstream) the constriction rises until it matches the subglottal pressure, causing the airflow through the glottis to stop. When the primary articulator starts to release the full closure, the initial release is accelerated by the force exerted by the pressure upstream of the constriction, causing an initial *transient* (stage 1) of acoustic energy as the airflow suddenly increases. This increase of airflow comes with a sudden pressure drop and the rate of increase of the area at the constriction becomes slower after this initial flow pulse. The small opening in the beginning of the release now causes turbulence in the airflow and thus *frication* noise (stage 2). As the constriction becomes larger, the friction noise turns into *aspiration* noise (stage 3) before the *voicing* sets in (stage 4) for the following vowel. The aspiration noise is generated at a secondary constriction arising from the articulatory context, i.e., not at the place of articulation itself. The time from the release of the closure to the beginning of the voicing of the following sound is called Voice Onset Time (VOT) and is an important feature that varies across different places of articulation (see examples in Figure 2.11), but also across languages [40] and many other factors, e.g., age [41]. Besides VOT, Figure 2.11 also illustrates how the other stages

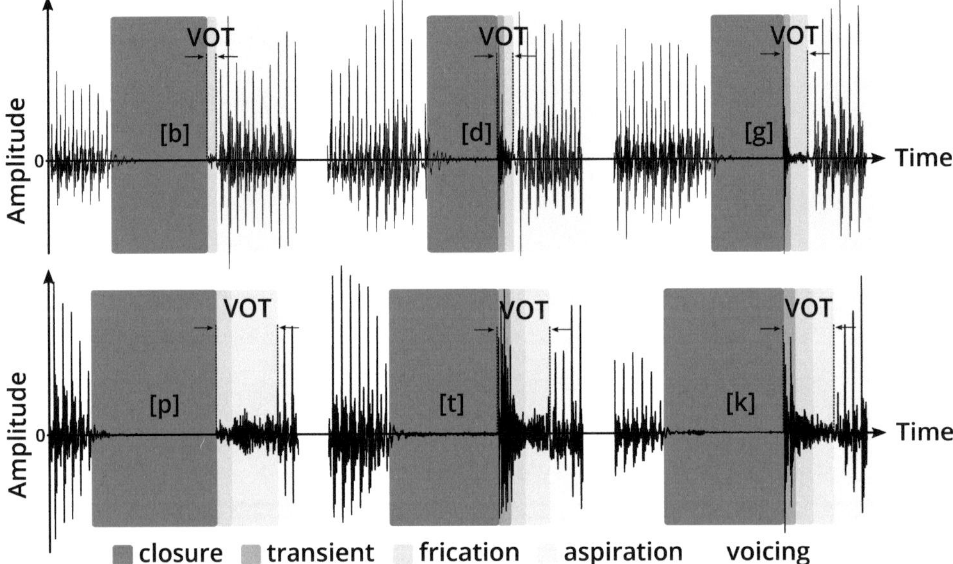

Figure 2.11.: Voice Onset Time (VOT) of voiced (top) and unvoiced (bottom) stops produced in an [aː] context. Not all stages are present in all sounds.

are also affected by the voicing of the stop and the place of articulation: voiced stops generally have hardly any aspiration noise as the vocal folds resume oscillating soon after the supra-glottal pressure drops in the initial transient. In (voiced and unvoiced) labial stops, the transient burst sound is barely noticable. In alveolar and velar stops, the transient burst is much more pronounced. The exact temporal composition, sequence and pattern of the four stages (and even the duration of the "stage 0" *closure*) may all contribute to the discrimination of the different stop sounds.

2.5. Coarticulation

So far, each phoneme (the smallest unit of speech that is used to distinguish different words [42]) was assigned a single articulatory realization or phone. However, the same phoneme may be realized very differently depending on the sounds preceding and following it (the *phonetic context*). This phenomenon is called *coarticulation*. In [43], the authors explain the concept by comparing the articulatory domain to the written word: When a typewriter produces a sentence, it produces it one letter at a time, using a separate hammer for each letter with no inter-dependencies or interferences between each individual symbol. When the vocal tract produces connected speech, it cannot "jump" from one articulatory configuration to the next one. Instead, it has to move along a path that is very distinctly defined by the starting and end point, all the while speech is being produced continuously. A more fitting analogy than the static typewriter, the authors claim, would be cursive handwriting, where the letters are produced in a connected, continuous fashion and each letter therefore may look slightly different depending on which letters came before or after it. While these metaphors are slightly contrived (since they, e.g., do not consider the motor task of hitting the sequence of typewriter keys), they serve to illustrate two main aspects of coarticulation: (1) The planning of the motor task of articulation and (2) the physical and biomechanical influence of the context on a particular realization of a speech sound. An example for coarticulated phones corresponding to the phoneme /k/ are the words *caw* [kɔː] and *key* [kiː]. In the former realization, the lips are likely already in the rounded configuration of the following [ɔː] while they are likely quite unrounded in the latter realization, as necessary to produce the [iː] following the stop. You could say that the vocal tract anticipates the later articulations, which is why this influence of a later sound on the articulation of one or more preceding sounds is called *anticipatory* coarticulation. Coarticulation can also have the opposite effect, where a preceding sound influences the articulation of one or more later sounds. This is called *carry-over* coarticulation and was, e.g., observed in the articulation of vowels in nasal contexts [44], where the vowels are nasalized due to the velum still being lowered from previous nasals. There are many studies regarding coarticulation (see [43] for a good introduction) and numerous models (see [45] for an overview) based on various assumptions of the underlying mechanics. A basic explanation for the observed effects can be found in the principle of economy of the speech motor system: A speaker only realizes the minimum requirements for their speech to be understandable. If an articulatory feature does not obfuscate the sound identity to the point that it might be mistaken for another sound, it does not have to be changed. The lowered velum of the first [n] in *banana* [bəˈnænə], for instance, can be kept in that position for the entire utterance even though it causes the vowel [æ] to be nasalized because nasalization of vowels is not a discriminant feature in English. That way the movement to lower and raise the velum does not have to be repeated for the second [n], which is more economical in terms of energy conservation but would also otherwise limit the speech rate because of the inertia of the velar movement. Similarly, an inter-vocalic fricative might look very much like the vowel vocal tract shape, except for the critical constriction used as a distinctive cure for the respective fricative.

The notion of economy is only a very shallow understanding of coarticulation, however, which is a complicated and deep issue, subject to many studies and analyses (as reviewed in [45]). Within the scope of this dissertation, the important concept to point out is that the actual observable number of different vocal tract configuration is much higher than the number of phonemes in a language and even higher than the number of canonical phones because the context in both directions (before and after the sound of interest) can have an effect on the specific realization of a sound.

2.6. Phonotactics

While the phenomenon of coarticulation greatly inflates the number of vocal tract shapes to consider in connected speech, there are also some constraints on the possible sequences of sounds permitted in any given language. These constraints are called *phonotactics* (from Greek phōné "voice, sound" and tacticós "having to do with arranging") and are not part of phonetics, because they are not part of the *speech* production processes, but of the linguistic discipline of phonology, because they are part of the structure of a *language*. They are therefore highly language-specific and can be formulated at the level of syllables as well as the level of phonemes. Syllables are divided into three parts: onset, nucleus (Latin for "core"), and coda (Italian for "tail"). Onset and coda are generally optional, while the nucleus is obligatory. Within each of these parts, not all combinations of phonemes are allowed. Onset and coda generally do not include vowel sounds. The nucleus usually contains a (monophthong or diphthong) vowel, but may also be a so-called syllabic consonant, e.g., the [n] in the two-syllable word *bitten* [ˈbɪt.n̩] (the . symbol marks the syllable boundary). This structure alone hardly reduces the number of possible sequences, however. To give a tangible example of the importance of phonotactics, we will follow the argument and rules for English presented in [46]: We can assume that an English syllable consists of zero to three consonants in the onset, always a vowel sound or syllabic consonant in the nucleus, and zero to four consonants in the coda. The long-form calculations necessary to arrive at the numbers in the following are given in section B.1. If all combinations of the sounds introduced in this chapter were allowed in English, there would be about 75 billion possible syllables. This staggeringly high number, however, is greatly reduced by a number of phonotactic rules. As mentioned above, these rules are very language- (and even dialect-) specific and cannot be generalized. For English, one very basic rule is that no consonants can be consecutively repeated in any part of a syllable. This constraint reduces the number of syllables to about 61 billion, a reduction of almost 20 %. Other phonotactic rules are that the velar nasal /ŋ/ never occurs in the onset of a syllable and the glottal fricative /h/ never occurs in the coda, which leaves about 45 billion possible syllables. The affricates /t͡ʃ/ and /d͡ʒ/ and the glottal fricative /h/ can only occur in the onset if they are the only sound. This slightly more complex rule leaves about 29 billion syllables. In two-consonant onsets, a number of rules can be applied. The first consonant must be an obstruent (so a fricative or stop) and the second consonant must not be a voiced obstruent. Also, if the first consonant is not an /s/, the second consonant must be /l/, /ɹ/, /w/, or /j/. These constraints on two-consonant onsets reduce the number to 28 billion. For longer sequences of consonants, every subsequence must itself obey all the phonotactic rules. For the onset, that means that the second consonant in a three-consonant onset must obey both the rules for the first *and* the second consonant in a two-consonant onset. Therefore, it can only be an obstruent (because of the rule for the first consonant) but it cannot be a voiced obstruent (because of the rule for the second consonant. This leaves only the voiceless obstruents /p/, /t/, /k/, /f/ and /θ/ as options for the middle consonant in a three-consonant onset. Since only voiceless obstruents are allowed as the second consonant, only /s/ is allowed as the first consonant and only /l/, /ɹ/, /w/, or /j/ are allowed as the third consonant, according to previously defined rules. This constraint on three-consonant onsets in addition to the rule that the syllable coda must not contain /w/ or /j/ reduces the number of possible syllables by several orders of magnitude to approximately 284 million. A final simple rule that can be applied to the coda is that the second consonant in a two-consonant coda cannot be /ŋ/, /ð/, /ɹ/ or /ʒ/. Also considering this for substrings in a three-consonant coda, this brings the number of syllables down to about 147 million syllables. These simple rules therefore eliminate more than 99 % of the possible combinations of articulations in General American English. This number can be reduced even further by more specific rules governing the co-occurrence of certain sounds to eventually arrive at only around 6 million syllables (a reduction of 99.99 %, see [46]).

For German, the phonotactic constraints are more easily defined explicitly, instead of formulating them as rules. Assuming the same syllable structure as for English, the total number of possible German syllables would be about 85 billion. According to [47], however, there are only 50 possible consonant sequences in the syllable onset in German and about 160 possible sequences in the coda (as shown in Table 2.1). This immensely reduces the total by more than 99.9 % to only 136 000.

—	h	j	z	f	ʃ	ʃp	ʃt	b	d	g	p	pf	t	ts	tʃ	k
l				fl	ʃl	pl		bl		gl	pl	pfl				kl
r				fr	ʃr	ʃpr	ʃtr	br	dr	gr	pr	pfr	tr			kr
v					ʃv									tsv		kv
m					ʃm											
n					ʃn					gn						kn
																sk
																skl

(a) Onset

—	l	r	m	n	ŋ	p	t	pf	k	f	ʃ	ç	x	
			lm	ln		lp	lt		lk	lf	lʃ	lç		
	rl		rm	rn		rp	rt		rk	rf	rʃ	rç		
						mp		mpf			mʃ			plus additional suffixes
										nf	nʃ	nç		
									ŋk					-s, -t, -st, -ts
											tʃ			
											pʃ			
							ft							

(b) Coda

Table 2.1.: Consonant sequences occurring within German syllables (according to [47]).

Other languages may have similar or different rules and may be more or less constraining regarding sound sequences. The large difference between the numbers of possible syllables in German and English can be easily demonstrated by the concept of a minimal set. All words that only differ in a single sound in the same position form a minimal set. In English, large sets can be easily found (e.g., *crock, creek, crook, crack, crick, crake, croak* - [kɹɑk], [kɹik], [kɹʊk], [kɹæk], [kɹɪk], [kɹeɪk], [kɹoʊk]), while in German, these sets tend to be smaller due to the phonotactic constraints.

Similar to the way that phonotactics limit the possible sequences of articulations that form a word, higher-order linguistic concepts can limit the sequences of words that form a connected utterance. A language-specific grammar, for instance, can define the part-of-speech of a word in a specific location, which may exclude certain words and thus limit the number of possible combinations, as well. These models are summarily called *language models* and are commonly used in Large Vocabulary Continuous Speech Recognition (LVCSR) to limit the number of words the system has to choose from for any given context. Sometimes these models are explicit (e.g., rule-based) and sometimes they are learned as part of the system (e.g., by using a Recurrent Neural Network (RNN)). In the former case, they are based on expert-knowledge and in the latter case they are based on a large set of labeled training utterances.

2.7. Summary and implications for the design of an SSI

Speech sounds are produced by airflow from the lung through the glottis and a variably shaped vocal tract. Speech consists of a finite, relatively small set of phonemes, which are the smallest units of speech that, when swapped, change the perception of the word. Each phoneme can be realized by one or more phones, which are the actual articulatory configurations of the vocal tract that result in the acoustic speech signal. The phonemes of English and German are summarized in Table 2.2. They can be grouped into vowels and consonants. Vowels are marked by a mostly open vocal tract, while consonants have a very narrow constriction or even closure somewhere inside the vocal tract. Consonants can be produced with a voiced excitation (the vocal chords are vibrating) or voiceless excitation (the vocal chords are not vibrating) and this voicing is a feature that is used to distinguish between phonemes. In connected speech, sounds before or after a particular sound can influence its articulation, which is an effect called coarticulation. The number of actual vocal tract configurations for any given language is therefore much larger than the number of its phonemes. Linguistic models (phonotactics or higher-order language models) can reduce the number of possible sequences of articulations by eliminating impossible or unlikely combinations, but must be explicitly specified or learned from a large number of examples.

From the perspective of an SSI, a number of challenges arise from this basic understanding of articulatory phonetics: The approximation of the vocal tract as a shapeable tube calls for a data acquisition frontend that is not only able to capture the position of the primary articulators, but also has to keep track of the secondary articulators (for consonants) or the vocal tract boundaries (for vowels) relative to them so that the tube shape can be extracted. The sensing of the articulators should also cover at least the entire oral cavity and the lips. Even though most articulations are well-defined by the mid-sagittal slices shown in the schematic figures in this chapter, some sounds are more precisely identified by additional lateral information. Besides for the obvious lateral sounds, this is also useful for the accurate measurement of the cross-sectional area of critical constrictions, which is very important for the noise characteristics of fricatives and stops in an Articulation-to-Speech (ATS) system. The temporal resolution also needs to be sufficiently high to not only correctly capture the transient movements from one phone to the next one, but also to resolve the various stages within stop sounds, at least in an ATS system. The spatial resolution of the measurement technique needs to be high enough to distinguish the various places of articulation, which can be just a few millimeters apart, especially near the incisors and the alveolar region. The number of phones is a challenge for the mapping algorithms employed in both Articulation-to-Text (ATT) or ATS systems, especially when also considering coarticulation. From the overview in Table 2.2, it is evident that the vowel systems are quite rich (especially the German one) and there are many vowels that have very similar articulations. Similarly, the various manners of articulation of consonants are also very similar in terms of articulation, even though they have quite different acoustic results. The sounds [ɹ], [z] and [d], for example, only differ by a few millimeters in distance of the tongue tip from the alveolar ridge, but the acoustic result ranges from harmonics-dominated (approximant) through noise-dominated (fricative) to silence (closure phase of the stop). These minute differences require a highly-precise measurement technique. Some shortcomings of a measurement technique may be compensated by using a language model, which can improve the recognition rate in an ATT system by eliminating impossible or unlikely combinations. In ATS, however, this kind of processing would impose language-specific constraints on a theoretically language-independent system (at least in direct ATS) and adds another layer of processing, which may be critical in a real-time application.

All of the requirements described above are difficult to quantify in a generalized way. Instead, as long as one can reasonably assume that a measurement technique meets them sufficiently well (i.e., there are no fundamentally unsuitable properties like a seconds-long measurement period), the technology should always be evaluated in terms of the recognition or synthesis result in an end-to-end fashion. Therefore, chapter 3 presents the current state-of-the-art of articulatory data acquisition techniques in SSIs by using those metrics as indicators for their performance.

Finally, some sounds can only be distinguished by their voicing, while the supra-glottal articulation is the same. Similarly, the fundamental frequency f_0 is generated by the vocal folds and as such not "visible" in the supra-glottal articulatory data. These issues are of general concern for all data acquisition techniques and thus form a somewhat separate problem than choosing the right measurement technology. Therefore, they will be separately investigated in section 6.7.

Sound	Example English	Example German	Sound	Example English	Example German
/ɑ/	palm	—	/ɪ/	kit	mit
/a/	—	Bahn	/ɔ/	thought	offen
/e/	—	Beet	/ʊ/	foot	Butter
/i/	fleece	Tiere	/œ/	—	Götter
/o/	—	Boote	/ʏ/	—	Mütter
/u/	goose	Bude	/a͡ɪ/	price	Mai
/æ/	trap	—	/ɔ͡ɪ/	choice	—
/ɛ/	dress	Bett	/ɔ͡ʏ/	—	Heu
/ø/	—	Höhle	/a͡ʊ/	mouth	Sau
/y/	—	Güte	/eɪ/	face	—
/ɐ/	strut	Ober	/oʊ/	goat	—
/ə/	about	viele			

(a) Monophthong and diphthong vowels.

Sound	Example English	Example German	Sound	Example English	Example German
/p/	pit	Post	/b/	bit	aber
/t/	tin	tief	/d/	din	Ader
/k/	cut	kurz	/g/	gut	Lager
/f/	fat	Fahrt	/v/	vat	Wange
/θ/	thigh	—	/ð/	though	—
/s/	sap	Last	/z/	zap	Wiese
/ʃ/	dilution	Schule	/ʒ/	delusion	Plantage
/ç/	—	ich	/j/	you	jung
/x/	—	Buch	/r/	run	rot
/h/	ham	Haus	/w/	we	—
/p͡f/	—	Topf	/m/	map	Mord
/t͡s/	—	Zaun	/n/	nap	Nord
/t͡ʃ/	cheap	deutsch	/ŋ/	thing	Ding
/d͡ʒ/	jeep	—	/l/	left	alle

(b) Voiced and voiceless consonants.

Table 2.2.: Examples of the (General American) English [48] and (Standard) German [49] monophthong and diphthong vowels and consonants.

3. Articulatory data acquisition techniques in Silent-Speech Interfaces

3.1. Introduction

As the previous chapter 2 has shown, many articulators are part of the speech produciton process. Unfortunately, most of them are not easily observed during articulation because they are hidden from view inside the vocal tract. In order to analyze, capture, and classify articulatory data, these movements need to be made accessible by technological means in the form of some kind of articulatory data acquisition technique. When comparing the technological landscape in SSIs with the one in traditional, acoustic signal-based speech interfaces, the major difference is the lack of an "articulatory microphone": There is no gold standard of a data acquisition technique, which makes comparing different approaches to SSIs and "cross-pollination" between different research groups is very limited, since the findings of one group using one particular technology may barely apply to another group's different technology. Even if both technologies major the same underlying processes of articulation, the nature of the captured data may be very different in terms of dimensionality, complexity, specificity, noise level, and so on. Therefore, algorithms that work well with one kind of data, do not necessarily work well with others. So while during the design of an acoustic speech processing system an engineer can easily pick and choose some well-established building blocks across the entire pipeline (e.g., denoising, beamforming, feature extraction methods, or pre-trained models language or speaker models), each SSI has to be created from the very bottom up and the data acquisition frontend is usually inextricably entwined with the recognition or synthesis backend. Consequently, this chapter presents an overview of the technologies that have been developed for and/or employed in Silent-Speech systems alongside with the studies and algorithms they were used in.

This overview was greatly facilitated by the review papers [50] and [51], but updated and expanded where appropriate. The structure of each entry in this chapter is as follows: after a brief review of the historical context, each articulatory data acquisition technology is discussed separately. Each discussion follows roughly the same pattern: the respective pioneering works are discussed in detail, then the development of the technology over the years is summarized, and finally the state-of-the-art in that particular area is presented in more detail once again. This structure was chosen to highlight how immediate any successes using this particular technology were from the start and where the bar was moved over the years until now. Since the field of SSI research is quite fragmented, the goal of this approach is to give an idea if a technology remains promising and may deliver even better results if a wider audience were interested in it, or if results have never really improved beyond the initial work because of some intrinsic shortcomings and idiosyncrasies of the respective technique. This chapter also deviates from the conventional structure of separating the summary of the state-of-the-art from the descriptions of the methodical background and instead explains the various pattern recognition and signal processing techniques in the context of the respective studies that used them. Again, the fragmentation and non-existence of standards and conventions in the field of SSI research led to a sprawling catalog of methods, where almost every study used entirely different processing pipelines. Therefore, these *in-situ* descriptions were preferred in order to have all the necessary information in the same place.

While there are of course numerous challenges inherent to every individual technology, some issues are more general problems in the context of SSIs. One of these issues is the modality of the speech that is used as input. As several studies using different technologies have shown (e.g., [52, 53]), there is a significant difference in both the static articulator positions and also their movement depending on the speaking mode of audible speech, whispered speech, and truly silently mouthed speech (sometimes called the *silent Lombard effect* because of a similar, well-known effect [54] occurring in acoustic speech in noisy environments). Another important sidenote is that most SSIs only capture supraglottal articulation, which means most importantly that no voicing and pitch information is directly available. For a practical SSI, these limitations have to be considered but since they are independent of the sensor technology, they are not explicitly discussed and not part of the review here. Another important challenge is the articulatory analog of Voice Activity Detection (VAD): articulatory movements are not easily distinguishable from background movements, e.g., swallowing or even their resting position. Without some kind of framing signal (either derived from the articulatory data itself or from some sort of external trigger), the intention of the user to communicate cannot be considered. Because of the technologically fragmented field, no concerted efforts have yet been made to develop such an *articulation activity detection* algorithm and this issue is therefore also not considered in this review. Instead, section 6.7 includes a brief discussion of the state-of-the-art of these issues before presenting some novel approaches to some of them.

For the sake of a concise and succinct comparison of the numerous reviewed studies, the various performance measures commonly used in the evaluation of ATT systems have mostly been converted to word accuracy (which is the number of correctly recognized words divided by the total number of words to recognize). This measure is usually only applied for isolated command word recognition but used throughout the entire chapter due its intuitiveness. Other measures (like Word Error Rate (WER)) were converted where applicable. In addition to the different metric, isolated command word and continuous speech recognition are also difficult to compare. Instead of discussing this difference for every study individually, I therefore preface the review here with a small caveat for the reader to consider when comparing between different paradigms: Intuitively, one would think that continuous word recognition is a much harder task because the number of words tends to be much larger than in isolated command word recognition studies. However, as has been briefly mentioned in section 2.6, speech phrases are not just a randomly chosen sequence of words sampled from the vocabulary but follow a certain syntactical structure (e.g., a noun often follows an article), which can be exploited to limit the search space when predicting the next word in a sequence. In isolated command word experiments, this is not the case. The performance of command word recognition systems therefore scales very poorly with the vocabulary size, while scaling the vocabulary of a continuous speech recognition is less punishing. The same basic principle can also be extended to lower-level speech units: isolated phoneme recognition is also a more difficult task than command word recognition, because just as sentences are a *syntactical* sequence of words, words are a *phonotactical* sequence of phonemes, which can also be used to limit the search space (see section 2.6). Generally speaking, for the same intuitive performance of an ATT system, one should expect the phoneme accuracy to be the lowest, the isolated word recognition accuracy to be slightly higher, and the continous word recognition accuracy to be the highest (assuming language models at the phoneme and word level).

3.2. Scope of the literature review

Even though the field of SSI research is quite young, it is very diverse and a plethora of sensor technologies have been used in studies to register and/or visualize articulatory movements. To distill the current state-of-the-art to a selection of the most relevant technologies, I excluded all techniques that are obviously non-portable (e.g., Magnetic Resonance Imaging (MRI)), potentially harmful to the user (e.g., X-ray), or cannot be used silently (e.g., Non-Audible Murmur (NAM) microphones). In addition to these, all Brain-Computer Interfaces (BCIs) are not included. BCIs are a subset of SSIs that use some sort of brain-related signal as an input modality, thus essentially constituting a "Thought-to-Speech" system. Technologies involved in this field are Electroencephalography (EEG), Magnetoencephalography (MEG) and Electrocorticography (ECoG) (measuring the electric activity of cortical neurons), and functional Magnetic Resonance Imaging (fMRI) and functional Near-Infrared Spectroscopy (fNIRS) (measuring the oxygenization of blood as an indicator of neural processing). However, research using these technologies is currently either lab-bound (ECoG, fMRI, MEG), offers extremely inconsistent results (EEG), or is even wrapped in scandalous controversies[1](fNIRS). Due to their highly experimental status, BCI-related works are therefore beyond the scope of this review and I instead point to the review in [55] for further information in this regard.

3.3. Video Recordings

The most intuitive approach to realize an SSI is probably by emulating lip reading, which essentially constitutes a natural SSI employed by humans as both a means of supporting and replacing acoustic speech perception. The term "lip reading" is however somewhat misleading, because human lip readers also incorporate cues from facial movements, jaw positions, arm and hand gestures, and even the tongue (when it is visible) into their interpretation. Therefore, this technique is also often more accurately called *speechreading*.

In a technical speechreading system, a video camera captures the speaker's upper body and/or face during articulation of words and the video data stream is then processed with machine learning techniques to classify the image sequences into utterances. So far, all published systems were ATT systems, but extending these systems by a Text-to-Speech (TTS) stage would be a trivial problem.

The first reported such system was developed in 1984 by Eric David Petajan in his dissertation [56] and then four years later published in an improved version in [57]. His goal was not, however, to develop an actual SSI, but to support a regular Automatic Speech Recognition (ASR) system with information from the lip reading subsystem to improve the recognition accuracy in noisy environments. This multi-modal approach is well-motivated by the fact that humans also use both acoustic and visual information when interpreting speech sounds; to the extent that the visual information can entirely override the acoustic information under certain circumstances (the so-called *McGurk effect* [58]).

Petajan's setup consisted of a solid-state camera (with a capture rate of 60 fps), two sets of incandescent lamps, and a microphone (for the ASR part of the system) mounted to a head band in a way that allowed the adjustment of the viewing angle and range. Since the mouth opening was assumed to be much darker than the facial area, the images were thresholded to produce binary images where an open mouth (and the nostrils) appeared black and everything else was white. In these binary images, the contour of the mouth opening was calculated for every frame. After recording a number of utterances, the contour images were clustered using a custom image distance measure (which was essentially a Hamming distance scaled by the total black area in the two operand images). From each cluster, a representative mouth image was taken and added to a codebook of mouth images (see Figure 3.1).

The system was evaluated using two vocabularies consisting of the spoken English alphabet and the English digit words zero through nine, respectively. Each utterance was repeated eight times by

[1] https://www.discovermagazine.com/the-sciences/the-fall-of-niels-birbaumer

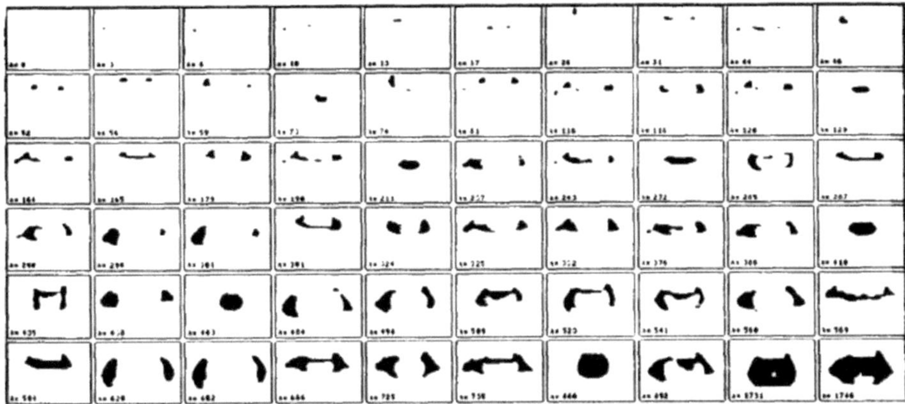

Figure 3.1.: Example codebook of binary mouth images taken from [57]. Each image represents one speech sound. The mouth opening is not necessarily continuous due to a visible tongue or teeth.

four subjects and two samples of each letter were used to create the speaker-dependent codebook for each subject. For each utterance, a binary image sequence was obtained as described above. To evaluate the system, each image sequence was used as a test sequence once and compared to all other image sequences of that subject in the respective data set (leave-one-out evaluation). The comparison was done with Nearest Neighbor classification in two different domains: either by calculating the distance between the test image sequence and the vocabulary image sequence in the image domain using the distance metric described above, or by first vector-quantizing all images using the aforementioned codebook and calculating a simple difference between the codebook indices. In both cases, the time alignment was done using dynamic programming. The speaker-dependent results using only the lip reading modality showed an average performance of 72 % to 80 % for the letter recognition task and 93 % to 100 % for the digit recognition task depending on the subject and whether or not vector quantization was used (with vector quantization generally degrading the performance).

The authors point out the limitations of their system in the error analysis, which is a general problem for visual speechreading systems: the set of visually distinguishable phonemes (the so-called *visemes* [59]) is a subset of all phonemes in a language. In their vocabularies, this was evident in the confusion of the letters A (/eɪ̯/) and K (/kʰeɪ̯/), B (/biː/) and P (/piː/), C (/siː/) and Z (/ziː/), D (/diː/) and T (/tiː/), S (/ɛs/) and X (/ɛks/), and Q (/kjuː/) and U (/juː/). This list shows that in addition to the inability to distinguish voiced-unvoiced minimal pairs, which is an often encountered problem in SSIs, lipreading systems are "blind" to consonants with posterior places of articulation (e.g., /k/ or /ç/) if only the shape of the mouth opening is considered as a feature.

Subsequent work has therefore focused mostly on improving the feature extraction component of such a system (see [60] and [61] for reviews of these efforts), using hand-crafted features processed by shallow (i.e., non-deep learning based) classification models. The state-of-the-art system from that era [62] reported recognition rates of approximately 50 % to 70 % on a ten word vocabulary when using manually corrected regions of interest in the image data, albeit in a more robust (i.e., speaker-independent) fashion. Still, even with these feature engineering efforts and the application of (at the time) state-of-the-art classifiers, the problem of distinguishing phonemes that emit the same viseme remained even in such small vocabularies.

After the meteoric rise of deep learning, Chung and Zisserman [63] were the first ones to significantly scale up the vocabulary size, which so far had generally been set at ten phrases or words (with the exception of the spoken alphabet dataset). Instead of relying on the small existing corpora of visual speech, Chung and Zisserman created their own, substantially larger dataset by automatically mining BBC broadcasts of news shows and their accompanying subtitle tracks to generate thousands of hours of spoken text covering thousands of different words with over 1 million word instances and more than 1000 different speakers. From this vast amount of essentially random data, a structured subset was selected to constitute the corpus: The 500 most frequently (and at least 900 times) occurring words between 5 and 10 characters in length. The lower bound of the word length is chosen to avoid homophenes, which are words consisting of identical visemes (e.g., "pat", "bat", "mat") and more likely to occur in short words. The upper bound of the word length is due to the fact that each word is represented by a one-second video clip, no matter how long the actual word is (i.e., there is word-level context information in the sequences). The dataset was partitioned into three non-overlapping subsets: one for training (containing at least 800 instances of each of the 500 words), one for validation and one for testing (each containing 50 instances per word). A sample of the speakers and a clip from the dataset is shown in Figure 3.2.

(a) A subset of the over 1000 speakers in the corpus

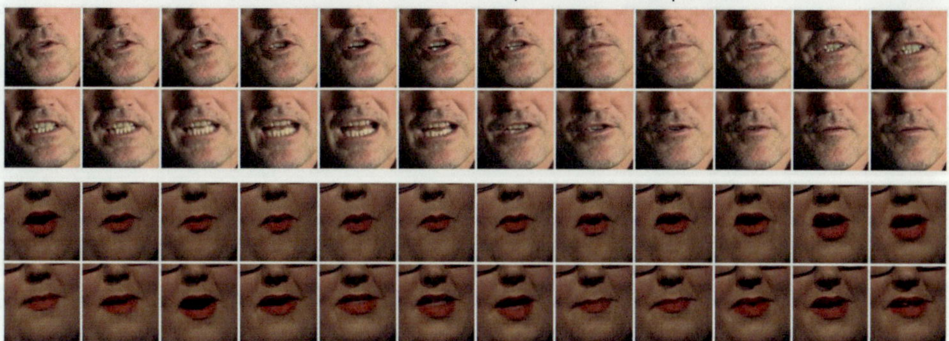

(b) Two one-second clips containing the word "about" (/əˈbaʊt/)

Figure 3.2.: The Lip Reading in the Wild corpus (both figures taken from [63])

In their landmark paper introducing the dataset, Chung and Zisserman also trained and tested a Convolutional Neural Network (CNN) to classify the 500 words. The best achieved word recognition accuracy was 61.1 %, while the best Top 10 accuracy (i.e., the true word label was within the first ten most likely guesses) was 90.4 %. Considering the fact that the vocabulary size was an order of magnitude larger than in all preceding works, these results were very impressive at the time and for the first time showed the promise of an actually practically relevant automatic speechreading system. However, the exclusion of short words somewhat tarnishes the results, since it is exactly the problem of resolving homophenes that is the hardest to solve for a speechreading system. Human speechreaders distinguish between homophenes by incorporating (among other things) syntactic and phonotactic knowledge, sentence-level context, and even discourse-level context. These temporal patterns are more efficiently learned by RNN and as Chung and Zisserman point out themselves in their conclusion, an RNN such as a Long Short-Term Memory (LSTM) to represent a language model might further improve the results. Indeed, the current state-of-the-art performance is achieved by Stafylakis et al. in [64] by using a combination of residual networks and LSTMs to score a word accuracy of 83.0 % and a Top-10 accuracy of 98.3 % on the Lip Reading in the Wild dataset. This basically models the phonotactics word-level patterns (since every sequence in the training set is essentially just one word with an uncontrolled, small number of words preceding and following it), but no higher-level patterns like syntax or discourse-level patterns (like the domain). The inference time for a single utterance was in the order of tens of seconds, according to an independent measurement in [65]. While these results are quite impressive compared to earlier work, the vocabulary size of 500 words is still rather small compared to acoustic-based ASR, where vocabulary sizes of several 1000 words are quite common. In [66], for example, the authors describe a mobile ASR system that achieves an accuracy of 88.7 % in an open-ended dictation task with a vocabulary size of 64 000 words.

Summary and conclusion

Visual speechreading is a well-investigated task with a major emphasis on improving the algorithms to classify individual words. Deep learning based systems are performing at a level where a meaningful system with a limited vocabulary size in the order of hundreds could already be constructed. The problem of homophenes has so far only been addressed by incorporating word-level context, but higher-level context has been ignored so far because no dataset is available that contains properly labeled data for this kind of modeling. Given the difficulty of the task, it seems unlikely that all homophenes can be resolved through higher-level context modeling, especially when considering very short words (which have been generously excluded from the state-of-the-art training set). Another issue is the data acquisition frontend: the current state-of-the-art systems were trained on data extracted from TV news broadcasting with an ideal broadcasting studio lighting scene and very frontal camera viewing angle. For a portable system, the algorithms would have to deal with different viewing angles on top of the already existing challenges. Lastly, the state-of-the art system has a very slow inference speed in the order of tens of seconds, which makes it unsuitable for a real-time system. Despite their limitations, speechreading systems have been successfully used to support acoustic-based ASR systems. They could therefore also be considered as an auxiliary modality in a multi-modal SSI, where the primary modality might be able to resolve the homophenes.

3.4. Ultrasonography

Ultrasonography (US) is a well-known medical imaging technique that exploits the different reflective characteristics of different tissue compositions. To obtain an image using ultrasound (a *sonogram*), high-frequency (above 20 000 Hz) sound pulses are emitted into the tissue under analysis using a transducer probe. Inside the tissue, at every interface of layers with different compositions and therefore different acoustic impedances, the ultrasound waves are partly reflected and partly transmitted. The reflected part (the *echo*) can be registered at the transducer probe and used to construct an image. The most common way to construct an image from these recorded echos is to associate the time delay between sending out the pulse and receiving an echo to a tissue penetration depth and the amplitude of the echo (which is a function of the reflection coefficient of the interface it originated from) is related to a brightness value. This procedure is therefore called *brightness mode* or, more commonly, *B-mode* imaging and is the mode exclusively used in SSIs applications to date. The images in all US-based SSIs are midsagittal images of the tongue, recorded with a transducer probe attached under the chin. An example image is shown inFigure 3.3.

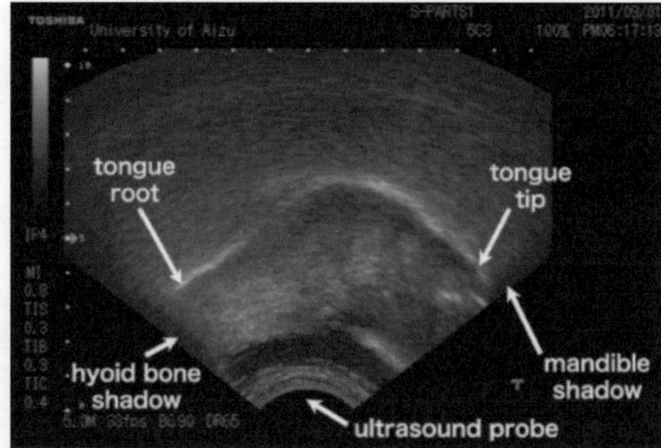

Figure 3.3.: An example sonogram (taken from [67]) similar to the ones used in US-based SSIs. At the interface between the tongue surface and the air in the mouth cavity, almost the entire sound wave is reflected, causing the bright white line in the B-mode image.

Both ATT and ATS systems have been developed using US as the data acquisition frontend. The first such system was presented by Denby and Stone in [68]. Since movement of the head or the transducer can greatly impact the image quality, a previously introduced support system [69] was used to immoblize the speaker's head and maintain a fixed position of the transducer (see Figure 3.4).

Figure 3.4.: The head and transducer support system (HATS) used in [68] (image taken from [69]). The head of the subject is completely immobilized to keep the relative positioning of the transducer under the chin as constant as possible.

With this setup, a dataset was recorded using one subject who read two repetitions of one six-sentence passage and one nine-sentence passage that were designed to contain multiple examples of all English phonemes. In total, the data consisted of roughly 2.5 min of speech represented by 4491 ultrasound images and a simultaneous audio recording. The authors then extracted 14 points on the tongue contour in each image using a maximum smoothed spatial intensity gradient criterion. The coordinates of these 14 points were then mapped to the 12 parameters of the synthesizer (a parametric vocoder) using a Multi-Layer Perceptron (MLP) with four layers containing 14, 20, 20 and finally 12 neurons per layer. Using a 90 %/10 % training/test split, the mapping was learned using backpropagation. According to the authors, the resulting audio was "not recognizable; but alternating between original and synthesized recordings, the listener can soon easily pick out most of the correspondences". A quantitative measure for the synthesis quality was not provided. Despite the poor performance of this first attempt, many subsequent studies have tried to improve on this system by using different synthesizers, different features, and most importantly, using a video recording of the mouth as an additional input modality.

The major driver of US-based SSIs was the French research project "Ouisper" [70] that ran from 2006 to 2009 and produced numerous studies that thoroughly advanced the state-of-the-art in the field. The data acquisition frontend of Ouisper extended the setup by Denby & Stone by a video camera pointed at the mouth (see Figure 3.5a).

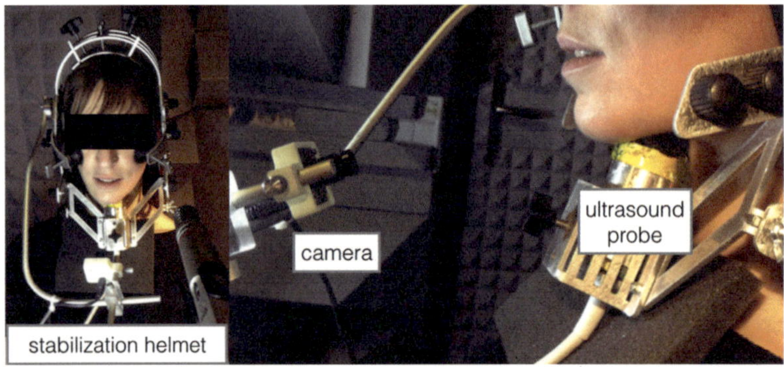

(a) Setup of the data acquisition component

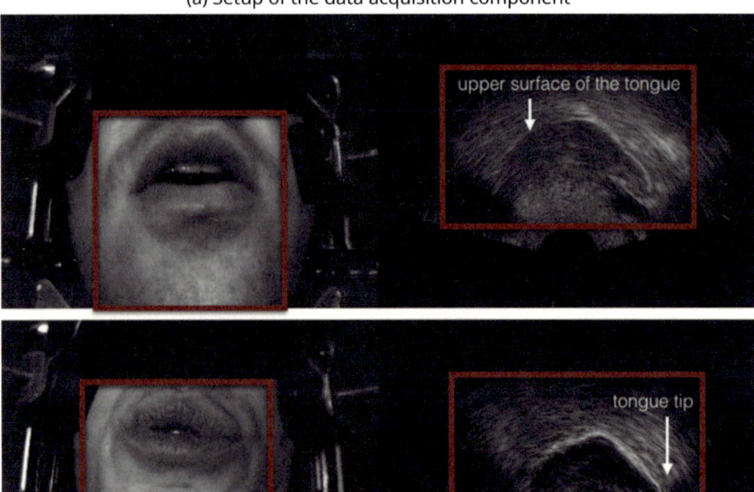

(b) Sample images during recording

Figure 3.5.: The Ouisper system (both images taken from [71])

With this setup, both ATT and ATS systems were developed and evaluated. During the original funding period of Ouisper, work mostly focused on engineering better features to represent the tongue shapes in the ultrasound images using statistical models [72] and to optimize the multi-modal data acquisiton setup [73]. Pilot studies on using the data for an ATS system were carried out as well. In [74], the group built a phoneme-level ATT system, which they then extended in [75] to an ATS by a unit-selection synthesis stage. They reported a phoneme recognition accuracy of 60 % on a dataset made up of 41 of the 44 English phonemes. Intelligibility evaluations of the synthesis were at this stage not possible due to the rather low accuracy.

The research efforts continued with the same general framework beyond the initial funding period of Ouisper and after some incremental improvements in the early 2010s (e.g., [52]), the ATT stage was finally dropped and a direct ATS system was presented in [71], using a statistical mapping from the hand-engineered tongue and mouth contour features to a statistical, parametric speech synthesizer without any intermediate recognition step. In order to still benefit from context modeling, the authors used full-covariance Hidden Markov Models (HMMs) with dynamic features, which allowed them to model the timing organization of the articulatory movements as well as the static tongue and lip shapes. The synthesis quality was evaluated by a transcription test, where ten native French speakers were asked to transcribe 30 synthesized French sentences with no prior knowledge of their content. The average word accuracy was around 60 %.

In the last few years, a number of studies (also from outside the original Ouisper group) have started to employ deep learning techniques both for only the feature extraction stage and for the mapping of the articulatory data to the synthesizer parameters [76]. In [77], CNNs were used to extract features from the video stream and sonograms, but the recognition itself used statistical models (HMM-Gaussian Mixture Model (GMM)) to classify the phonemes. The reported phoneme accuracy was 80.4 % trained on a dataset using 34 French phonemes in 488 sentences. The study in [78] trained a feed-forward Deep Neural Network (DNN) to map hand-crafted features of the articulatory data to vocoder parameters. The mapping was evaluated in a listening test with 23 Hungarian native speakers rating the naturalness of 15 synthesized Hungarian sentences. The average naturalness rating was approximately 3 out of 10 (where 10 is very natural and 0 is very unnatural). Systematic intelligibility tests were not conducted. The same group recently published a study [79] using an autoencoder network to compress the US images and was able to improve the naturalness rating to 4 out of 10.

The current state-of-the-art in US-based SSIs was, however, set by [80], using Discrete Cosine Transform (DCT) features to compress the input images, a feed-forward DNN combined with HMM decoding to classify the sequences into words, and a language model to constrain the decoding. This system achieved a word accuracy of 94.13 % on a set of 1023 words, greatly improving their own previous benchmark of 84.3 % [81] using the same data and feature extraction technique, but no DNN and instead going straight to the HMM stage.

Summary and conclusion

Ultrasonography-based SSIs are quite mature and ongoing research is mostly concerned with better feature extraction and mapping techniques, while the design of data acquisition composition seems relatively stable: a transducer probe attached below the chin and a frontal view video camera directed at the mouth. One major drawback, however, is the rigidness of the setup and the necessary immobilization of the subject. US image quality depends strongly on the coupling between the transducer and the tissue. Even small disturbances of the coupling can lead to strong artifacts in the images to the point that any small air gap between the transducer and the tissue causes total reflection before the ultrasound even penetrates the skin. To improve the coupling, a hydrogel is used, which needs to be reapplied over time as it wears off during use. It is true, as most authors in the field point out in their papers, that US is conceptually a portable technology. Since the setup commonly used in the published studies, however, imposes these restrictions, the factual portability is severely limited.

On the algorithmic side of the system, achievable word accuracy on practically relevant vocabulary sizes has reached a level that useful out-of-lab ATT systems seem feasible, thanks to deep learning techniques. For direct ATS systems, the limited number of visible articulators seems critical: only the tongue back and the mouth opening are clearly visible. The tongue tip is often invisible in the sonogram, as are the palate and the velum. Many minimal pairs can therefore not be distinguished using only the visible information (e.g., the nasal /n/ and the stop /d/, which only differ in the velum position, see chapter 2), although some of them may be resolved using temporal information and language models. The technique therefore intrinsically suffers from the same homophene problem (albeit with different homophenes) as video-only-based systems (see section 3.3). Lastly, it is currently unknown how speaker- and session-dependent the trained models are. Given the diverse anatomy of speakers and the difficult reproducible placement of the transducer probe (especially without an immobilizing head fixture), it seems unlikely that the systems can be scaled up to more speakers (or even across several sessions of the same speaker) without severe performance losses.

3.5. Electromyography

Electromyography (EMG) is a technique to capture the activity (contraction and relaxation) of skeletal muscles. The history of EMG runs in parallel with the history of electricity and the slow discovery of the underlying physiology of what causes muscle contractions [82]: from Luigi Galvani's discovery that electricity can cause a muscle contraction in frog legs in 1797 [83] all the way to the Nobel Prize in 1932 awarded to Edgar Douglas Adrian and Charles Sherrington for their work on the function of neurons [84], progress in the neurology and physiology was slow but steady, finally culminating in the understanding of the underlying processes we have today. The contraction of muscles is controlled by neural activity [85, Chapter 5-6]: A bunch of muscle fibers are connected to the nervous system through the endings of a *motor nerve*. Along that motor nerve, a small electric potential called an *action potential* can be sent by the nervous system to signal contraction. Due to chemical imbalances between the inside and the outside of a nerve cell, the resting potential difference across the cell membrane is −80 mV to −90 mV (inside is more negative). An action potential is a rapid depolarization of this membrane potential, i.e., it suddenly becomes less negative, that spreads along the nerve fiber membrane and can thus establish communication between distant neurons. The sudden depolarization is caused by the rapid inflow of positive sodium (Na^+) ions, allowed access by voltage-gated sodium channels, and quickly approaches zero or, in case of large nerve fibers, even overshoots the zero level and becomes positive. After a few microseconds, the sodium channels begin to close again and potassium (K^+) channels begin to open (more than during the resting state), allowing the diffusion of positively charged potassium ions to the exterior and thus the repolarization of the membrane. A typical action potential is shown in Figure 3.6.

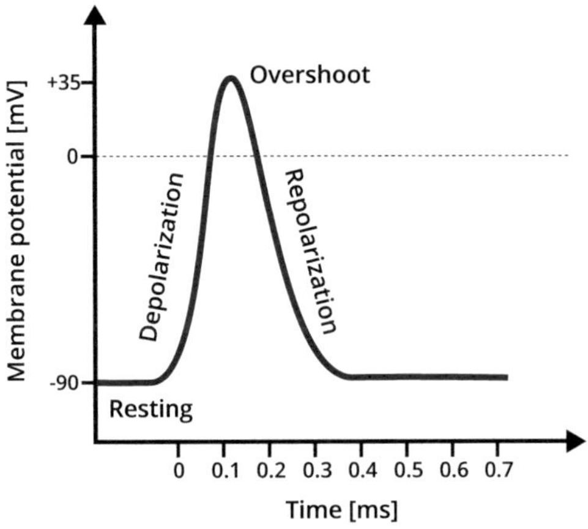

Figure 3.6.: Typical action potential (recreated from [85, Figure 5-6]). The exact timing and amplitudes vary across the different kinds of cells.

When such an action potential reaches the nerve endings innervating muscle fibers, it triggers the secretion of a neurotransmitter (acetylcholine). The neurotransmitter in turn triggers an action potential at each muscle fiber membrane, which travels along the membrane in the same way it would trave along a nerve fiber membrane. The action potential depolarizes the muscle membrane and causes the release of calcium ions from a membrane-bound pocket called the sarcoplasmic reticulum within the tissue. These calcium ions then cause attraction between the components that mostly make up the muscle fiber (large polymerized protein molecules called actin and myosin) and the fiber contracts. After a few milliseconds (the exact number depends on the type of muscle), the calcium ions are pumped back into the sarcoplasmic reticulum causing the contraction to cease and the fiber is relaxed again until the next muscle action potential comes along.

Multiple muscle fibers are usually innervated by the same neuron and form a *motor unit*. On average, a motor unit consists of about 80 to 100 muscle fibers, but the exact number depends on the type of muscle: fast-reacting muscles with fine-grained control have more neurons but fewer muscle fibers per neuron than comparatively slow and imprecise but very strong muscles. Within a muscle, motor units are not necessarily separate, distinct entities but can also overlap other motor units to allow supporting contractions without being individually triggered. The intensity of the muscle contraction can be increased by adding together several of the individual twitch contractions described above, either by recruiting more motor units to contract simultaneously (multiple fiber summation) or by increasing the frequency of contraction (frequency summation). In summary: even a "simple" movement consists of many, many well-coordinated twitch contractions and many, many action potentials overlapping each other in time and space. Physiological studies and diagnoses therefore often used needle electrodes [86] to better individually select motor units or even individual fibers instead of recording only the sum activity. For non-clinical studies, however, a non-invasive measurement was desirable. Since the electric signals involved in the muscle control are detectable on the skin surface, a variant called Surface Electromyography (sEMG) was developed that used surface electrodes to measure the action potentials of the motor neurons on the skin surface. These electrodes are glued to the skin and measure the compound activity of all motor units in a comparatively large area with a diameter of up to several centimeters. The signal quality is therefore much lower than that of intramusculuar EMG: The clearly defined peaks of the action potentials of the motor unit of interest are "drowned out" by a noise floor caused by a large number of nearby motor units and even other effects like varying coupling impedance, mechanical disturbance of the electrode and so on. An example of the difference in signal quality is shown in Figure 3.7.

SEMG has such low specificity that as of the technological state in the year 2000, the American Academy of Neurology did not recommend it for diagnosis of neuromuscular diseases or lower back pain in a report that analyzed more than 2500 articles, reviews and books on the subject matter [88]. The Academy did find sEMG suitable to record bursts of activity as in chewing, walking, and breathing and so considered it an "acceptable tool" (a Type C recommendation) for kinesiologic analysis of movement disorders, evaluating gait and posture disturbances, and similar applications. The report notes that sEMG offers only low signal resolution and is highly susceptible to movement artifacts. Others have even found an effect of body temperature on the frequency components of the sEMG signal [89]. Because it is so difficult minimize such interferences, an entire body of work exists that is only concerned with the right positioning of the electrodes for various applications and even different subjects (see, e.g., [90–92]).

Nevertheless, articulator activity is a kind of movement and since sEMG is an acceptable tool for movement analysis (see above), various groups were motivated to explore its suitability for an SSI. The first documented attempts to use sEMG data in this context were attempted by Sugie and Tsunoda in 1985 [93] and Morse and O'Brien in 1986 [94] at a time, when microprocessor-controlled sEMG systems were starting to enter the market [95]. The study by Sugie and Tsunoda aimed at a full speech prosthesis: recognizing the articulated speech and synthesizing the corresponding sound (indirect ATS). Since this was the first foray into this application for an at the time still fairly new technology, they limited the vocabulary to the five Japanese vowels $/\mathrm{a}/$, $/\mathrm{e}/$, $/\mathrm{i}/$, $/\mathrm{o}/$ and $/\mathrm{u}/$. They employed an sEMG system using off-the-shelve components available at the time to acquire data with three differential pairs of sEMG electrodes. The electrode pairs were positioned around

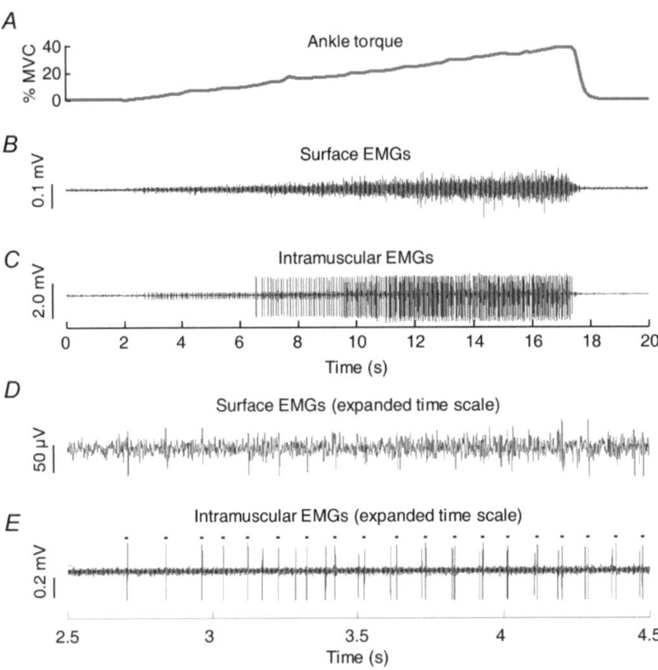

Figure 3.7.: Example comparison between an intramuscular EMG signal measured with a needle electrode and a an sEMG signal measured with a surface electrode (image taken from [87]). A: Plantar flexion torque during an isometric ramp contraction from 0 % to 40 % Maximum Voluntary Contraction (MVC). B: Surface and C: intramuscular EMG signals recorded from the medial gastrocnemius muscle. D+E: zoomed-in segment of each signal. While the overall contraction level appears reflected in the signal *level* of the sEMG, the individual discharge instants of the motor unit seem much more difficult to derive from the sEMG than from the EMG.

the mouth opening of the subject: one pair on the upper lip, one on the chin, and one on the right cheek. The envisioned speech prosthesis used a two-step technique: *recognize* the sound based on the muscle activity (i.e., obtain a text label representing the articulated sound) and *then synthesize* audio from the text label. Unfortunately, the authors used a (at least in the field of speech recognition) non-standard evaluation metric, which makes it necessary to introduce their classifier in greater detail: The three-dimensional feature vector used for the classification contained the binary activation of each of the three muscles associated with the electrode positions (0: muscle is not active, 1: muscle is active). This activation pattern was obtained every 10 ms and fed into a finite state machine (FSM). An FSM is a way to model the output to a given input sequence [96, Chapter 3]. The (purely abstract) "machine" starts in a *start state* X and can receive input in the form of an element from a finite set (the *input alphabet*). In the case of above vowel recognition study, the input alphabet consisted of all possible combinations of muscle activations, i.e., all binary vectors from $(0, 0, 0)$ to $(1, 1, 1)$. The machine can then *transition* into another state (or even into the same state again) depending on the input according to a state transition table. It then waits for another input and continues to transition between states until it reaches a *final state*, which is associated with a certain output. Here, the final states are associated with the five vowels so that if the machine gets to such a state, the corresponding vowel has been recognized. The excerpt of the state transition diagram from [93] is reproduced in Figure 3.8 to illustrate the principle of their classifier.

The rules for the transitions of the FSM of course critically affect the accuracy of the detection. Unfortunately, even though the authors state the *ad hoc* transition rules for this particular study

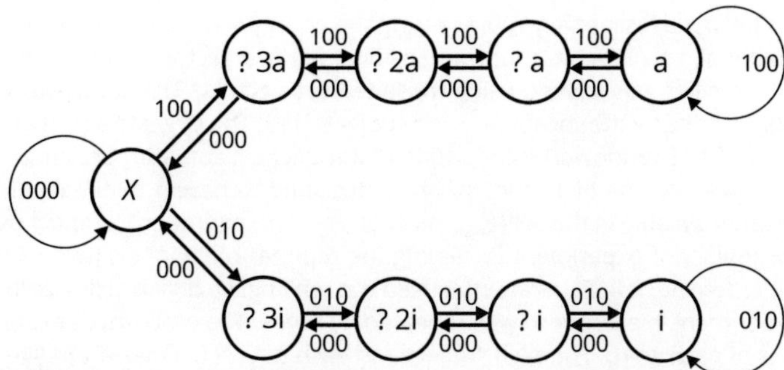

Figure 3.8.: Excerpt of the state transition diagram, reproduced from [93, Fig. 5]. *X* is the start state representing articulatory "silence", "a" and "i" are two of the five final states representing the corresponding vowels, and the remaining states represent intermediary states that hint at a particular vowel detection but need further input to give a confident output. The binary triplets are the muscle activation patterns extracted from the sEMG data used as input.

in [93, Table I], they do not explain how those were generated or how to adapt them to different vocabularies. To evaluate the classifier, data from three adult male subjects were recorded during the articulation of the 50 Japanese consonant (C)-vowel (V) monosyllables (e.g., /a/,/e/,/i/,/ka/,/ke/,/ki/ and so on). Without the authors stating this explicitly, the various signal traces in [93, Fig. 6] indicate that the subjects were instructed to sustain the vowel parts of the utterances for approximately 1 s. The output of the FSM was generated at a frame rate of 100 Hz and evaluated at every output transition of the FSM, i.e., every time the classifier changed its output, it was compared to the ground truth. The reported error metric was therefore the number of correct output transitions divided by the total number of output transitions, i.e., the *correct rate*. Using the same transition table for all three subjects, the correct rates for each vowel instance (calculated over the duration of each vowel) ranged from 42 % to 100 %, depending on the subject and context. The global average was 64 %. The result from the classifier was used to synthesize vowel sounds using a partial autocorrelation (PARCOR) synthesizer. The output of the synthesizer was rated by 10 listeners on a scale from 1 (very poor) to 5 (excellent). The result was an average rating of 2.9 for all synthesized sounds with the rating correlating rather strongly with the objective correct rate of the FSM output transitions.

There are numerous possible criticisms to this study, but the most glaring ones are the lack of generalization of the transtioning table, making the setup very hard to adapt or extend. The significance of the results is also somewhat limited by the artificially sustained articulations. Given the high frame rate of the system of 100 Hz, the speech could have easily been produced in a more natural manner while still acquiring enough data frames for the FSM to reach a final state. The reason this was not done most likely lies in one of the disadvantages of EMG: the high noise level. The FSM approach with several intermediary states and the long durations of the vowel sounds were both used in an effort to counter the fluctuations of the EMG signal and to get a more stable output. But in spite of these harsh limitations, the correct rates still went down to 42 % in some cases because of the extremely noisy signal. Nevertheless, the study was pioneering work in the field and the paper even introduced a real-time system implementing the entire pipeline and thus representing the first closed-loop direct speech synthesis voice prosthesis, albeit with a very limited vocabulary of just five vowels.

The second, almost concurrently published, pioneering study by Morse and O'Brien [94] did not try to synthesize the intended speech but focused on the recognition of entire words instead of just isolated vowels. They used four electrode pairs (i.e., four channels of differential data), three of which were placed at the neck and the fourth was placed on the forehead. The EMG signal was processed so that the output was the average magnitude of each channel over 50 ms. For each channel, the averaged magnitude signal was integrated over the duration of an utterance to calculate a feature value (essentially representing the energy level of the corresponding channel during the articulation), resulting in a fourdimensional feature vector for every utterance. A maximum likelihood classifier was trained using these feature vectors. The study was comprised of five experiments differing by the vocabulary and subject used: The largest vocabulary (used in experiment 2) was a set of 17 pseudowords consisting of a trigger syllable with presumed high muscle activity (/tɹoʊ/) followed by one of 17 CVC syllables designed to have a minimal pair relationship with at least one other syllable in the set (e.g., /pat/ or /ɹat/). Experiment 1, 3 and 4 used a 12 word subset of the vocabulary of experiment 2, varying the number of channels (two or four) and the subject (male, 24, or female, 24). Experiment 5 used the ten English digit words ("zero", "one", "two" and so on). In experiment 1, each word was repeated 10 times. The other three experiments contained 20 repetitions of each word. For each subject and each data set, a maximum-likelihood classifier (also called a Naive Bayes classifier) was trained using all the available data of each set. A maximum-likelihood classifier models the probability $P(k|\vec{x})$ that an observed feature vector $\vec{x}$ belongs to a class $k \in K$, where K is the total number of classes. Since this *a-posteriori* probability is unknown, it is derived from the *a-priori* joint probability density function (PDF) $p(\vec{x}|k)$ (modeling the probability to observe a feature vector $\vec{x}$ given the class k) using Bayes' theorem:

$$P\left(k|\vec{x}\right) = \frac{p\left(\vec{x}|k\right) \cdot P(k)}{p\left(\vec{x}\right)} \tag{3.1}$$

The classification result is the most likely class, i.e., the class k for which $P\left(k|\vec{x}\right)$ is largest. For this decision, the probability $p\left(\vec{x}\right)$ of observing a given vector $\vec{x}$ in the first place is the same for all classes k and is thus just a linear factor that can be ignored when looking for the maximum value of $P\left(k|\vec{x}\right)$. The decision rule e for this classifier can be written as:

$$\begin{aligned} e &= \underset{k=1,\dots,K}{\arg\max}\, P\left(k|\vec{x}\right) && (3.2)\\ &= \underset{k=1,\dots,K}{\arg\max}\, \frac{p\left(\vec{x}|k\right) \cdot P(k)}{p\left(\vec{x}\right)} && (3.3)\\ &= \underset{k=1,\dots,K}{\arg\max}\, p\left(\vec{x}|k\right) \cdot P(k) && (3.4)\end{aligned}$$

In their study, Morse and O'Brien presumably assumed an equal prior probability $P(k)$ of each class, meaning that every word was equally likely to occur. In that case, the $P(k)$ can also be omitted since it does not affect the arg max result and the final decision rule therefore becomes simply:

$$e = \underset{k=1,\dots,K}{\arg\max}\, p\left(\vec{x}|k\right) \tag{3.5}$$

So in order to train the classifier, the joint PDF $p\left(\vec{x}|k\right)$ needs to be estimated from the training data for each class k. This is usually done by assuming that $p\left(\vec{x}|k\right)$ has the general shape of a multivariate Gaussian distribution of the the same dimensionality D as the vector $\vec{x}$:

$$p(\vec{x}|k) = \frac{1}{\sqrt{(2\pi)^D\,|\Sigma_k|}} \exp\left\{-\frac{1}{2}(\vec{x}-\vec{\mu}_k)^T \Sigma_k^{-1} (\vec{x}-\vec{\mu}_k)\right\}, \tag{3.6}$$

where the class-related means $\vec{\mu}_k$ and the class-related covariance matrices Σ_k can be readily calculated using the labeled training data set.

The overall accuracy (number of words correctly recognized divided by total number of words) for the experiments using 12 words hovered around 50 % and dropped to 35 % for 17 words. The accuracy when classifying the numbers data set was approximately 65 %. The study also investigated the accuracy of a classifier trained with data from one speaker and tested on data from the other speaker (inter-speaker dependency) and with data from the same speaker but from another recording session (inter-session dependency). The result was that the accuracy for the 12 word vocabulary dropped from around 35 % when training and testing with data from the same speaker and session to 30 % when using data from the same speaker but different sessions, showing the high session dependency of the technique. When data from different speakers was used for training and testing, the even higher speaker dependency caused the accuracy to drop below chance level. After further analyses of their system in [97], the authors conclude that one of the major problems was the signal noise.

In follow-up studies [98, 99] using the same experimental setup and classifier, the effect of additional features (average energy and the standard deviation of each channel) on the accuracy was examined but yielded no additional improvement. When the backpropagation algorithm moved into the mainstream (for the first time) in the early 1990s [100], Morse et al. [101] even employed a (unspecified) neural network to the same task, using 16 (also unspecified) spectral features obtained from the power spectral density of each utterance. The results are not presented in a systematic way and are therefore somewhat anecdotal, but the authors report a "dramatically better" accuracy when compared to using time-domain features, citing the noise robustness of spectral features as the biggest contributor. The final publication from the group regarding this topic in 1990 [102] made some methodological improvements to the experimental setup by using eight subjects and three non-overlapping vocabularies of the same size: one with ten pseudwords following their established pattern, one with the ten English digit words, and one set of ten two-syllable English words. For all eight subjects, the reported accuracy ranged from 20 % to 30 % but the probability of the correct response being among the first five guesses of the classifier (Top-5 accuracy) was much higher (approximately 70 % to 80 %). While the studies by Morse et al. had numerous issues regarding the experimental (non-systematic variation of vocabulary size, subject, number of channels) and evaluation setup (different number of channels used for intra- and inter-speaker analyses, unspecified experimental settings, unsystematic report of results), they identified some of the main issues of the application of sEMG to SSIs: the reproducibility of the data for different sessions and subjects, and the generally noisy signal.

It took about a decade for the research community to rediscover sEMG for silent-speech recognition (or synthesis, for that matter) and in the early 2000s, quick improvements were made using the more advanced analog (for the measurement hardware) and digital (for the signal processing and pattern recognition) technology of the time. In [103], the authors tackled the problem of session dependency, i.e., the variance of the accuracy when training and testing with data from the same subject but different recording sessions. The study used seven pairs of electrodes to collect sEMG data from three subjects (one female, two male) in four sessions, each recorded on four different days. The vocabulary consisted of the silently articulated ten English digit words from "zero" to "nine" and each session contained thirty repetitions of each word. The first measure to reduce the session dependency was to prepare a plaster mask for each subject that would cover their faces and leave holes for the sEMG electrodes to be wired through. This was supposed to ensure a reproducible positioning of the electrodes and thus was expected to reduce the session variance. Using spectral features obtained from a Short-time Fourier transform, HMMs were used to classify the data. The study used a five-state left-to-right HMM with 12 Gaussians per state for every word in the vocabulary. For in-session training and testing, a leave-one-out cross-validation scheme was used. For inter-session training and testing, the training sessions were split into subsets of equal sizes, each containing 30 instances of each vocabulary word, and a different model was trained for each subset. The reported testing result was the average of the test results using these models. The accuracy of the recognition for the in-session condition using all available channels ranged from 96 % to 98.8 % for the ten words, averaged across all four sessions for each speaker. When using a different session for training and testing (but just one of each) without any further normalization, the accuracies dropped down to up to 48.8 % with an average of 76.2 %. By using three of the four available sessions for training and and the fourth for testing, and by additionally standardizing the feature vectors to zero mean and unit variance, the session dependence could be greatly reduced to an average of 87.1 % across the three subjects.

In the 2010s, many more improvements were made, driven by essentially two groups: the group around Geoffrey Meltzner in the United States, and the group around Michael Wand in Germany. Both groups individually settled on a particular electrode setup and kept it mostly constant throughout their work. The Meltzner group arranged the sensors unilaterally (see Figure 3.9a), motivated by the possibility of using a handheld device similar to a mobile phone that would hold an array of sensors and would be used in much the same way, except that instead of a microphone capturing the acoustic speech, the electrode array would capture the sEMG signal. This handheld device was never realized, though, but the sensor arrangement was kept regardless. The Wand group, while also dabbling in a sensor array setup for a bit (see, e.g., [104]), generally used the bilateral setup shown in Figure 3.9b. Neither group developed the respective hardware themselves and instead used commercially available (and slightly modified) sEMG equipment.

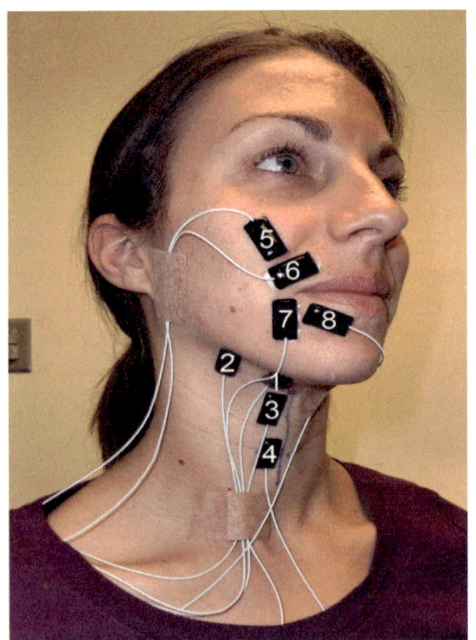

(a) Setup according to the Meltzner group [105–107]

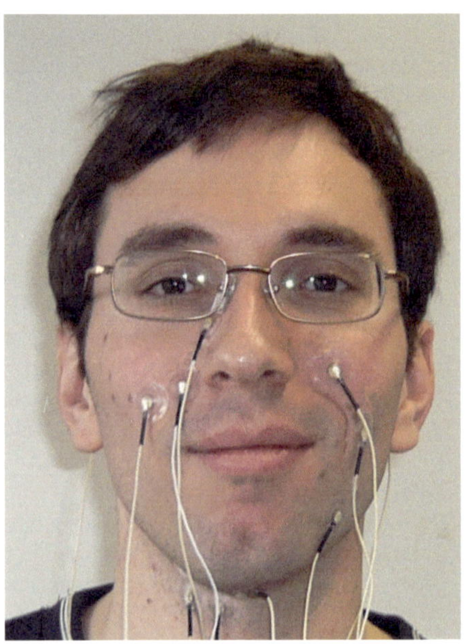

(b) Setup according to the Wand group [108–110]

Figure 3.9.: Sensor setups used by the two main research groups driving development of sEMG-based SSIs

After several years of steady improvements, both groups have published their (as of today) best results using an ATT paradigm. The Meltzner group used HMMs for the classification and reported in [111] a recognition accuracy of 90.4 % for isolated word recognition using a vocabulary of 65 words. In a continuous word recognition task (which allows the use of language models to constrain the search), they achieved an accuracy of 91.1 % across various domains with a vocabulary of 2200 words. The system was speaker-dependent and required 2 h to 3 h of training material from each new speaker to train an individual model. It is unknown how the performance varied across multiple sessions using the same speaker because both training and testing data were recorded in a single session. Given the noisiness of the data and the sensitivity with respect to the sensor positions, session-invariance is, however, of vital importance for a practically relevant system.

The Wand group published their best ATT results in [104], where they used an HMM classifier and reported an accuracy of 89.9 % in a continuous word recognition task using a vocabulary of 108 words. While the Meltzner group has exclusively employed shallow models, the Wand group eventually graduated to deep learning in [112], where they used a DNN as a frontend, whose outputs were decoded by an HMM. For this setup, they reported a session-dependent recognition accuracy of 23.8 % for the same continuous speech recognition task with a vocabulary of 108 words.

Instead of scaling up the vocabulary for the session- (and thus speaker-) dependent paradigm, their following work focused on improving the reproducibility and lowering the session-dependency (see, e.g., [108, 109]). Their most recent effort was published in 2018 in [110] and applied domain-adversarial training of the DNN stage to achieve an average across-session accuracy of 28.5 % with a reported floor accuracy for some sessions of approximately 25 %, in which case the adversarial training even lowered the accuracy.

While all of the studies discussed so far have investigated an ATT paradigm, the Wand group has also looked into the development of an sEMG-based, direct ATS system: Using sEMG to predict vocoder parameters [113], the result was, in the authors' own words, a "mostly unintelligible [...] speech-like audio" signal. A systematic evaluation was not conducted. In a follow-up study in [53], they used a joint distribution of the EMG signals and the target vocoder parameters as a mapping and conducted an objective evaluation using a spectral distortion measure on the synthesized speech. The lowest speaker- and session-dependent average distortion was 4.53 dB, while the best session-independent, but speaker-dependent distortion was 6.04 dB. The results are difficult to contextualize, however, because spectral distortion measures are a good way to rank various variants of a speech processing pipeline, but cannot be quantitatively or qualitatively related to the intelligbility or naturalness of the ouput. Finally, a DNN was applied to map the EMG data to the vocoder parameters in [114] and achieved a distortion of 4.56 dB to 5.61 dB. A test to transcribe the ATS result or compare it to natural speech was not conducted because of the generally low intelligibility. Curiously, using the synthesized speech as input to an HMM-based ASR system, the word accuracy was higher than in their previous ATT system (92.7 % vs. 89.9 % in [104]), even though the same data was used and human intelligibility was considered too low by the authors to warrant a listening test. The real-time factor of the DNN system on a desktop PC (Intel Core i7-2700 CPU running at 3.5 GHz) ranged from 2.9 s to 16.2 s, depending on the feature set used.

Summary and conclusion

SEMG-based SSIs have been under heavy developement in the last decade, although both main research drivers in the field appear to have moved on to other topics given the lack of published work in the last year (especially compared to their previous output pace). Sensor positioning and attachment is challenging, even in a lab environment. The signal quality is generally low, the sensors are very unspecific in the muscle activity they register, they are prone to (non-articulator-related) movement artifacts and to Electromagnetic Compatibility (EMC) isses due to the small analog voltages involved. The current state-of-the-art has produced continous speech recognition ATT systems with vocabulary sizes that are already suitable to domain-specific applications, although still at least one order of magnitude lower than acoustic-based ASR (2200 vs., e.g., 65 000 [66]). A major limitation on the systems' relevance in practical application is, however, the heavy speaker- and session-dependence. While many attempts were made to lessen the performance drop when using the systems with speakers that it was not trained with, no satisfying solution has been found yet. The training material needed to adapt a system to a new speaker and/or session is also quite extensive (e.g., 2 h to 3 h), making an individually trained system impractical. Authors in the field have mentioned the possibility of transfer learning or other adaptation strategies involving less training material from the target speaker, but no algorithms or models have been proposed for this yet. Deep learning techniques have been successfully applied to both of the SSI paradigms (ATT and direct ATS), but have not yielded the performance boost they have facilitated in other fields. It is possible that more (and more diverse) data from more speakers are necessary to fully exploit the potential of DNNs.

3.6. Permanent-Magnetic Articulography

In 2005, a research group around Fagan filed a patent for a new measurement device specifically designed to capture speech movements for silent-speech processing [115]. In their application, they describe the operation of the device as follows: a number of small magnets are attached to the tongue, lips, and/or teeth of a subject. In addition, the subject wears a support structure (similar to the frame of a pair of eyeglasses) carrying a number of magnetic field sensors. During (silent or audible) speech, the magnetic field changes at the sensor positions because of the relative movement of the magnets in and on the mouth. These changes are registered by the sensors and passed to a processor that can then further analyze and interpret the signals. This measurement modality was (later) named Permanent-Magnetic Articulography (PMA). In their patent, the authors pointed out the possible applications of recognizing the spoken words, using the device as an input modality to control other devices or machines, and to use it to identify the individual wearing it. In their first paper based on their invention three years later [116], the group started investigating the suitability of their system to be used in an SSI. To evaluate if the magnetic field sensor data contains information that can be related to the spokent utterances, they devised two experiments: one experiment using a vocabulary of 13 phonemes and one experiment using a vocabulary consisting of 9 words. Each word or phoneme was spoken 10 times by a single subject. For this study, one magnet was attached to the center of the subject's tongue tip and two pairs of magnets were attached to the upper and lower lips symmetrically positioned with regard to the face's center line. The magnetic field of these five magnets was sensed by a total of six dual axis magnetic sensors mounted on the frame of a pair of eyeglasses (see Figure 3.10).

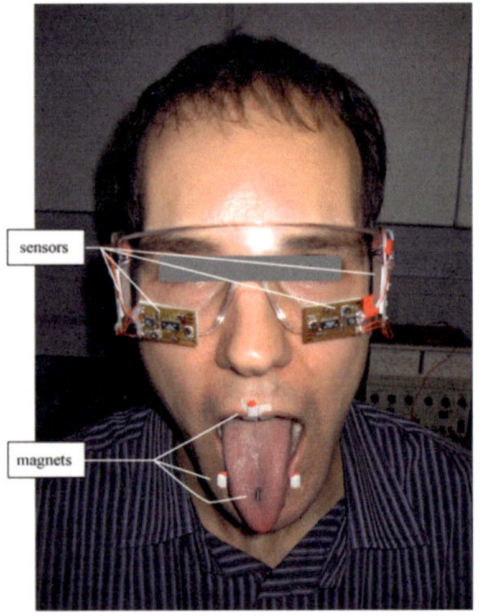

(a) Setup from Fagan's pilot study [116]

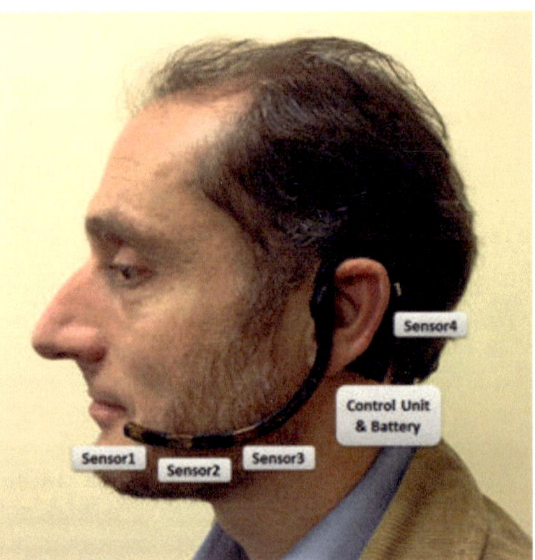

(b) Most recent iteration used in [117]

Figure 3.10.: Permanent-Magnetic Articulography setups

The data used for classification were the twelve (2 channels times six sensors) magnetometer signals, which were low-pass filtered with a cut-off frequency of 40 Hz for noise suppression. The classifier was a nearest-neighbor classifier using all 10 repetitions of each of the vocabulary entries as templates and Dynamic Programming using a Euclidean distance measure to implement Dynamic Time Warping (DTW) and find the most similar match to a given test sample among the templates. Unfortunately, the authors failed to explain how they generated test samples but it can be assumed that they recorded one additional repetition of each word/phoneme to use for the testing. The recognition accuracy with this setup was 94 % for the 13 phonemes and 97 % for the 9 words. Two years later, the same group published the results of a follow-up study in [118], that used the same measurement device and classifier, but different vocabularies: one vocabulary consisting only of the 10 English digit words "zero" to "nine" (the numbers set) and one vocabulary additionally consisting of 47 other words (the words set) chosen to cover a wide range of phones. Using ten repetitions of the numbers set and five repetitions of the words set, the DTW classifier was evaluated using leave-one-out cross-validation for three speakers using only the data from each speaker, i.e., not evaluating inter-speaker performance. The recognition rates ranged from 82 % to 100 % for the numbers set and from 76 % to 99 % for the words set, depending on the speaker.

Acknowledging the small vocabulary size and thus the limited usefulness of the system at this stage, the authors identified a few ways to improve the system, mostly by using more elaborate data processing and pattern matching techniques. Consequently, the next few publications by members of the group [117, 119, 120] focused on these aspects to improve the results, while also increasing the vocabulary size:

In [121, 122], they replaced the DTW-based recognizer with statistical sequence modeling using HMMs and thus achieved a leave-one-out cross-validated word accuracy of 92 % to 98.8 % on the words set for a single speaker, depending on the signal condition used (time signal, plus first time derivative, plus second time derivative, first time derivative only). Going a little further in [122] they also performed a digit sequence recognition experiment using HMMs and achieved a sequence accuracy of 61.1 % to 81.7 %, again depending on the signal condition.

While these results were all obtained using only a single speaker, in [123] the same general setup was used to train and test models for three speakers individually (again using only data from the same speaker for training and testing). The results for the word accuracy ranged from 82.72 % to 90.97 % and the sequence accuracy from 74.89 % to 86.76 %.

Most work around PMA-based ATT has focused on PMA as the only modality, with the notable exception of the study by Sahni et al. [124], which additionally included an intra-aural sensor that measured the miniscule deformations in the ear canal caused by jaw movements. They achieved a speaker-dependent, sentence-level accuracy of 83.3 % to 96.4 % on a set of 11 sentences from a medical domain (e.g., "I need water" or "It hurts"). Since this study was a one-off project by the group and had numerous methodological weaknesses, the results have to be considered anecdotal, although it is still noteworthy because of the multimodal approach.

Lately, PMA was also used for a direct ATS system. Recording simultaneous audio and PMA, Gonzalez et al. [125] tried a statistical approach using joint distributions of PMA data and vocoder parameters. The synthesis was trained and tested using two vocabularies: one consisting of the ten English digit words ("zero" to "nine"), and one consisting of 48 consonant-vowel (CV) syllables containing all combinations of four vowels and twelve consonants. The joint distributions were trained in a speaker-dependent fashion and the mapping was objectively evaluated using 10-fold cross-validation and a spectral distortion measure. Depending on the mixture components in the mapping and the window length of the PMA data , the spectral distortion was around 3 dB to 7 dB (similar to sEMG-based ATS, see section 3.5) for both the digit words and the isolated consonants and vowels. A listening test was conducted to evaluate the subjective quality and naturalness of the synthesis[2]. The naturalness was rated by 25 human listeners as approximately 2.25 out of 5 (where 5 is very natural) when no additional information was used and apporx. 3 out of 5 when voicing information from the original audio files was used. For the CV syllables, the intelligibility was subjectively evaluated by a transcription experiment involving 25 human transcribers. The average accuracy was 68 % but showed great variance across the various possible CV combinations, to the extreme that some syllables were always correctly transcribed (e.g., "shoo" - /ʃu/) and other syllables were never correctly transcribed (e.g., "rue" - /ru/).

Following up on this study, Gonzalez et al. replaced the statistical mapping with an RNN consisting of Gated Recurrent Units (GRUs) [117]. Data from six speakers were used for training speaker-dependent mappings with the number of sentences ranging from 353 to 519. The synthesis quality was rated about the same as with the statistical mapping (40 on a 100 point scale), but the intelligibility was improved significantly by the RNN in a direct comparison with an average word accuracy of 73.49 % (vs. 65.25 % using statistical mapping) across speakers and a peak accuracy of 91.53 % (vs. 79.18 %) for one of the six speakers.

Gilbert et al. [126] used an LSTM network for the same task of mapping the PMA data to the

[2]The intelligbility was not assessed for the digit words because the authors found the synthesis completely intelligible. This underlines the aforementioned fact that spectral distortion measures are difficult to interpret: For a very similar distortion level, the authors in [114] described their synthesis' intelligibility as "overall very low" (see section 3.5).

vocoder parameters using the same training data and achieved a similar objective distortion level. They have not, however, reported any subjective test results.

While most studies involving PMA did not consider session-dependency or robustness against various possible interferences (movement or EMC issues), two notable exceptions exist. In [120], an algorithm to remove motion artifacts in the PMA data is presented. The results showed that the word accuracy of a PMA-based ATT system using a vocabulary of eleven English digit words ("zero" and "oh" representing the number 0 and the digits "one" through "nine") degraded from about 90 % during no head movement down to 2 % during normal conversational movement. The proposed algorithm was able to reduce the impact significantly and retain a word accuracy of approximately 80 % despite conversational movement. In [127], the session-dependency of the PMA-based ATS system [125] was evaluated using the aforementioned spectral distortion measure. Without a session adaptation strategy, the distortion level more than doubled from 4.5 dB to approximately 9.8 dB. Using an MLP-based adaptation technique, the distortion could be lowered to approximately 5.5 dB. This analysis was only done for the digit synthesizer described in [125] but not for the CV setting, and no subjective tests of the adaptation technique were conducted.

Summary and conclusion

PMA is an extremely promising technique regarding both ATT and ATS and, in fact, can be regarded as the current state-of-the-art in the field, given the good results presented by the group around Gilbert and Gonzalez and the technological maturity of their device. Unfortunately, attaching the magnets to the tongue in a safe and reliable way is a non-trivial issue. The authors have used tissue adhesive in their studies but pointed out that, ultimately, the magnets would have to be implanted into the tongue for the device to be used longer than just a single recording session in a lab environment and to avoid accidental swallowing of the magnets, which can be very harmful to the subject. So even though the reported results have been quite impressive so far, an actual user study has yet to be conducted, possibly due to this issue. Another open question is the speaker dependency in the recognition paradigm: the accuracy can swing quite significantly depending on the speaker, even when trained on the same speaker's data. It is yet to be seen how the system will perform when training with data recorded with different speakers than the test data (inter-speaker evaluation). The session dependency has been briefly described but not systematically explored. Similarly, the impact of movement artifacts was successfully reduced for the ATT paradigm, but it is unclear if this strategy can be generalized to more scenarios (e.g., walk-and-talk), to the ATS paradigm, and to other sources of interference (i.e., EMC-related issues).

3.7. Electromagnetic Articulography

Electromagnetic Articulography (EMA), or sometimes called Electromagnetic Midsagittal Articulometry (EMMA) when only used in the midsagittal plane, is a technique to track fixed points on the articulators during speech production and is a commonly used tool in instrumental phonetics. Since the mid-90s, several systems have been commercially available (see Figure 3.11 for an example), but their basic principle is the same: Small sensor coils are attached to the subject's articulators (usually the tongue, the lips, and the jaw). The subject is placed into an alternating electro-magnetic field, created by a field generator. The varying field induces a small Alternating Current (AC) voltage in the sensor coils, which changes depending on the relative orientation and position to the surrounding field and these spatial data can therefore be reconstructed from the sensor signal. While the reconstruction is fairly complex, it is possible with a very small error (e.g., less than 1 mm [128]) and at a high temporal resolution (e.g., 500 Hz [129]). Some SSI-related studies have used EMA in conjunction with other input modalities (see section 3.9), but the first EMA-only system was proposed by Heracleous and Hagita in [129]. The authors used the positional information of three coils on the tongue, two coils on the lips and one coil on the lower jaw as features (after decorrelation) and trained a speaker-dependent HMM-based ATT system to recognize 16 different French consonants

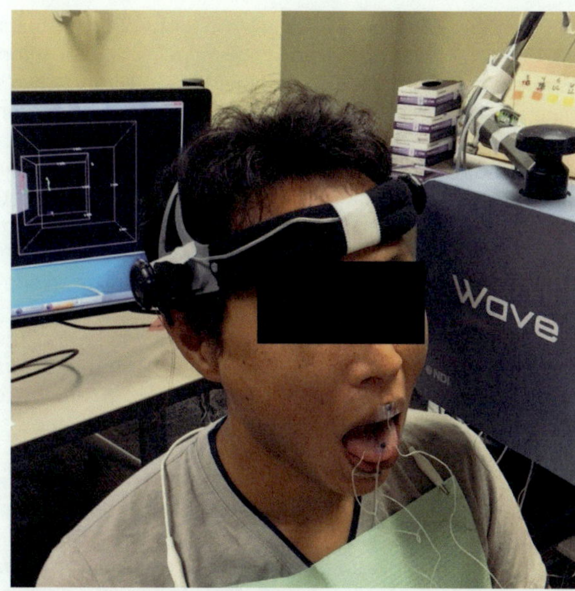

Figure 3.11.: A subject using an EMA system (here: NDI Wave). The sensor coils are individually glued to the subject's articulators and the wires are required to pick up the small signals induced by the alternating electro-magnetic field generated by the field generator next to the subject's head.

and 14 different French (oral and nasal) vowels. On a test set of 682 vowel instances and 568 consonant instances, they achieved a phoneme-level accuracy of 93.1 % for the vowels and 75.2 % for the consonants. In 2015, Hahm & Wang [130] presented a speaker-dependent ATT system that uses a DNN for the articulatory modeling and an HMM-based decoding stage. The authors used the positions of five coils (three on the tongue and two on the lips) on the midsagittal posterior-anterior (x) axis and superior-inferior (y) axis, but also added their time derivatives (delta features) to the feature vector (five coils × two positions + their first and second derivatives for a feature vector size of 30). With a vocabulary of 44 English phonemes, the system achieved a phoneme accuracy of 64.5 % for a male speaker and 62.9 % for a female speaker. In a more recent study in 2016 [131], the authors used a very similar setup (midsagittal positions as features and a DNN-HMM classifier), except with only four sensor coils (two on the tongue and two on the lips) and achieved a phoneme-level accuracy of 27.2 % on a set consisting of 39 phones. Since they only used monophones (which means less restrictions on the search space), this seemingly low accuracy was compared to a baseline acoustic ASR system which achieved a phoneme accuracy of 37 %. While all of these systems were speaker-dependent, Kim et al. [132] described a speaker-independent system that used articulatory normalization (both physiologically and statistically driven) and i-vector methods (a sparse representation of a feature vector sequence commonly used in speaker and language recognition) to achieve a speaker-independent phoneme accuracy of 44 % on a set of 278 unique words consisting of 39 unique phonemes. Using a bigram language model, they also achieved a word accuracy of 44.8 %.

A larger number of studies have proposed EMA-based ATS systems. The first such system was introduced in 2011 by Toutios et al. [133] and was actually motivated by studying acoustic-to-articulatory inversion (so the inverse mapping of an ATS system) in an analysis-by-synthesis paradigm. While the study does not conduct a subjective intelligibility or naturalness test, it is noteworthy due to the fact that it is one of the two only ATS studies (across all proposed technologies) that used an articulatory synthesizer as a backend instead of a statistical vocoder. The input EMA data was recorded using four sensor coils on the tongue, four on the lips, and one on the lower incisor. The mapping was found by linear regression. The results were given in terms of the formant frequencies of the vocal tract shapes of six French vowels produced by the mapping but not summarized by the authors. It is evident, however, that the formant error is generally within one to two standard deviations from the statistical mean of the formant frequencies of human French speakers.

A much more thoroughly designed EMA-based ATS system was introduced five years later by Bocquelet et al. in [134]. The authors presented two experiments: one speaker- and session-dependent experiment and one speaker-adaptation experiment. For the first one, they used the same basic sensor setup as Toutios et al. but extended it by a sensor on the soft palate and recorded the movement in all three dimensions instead of just the midsagittal plane. With this setup, they recorded about 45 min of audio and EMA data from one speaker containing an unevenly distributed number of each of the 34 phonemes of French. The synthesizer was a vocoder and its parameters were predicted from the EMA data using a DNN with three hidden layers. The intelligibility of the synthesis was evaluated subjectively in a listening test with 12 human listeners. Without any further information from the audio (i.e., without the original pitch contour), the recognition accuracy of 10 synthesized vowels was 87 % and of 16 different consonants was 45 %.

The second experiment used fewer sensor coils (three on the tongue, two on the lips, and one on the jaw) to enable real-time data processing, but more speakers (three male and one female). The goal of the second experiment was to use the mapping trained in the first experiment for new speakers without the need of recording another large training dataset. Because the new speakers' articulation may differ, the input EMA data had to be transformed into the articulatory space of the reference speaker from the first experiment. To find this articulatory-to-articulatory mapping, the new speakers were asked to repeat a set of 50 sentences from the training set of the first experiment. Using these sentences, a linear mapping was trained and inserted as a speaker adaptation module in the framework between the data acquisition and the (pre-trained) mapping of the adapted EMA data to the vocoder parameters. The speaker-adapted real-time synthesis was also evaluated in terms of its subjective intellibility and achieved an accuracy (averaged across the four speakers) of 86 % for the vowels and 49 % for the consonants. However, nasal and unvoiced sounds were excluded from the evaluation because no velum sensor was used and voiced and unvoiced sounds had been difficult to distinguish in the first experiment. The recognition accuracy of the reduced set in the first experiment (with a matched training and testing speaker and session) was 99 % for the vowels and 61 % for the consonants. Given the mismatch of training and testing speaker in the second experiment, the reduction in accuracy was statistically significant but not catastrophic.

Around the same time of the landmark study by Bocquelet et al., Liu et al. [135] investigated if excitation information (power, voicing, and pitch) can be predicted from the EMA data alongside the spectral parameters or even from both EMA *and* the predicted spectral parameters using a cascaded mapping. Their best-performing systems used the EMA data (including the first and second order time derivatives to represent the time dynamics) as input and achieved a spectral distortion of 3.09 dB (using an LSTM-RNN), a Root-Mean-Square Error (RMSE) of the power prediction of 0.56 dB (also using an LSTM-RNN), an error rate of the voicing decision of 20.29 % (using a non-recurrent DNN), and an RMSE of the pitch prediction of 22.76 Hz (also using a feed-forward DNN). A subjective evaluation was only carried out with regards to the subjects' preference of different variations of their system, which is difficult to contextualize. Still, the group managed to show that even though only superglottal articulation is captured by EMA, the excitation information can still be derived to some extent using deep learning techniques. A similar study was conducted in [136] and essentially validated the results by Liu et al. using a DNN for the mapping.

Summary and conclusion

EMA is a highly precise and well-established, commercially available measurement technique in the field of instrumental phonetics and speech and language esearch. The tracking of the sensor coils is very robust and the collected data can be qualitatively and quantitatively related to articulatory movements and even adapted between different speakers. The only "blind spot" of EMA is the hard palate, which can, however, be approximated by asking the subject to trace the hard palate with their tongue at the beginning of a session. EMA is also sometimes accompanied by other measurement modalities more suitable to covering the palate (see section 3.9). The number of the captured articulators is otherwise only limited by the number of channels of the particular system in use. However, not all subjects tolerate all sensor positions: while it is, for example, possible to attach a sensor to the velum, the gag reflex of many subjects prevents its use. This is even true for posterior tongue positions, which can also trigger gag reflexes for some subjects. Even in more convenient positions, the sensor coils are wired and, even though they are themselves quite small, the very limited real estate on the tongue makes it difficult to find a good compromise between a high spatial resolution and a tolerable level of discomfort for the subject. Despite the so-far unconvincing performance of EMA-based ATT systems, EMA-based ATS systems are very mature and are even already trying to move towards predicting other speech characteristics then just the spectral features (e.g., voicing and pitch) with promising results. Because of the availability of several large datasets, deep learning techniques have been used extensively on EMA data to great effect. The major disadvantage of EMA besides the discomfort for the subjects is that no truly portable system exists as of the time of this writing. Given the alternating magnetic field necessary to induce the sensor voltages, EMC-related issues are to be expected but currently uninvestigated.

3.8. Radio waves

A very small number of studies have investigated the suitability of High-Frequency Radio Waves as a sensing modality for SSIs. In their 1998 patent [137] and then in two accompanying papers [138, 139], Holzrichter et al. described (but never evaluated) a system, that used low-power radar sensors at a frequency of 2.3 GHz to measure the movement of various articulators (see Figure 3.12a) and to (potentially) use those measurements in an ATT or ATS system. Their approach was to spatially resolve the signals modulated by the different organs and thus get interpretable, articulatory information on their respective activity. Instead of attempting to use several HF-antennas to sense individual articulators, Eid & Wallace [140] used only one antenna placed 2 cm in front of the subject's mouth (see Figure 3.12b). Sending out a sweep signal over the range of 500 MHz to 10.000×10^3 MHz with a resolution of 100 kHz, they recorded the time-varying complex reflection coefficients for each frequency during the articulation of the ten English digit words ("zero" to "nine"). After reducing the data to the points from 3 GHz to 10 GHz, they classified 25 instances of each target word by comparing their feature vectors to a vocabulary of 30 (different) instances of each word and finding the closest match (Nearest Neighbor classification). The word accuracy was remarkably high for such a simplistic approach at 93 %. Subsequent studies by the group focused on the antenna design [141, 142] but did not further pursue any applications in SSIs. A similar setup was devised in [143] (see Figure 3.12c), which used one antenna for transmitting and one antenna for receiving. They used a pulsed radar signal with a frequency range from 6 GHz to 10.2 GHz directed at the subject's mouth at a distance of 10 cm to 16 cm (to simulate the distance of a hand-held device). The reflected signal was then captured by the receiving antenna and the distance of the reflecting surfaces is estimated, resulting in a "distance spectrum" where a set of equally spaced distances (4 mm resolution) were associated with the received signal amplitude captured at the time delay that corresponds to that distance. The frame rate of the measurements was 100 Hz. Using this setup, the authors conducted two ATT experiments: a vowel recognition and a command word recognition task. For each tasks, a Nearest Neighbor template matching classifier with DTW was applied. The leave-one-out cross-validated vowel recognition accuracy for a single speaker and five English vowels (/a/, /æ/, /i/, /ɔ/, /u/) was 94 %. The command word recognition was studied with five different speakers and the ten English digit words ("zero" to "nine"). The leave-one-out cross-validated speaker-dependent word accuracy was 85 % and thus slightly lower than in the previous study in [140] mentioned above, possibly due to the larger number of subjects. No follow-up study to this initial attempt has been published since.

The most recent HF-based SSI research was published by Birkholz et al. in 2018 [144]. Their setup

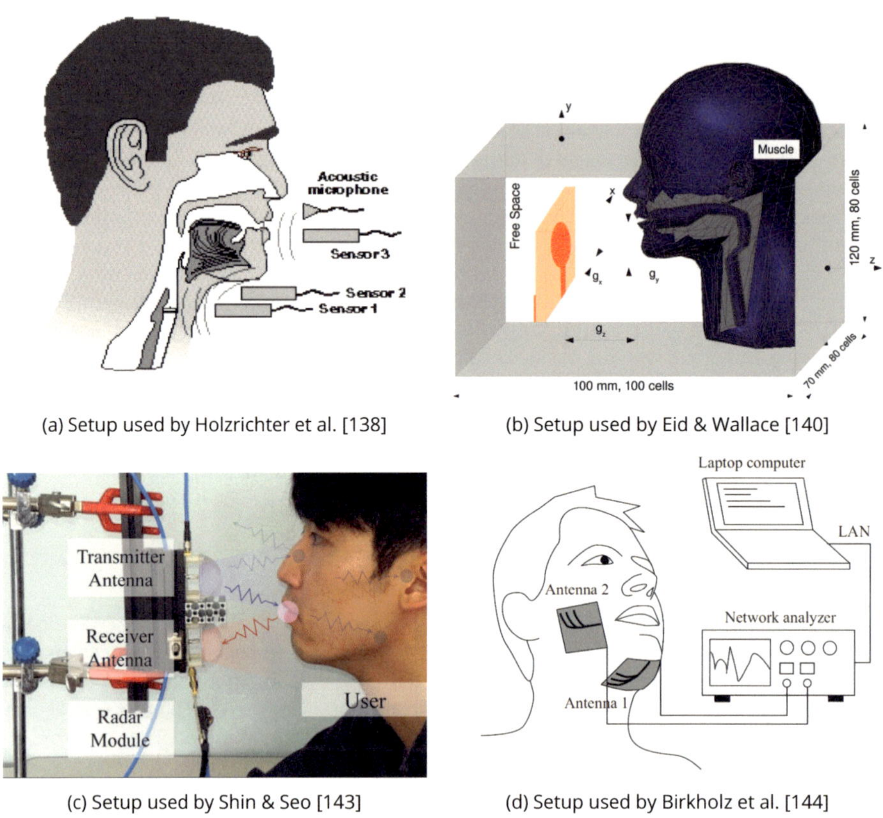

(a) Setup used by Holzrichter et al. [138]

(b) Setup used by Eid & Wallace [140]

(c) Setup used by Shin & Seo [143]

(d) Setup used by Birkholz et al. [144]

Figure 3.12.: Setups for HF-based SSIs. Figures taken from the respective publication.

also consisted of two antennas (see Figure 3.12d), but attached them to the subject's skin and used both of them for sending and reception of high-frequency sweeps ranging from 2 GHz to 12 GHz. Because of their chosen geometric setup, the authors were able to capture the transmission through the vocal tract from one antenna to the other one as well as the reflection (which was the only quantity used by all previous studies). The spectral magnitudes of the signals recorded along all possible paths between the two antennas were calculated and averaged across the entire duration of a target utterance to form a feature vector representing this utterance (using no dynamic, time-related information). The authors conducted an ATT experiment with this setup using two subjects and sustained articulations of 25 different German phonemes. The best phoneme accuracy was 93 % for subject 1 and 85 % for subject 2, achieved using a Linear Discriminant Analysis (LDA) classifier and all available signal paths (two reflection spectra and one transmission spectrum). Of the three signal paths, the transmission path from one antenna to the other was the one with the highest predictive power, achieving a phoneme accuracy of up to 86 % even when only features derived from that path were used.

Summary and conclusion

HF-based SSI research is extremely underdeveloped compared to the various other technologies but already shows great promise, at least with regards to ATT systems. ATS systems, while mentioned as a possible application, are yet to be actually presented. The different antenna setups proposed in the literature offer different advantages: the approach by Eid et al. and Shin et al. is contactless, but does not offer a lot of information about posterior places of articulation and the setup is difficult to control in a real-life application. The approaches by Holzrichter et al. and Birkholz et al. require the antennas to be attached to the user, but the setup is easier to keep constant and therefore potentially less speaker- and/or session-dependent. The most salient advantage of the Birkholz setup is, however, the possibility of measuring the transmission path between the two antennas, which appears to be the path containing the highest amount of information on the vocal tract configuration and thus the sound identity and sets the method more distinctly apart from a video-based speechreading system. While the initial results using HF-sensing are very promising, the technology is structurally just as sensitive to speaker- and session-dependency as the other techniques described in this report but no systematic studies in this regard have been conducted yet. For a practically relevant system, the measurements also need to be both robust against incoming electro-magnetic interferences and must at the same time not interfere with other electronic devices in the immediate vicinity (EMC).

3.9. Palatography

Palatographic measurements originate in instrumental phonetics and are a class of techniques to capture the lingual (i.e., tongue-related) articulation. In most cases, palatography records the palato-lingual contact pattern, i.e., the area of contact between the tongue and the palate, usually during articulation of speech sounds. For the very first iterations of palatography (see [145] for a historic review), researchers used to paint the roof of the mouth with, e.g., a mixture of flour and mucilage [146] or a mixture of charcoal and powdered chocolate [147]. After applying the mixture, the subject articulated a single utterance. In case of the flour mix, the malleable mass was shaped by the tongue and could be extracted from the mouth for further study. The charcoal mix was wiped off at the locations of tongue contact with the palate and, using a set of mirrors, the result could be photographed for further analysis. Any time characteristics inherent to the studied utterance were therefore integrated and only the superposition of a sequence of tongue contacts could be analyzed with a single measurement. The first palatographic technology to capture the *time-varying* palato-lingual contact pattern was Electropalatography (EPG), which uses an artificial "pseudopalate": a plastic plate form-fitted to the subject's actual palate. On the pseudopalate sits an array of small metal electrodes. A small reference voltage is applied to the subject wearing the pseudopalate. When the tongue touches any of the electrodes, this reference voltage is then picked up by the electrode. By sampling all electrodes repeatedly, the time-varying palato-lingual contact pattern can be recorded during continuous speech (or non-speech articulator movements, e.g., swallowing [148]). Different EPG systems use different numbers and distributions of the small metal contacts on the pseudopalate. The first EPG system, also known as the "Palatometer", introduced in 1972 by Hardcastle [149] and patented in 1977 by Fletcher & McCutcheon [150]. The patent described the pseudopalate as an acrylic base and top layer between 0.1 mm and 0.5 mm thick. The two layers were vacuum-formed to a plaster model of a subject's upper jaw and covered the entire hard palate, as well as extending over the teeth, providing a tight fit that did not require additional fixture. On the lingual top layer (facing the tongue), a 96 electrodes were arranged in a regular grid pattern for general purpose investigations (see Figure 3.13, left).

In [150], Fletcher et al. stated that specialized pseudopalates with electrode patterns matching specific sounds of interest (e.g., an alveolar cluster of electrodes for investigations of /s/) could also be manufactured. For each electrode, a thin conductor was sandwiched between the top and base layer and routed towards the posterior end of the pseudopalate. The conductors were led towards the mouth opening between the buccal side of the teeth and the inside of the cheeks and exited the mouth in two bundles (see Figure 3.13, left). The reference voltage used in the system was an AC voltage of 200 mV at a frequency of about 10 kHz. The original patent suggested an extra-oral electrode secured to the subject's wrist but according to [151], the Palatometer system manufactured by Kay Elemetrics in the 1990s (the so-called "Kay palate") used an additional four electrodes, two on each buccal surface of the teeth, that made permanent contact with the cheeks

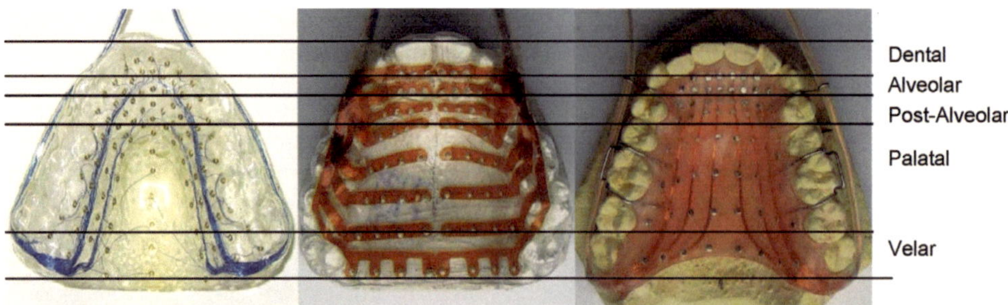

Figure 3.13.: Comparison of (from left to right) the Kay, Articulate, and Reading palate (taken from [151]).

and were used to apply the reference voltage intra-orally. The system was discontinued in 1998 with the high cost of the manufacture of the palates being cited as a significant factor [151].

Building on the works of Fletcher et al., a group around William J. Hardcastle at the University of Reading (Scotland, UK) developed another palate, dubbed the Reading palate (seeFigure 3.13, right), in the 1980s [152,153]. The Reading palate was conceptually very similar to the Kay palate but used only 62 silver electrodes. The pseudopalate was made from an acrylic resin and did not cover the teeth but instead used stainless steel Adams clasps (specialized orthodontic fixtures). Similar to the Kay palate, each electrode was soldered individually to a fine copper wire embedded in the base plate and the 62 wires exited around the back of the posterior molars in two bundles sealed in flexible tubing. This manufacturing process was intricate and expensive and so in 1979, Rion Co Ltd in Japan developed a flexible circuit board that contained the contact sensors and could directly be applied to the subject's palate [154]. It was discontinued shortly after due to materials-related safety issues. In 1989, Hardcastle [152] also developed a flexible circuit design intended to be used as an EPG device but it was deemed too uncomfortable [151] and thus never saw much use.

EPG is well-known and widespread in experimental and clinical phonetics and has been used in numerous scientific studies (see [152,155]) from a host of different fields (see Figure 3.14). Table 3.1 shows a summary of the existing systems and some of their key features.

Name	Technology	No. of palate electrodes	Sample rate [Hz]	Palate cost [€]	Status
Kay Palatometer	wired	96	100	ca. 300	discontinued
Reading	wired	62	100	ca. 220	available
Rion	flexible circuit	63	N/A	N/A	discontinued
SmartPalate	flexible circuit	122	100	ca. 230	available

Table 3.1.: Properties of several EPG systems described in [151] (pricing according to manufacturer inquiry).

Several studies have been conducted regarding EPG-based ATT systems. The first one to explore the feasibility of recognizing words by their EPG patterns was Fletcher in [156]. However, he trained human subjects to identify 16 different words based on their contact pattern, similar to historic ASR research where human subjects were trained to read spectrograms of acoustic speech [157]. The subjects learned to identify the words quickly and some of them achieved 100 % accuracy, proving the distinctiveness of the patterns. The first automatic ATT system involving EPG data in [158] used a hybrid EMA-EPG frontend and a statistical HMM-based classifer to achieve a peak word accuracy of 55 % on a set of 460 sentences (using 5-fold cross-validation). The weight of the EPG features versus the EMA features was not discussed. In another study using the same data [159], the authors achieved a phoneme-level accuracy of 33.2 % using EMA and EPG data (and additional voicing information) and 33.9 % when using only EMA (plus voicing). The EPG data was therefore apparently largely redundant with the EMA data, but unfortunately no results were reported for the only-EPG condition. In the various studies making up the dissertation in [160], only EPG data was used to

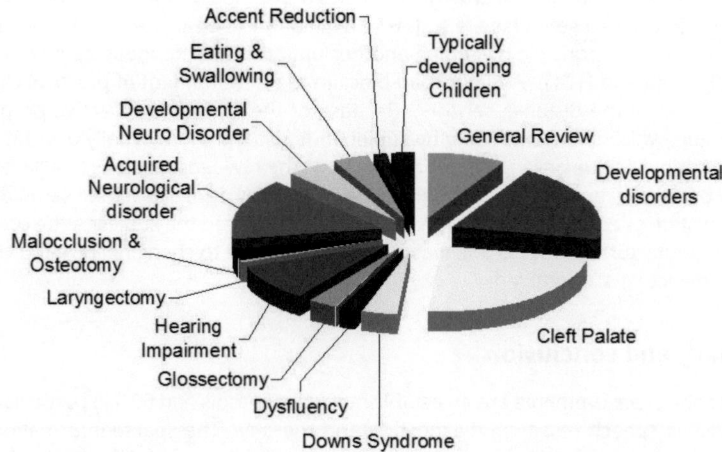

Figure 3.14.: Distribution of the research topics covered by EPG studies (image taken from `http://www.articulateinstruments.com/epg-in-clinical-practice/`).

recognize a set of 50 English words. Using various different features and (shallow) classifiers, the best setup achieved a reported word accuracy of 94.14 % on non-rejected words, but the system was allowed to reject unknown input causing 17.74 % of the presented words to be rejected. The best system without a rejection stage achieved only 82.5 % word accuracy. Most recently, a group at Google [161] presented an EPG-based ATT system with a vocabulary of 21 words. Using four speakers and a Support Vector Machine (SVM) classifier, they achieved speaker-dependent word accuracies of 74 % to 93 %. When using data from all speakers in a 75 % to 25 % holdout validation (i.e., the data was not partitioned by speaker so material from the test speakers could be part of the training set), the word accuracy was 84 %. Attempts to create an EPG-based ATS system have not been reported yet. The main disadvantage of EPG is the lack of information gained during articulation of sounds with little to no palato-lingual contact, e.g., vowels and the lack of lip information. Given the numerous minimal pairs of words that are only distinguishable by the vowel sound (e.g., "moon" /muːn/ vs. "man" /mæn/), this is a major limitation that needs to be compensated by a second input modality if any meaningful system is to be designed. Because of this "blind spot" of the EPG, another palatographic method called Optopalatography (OPG), or sometimes glossometry, was proposed by [162]. Instead of contact sensors, it used optical distance sensors mounted on a pseudopalate that measure the distance between the tongue and the hard palate along their respective optical axes. The resultant points can then be connected to form the midsagittal tongue contour, which is especially characteristic of vowel articulations. Several measurement setups exist to perform the optical distance sensing: Masuda et al. [163] proposed a combination of two sinusoidal light sources of 90° relative phase arranged around one detector, where the phase of the detected signal was related to the distance between the sensor and a reflector. However, this technique does not lend itself well to an application in the vocal tract, so instead the basic principle proposed in [162] has been commonly adopted and extended in subsequent works: A light source of constant brightness emits a beam of light onto the tongue surface which diffusely reflects the incident light. The reflected light intensity is detected by a light detector located directly next to the source. The detected light intensity can then be related to the reflector distance, as the intensity decreases the further the reflector is away. To measure the palato-lingual distance at several locations, multiple sensor units are used. In most studies, the light sources are switched in sequence and only the directly adjacent detectors are sampled to reduce cross-talk between sensors (see, e.g., [164], [165]). Wrench et al. [166] experimented with a setup where all light sources are turned on at the same time and the detectors are sampled in sequence but they also returned to the single-switched setup (see, e.g., [167, 168]). Birkholz et al. also further developed OPG and expanded upon the principle by adding another optical sensor to measure lip movements as well (see [169], [170] and [171]). A major road block in the development of practical OPG systems was the calibration of the distance sensors. Because of the individual reflective properties of a subject's tongue, which change not only by subject but also intra-individually over time, e.g., because of food or drink residue or saliva, the mapping from the raw sensor values to a distance needs to be adapted both inter- and intra-individually. A basic method using spacers to sample the mapping at discrete distances extra-orally was devised [170] but required the subject to be present during the devices manufacturing process and was also not adaptable to changing intra-individual conditions once the device was assembled.

Summary and conclusion

Palatographic measurements are an established suite of tools and EPG in particular has been used extensively in speech research, diagnostics, and therapy. The sparse information during articulations with little to no palato-lingual contact, especially during vowel articulations, greatly limits the suitability of this technique for SSI applications. OPG measurements could potentially capture such articulations more accurately, but there is no commercially available system and the lack of an adaptable calibration procedure that does not require the targeted individual subject to partake in the device assembly process makes it equally unsuitable for the task.

3.10. Conclusion and Discussion

As has been mentioned before, the data acquisition technologies for SSIs are difficult to compare due to the lack of standardized (or at least just conventions regarding) datasets, vocabularies, metrics, and more. The individual strengths and weaknesses of the techniques have already been described above in the respetive sections. For the purposes of this dissertation, a single technology needed to be identified to develop further into an SSI. Most of the presented techniques have already been extensively developed and have therefore probably hit their respective performance ceilings, which narrows the field down to video recordings and PMA as the techniques with the highest performance ratings, and HF, EPG, and OPG as the currently underdeveloped techniques. To choose a candidate to use among these remaining technologies, several factors should be considered. Firstly, it is clear that session- and speaker-dependency are a general problem for all sensor modalities. Due to the insular and fragmented research landscape, no data-driven adaptation algorithms have been successfully applied. Therefore, more interpretable data as in speechreading, EPG, and OPG should be preferred over the more opaque data acquired by PMA or HF. Secondly, there should still be reasonable room for improvement so that a performance increase is likely. For video-based speechreading systems, there is very little that can be done to improve the data acquisition. Since the problem of the homophenes remains, current state-of-the-art performance is likely as good as it can get and the technology should only be used as an additional, auxiliary sensor modality. PMA is also quite advanced at this point, but the use of a permanent magnet at the core of the measurement principle limits its usefulness in both non-permanent and permanent SSI applications, because users probably would not want to get a tongue piercing or have a magnet implanted into their tongue for various reasons, chief among them the hazardous prospect of accidentally swallowing the magnet. This leaves HF and palatographic techniques as the most promising options. Since HF-based hardware is immensely complex and a system that goes beyond the initial proof-of-concept presented in [144] goes far beyond the scope of a doctoral project, only the palatographic techniques remain as viable candidates. As has been pointed out in section 3.9, EPG and OPG are remarkably complementary and work on combining them has already begun but ultimately stalled when the issue of an adaptable calibration technique arose. However, in this dissertation, I present a new approach to a multi-modal palatographic measurement technology that removes this road block using a calibration technique that can be adapted to a new user or varying tongue surface conditions even while the user is wearing the device. Great care was taken to develop not another lab-only system (like, e.g., EMA-based SSI) but to contribute the foundations for an actually practically useful and relevant device that may be further developed to reach end-users "in the wild". The following chapter 4 is dedicated to the description of the hardware and the calibration process of this new technology.

4. Electro-Optical Stomatography

As described in section 3.9, the already existing technologies EPG and OPG are complementary in nature and using both modalities in a multi-modal system is a promising idea. Initial work to combine them in a single device was already conducted [169, 171]. As part of this dissertation, I continued these efforts and present the most advanced prototype of the multimodal palatography called Electro-Optical Stomatography. This chapter is dedicated to the description of all system components, ranging from the sensor specifications and characteristics, to the calibration methods involved, and the available software frontends designed for different use-cases of the hardware. The schematics and layouts of all hardware components are reprinted in Appendix C and available on the optical disc accompanying this dissertation in the subfolder *Hardware*. Some subcircuits (like the sensor detector circuits) are shown in this chapter in simplified drawings for ease of reference. The software source code and executables for 64-bit Windows 7 or above are also available on the accompanying optical disc in the subfolder *Software*. The measurement system was designed with its applications in an SSI context in mind. Therefore, portability was a key requirement, in terms of the form factor as well as the energy and computational demands. Since EOS was a new invention, however, accessibility of all components for hardware and software debugging was also desirable. As a workable compromise, I opted for a system design consisting of three parts (see Figure 4.1): (I) a sensor unit, which is worn by the user and carries all EOS sensors on a pseudopalate, (II) a control unit, which is connected to the sensor unit by a wired connection, gathers and preprocesses the data, and (III) a desktop computer or laptop, which receives the data from the control unit and further processes it in analysis, recognition, or synthesis software.

Another requirement for the system was low cost. While custom-made sensor chips or elaborately produced pseudopalates might certainly produce the best possible sensor system, off-the-shelf components and simple assembly drives down the cost even for a small number of units, which is very desirable for this proof-of-concept work.

The following sections describe the three main components of the system in detail, following the flow of the articulatory data (from sensors, to the sensor unit, to the control unit, to the software). While several iterations of each component were developed and produced, only the final ones are presented, except where earlier versions add some special insights or motivated otherwise less-obvious design choices.

4.1. Contact sensors

The general principle of the contact sensor measurement is shown in Figure 4.2 (ignoring the additional components for now, they will be explained in section 4.5): A small reference voltage is applied to the user's body (V_{body}). The tongue now essentially acts as a switch with the contact sensor being the throw and when the switch is closed (the tongue touches the sensor), the voltage

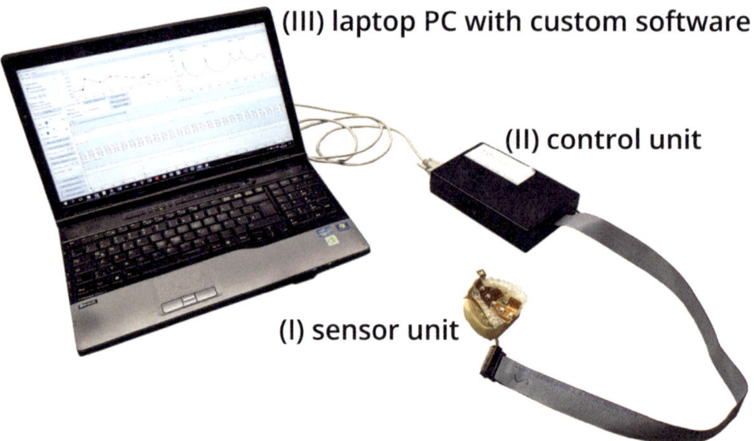

Figure 4.1.: Components of the proposed EOS system: (I) An individually fitted sensor unit (see section section 4.4) is connected to (II) a control unit (see section 4.5), which preprocesses the raw sensor data and passes the processed data to (III) a laptop computer for visualization, analysis, and/or further processing in various application-specific software frontends (see section 4.6).

$V_{contact}$ can be measured at the contact sensor.

The design of the contact sensors was largely informed by the EPG systems mentioned in section 3.9 and the review conducted in [166]. In EOS, the contact sensors were realized as exposed conductor track endings. While the conductor tracks themselves were usually made from copper, the endings were plated with gold for improved conductivity, which directly impacts the sensitivity of the sensor regarding tongue contact. While silver would offer even better conductivity (and was therefore used in the commercial Reading EPG system), it is prone to corrosion when exposed to moist air. Since the sensors are often exposed and the mouth cavity is a very damp environment, this severely impacts the suitability of silver for the contact sensors, especially if long-term use is considered. While soft gold is commonly used for plating contacts (e.g., in the Kay palate [150]) and has considerable advantages like solderability and ideal biocompatibility, the contact sensors in the EOS system were plated with hard gold (cobalt alloyed with pure gold). Hard gold, while

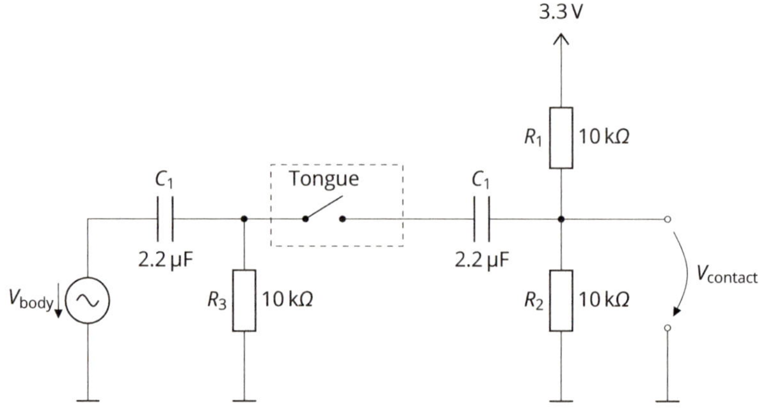

Figure 4.2.: Simplified equivalent circuit of the contact sensor measurement

being potentially slightly less biocompatible due to the cobalt, has the added advantage of being much more resistant to wear caused by repeated, sometimes even sliding contact events with considerable force (the force exerted by the tongue can easily go beyond 10 N [172]). Since cobalt is an element that is already present in the human body [173], the biocompatibility was expected to be only minimally affected by it (although this assumption was admittedly never tested and other chemicals involved in the bonding process of the hard gold could also theoretically affect the biocompatibility).

Besides the surface material of the sensors, the contact area is another major factor to consider: Using a smaller contact area, more sensors can be fitted onto the a pseudopalate but a larger contact area increases the conductance of the connection (see section B.3. Previous systems (in chronological order) used 1 mm (Kay), 1.4 mm, (Reading), and finally 1.5 mm (Articulate). The EOS system uses circular contact sensors with a diameter of 2 mm to ensure good conductivity at the expense of spatial resolution. Since the commerical EPG systems were all designed with the analysis of pathological speech in mind (see Figure 3.14), they needed to have a higher spatial precision to be able to, e.g., differentiate a "good" /ʃ/ from a "bad" /ʃ/ in a cleft-palate patient. In an SSI context, it should be enough to capture the general place of articulation, which requires much less precision: There are only nine places of articulation in the anterior mouth cavity (bilabial to uvular, see chapter 2) that need to be distinguished, even fewer for some languages.

The contact sensors are arranged in an irregular grid (see Figure 4.3). To prevent saliva from short-circuiting two or more sensors, the distance between the sensors should be not too small. Since the exact distance depends, among other things, on the conductivity of the saliva, which in turn depends on various influence factors including recently consumed food and drink, only a best-practice value can be assumed here. Previous systems used between 1 mm in very dense parts of the layout to 3 mm in more sparse areas. As a compromise between these extremes, EOS contact sensors are spaced approximately 2 mm apart (edge to edge). There were iterations of the sensor unit that included 124 and 64 contact sensors of reduced diameter and increased density, but these units were very unreliable due to issues with the additional components necessary to address the additional sensors (see subsection 4.4.2). The final number of contacts used was 32. This puts EOS at the lower end of the spectrum in comparison with other EPG systems (see Table 3.1), but given the limited application scope described above, robustness was preferred over spatial resolution.

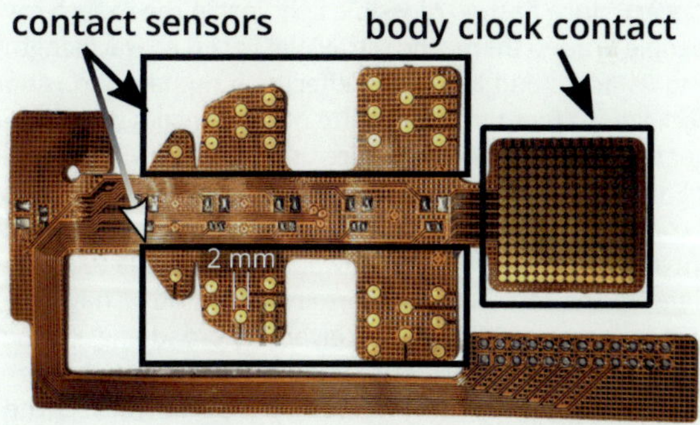

Figure 4.3.: Contact sensor arrangement on the unmounted circuit board (see section 4.4 for more details on the assembled sensor unit).

4.2. Optical distance sensors

Figure 4.4 summarizes the basic principle behind the optical distance sensing in its simplest form (a more complex model will be derived in subsection 4.2.3): A light source of some kind emits light into free space. If an object is placed in front of this light source, some of its emitted light is absorbed and some of it is reflected at the object's surface. Some of this reflected light is scattered at an angle that it eventually hits a light-sensitive detector, which measures the incident light intensity. This light intensity can be related to the distance of the detector from the object: the further the object is from the detector, the lower the measured light intensity becomes. Even with this high-level

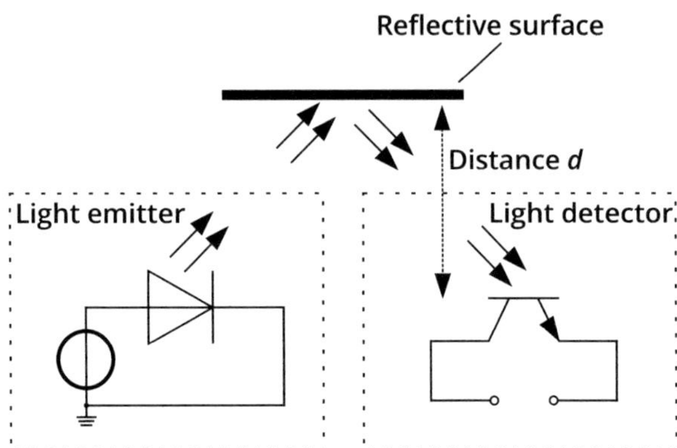

Figure 4.4.: The basic principle of optical distance sensing: A light source emits light, which is reflected by an object's surface and captured by a detector. The light intensity at the detector is related to the distance *d* of the object.

understanding of the measurement setup, a few design considerations are immediately apparent: What kind of light source and detector should be used and how should they be arranged? What kind of circuit should drive the light source and detect the received light intensity?

4.2.1. Selection of the source and detector components and setup

The bandwidth of the light used in the system should be in the infrared range (i.e., wavelengths of 700 nm and longer), since flashes of visible light inside the mouth cavity would be irritating to the user and the people around them, and ultraviolet light (i.e., wavelengths of 400 nm and shorter) was excluded due to its acute and long-term effects on human skin. Another important requirement was a small package, so that the overall size of the sensors would be as small and unobtrusive as possible. Earlier iterations of the EOS device used a Vishay VSMY2850 infrared (peak wavelength of 850 nm) Light Emitting Diode (LED) as a light source, since it was previously identified as the best candidate in a comparison made by Birkholz *et al.* [171]. Due to its focusing miniature lens, it offered a narrow beam angle of only $\pm 10°$, which was very desirable to achieve a high directivity and long range of the sensor. The same study determined that the Vishay TEMT7100 phototransistor (peak sensitivity at 870 nm) was the optimal receiver. Its broad angle of half sensitivity of $\pm 60°$ further increased the range of the sensor setup. Both of these components are shown in Figure 4.5b and Figure 4.5a, respectively. The circuitry necessary to power the led (the driver circuit) and sense the photocurrent through the transistor (the detector circuit) were also adopted from [171] in earlier iterations and is shown in Figure 4.6. The driver circuit is a voltage-controlled current source using an operational amplifier to stabilize the output under load. However, since portability was a major design goal of EOS, the relatively high current consumption of the VSMY2850 LED was rather concerning. Therefore, a TT electronics OP280V vertical-cavity surface-emitting laser (VCSEL) diode was selected as the light source for the final prototype, which offered a similar beam width of $\pm 18°$ at the same peak wavelength of 850 nm but was rated at a much lower forward current of only 7 mA, which could be sourced by the microcontroller used in the control unit (see section 4.5) directly and made the inclusion of a dedicated driver circuit obsolete in later iterations. The detector circuit produces an output voltage that is inversely proportional to the incident light and thus an inverse function of the reflector distance: the *closer* the reflector, the more light falls onto the phototransistor, the

(a) Vishay TEMT7100 phototransistor

(b) Vishay VSMY2850 infrared LED (only used in early iterations)

(c) TT electronics OP280V VCSEL diode (used in later iterations)

Figure 4.5.: Optical components for the distance sensors. The VSMY2850 LED was replaced by the OP280V vertical-cavity surface-emitting laser (VCSEL) diode in the later iterations of the EOS system.

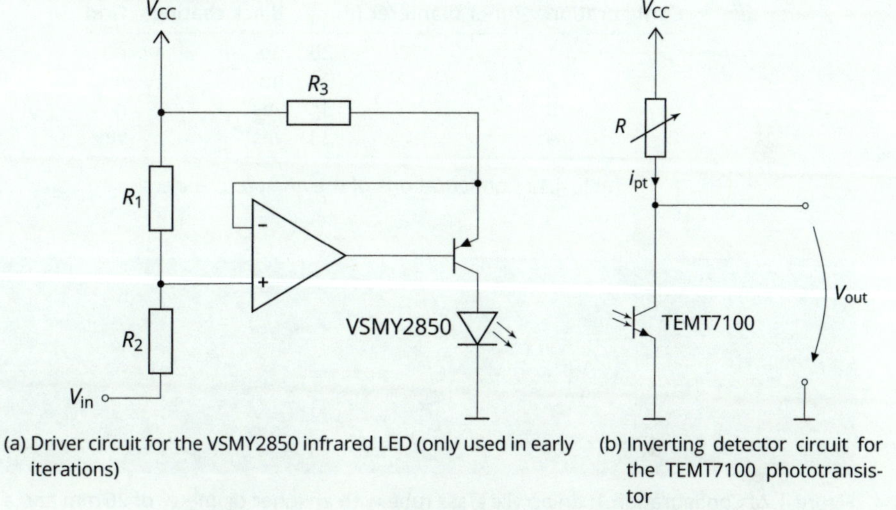

(a) Driver circuit for the VSMY2850 infrared LED (only used in early iterations)

(b) Inverting detector circuit for the TEMT7100 phototransistor

Figure 4.6.: Circuitry surrounding the optical components.

higher the collector current gets, the higher the voltage drop across resistor R and thus the *lower* the measured voltage becomes. The variable resistor R can be adjusted to change the sensitivity of the circuit. Given the same current, a larger value of R means a larger voltage drop compared to a smaller value of R and thus a higher sensitivity. However, the sensor becomes "saturated" when the collector current i_{pt} of the phototransistor becomes large enough so that $i_{pt} \cdot R = V_{CC}$. Therefore, the sensitivity needs to be adjusted to a level that allows both a good sensitivity, so that larger distances can be measured, but that does not at the same time drive the voltage V_{out} to ground at too large distances, as well. However, the relationship between the phototransistor current and the distance of the tongue cannot be easily defined analytically and thus this trade-off can also not be determined without experimental exploration.

Measuring the distance sensing characteristic

A measurement setup was devised similar to the one described in [170] to define the mapping of the phototransistor current to the distance of the tongue in millimeter. Instead of deriving the mapping analytically (as was attempted by [162]), the characteristic is approximated by sampling the sensor value at a discrete set of distances and then interpolating linearly between these known points. To that end, the tongue is placed at a number of fixed distances from the sensor. The sensor output voltage is digitized and recorded for each distance. To get precise and reproducible results, the tongue needs to be held at a fixed distance by some sort of spacer during the measurement. At the same time, the spacer should not cause additional reflections, which could strongly impact the sensor reading. In one of the studies leading up to this dissertation in [170], Birkholz and Neuschaefer-Rube used a set of acrylic glass tubes (inner diameter of 26 mm) of various lengths, capped with an acrylic glass grid to keep the flexible tongue tissue from protruding into the tube and thus inadvertantly shortening the effective measurement distance. While the design of these spacers was well-motivated, there was no experimental validation of the impact of these spacers on the measured sensor values compared to the "free-floating" tongue. As part of this dissertation, a series of measurements was conducted on various modified versions of the original spacer design to quantify the difference of measurements using these spacers to a reference measurement performed without a spacer [174]. The spacers were all made of the same acrylic glass used in [170] but in the following four configurations (also summarized in Table 4.1): The most basic design was

Configuration	**Inner diameter** [mm]	**Black coating**	**Grid**
1	26	no	no
2	34	no	no
3	34	yes	no
4	34	yes	yes

Table 4.1.: Configurations of the analyzed spacers

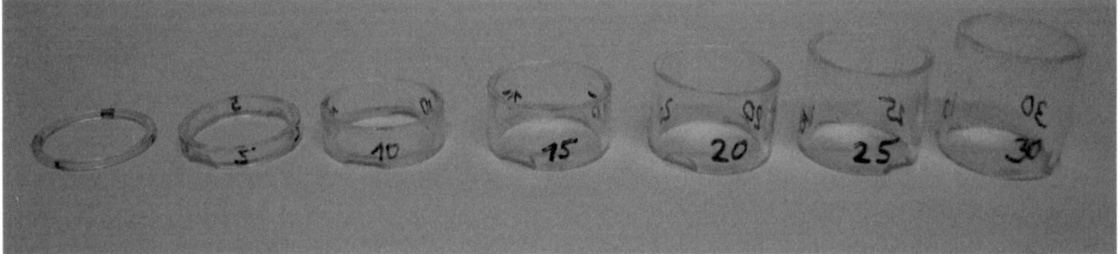

Figure 4.7.: Configuration 1: an acrylic glass tube with an inner diameter of 26 mm and a length as labeled on the tube (in mm).

a set of seven acrylic glass tube sections with an inner diameter of 26 mm and lengths of 2, 5, 10, 15, 20, 25, and 30 (all in mm), as shown in Figure 4.7. Even though the acrylic glass transmitted 99 % of the incident light (according to the manufacturer), under visual inspection very noticable reflections (at least of visible light) were apparent, most likely due to the curved shape. A set of similar tube sections of the same material and the same lengths but a larger inner diameter of 34 mm were therefore manufactured and included in the study. To avoid even more reflections on the inner wall of the tubes, a third set with the larger inner diameter and additionally with a black inside coating made of thin black matte cardboard was created (configuration 3). Finally, because as was already pointed out in [170], the tongue tissue tends to protrude into the spacer and needs to be restrained in some way. Following the example of [170], a configuration 4 was created by adding an acrylic glass grid with square grid openings with a width of 4.5 mm and a strut thickness of 0.5 mm. To identify the optimal configuration between these four, all other influencing factors during the measurements have to be kept constant. In particular the tongue, however, is a major source of uncertainty because its surface tissue is not homogenous and saliva or residue from food or drink may change the reflective properties between measurements, invalidating the comparisons between the spacer configurations. To eliminate this problem for the purpose of identifying the optimal spacer, an artificial reflector was used that consisted of a 5 cm × 5 cm piece of solid cardboard covered with red velour (see Figure 4.8). The fabric was chosen because it resembled the tongue both in color and texture. Because of possible deviations across sensor units due to the production and assembly processes, the measurements were conducted using five sensor units, arranged on a flexible circuit board strip taped to a matte black surface to avoid stray reflections (see Figure 4.10a). The sensors used the OP280V laser diodes and were controled and sampled using an EOS control unit, which used an Atmega SAM3S4B 32-bit ARM Cortex-M3 RISC processor to source the current for the VCSEL diodes and to convert the detector circuit output voltage to digital values using the built-in 12-bit Analog-to-Digital Converter (ADC) (more details follow in section 4.5). To ensure the same conditions as during the actual application of EOS, the same basic measurement protocol was used but with slightly different timing (see subsection 4.5.1): The light sources were switched on one at a time in sequence for 500 µs each. During the on-time, the ADC gathered 160 samples of the detector voltage continuously with a sampling frequency of $f_{\mathrm{adc}} = 320\,\mathrm{kHz}$. Of these 160 samples, the first 32 were discarded (corresponding to the first 100 ms of the on-time) to avoid transient effects. The remaining 128 samples were averaged to obtain the final sensor reading for a single measurement frame. The frames were sampled and sent to a desktop PC for further processing at a frame rate of $f_{\mathrm{S}} = 100\,\mathrm{Hz}$. Each measurement value in the spacer study was obtained by averaging again over 1 s ($\widehat{=}$100 frames) to further reduce the measurement noise (see subsection 4.4.1). In order to find the optimal spacer configuration, a ground truth sensor

Figure 4.8.: Reflectors used in the spacer study: large reflector (15 cm × 15 cm, left) for the reference measurement and small reflector (5 cm × 5 cm, right) for the spacer measurements.

value needed to be determined for each distance. These reference values were obtained with a 15 cm × 15 cm large reflector made of the same material as the smaller one, which was put in front of the sensor by resting it on three configuration 1 spacers placed at the very edge of the large reflector, which ensured that they would not have any impact on the measured value (see Figure 4.9). Using this setup, a reference value was recorded for each of the seven distances of interest and each of the five sensors. Because the slightly inhomogenous surface of the reflector may also impact the measurement, every measurement was repeated three times after fully disassembling and reassembling the setup between measurements. Finally, the mean and standard deviation across these 15 data points (three repititions measured at five sensors) were calculated and recorded. Using the spacers of the four configurations, a similar protocol was followed: each spacer (in each configuration and of each length) was placed so that one of the five sensors was in its center. The small reflector was then placed on top of the spacer and the sensor was sampled and averaged over 1 s. The reflector and spacer were then removed and the same procedure repeated two more times for the same spacer for a total of three samples (each representing the 1 s average) from each of the five sensors. As with the reference measurements, the mean and standard deviation across these 15 repetitions were calculated and recorded for each spacer configuration and length. To

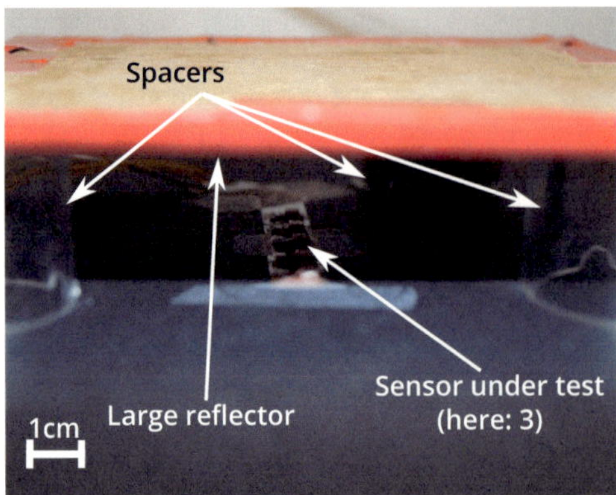

Figure 4.9.: Setup for measuring the reference sensor value: The spacers were moved relatively far away from the sensor under test to emulate a "free-floating" reflector.

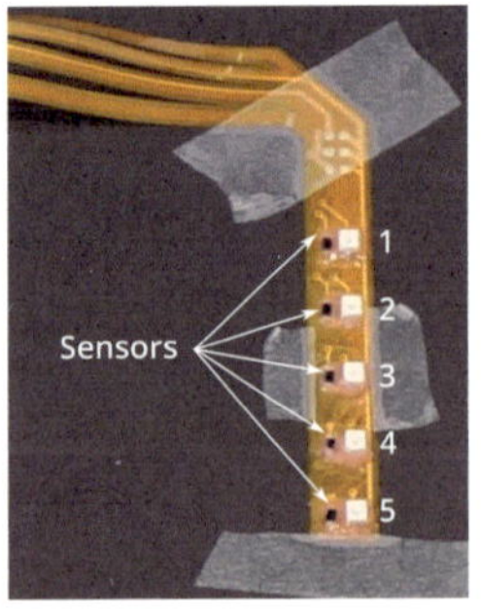

(a) Flexible circuit board with the five sensors

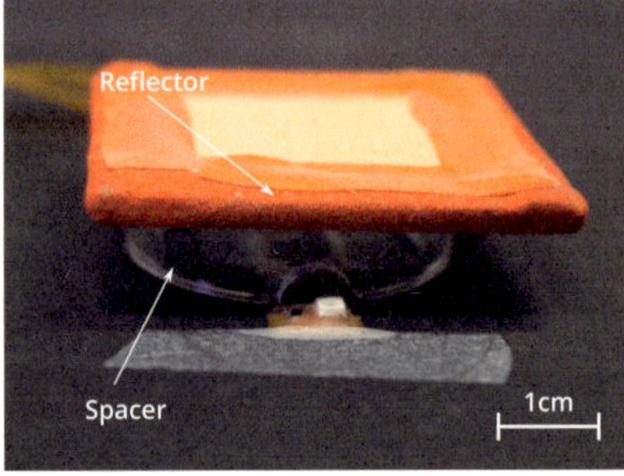

(b) Artificial reflector on a (configuration 2) spacer and centered on sensor 3

Figure 4.10.: Setup of the spacer comparison study

compare the characteristics obtained in this way to the reference characteristic, the RMSE would intuitively seem like a good choice. But due to the non-linearity of the sensor characteristic, it is not advisable to calculate any such global metric across the entire characteristic. Instead, the point-wise differences δ_i were calculated for each of the spacer configurations $i = 1, \ldots, 4$ between the mean sensor value at each distance (averaged across all five sensors) and the corresponding reference value. The final results are shown in Table 4.2.

The first finding was that measured sensor values are generally lower than the corresponding reference values for configuration 1 and 2. Given the inverting behavior of the detector circuit (see Figure 4.6b), this equated to more light getting reflected back to the detector. Since these two configurations were the only two with no black lining, the most likely explanation is that the acrylic glass walls of the spacers reflected a significant amount of light, as was already suspected from the observations under visible light. This hypothesis was further supported by the fact that configuration 2, which used a larger inner diameter and thus had a larger distance between the detector and the inner wall of the spacer, was also causing lower sensor values than in the reference setup but was closer to the ground truth overall. Between the two black-lined configurations, configuration 3 was slightly closer to the reference values than configuration 4, but both were well within the first standard deviation of the respective distribution, showing that the grid on top of the spacer has only a minimal impact on the measured value. Although configuration 3 was best overall, the lack of a grid

Distance	Reference		Configuration 1			Configuration 2			Configuration 3			Configuration 4		
d	μ_{ref}	σ_{ref}	μ_1	σ_1	Δ_1	μ_2	σ_2	Δ_2	μ_3	σ_3	Δ_3	μ_4	σ_4	Δ_4
[mm]	[ADC]	[ADC]	[ADC]	[ADC]	[ADC]	[ADC]	[ADC]	[ADC]	[ADC]	[ADC]	[ADC]	[ADC]	[ADC]	[ADC]
2	208.1	24.5	–	–	–	209.7	21.3	1.6	209.2	22.7	1.1	199.4	17.2	-8.8
5	605.6	354.9	526.9	264.7	-78.7	557.3	251.8	-48.4	614.5	238.2	8.9	517.3	304.9	-88.3
10	2654.9	134.0	2580.9	123.0	-74.0	2623.8	96.9	-31.1	2685.5	99.1	30.7	2715.0	143.9	60.1
15	3380.7	63.0	3278.9	59.7	-101.8	3334.9	50.3	-45.8	3394.7	40.4	14.0	3402.5	57.5	21.8
20	3665.9	32.0	3566.3	33.7	-99.5	3612.4	27.2	-53.5	3662.8	23.8	-3.1	3671.2	35.1	5.3
25	3816.3	19.4	3715.9	26.9	-100.4	3767.6	18.0	-48.7	3810.7	15.7	-5.7	3810.5	24.6	-5.8
30	3900.1	11.9	3805.0	20.9	-95.1	3845.0	13.9	-55.1	3889.6	11.8	-10.5	3884.7	17.0	-15.4

Table 4.2.: Mean μ_i and standard deviation σ_i measured across the five sensors under test for each configuration $i = 1, \ldots, 4$ of the spacers and the reference setup using the free-floating reflector (subscript ref), and the difference $\Delta_i = \mu_i - \mu_{ref}$. The smallest errors were achieved using configuration 3 (black lined spacer with no grid), followed very closely by configuration 4 (black-lined spacer with grid).

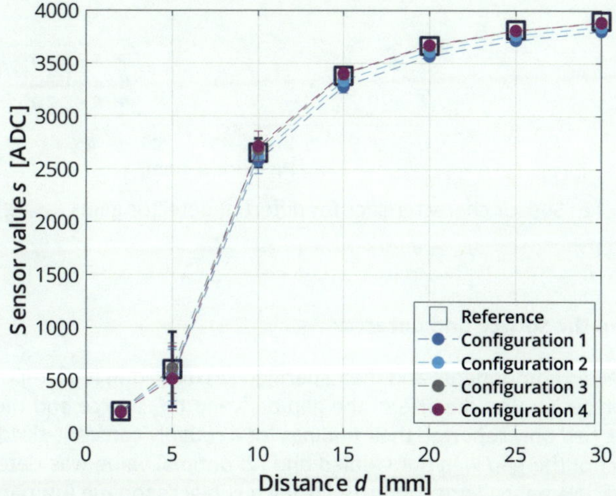

Figure 4.11.: Sampled characteristics using the four spacer configurations (see Table 4.1) with the free-floating reflector as a reference. The whiskers extend to $\pm\sigma$.

makes it a poor choice for use with an actual tongue, because the tongue tissue would protrude into the spacer. Therefore, configuration 4 was ultimately identified as the optimal choice.

Detector sensitivity setting

As mentioned above, the resistor R in the detector circuit (see Figure 4.6b) can be used to adjust the sensor characteristic to find the optimal trade-off between sensitivity at large distances versus sensitivity at very small distances. This adjustment ideally is made at an individual level, because every subject's tongue is likely to be slightly different in its reflective properties. Although some of these differences can be alleviated by the *in-vivo* calibration scheme developed later in subsection 4.2.2, it is advisable to adapt the detector gain to obtain a baseline characteristic that should be as similar as possible across all subjects. As a reference to guide this manual process, a series of measurements was conducted to illustrate the influence of the detector gain on the characteristic. The basic measurement setup followed the design described above using spacers. However, in this case a subject's tongue (male, 28 years old) was used to record the characteristics. The light source used in the sensors was the VSMY2850 infrared LED at a forward current of $I_F = 200\,\text{mA}$. The measured characteristics (see Figure 4.12) show that for smaller detector gain resistors the resolution in terms of ADC-values per mm was significantly larger, but at the expense of a very poor resolution of larger distances. For larger values of R, the sensitivity at larger distances becomes much higher but a saturation effect can be observed at small distances. The characteristic for $R = 372\,\Omega$ was found to be a good middle-ground between these conflicting requirements and this value was therefore used for the measurements using the VSMY2850 as a light source. For the OP280V, the measurement was informally repeated and a resistor value of 3.5 kΩ was determined to achieve a similar trade-off and used in all measurements using the OP280V as a light source.

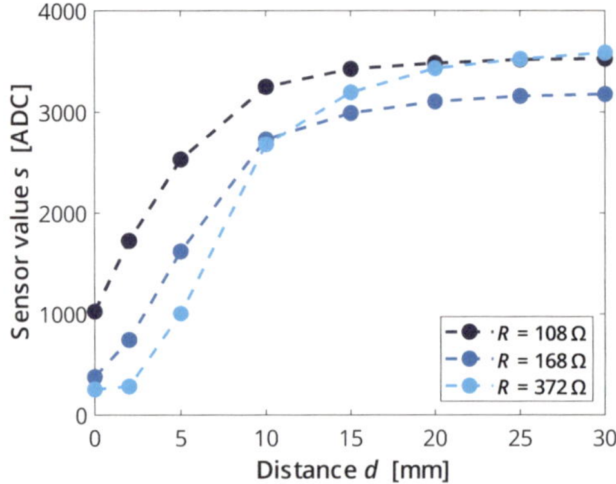

Figure 4.12.: Sensor characteristics for different detector gains (using the VSMY2850 LED)

Gap between the source and detector

With the selected components and their specified circuitry, one final important degree of freedom in the sensor design was the size of the gap between the source and the receiver. The study by Birkholz *et al.* had only reported their findings for a roughly constant-sized gap of 3 mm to 3.5 mm, but the effect of the gap was not studied and no optimal value was determined. Therefore, two series of measurements were conducted using a subject's tongue (human male, 28 years old), the VSMY2850 light source at $I_F = 200$ mA, and an older EOS control unit using a 10-bit ADC. The measurements followed the protocol to measure the distance sensing characteristic for two different sensor-detector gaps (3.2 mm and 3.8 mm), measured between the centers of the two components. The results are shown in Figure 4.13.

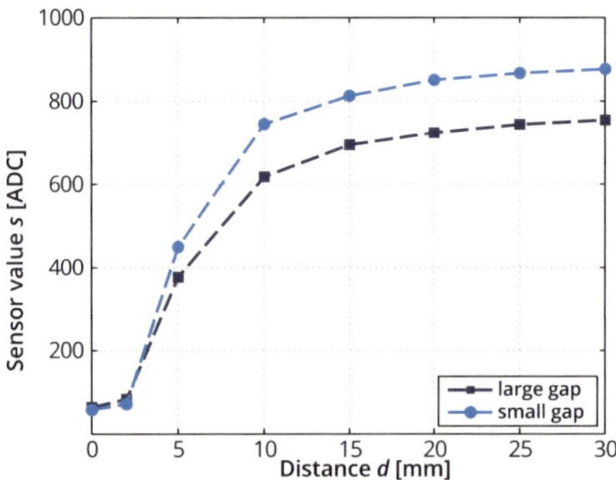

Figure 4.13.: Distance sensing functions for two sensor units with different distances between the light source (VSMY2850) and the receiver (TEMT7100): 3.2 mm (small gap) and 3.8 mm (large gap)

The larger gap caused a higher light intensity to be measured at the detector position, which was most likely due to an increase in optical cross-talk. Nevertheless, both measured characteristics are essentially parallel-shifted copies of each other, which means that the cross-talk only added a constant offset to the measurements. Given the much easier handling of the sensor units with a larger gap during the assembly of a pseudopalate (see section 4.4), a layout with a gap of 3.6 mm was chosen for the final sensor layout as a compromise between the level of cross-talk and the practicality constraints.

Comparison between the VSMY2850 and the OP280V

As mentioned above, the high current consumption of the VSMY2850 LEDs was a concern during the development of the system. While this component was the most suitable one available at the time the development process began, in another round of market research later in the development process the OP280V VCSEL diode (see Figure 4.5c) was discovered as an even better option, since it promised a much lower current consumption while also offering similar beam angle and optical power. In order to avoid the repetition of all the experiments already conducted using the VSMY2850 but still be able to use the findings gleaned from them, it was desirable to reproduce the distance sensor characteristic of the VSMY2850 using the OP280V. The assumption was that if the distance characteristic was very similar, all other properties should also be very similar. To that end, a series of measurements was conducted using a single subject's tongue (male, 29 years old) and the OP280V as the light source, otherwise following the established protocol (see above) to measure the sensor output at eight distances. The forward current through the VCSEL diode was varied in three steps from a very low current to the maximum forward current recommended in the data sheet. The exact values were chosen due to the available values for the series resistor in the driver circuit (see section B.4 for details and the actual calculation). According to the results of these measurements (see Figure 4.14), the best approximation of the VSMY2850 characteristic was achieved using a forward current of 11.5 mA. With this setting, the sensor is slightly more sensitive to small distances which is likely due to the larger beam angle of the OP280V (18°) compared with the VSMY2850 (10°). However, due to the non-linearity of the characteristic, it was more important to achieve a good approximation at large distances, since small errors in raw output would translate to large errors in mm here. Therefore, the OP280V was used at a forward current of 11.5 mA for the remainder of this work. All studies and results presented below were conducted and obtained using this setup, while some references to the VSMY2850 are made only to describe earlier design approaches.

4.2.2. Calibration

So far, the mapping between the sensor values and the distance in mm was determined by interpolating between known reference points. While this technique works well for measurements to characterize the sensors in a lab setting, it does not lend itself well to *in-vivo* measurements in an actual use-case scenario: Once the sensors are intergrated into a pseudopalate, it is impossible (or at least very impractical) to establish the conditions necessary to follow the measurement protocol and so the distance sensing function cannot be adapted should the properties of a subject's tongue change due to food residue, saliva, tissue changes, or similar outside influence. Some sort of parametric calibration scheme that allows the reconstruction of the entire distance sensing function based on just a few, easily *in-vivo* obtainable parameters was therefore very desirable. Two basic options present themselves to define the mapping: Either by implicitly modeling the analytic function, or a regression-based approach. Both approaches are presented here, while the latter was also published in [175].

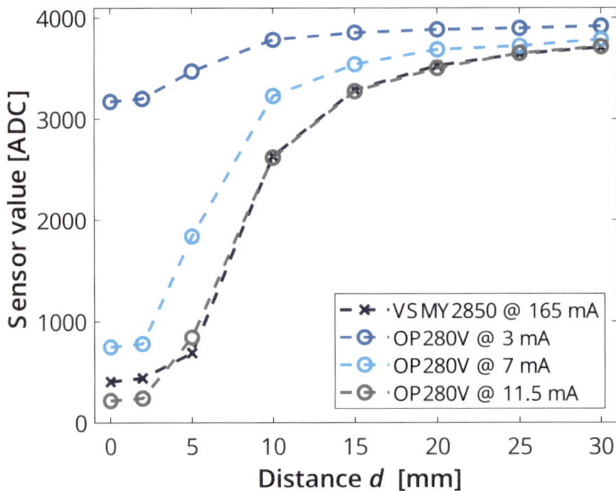

Figure 4.14.: Comparison of the OP280V at different forward currents and the VSMY2850 at the previously determined optimal setting. The best agreement was achieved using a forward current of 11.5 mA.

Analytic approach

In the first publication on optopalatography by Chuang and Wang [162], the authors derived an analytic approach to model the mapping from received light intensity to reflector distance, based on the assumption that the tongue surface behaves like an ideal Lambert reflector and diffusely reflects the entire incident light. They arrived at the following equation (notation adapted to the conventions of this dissertation):

$$s_C(d) = \frac{B\,(d + d_e)}{\left((d + d_e)^2 + x_0^2\right)^{3/2}} + A, \tag{4.1}$$

where $s_C(d)$ is the sensor output for a given reflector distance d, B is a free parameter proportional to the maximum intensity of the light source, d_e is a correction term that takes the tongue's surface structure into account, x_0 is the distance between the light source and the detector, and A is another free parameter. Because the detector circuit used in EOS was inverting, equation 4.1 was inverted as well and offset by the maximum possible digital sensor output value of 4095. Since the ultimate purpose of the distance sensing function would be to use it for calibration, the function also needed another degree of freedom that would allow its adaptation to different sensor and tongue properties. This degree of freedom should be representative of the inter-sample variance (the variance across both subjects and sensors) and at the same time easy to obtain both *in vivo* and after the assembly of an EOS unit. The sensor value measured at a distance of 0 mm (so during gentle tongue-sensor contact) would be such an accessible data point and so the final equation was written as:

$$s(d) = 4095 - \frac{B(s_0)}{2\pi} \cdot \frac{d + d_e(s_0)}{\left((d + d_e(s_0))^2 + x_0^2\right)^{3/2}} + A(s_0) \tag{4.2}$$

$$\text{with} \tag{4.3}$$

$$A(s_0) = A' \cdot (4095 - s_0)^{3/2} \tag{4.4}$$

$$B(s_0) = B' \cdot (4095 - s_0)^{3/2} \tag{4.5}$$

$$d_e(s_0) = d_e' \cdot (4095 - s_0)^{3/2} \tag{4.6}$$

So in equation 4.3, the original free parameters from equation 4.1 were replaced by functions of s_0, which introduced new free parameters A', B' and d'_e. These parameters could be determined to optimally fit a set of given measured distance characteristics as long as the sensor output value s_0 at a distance of $d = 0$ mm was known for each series of measurements. Once optimal values for A', B' and d'_e were determined in this way, only s_0 remained as a degree of freedom of $s(d)$ and would thus allow the adaption of the distance mapping by inserting the measured sensor output while gently pressing against the sensor with the tongue.

The necessary data for evaluating this approach were recorded using 5 subjects (all male, 29-62 years old), the OP280V light source, 5 different sensor units, and following the established measurement protocol, except that the sensors were sampled at seven distances from 0 mm to 30 mm, spaced in equal 5 mm steps. The 25 characteristics (5 subjects times 5 sensors) measured in this way are shown in Figure 4.15a.

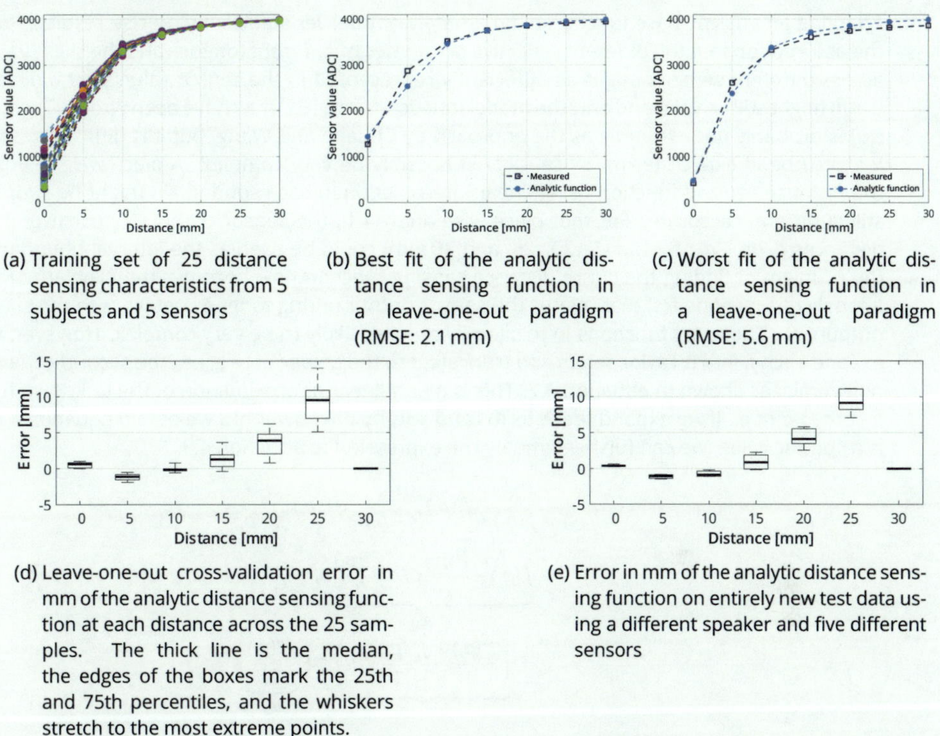

(a) Training set of 25 distance sensing characteristics from 5 subjects and 5 sensors

(b) Best fit of the analytic distance sensing function in a leave-one-out paradigm (RMSE: 2.1 mm)

(c) Worst fit of the analytic distance sensing function in a leave-one-out paradigm (RMSE: 5.6 mm)

(d) Leave-one-out cross-validation error in mm of the analytic distance sensing function at each distance across the 25 samples. The thick line is the median, the edges of the boxes mark the 25th and 75th percentiles, and the whiskers stretch to the most extreme points.

(e) Error in mm of the analytic distance sensing function on entirely new test data using a different speaker and five different sensors

Figure 4.15.: Fit and evaluation of an analytic distance sensing function proposed in [162]

The most important observations from this (admittedly slightly convoluted) plot is that the characteristics had larger variances at small distances and converged towards large distances, but were generally of the same shape. This supports the assumption made above that the entire shape of a sensor characteristic can be derived from s_0. The equation proposed by Chuang and Wang, adapted into the form given in equation 4.3, was then fitted to the measured data points in a least-squares sense using the Matlab function `lsqcurvefit` from the Optimization Toolbox and the trust-region-reflective algorithm. Each fit used the data of 24 of the 25 measured characteristics and was evaluated on the remaining one (leave-one-out cross-validation) by calculating the pair-wise differences between the measured sensor outputs s_d and the analytically calculated function values $s(d)$ at the corresponding distances d. When comparing the goodness-of-fit at the various distances across the characteristics, the non-linearity of the characteristic required special attention. Instead of calculating the RMSE in ADC values, which would not represent the non-linearity of the characteristics, the differences $|s_d - s(d)|$ were converted to mm taking the local resolution (slope of the section) into account and the RMSE was therefore calculated in mm. The best fit achieved an RMSE of 2.1 mm (see Figure 4.15b) and the worst fit had an RMSE of 5.6 mm (see Figure 4.15c). This error was also unevenly distributed across the seven evaluated distances, as shown by Figure 4.15d: at larger distances, the error was also generally larger and in extreme cases went up to almost 15 mm. This was most likely due to the fit being optimized using the digital values and a fit after converting to mm might have reduced these outliers, but the overall accuracy was still severely limited. In summary, the analytic approach, even when determining the unknown parameters through experimental data, did not accurately reflect the complex processes resulting in the observered variance of distance sensing characteristics across subjects and sensors.

Regression-based piece-wise approach

Adapting an analytic base function did ultimately not deliver sufficiently precise results. However, the assumption that the different reflective properties of different tongues and the slight variations across different sensors might be sufficiently represented in the sensor value s_0 at a distance of 0 mm might still be valid and only the model function from [162] may have been wrong. The function $s(d)$ is probably not as simple as the approach by Chuang and Wang, but it is difficult to say what it *should* be in explicit terms, since it could possibly be very complex. A piece-wise definition of the distance sensing function using linear interpolation in each subdomain might be simpler and still sufficiently accurate. For that piece-wise approach, the sensor outputs s_{d_i} corresponding to distances d_i (d_1 - d_6: 5, 10, 15, 20, 25, and 30 mm) could be used as the interval boundaries. So the problem of finding the entire distance sensing function now becomes the problem of finding a family of functions $f_i(s)$ that relates the sensor output during tongue contact s_0 to the six sensor outputs s_{d_i}. The exact functions in this family are also likely to be very complex. However, we can expand each f_i into a Taylor series and truncate it to the power of two, i.e., the second-order Taylor polynomial as shown in equation 4.7. This is a non-linear approximation of the unknown function f_i at the point p_i. If we expand these terms and sort by the power of s we obtain equation 4.8. As p_i is a specific value, we can further simplify the expression to equation 4.9.

$$f_i(s) = f_i(p_i) + \frac{f_i'(p_i)}{1!}(s - p_i) + \frac{f_i''(p_i)}{2!}(s - p_i)^2 \tag{4.7}$$

$$= \underbrace{f_i(p_i) - \frac{f_i'(p_i)}{1!}p_i - \frac{f_i''(p_i)}{2!}p_i^2}_{a_{i,0}} + \underbrace{\left(\frac{f_i'(p_i)}{1!} - \frac{f_i''(p_i)}{2!}2p_i\right)}_{a_{i,1}} s + \underbrace{\frac{f_i''(p_i)}{2!}}_{a_{i,2}} s^2 \tag{4.8}$$

$$= a_{i,0} + a_{i,1}s + a_{i,2}s^2 \tag{4.9}$$

A mathematically equivalent approach would be to simply describe the unknown mappings from s_0 to s_{d_i} by linear regression using a a second-oder polynomial basis function, leading to the same equation as equation 4.9.

We now would have to determine the scalar coefficients $a_{i,0}$, $a_{i,1}$, and $a_{i,2}$ so that $f_i(s_0)$ becomes s_{d_i}. Because a single exact solution to this problem that holds for all tongues and sensors with just a single set of coefficients for each distance is not possible, we need to find optimal sets that yield a good approximation $f_i(s_0) = \hat{s}_{d_i} \approx s_{d_i}$. To that end, we need a number of known tuples (s_0, s_{d_i}) for each distance d_i to set up an overdetermined set of (in the coefficients) linear equations as in equation 4.10, where $\mathbf{s_{d_i}}$ is a column vector containing sensor values measured at distance d_i, $\mathbf{S_0} = (1,\ \mathbf{s_0},\ \mathbf{s_0}^2)$ (where $\mathbf{s_0}$ is a column vector of sensor values at a distance of 0 mm and $\mathbf{s_0}^2$ denotes the element-wise square of $\mathbf{s_0}$), and $\mathbf{a_i} = (a_{i,0},\ a_{i,1},\ a_{i,2})^T$.

$$\mathbf{s_{d_i}} = \mathbf{S_0} \cdot \mathbf{a_i} \tag{4.10}$$

This system of equations was set up for each distance d_i and solved for $\mathbf{a}_i$ in a least-squares optimal sense using a standard QR decomposition algorithm implemented in the Matlab built-in function `mldivide`. This eventually yielded one set of coefficients for each distance of interest.

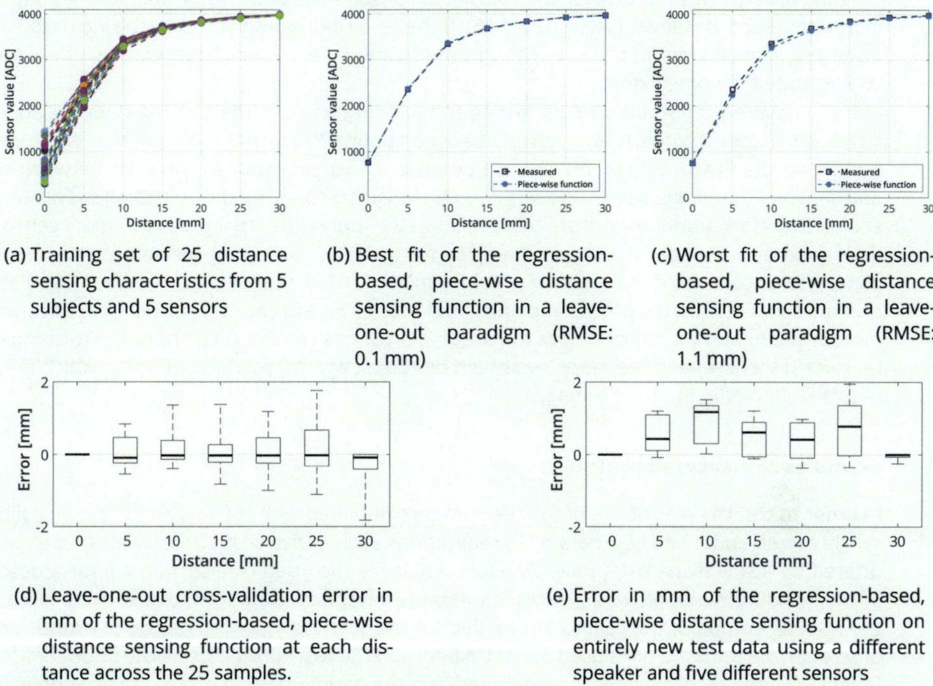

(a) Training set of 25 distance sensing characteristics from 5 subjects and 5 sensors

(b) Best fit of the regression-based, piece-wise distance sensing function in a leave-one-out paradigm (RMSE: 0.1 mm)

(c) Worst fit of the regression-based, piece-wise distance sensing function in a leave-one-out paradigm (RMSE: 1.1 mm)

(d) Leave-one-out cross-validation error in mm of the regression-based, piece-wise distance sensing function at each distance across the 25 samples.

(e) Error in mm of the regression-based, piece-wise distance sensing function on entirely new test data using a different speaker and five different sensors

Figure 4.16.: Fit and evaluation of the regression-based, piece-wise distance sensing function

The regression-based distance sensing function was also evaluated in a leave-one-out paradigm using the data set described above and the result is summarized in Figure 4.16. The best fit (see Figure 4.16b) achieved an overall RMSE of 0.1 mm, while the RMSE of the worst fit was 1.1 mm (see Figure 4.16c). The error distribution at each of the six evaluated distances was slightly less dispersed compared to the results using the analytic approach, both for the leave-one-out cross-validation (see Figure 4.16d) and the test data (see Figure 4.16e). The median error in the leave-one-out setting was less than 0.1 mm at all distances while the maximum error was 1.8 mm at an actual distance of 30 mm. The median error on the test set, recorded with a sixth subject and five additional sensors not used for the training data set, was less than 1 mm at most distances except at 10 mm where it amounted to 1.17 mm, the maximum error was 1.95 mm at an actual distance of 25 mm.

Discussion

The regression-based, piece-wise approach achieved much smaller errors than the analytic approach. The results in the leave-one-out cross-validation setting were significantly better and more consistent than the results on the second evaluation set. This was due to the fact that by leaving only one trial out, data from the tongue that was used in this trial was still present in the training set, albeit recorded with another sensor. Analogously, the one sensor used in the left-out trial was still represented in the training set through measurements with different tongues. Therefore, the results from the second evaluation set with the entirely new speaker should be considered indicative for the true quality of generalization and representative for the error one should expect to find in real-world applications. By adding trials with more sensors and more subjects to the training corpus, the results are likely to further improve as the generalization error most likely goes down. The results also showed that the error can become generally larger at greater distances than at closer distances. Because of the decreasing $\frac{\text{ADC}}{\text{mm}}$ resolution between the calibration points with increasing distance, a small error in the calculated sensor value becomes an increasingly larger error in mm at greater distances (see Figure 4.16). If the resolution could somehow be increased at these distances, maybe even at the expense of the resolution at closer distances, this effect might be compensated to some extent.

The measured calibration points during tongue contact s_0 in the training data set also varied significantly across subjects and sensors between about 300 to 1400 ADC counts. While small differences in the sensor values could be attributed to the varying optical properties between subjects and sensors, this range seems too large to be explained solely by these variables. Future studies should therefore somehow ensure that the subjects apply consistent pressure to the sensor when their tongues are placed directly on it, e.g. by fixing the sensor-under-test on a pressure-sensitive plate. A less scattered distribution of s_0 values might further reduce the error when calculating the calibration points. On the other hand and in defense of the approach taken here, an unconstrained measurement of the s_0 value makes the acquisition of this calibration point easier to complete in a real-world scenario and the mapping should be robust against this kind of noise, which may add a regularization effect to the training.

Examples of measured contours

In order to test the plausibility of tongue contours obtained with the regression-based calibration, synchronized audio and EOS data of 10 realizations each of five sustained vowels (/aː, eː, iː, oː, uː/) uttered by a single speaker (male, 29 years old) were recorded (see section 4.6 for a description of the measurement software and visualization techniques). Data from this speaker were part of the training corpus of the calibration model but the sensors mounted on the pseudopalate were different from both the ones used in the training and the test corpus. Using the phonetics software Praat [176], the recordings were segmented and the middle section of each realization extracted, keeping the section length approximately constant at about 300 ms. We then averaged the EOS data over these intervals. The resulting mean, lowest and highest contours of the five vowels are presented in Figure 4.17. The tongue shapes were generally plausible and in line with the phonetic features height and frontness/backness (see Figure 2.2). There was also only a very small difference between the lowest and highest shapes within the 10 repetitions of each vowel which indiciates a high reproducibility within a series of measurements.

The tongue shape of /oː/ shows one potential weakness of this method of drawing the tongue contour: When an optical sensor (especially the most anterior one near the incisors) measures a distance of 30 mm, it cannot be determined for certain if the tongue is indeed very low or if it is so far back that the light is actually reflected by the floor of the mouth. Therefore the system cannot precisely locate the tongue tip. However, it is also possible to predict the entire tongue contour from the measured data and section 4.6 discusses this approach in greater detail.

Conclusions

As the results on the test set and the contours given in Figure 4.17 show, the automatic calibration using equation 4.9 and the coefficients determined in this study performed sufficiently well to yield realistic and meaningful measurements. The small errors were outweighed by the ability to quickly adapt to varying optical conditions during a measurement and the fact that a subject no longer has to do a calibration trial at several distances with each sensor before or after the pseudopalate is assembled. Future work should focus on further reducing the calibration error by increasing the size of the training data and reducing the variance of the s_0 distribution by controlling the level of force the tongue exerts on the sensors. Another important future experiment is to perform some other articulometric technique with a known precision (e.g., sonography or EMA) in conjunction with EOS measurements to evaluate the absolute precision of this system *in situ*.

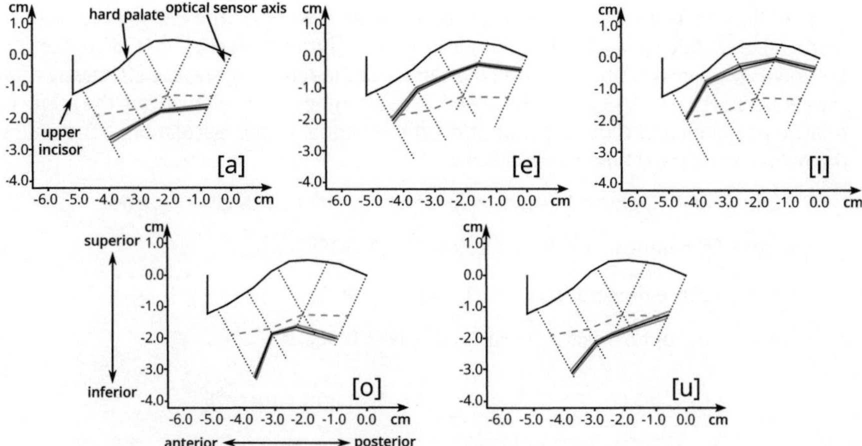

Figure 4.17.: Tongue shapes of five vowels obtained with the regression-based calibration. The solid black line is the mean shape (of 10 repetitions each), gray solid lines are highest and lowest shapes, and the dashed gray line is the contour of the neutral vowel /ə/ as a reference.

4.2.3. Angle correction

The calibration so far relies on a single sensor reading and was trained using a parallel surface as the reflector. If the reflector is not perpendicular to the optical axis of a sensor, however, the sensor output is likely to change as a function of the reflector angle even while the nominal distance stays the same. This section, the contents of which were also published in [177], investigates the relationship between the reflector angle and the sensor output both by means of a simulation and experimental validation. Based on these findings, a correction term is derived that uses the output from multiple adjacent sensors to reduce the distance measurement error introduced by the reflector angle. To conduct these analyses, a model of the light propagation for optical distance measurements is needed.

During the optical distance measurements, light travels from the source to the reflector and from there to the detector (assuming no significant source-detector-crosstalk). To model the propagation, we need to accurately describe the irradiance of light from the source onto the reflector and the irradiance onto the detector from the reflector. To that end, we need to model the setup during the optical distance measurement first.

Source-reflector-detector geometry

We define the geometric setup of the source, the reflector, and the detector during the optical distance measurements inside the mouth cavity as follows (see also Figure 4.18): A punctiform light source (representing the Optek OP280V infrared laser diode used in EOS) is located at a point $S = (S_x, S_y, S_z)$ in three-dimensional space, and a punctiform detector (modeling the Vishay TEMT7100 phototransistor used in EOS) at point $D = (D_x, D_y, D_z)$. Because we only have one lit light source at any given moment, it is convenient to put that source in the *xy*-plane (i.e., $S_z = 0$), which corresponds to the sagittal plane of the vocal tract. The detectors on the other hand can theoretically be arbitrarily placed, though on the EOS sensor units, they are always laterally displaced by 3.6 mm from the source in *z*-direction. The reflecting plane is located in the *xz*-plane at $y = 0$. The point of origin is moved to the intersection of the optical axis of the source and the reflector plane. The orientation of the optical axes of the source and detector are given by $\vec{n}_S$ and $\vec{n}_D$, respectively. The normal of the reflector plane is given by $\vec{n}_P$. To examine different inclination angles of the reflector, the source and detector are rotated around the origin by the corresponding angle, therefore the

z-component of all optical axes is assumed to be zero whereas the normal vector of the reflector plane is constantly $\vec{n}_P = (0,1,0)^T$. In measurements during speech, this is of course the other way around as the sensors' positions stay the same but the reflecting surface effectively rotates around the sensors, which only changes the absolute coordinates of the elements in the scene but not their relative positions and thus does not affect the outcome of the calculations. The entire scene has the following Degree Of Freedoms (DOFs):

- Position of the light source in the xy-plane in polar coordinates (2 DOFs).
- Angle of the optical axis $\vec{n}_S$ in the xy-plane (1 DOF).
- Position of the detector $D = \left(D_x, D_y, D_z\right)^T$ (3 DOFs).
- Angle of the optical axis $\vec{n}_D$ in the xy-plane (1 DOF).

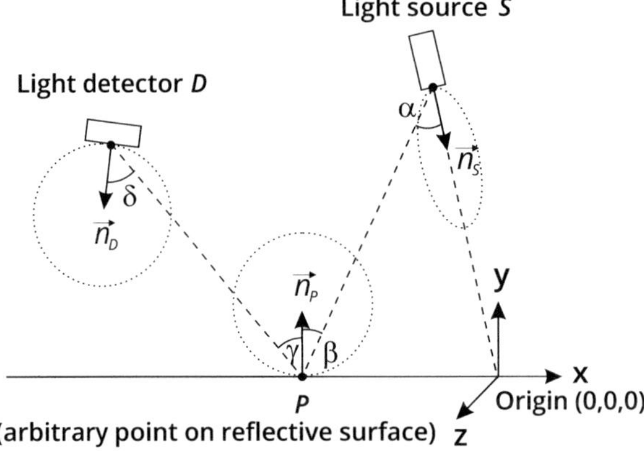

Figure 4.18.: Principal geometry of the optical distance measurement setup

Calculation of the Irradiance at a Detector Position

For this geometry, we are ultimately interested in the irradiance E_D at the position of the detector. Under the assumption that there is no significant crosstalk between the light source and the detector, the irradiance E_D solely depends on the light that is reflected from the reflector plane, i.e., the radiance M of the xz-plane, which is non-uniformly distributed on the surface. To determine the radiance at any point P on the reflector, we use the radiosity equation, as first introduced in the context of computer graphics by [178]. This equation yields the sought radiance $M(P)$ as

$$M(P) = M_{\text{self}}(P) + \rho(P) \cdot E(P) \qquad (4.11)$$

Here, $M_{\text{self}}(P)$ is the self-radiation, $\rho(P)$ the reflectivity of the surface and $E(P)$ is the incident irradiance (at the point P, respectively). Since the tongue does not emit any self-radiation, to compute the radiance $M(P)$ we only need the incident irradiance $E(P)$ given by[1]:

$$E(P) = \int_{P' \in S} M(P') \frac{1}{\pi r^2} \cos(\varphi_P) \cos(\varphi_{P'}) \, \mathrm{d}P' \qquad (4.12)$$

In this equation, S are all points P' on light emitting surfaces in the scene, r is the distance between the points P and P', and φ_P and $\varphi_{P'}$ are the angles the normal vectors at P and P' form with the line through P and P', respectively.

[1] This equation is given in discrete form in [178].

The major assumption underlying this equation is that all surfaces (reflectors and sources) are ideally diffuse actors (i.e., Lambertian scatterers and radiators), which means they emit or reflect light equally well in all directions. However, the OP280V light sources used in EOS are not Lambertian (i.e., diffuse) radiators. The radiation lobes of these laser diodes are not perfect circles but instead significantly more focused. We model this behavior by introducing an exponent $\theta > 1$ to the second (source-related) cosine term in equation 4.12, which is borrowed from the Phong reflection model where this technique is used to model specular reflections (see [179] for details). By solving $0.5 = \cos^{\theta}(\alpha_{\text{half}})$ for θ, where α_{half} is the half-power angle of the VCSEL diode provided by the data sheet, we obtain an exponent of $\theta = 13.8$ for the light sources used in the EOS system.

Considering that the light source in our scene is punctiform (i.e., S in equation 4.12 becomes only a single point), the angles φ_P and $\varphi_{P'}$ correspond to β and α in Figure 4.18, and the distance becomes $r = |P - S|$. This yields

$$E(P) = \frac{I_0}{\pi |P - S|^2} \cos(\beta) \cos^{\theta}(\alpha), \tag{4.13}$$

where I_0 is the radiant intensity of the source along the optical axis. According to equation 4.11, the resultant *radiance of* the reflector is the *irradiance on* the surface multiplied by the reflectivity. The radiance of a homogeneous reflector (where ρ is constant) therefore becomes:

$$M(P) = \rho \cdot E(P). \tag{4.14}$$

However, the tongue is far from a simple, perfectly homogenous surface reflector: The incident light is only partially reflected at the surface. It also partially penetrates the surface, is repeatedly scattered and reflected between non-uniform protrusions on the tongue called lingual papillae (which give the tongue its distinctive rough texture) and is finally either absorbed by the tissue or contributes to the tongue surface's total radiance as an additive diffuse component. This complex response to incident light is in fact desirable because it is what makes continuous distance sensing even possible, as already described in [162]. In the same paper, Chuang and Wang modeled the partial transmittance of light into the tongue tissue by an additional observed measured distance, which basically assumes a "virtual reflective plane" inside the tissue (see d_e in equation 4.1). This simplification, however, was likely contributing to the unsatisfying precision of their analytic approach to the distance sensing function (see subsection 4.2.2) and so it seemed advisable to adopt a more refined model of the response. To that end, consider the tongue to be a linear system, where the input (the irradiance distribution E caused by the light source) is convolved with the impulse response h to yield the output (the tongue's radiance M)[2]. Therefore, we replace equation 4.14 by

$$M(x,z) = (E * h)(x,z) \tag{4.15}$$

$$= \int_{-\infty}^{\infty}\int_{-\infty}^{\infty} E(\chi,\zeta) \cdot h(x-\chi, z-\zeta)\, d\chi\, d\zeta \tag{4.16}$$

where χ and ζ are the dummy variables necessary for the integration. To model the impulse response h, we first need to determine the general shape of the model function. The parameters of that model function can then be adjusted until it produces results that approximate *in-vivo* measurements. To obtain an initial guess of the impulse response shape, the following experiment was conducted: An LED emitted a bright red light dot directly onto a human subject's tongue dorsum via an optical fiber of a diameter of 0.5 mm. The dot, even though not infinitely small and bright, was assumed to be sufficiently so to approximate an actual impulse. Using visible red light with

[2]Technically, this approach implies that the tongue is a linear translation-invariant system. Even though the linearity seems intuitively plausible due to the fact that non-linear optical systems are highly complex crystalline structures and non-linear effects typically only occur at very high light intensities [180], the translation-invariance seems not to be. However, we assume the light spot on the tongue from the light source to be small enough to consider the tissue locally homogeneous in that very confined area.

a wavelength of approximately 650 nm instead of the near-infrared light used in EOS (peak wavelength of 850 nm) was possible because the optical properties of the tongue could be expected to be sufficiently similar within this narrow band. The tongue's response to the bright dot was photographed with a digital Single-Lense Reflex (SLR) camera on a tripod (Sony A580, Tamron 18 mm to 200 mm lense, 1/4 s shutter speed). Ambient light was eliminated by conducting the experiment in an unlit, windowless room. The resultant image can be seen in Figure 4.19. The raw digital data of the camera's image sensor for the red color channel is shown in Figure 4.20, represented by the horizontal and vertical brightness profiles.

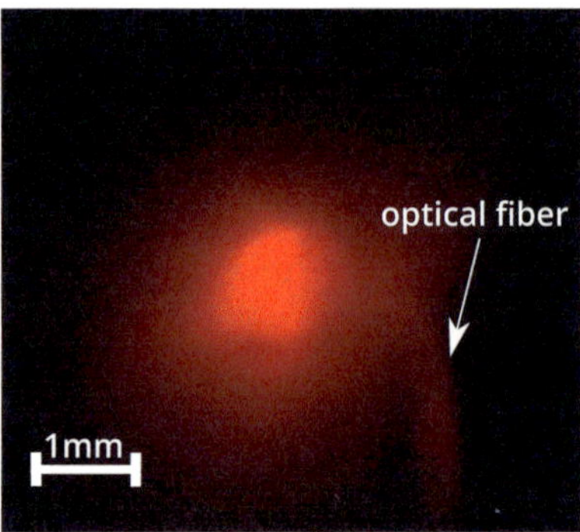

Figure 4.19.: Photo of the tongue's radiance when reflecting a light dot. The small dot, emitted onto the tongue through the 0.5 mm wide optical fiber, is spread into a blurred spot by the sub-surface scattering inside the tongue tissue.

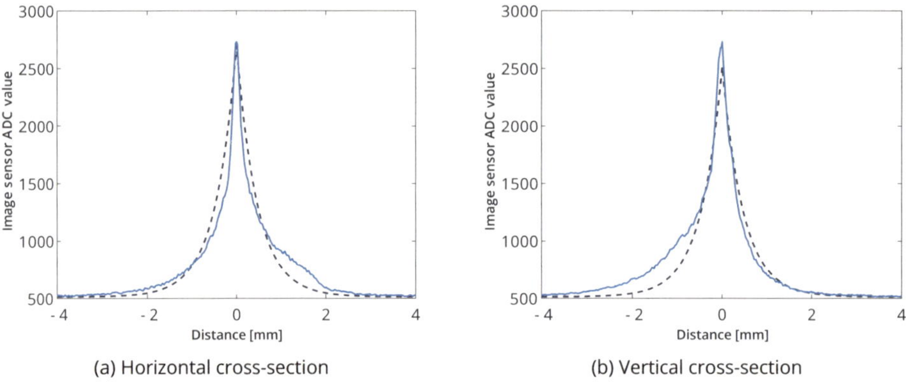

Figure 4.20.: Brightness profiles of the blurred spot in Figure 4.19, red color channel only. Due to the left-aligned data format of the SLR camera, an ADC value of 512 corresponds to a brightness value of 0. Distance is measured from the point of maximum brightness. The dashed lines show the shape of an optimally fitted 2D exponential function.

The "dot response" suggests an exponential shape for the underlying impulse response along both the horizontal and vertical dimension, as illustrated by the fitted exponential (dashed lines) in Figure 4.20. The choice of an exponential as the model function is further motivated by Stam's modeling of multiple scattering in [181], wherein he also describes an exponential reduction of the incident intensity as the incident light is diffused by sub-surface scattering. Therefore, we assume the impulse response h in our model to be a 2D exponential function of the form:

$$h(x,z) = \rho_0 \cdot e^{-\sqrt{\left(\frac{x}{r_x}\right)^2+\left(\frac{z}{r_z}\right)^2}} \tag{4.17}$$

Here, ρ_0 is a linear reflection coefficient and r_x and r_z are the parameters to control the decay of the function in *x*- and *z*-direction. Because the exact impulse response of a human tongue is likely to be slightly different across different tongues, we need to find the optimal parameter pair (r_x, r_z) by comparing the results produced with our model to results measured on actual tongues and minimizing the squared Euclidean distance between them as a function of (r_x, r_z).

To model a detector value for a given geometry that considers sub-surface scattering, we insert equation 4.17 into equation 4.16 to calculate the radiance "output" *M* of the tongue to a given irradiance "input" *E*:

$$M(x,z) = \int_{-\infty}^{\infty}\int_{-\infty}^{\infty} E(\chi,\zeta)\cdot\rho_0\cdot e^{-\sqrt{\left(\frac{x-\chi}{r_x}\right)^2+\left(\frac{z-\zeta}{r_z}\right)^2}}\,\mathrm{d}\chi\,\mathrm{d}\zeta \tag{4.18}$$

To proceed, we need to derive *E* in its Cartesian notation: If we replace the cosine terms in equation 4.13 by the dot product of the normal vectors enclosing the respective angles, we obtain:

$$E(P) = \frac{I_0}{\pi\,|P-S|^2}\cdot\frac{\vec{n}_P\cdot(S-P)}{|P-S|}\cdot\left(\frac{\vec{n}_S\cdot(P-S)}{|P-S|}\right)^{\theta} \tag{4.19}$$

which becomes

$$E(P) = \frac{I_0}{\pi}\frac{[\vec{n}_P\cdot(S-P)]\cdot[\vec{n}_S\cdot(P-S)]^{\theta}}{|P-S|^{3+\theta}} \tag{4.20}$$

and considering $P = (x,0,z)^{\mathsf{T}}$ we obtain finally:

$$E(x,z) = \frac{I_0}{\pi}\frac{S_y\cdot[n_{S_x}\cdot(x-S_x)+n_{S_y}(-S_y)]^{\theta}}{\left[(S_x-x)^2+{S_y}^2+z^2\right]^{(3+\theta)/2}} \tag{4.21}$$

Next we insert equation 4.21 for *E* in equation 4.18:

$$M(x,z) = \frac{\rho_0 I_0}{\pi}\int_{-\infty}^{\infty}\int_{-\infty}^{\infty}\frac{S_y\left[n_{S_x}(\chi-S_x)-n_{S_y}S_y\right]^{\theta}}{\left[(\chi-S_x)^2+S_y^2+\zeta^2\right]^{(3+\theta)/2}}\cdot e^{-\sqrt{\left(\frac{x-\chi}{r_x}\right)^2+\left(\frac{z-\zeta}{r_x}\right)^2}}\,\mathrm{d}\chi\,\mathrm{d}\zeta \tag{4.22}$$

To finally obtain the irradiance E_D at the detector, we use equation 4.12 for our specific geometry:

$$E_D = \int_{P\in\Pi} M(P)\cdot\frac{1}{\pi\,|P-D|^2}\cos(\gamma)\cos(\delta)\,\mathrm{d}P \tag{4.23}$$

where Π is the set of all points on the reflector, *M* is the radiance of the reflector and γ and δ are the angles as denoted in Figure 4.18. The directional sensitivity of the detector in the EOS system is described by the cosine function according to its data sheet, therefore making an exponent here redundant. In this equation, we now insert equation 4.22 for *M*(*P*), replace the cosines as before and, after expanding and rearranging, obtain an equation to calculate the scalar irradiance at a given detector position E_D as a function of the given geometry that considers sub-surface scattering of an inhomogeneous reflector:

$$E_D = \frac{\rho_0 I_0}{\pi^2}\int_{-\infty}^{\infty}\int_{-\infty}^{\infty}\int_{-\infty}^{\infty}\int_{-\infty}^{\infty}\frac{S_y\left[n_{S_x}(\chi-S_x)-n_{S_y}S_y\right]^{\theta}}{[(\chi-S_x)^2+S_y^2+\zeta^2]^{(3+\theta)/2}}\cdot e^{-\sqrt{\left(\frac{x-\chi}{r_x}\right)^2+\left(\frac{z-\zeta}{r_x}\right)^2}}\,\mathrm{d}\chi\,\mathrm{d}\zeta\cdot\frac{D_y\left[n_{D_x}(x-D_x)-n_{D_y}D_y\right]}{\left[(x-D_x)^2+D_y^2+(z-D_z)^2\right]^2}\,\mathrm{d}x\,\mathrm{d}z. \tag{4.24}$$

Evaluation of the light propagation model

To evaluate the model, simulation results for a specific geometry with a given pair of parameters (r_x, r_z) should be compared with *in-vivo* measurement results obtained with the same source-detector-reflector setup. To that end, the same data as in the previous section was used (see subsection 4.2.2). For this study, however, three detectors were sampled: one detector only laterally displaced from the source, one detector positioned more posterior and one more anterior in addition to the same lateral displacement. This was translated to the geometry shown in Figure 4.21 (when $\varphi = 90°$).

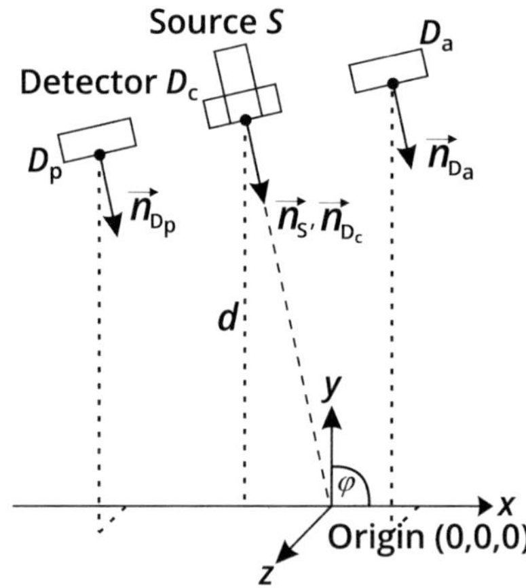

Figure 4.21.: The geometry of the *in-vivo* measurements translated to the model scene. To find the optimal pair of model parameters, φ was set to 90° and d was varied.

For each detector position D_i and each distance d_i, an irradiance value $E_{D_i}(d_i)$ was computed using a discretized version of equation 4.24 in a Matlab script with a reflector plane of 10 cm by 10 cm represented by a grid with equidistant 0.1 mm gridlines along both dimensions. Additional values E_{D_i} were computed for distances between the *in-vivo* samples (i.e., 0.25 cm, 0.75 cm, 1.25 cm, and so on). The simulated results were compared to the measured samples by calculating the RMSE for each detector position (center, posterior, anterior) across all distances. Both sets (model results and measured results) were normalized to their individual maximum, because it was only of interest to fit the relative shape, not the linear scaling factor of the model function. The parameter set (r_x, r_z) that produced the smallest summed RMSE across all five averaged *in-vivo* trials and the three detector positions was considered to be optimal. After performing an exhaustive search through the set $[0.1, 10]$ cm $\times$ $[0.1, 10]$ cm in 0.01 cm increments the results calculated with the pair ($r_x =$ 0.42 cm, $r_z =$ 1.25 cm) produced the best fit and are shown in Figure 4.22.

To validate the model with these optimal parameters, both the inclination angle and the distance of the reflector were varied in a second run of the simulation and the results were compared to *in-vivo* EOS data at two different reflector distances (1.7 cm and 2.2 cm) and eight inclination angles between 90° and 125° (in 5° steps). These data were recorded following the same protocol as before, except that instead of using spacers of different length, spacers which put the the tongue at different angles towards the optical sensor axes were used. All other parameters during the measurements were the same and the same subjects were used. For the simulations, the general geometry of the scene was kept the same, except that now measurements at 11 distances $d_i = \{0.5, 0.75, 1.0, \ldots, 3.0\}$ mm and at 15 inclination angles between 55° and 125° (in 5° steps) for 3 detector positions (relative positions as above) were simulated, for a total of $11 \times 15 \times 3 = 495$ simulations. As Figure 4.23 shows, the thusly computed irradiance profiles on the tongue surface under different inclinations exhibited a shift of the maximum depending on the angle. This shift was consequently also present in the radiance profile and caused a change in the irradiance sampled at the

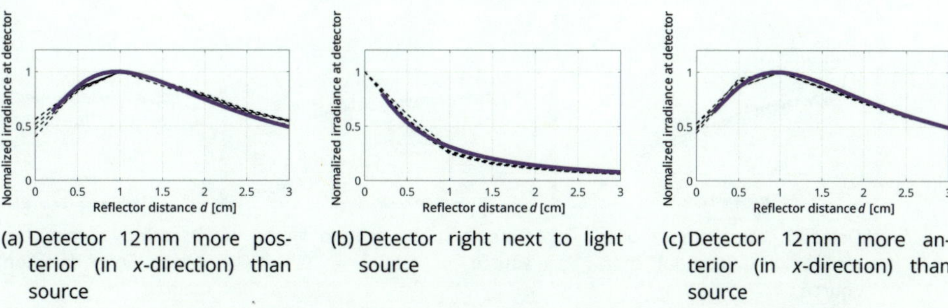

(a) Detector 12 mm more posterior (in *x*-direction) than source

(b) Detector right next to light source

(c) Detector 12 mm more anterior (in *x*-direction) than source

Figure 4.22.: The normalized simulated irradiance (solid line) calculated at three different detector positions compared with the normalized measured irradiance (averaged across five sensors in three configurations for each subject; black dashed lines) at different distances for a fixed inclination angle of 90°. All three detectors were laterally (in *z*-direction) displaced from the source by 3 mm.

three detector positions. As shown in Figure 4.24, this change was also present in the *in-vivo* measurements. The model therefore accurately represented real-world measurements even beyond the conditions it was trained with (i.e., with a perpendicular reflector) and allows the examination of the influence of the reflector inclination on the sensor value.

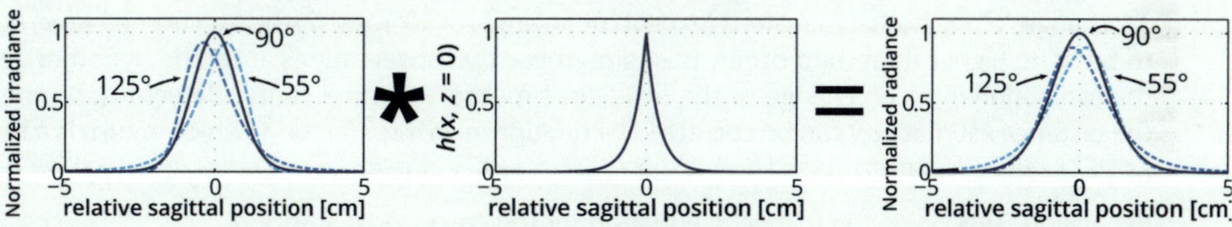

Figure 4.23.: Normalized irradiance, impulse response and radiance of the tongue surface (sagittal slice) for three reflector angles at a source-reflector distance of 3 cm. The irradiance distribution is convolved with the impulse response to obtain the radiance distribution. Changing the angle of the reflector moves and scales the maximum of the irradiance and radiance distributions.

Compensation of the reflector angle's influence on the sensor output

As shown in Figure 4.24b, a non-perpendicular reflector introduces a change of the irradiance at the detector, which subsequently results in an erroneous distance if a calibration characteristic is used that was obtained for a perpendicular reflector (e.g., using the calibration scheme derived in subsection 4.2.2): Instead of the true source-reflector distance d, an erroneous distance d' is measured, which is gained from linear interpolation between known calibration samples taken at a 90° reflector angle, and carries both the error due to the piece-wise linearization of the non-linear mapping between distance and irradiance (see Figure 4.22b) and the error due to the reflector inclination. Therefore, d' is only correct at the calibration distances when at the same time the reflector is perpendicular to the optical sensor axis. However, in both the simulation results and the *in-vivo* data, the change of the measured irradiance is not independent of the detector position (see Figure 4.24a and Figure 4.24c). If the irradiance is measured at three positions (one directly next to the source, one more posterior, and one more anterior), it seems possible to combine the information from the more anterior and more posterior detector to adjust d' derived from the central detector value by a correction term to obtain a corrected distance $\hat{d}$.

To further examine this notion, we take a look at the ratio of posterior to anterior detector values $\frac{E_{D_p}}{E_{D_a}}$ for different angles φ and distances d, where D_p and D_a are the posterior and anterior detector

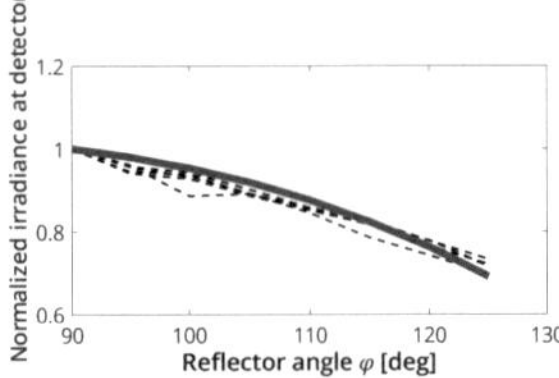

(a) Detector 12 mm more posterior (in x-direction) than source

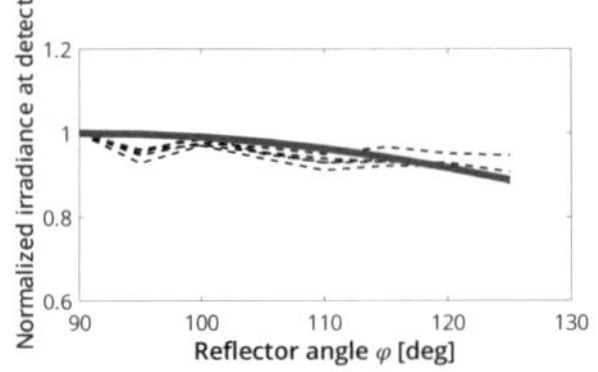

(b) Detector right next to light source

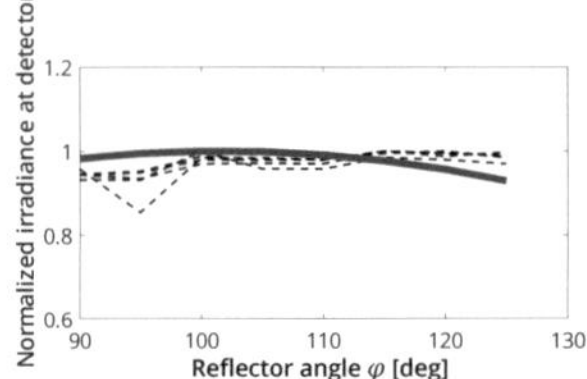

(c) Detector 12 mm more anterior (in x-direction) than source

Figure 4.24.: The normalized simulated irradiance (solid line) calculated at three different detector positions is compared with the normalized measured irradiance (averaged across five sensors for each of the five subjects; black dashed line) at different angles for a fixed distance of 1.75 cm. While the trends are mostly the same, the difference between *in-vivo* data and the simulation results becomes slighty larger at large angles. However, for large angles, it also becomes increasingly difficult for the subject to cover the entire top area of the spacer used in the experiment, especially in the anterior area, which makes the *in-vivo* results less reliable for large angles.

position respectively, which is shown in Figure 4.25. Two things are evident: (1) the irradiance ratio $\frac{E_{D_p}}{E_{D_a}}$ changes along both dimensions (except for an angle of 90°) and (2) the function $\frac{E_{D_p}}{E_{D_a}}(d, \varphi)$ appears to be of no higher than third order. Based on these two observations, it can be hypothesized that the inclination-induced change of the irradiance measured at the center detector (and therefore the distance estimate d') can be corrected by multiplying d' by a factor w, which in turn is a function of $\frac{E_{D_p}}{E_{D_a}}$. As the exact function $w\left(\frac{E_{D_p}}{E_{D_a}}\right)$ is unknown, it is instead approximated by its third-order series expansion. This yields the following equation for the corrected distance $\hat{d}$:

$$\hat{d} = d' \cdot \left(a_0 + a_1 \left(\frac{E_{D_p}}{E_{D_a}} \right) + a_2 \left(\frac{E_{D_p}}{E_{D_a}} \right)^2 + a_3 \left(\frac{E_{D_p}}{E_{D_a}} \right)^3 \right). \tag{4.25}$$

The unknown coefficients a_i ($i = 0, \ldots, 3$) are estimated in a least-squares regression scheme using the simulation results with varying angle above to set up an overdetermined system of equations according to equation 4.25, where $\hat{d}$ is substituted by the known true distance d. The thusly found optimal coefficients were than evaluated by calculating $\hat{d}$ for every simulated trial. The improvement of $\hat{d}$ over using d' is illustrated by Figure 4.26. The corrected distance $\hat{d}$ was consistently much closer to the true distance: Across all distances, the mean relative error (i.e., the relative accuracy) is significantly reduced from 4.71 % to 0.06 % while the standard deviation of the overall error distribution (i.e., the precision) is also significantly improved from 4.07 % to 2.53 % (unpaired t-test: $p < 0.0001$).

The same coefficients found with the simulated results can also be used to correct the distances in the *in-vivo* measurements, because the simulations replicated the same geometric setup in and only the derived quantity d' and the ratio $\frac{E_{D_p}}{E_{D_a}}$ (where the linear scaling factor, which is independent of the sensor position, cancels itself out) were used. The results are shown in Figure 4.27. Even in these real-world data that were not part of the training set the overestimation of the distance caused by linear interpolation and inclination is reduced significantly (unpaired t-test: $p < 0.0001$) both in terms of accuracy (from 7.38 % to 2.25 %) and precision (from 2.79 % to 1.9 %). It can therefore be concluded that the model is suitable to simulate real-world measurements of a given geometry and that the coefficients a_0 to a_3 in equation 4.25 can be trained with those simulation results to help improve the accuracy and precision of real-world measurements of the same geometry.

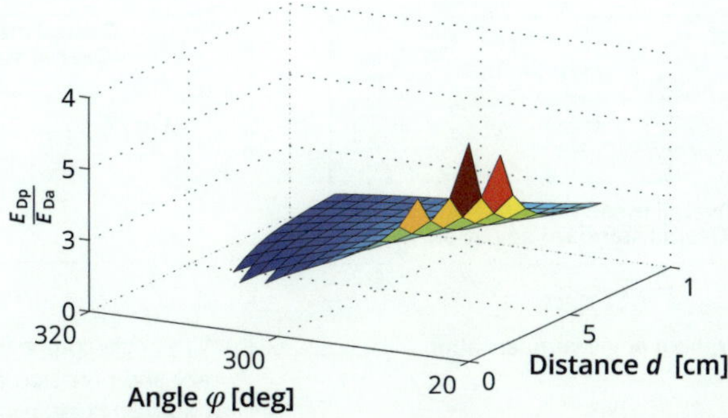

Figure 4.25.: Ratio of the irradiance at the posterior detector E_{D_p} to the irradiance at the anterior detector E_{D_a}.

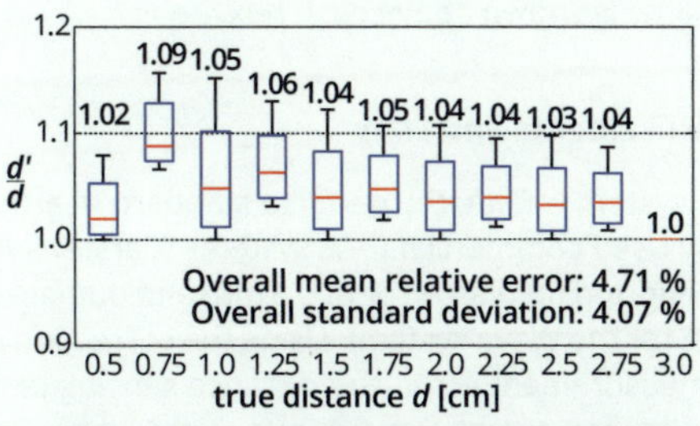

(a) Without angle compensation. The ratio is always 1.0 across all angles at 3.0 cm distance because the inclination angle causes overestimation of the distance but the measurement range is clipped at 3.0 cm

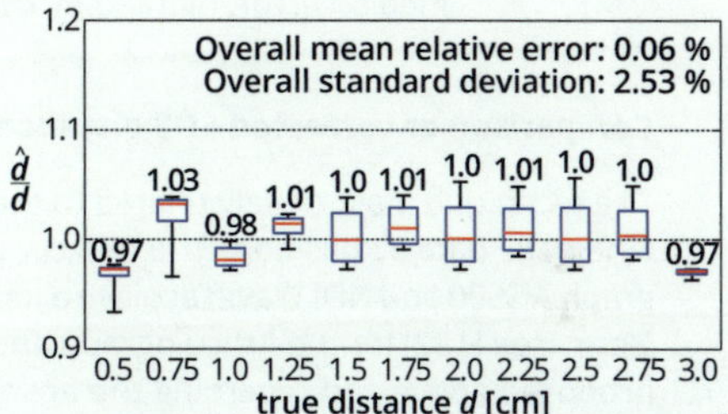

(b) With angle compensation. Both overall accuracy and precision are significantly improved (unpaired t test: $p < 0.0001$).

Figure 4.26.: Model data: Ratio of measured distances to true distances across all 11 angles. The respective median error, marked by the red line, is shown above each box.

Accurate tongue contour visualization in real-time EOS measurements

The compensation method proposed in this paper was tested with a real EOS palate (see section 4.4) and a human subject. The technique was applied to the measurements of the three center sensors, where both a more anterior and a more posterior detector was available. The geometric setups (relative positions and angles) of the three possible combinations of one light source and its respective three nearest detectors were extracted from a 3D scan of the pseudopalate and a simulation was performed for each setup to obtain coefficients for equation 4.25 as described above. The equations were adapted to each sensor geometry and then used in real-time EOS measurements to correct the distance at runtime. Figure 4.28 shows tongue contours acquired in this way for one subject's sustained realizations of the five German vowels /aː, eː, iː, oː, uː/, averaged over 10 utterances each. The tongue contours are both physiologically plausible and the articulatory features frontness/backness and height show the expected pattern. When comparing the measured distances with the distances obtained using a single-detector setup, the corrected value is always smaller. This is plausible because an inclined reflector causes less light to be registered by the detector, which in turn leads to an overestimated distance. The tongue contours also appear to be most strongly curved in the central region during articulation of high vowels, as shown by the relatively large corrections during /eː/ and /iː/ for d_2.

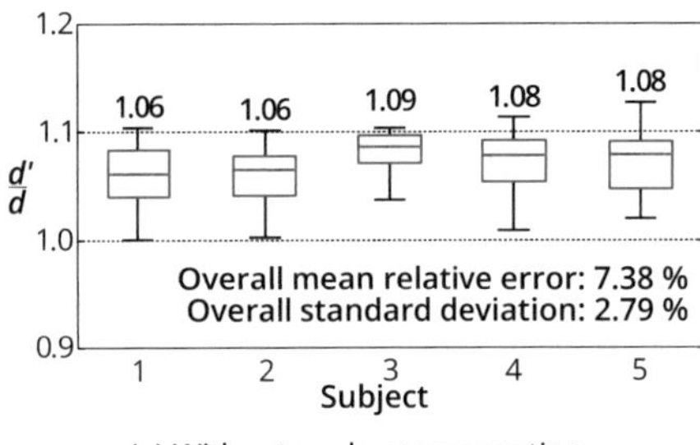

(a) Without angle compensation

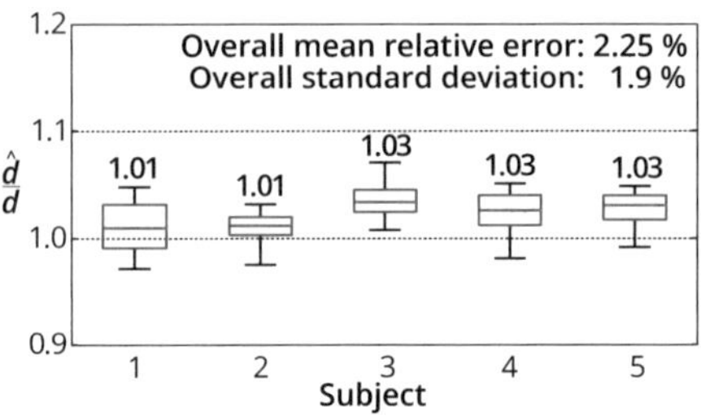

(b) With angle compensation. Both overall accuracy and precision are significantly improved (unpaired t test: $p < 0.0001$).

Figure 4.27.: Subject data: Ratio of measured distances to true distances across all angles. Each box represents the deviation from the true distance d across eight angles between 90° and 125° in combined trials at two different distances (1.7 cm and 2.2 cm). The respective median error, marked by the red line, is shown above each box.

Comparison of corrected EOS distance measurements and EMA

The technique most closely related to the EOS system is EMA, the de-facto standard in articulatory kinematic data acquisition. The two commonly used commercial EMA systems (Carstens Articulograph AG500 and NDI Wave) achieve a lowest reported median error of 0.5 mm and outliers of up to 2 mm (see [182] for the Articulograph and [128] for the Wave system). Using the correction scheme proposed above and regarding the absolute measurement error, the distance sensing in the EOS system achieved a median error of 0.4 mm (averaged across five subjects, eight angles, and two distances) with the largest outlier at 1.2 mm. Therefore, even when the angle between the tongue and the sensor axis is varied, the results of the optical distance sensors in EOS generally stay within the reference error margin set by EMA. While this is an encouraging estimate, further studies with larger sample sizes of EMA and EOS data are advised.

Conclusion

A novel approach was proposed to model propagation of light during optopalatographic distance measurements inside the vocal tract as performed in EOS, using a computer-graphics and systems-theory-based approach. By simulating optical distance measurements with this model, a linear regression model was trained that allowed the correction of the erroneous distances gained from a calibration characteristic that assumed a 90° reflector angle to account for the influence of the reflector's actual inclination angle. In the training data, the overall mean distance error was reduced from 4.71 % to 0.06 % and the overall standard deviation from 4.07 % to 2.53 %. In *in-vivo* data unseen by the training algorithm used to optimize the compensation coefficients, the improvement of the corrected distance over the interpolated distance was consistently significant across the EOS measurements from five evaluated subjects: the overall mean error (accuracy) was reduced from 7.38 % to 2.25 %, while the standard deviation of the error was reduced from 2.79 % to 1.9 %. These error margins were comparable to the measurement errors of the established EMA systems. The technique yields plausible (in terms of frontness/backness and height) and consistent (i.e., low variance) tongue contours in real-time measurements.

Since the simulations need the exact, subject-dependent geometric setup of the sensors and detectors, a method still needs to be devised to efficiently capture this geometry. For the purposes of this study, the palate contours were traced by hand and the sensor positions were determined manually. Unfortunately, this process is laborious and time and resource consuming. Since one of the major design goals of EOS was to create a system that can be easily produced en masse and the current technique to obtain the sensor geometry was incompatible with that goal, some preliminary work has been undertaken in a student's thesis [183] to automatically capture the geometry using a

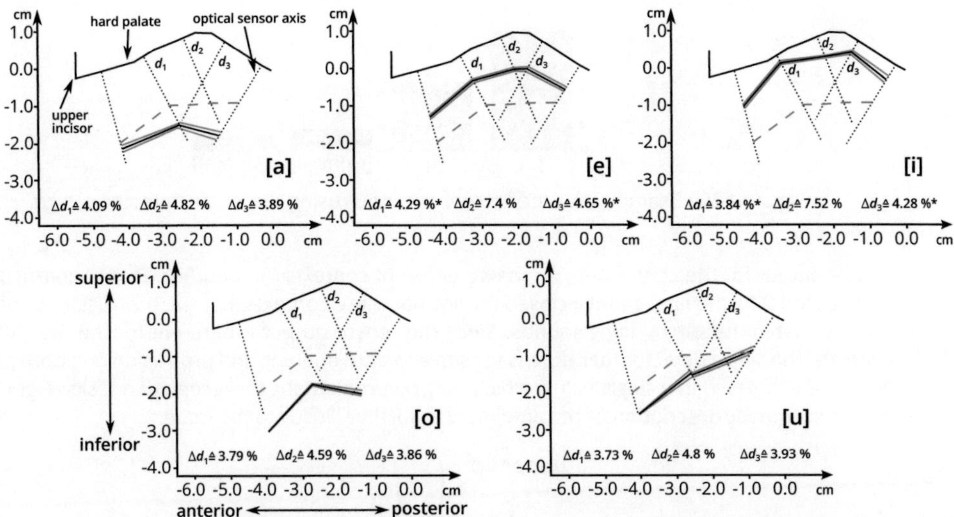

Figure 4.28.: Electro-Optical Stomatography tongue contours of five German vowels, averaged over 10 realizations of the same speaker. The solid black line is the mean tongue contour across all 10 realizations, the solid gray lines are the highest and lowest contour, and the dashed gray line is the mean contour of the neutral vowel /ə/. The measured distances d_i along the central three sensors' optical axes were adjusted to compensate the influence of the reflector angle. The relative change by applying the angle-correction to the single detector measurements is denoted as Δd_i. Except for the four values marked by *, all improvements are statistically significant (unpaired *t*-test, $p < 0.05$).

desktop 3D scanner and a custom image processing software. This work is currently on-going and has not yet yielded results that could be integrated into the EOS production workflow, therefore the measurements for the ATS and ATT studies (see chapter 5 and chapter 6) were conducted without the angle correction described above.

4.3. Lip sensor

Previous optopalatographic systems have exclusively captured tongue movements. As described in chapter 2, however, the lips are another major articulator and should not be ignored by the articulometric frontend of an SSI. For EOS, three different designs for an optical lip sensor were explored: one using a single light source and a single detector, one using a single light source and two detectors, and one using two light sources and two detectors.

4.3.1. Single-source, single-detector design

The most basic design followed the example of [169] and used the same layout as the optical tongue distance sensors (see section 4.2) and thus consisted of a single light source and a single detector, positioned on the upper incisors so that the sensor's optical axis was directed towards the upper lip. As illustrated by Figure 4.29, there were indeed different sensor outputs for different sounds.

However, the example sounds also show a problem inherent in the single-detector design: The lip configuration for the two sounds /aː/ and /uː/ does not just differ by the degree of the lip opening (/aː/ very wide lip opening, /uː/ very narrow opening), but also by the degree of lip rounding or protrusion (/aː/ neutral protrusion, /uː/ very protruded). The output of the single-detector lip sensor depends on both of these orthogonal parameters of the lips, however, as is evident in the

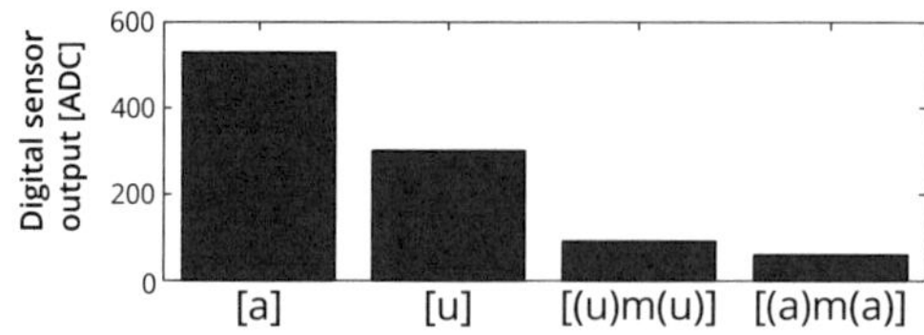

Figure 4.29.: Examples for the lip sensor output using the single detector design

sensor output for the consonant $/\mathrm{m}/$ in two different contexts ((a) and (u)). Due to coarticulation (see section 2.5), the lips are fully closed for both of these contexts, but the protrusion is coarticulated to match the surrounding sounds. Since the sensor output is different for the two different contexts, the single detector therefore is sensitive to both opening and protrusion and both parameters are expressed in a single value, which may be problematic for recognition tasks. Figure 4.30 gives a schematic description of the ambiguity to further illustrate the issue.

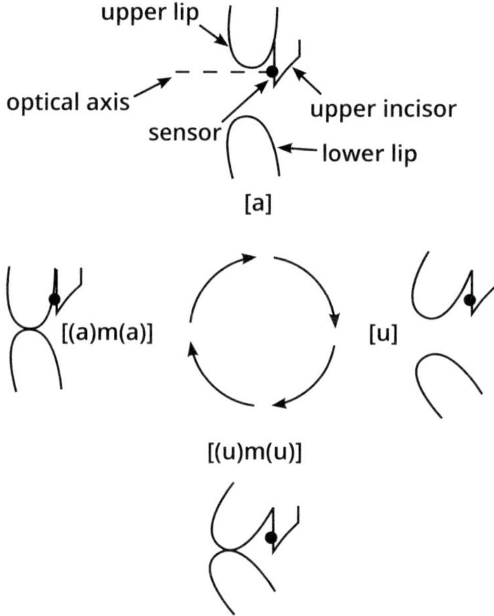

Figure 4.30.: Schematic description of the ambiguity inherent to the single detector design: There are several combinations of protrusion and opening that can lead to the same sensor output value if only a single detector is used.

4.3.2. Single-source, dual-detector design

To resolve the ambiguity of the single-detector paradigm, a second detector was placed closer to the lower edge of the incisors and the other detector was moved further towards the gums. The hypothesis behind this approach, illustrated by Figure 4.31, was as follows: The lip sensor, even though capturing the articulatory dimensions opening and protrusion, is essentially still an optical distance sensor. Since the lip forms a slope when it is protruded, the two detectors in the indicated positions would measure different intensities (which would normally be related to different distances) for protruded lips, with the difference increasing with increasing protrusion.

To validate this hypothesis and evaluate the suitability of this single-source, dual-detector setup, a study was conducted as part of a student's thesis [184]. The study gathered optical lip sensor data

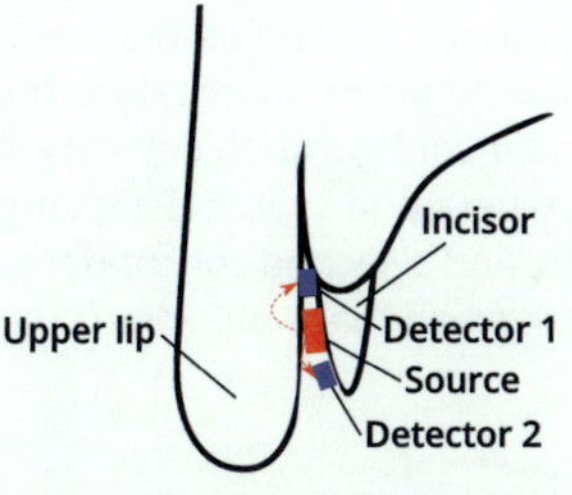

(a) Optical paths when the lips are closed: light travels through the tissue to both detectors approximately symmetrically.

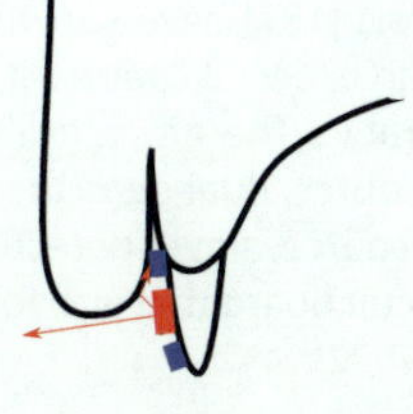

(b) Optical paths when the lips are open: the lower detector captures very little light, while the upper detector still captures as much light as in the closed configuration.

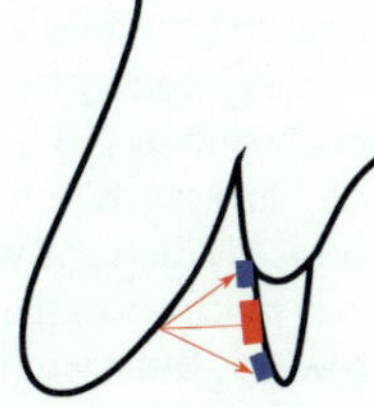

(c) Optical paths when the lips are protruded: The slope of the protruded lips causes the radiated light to be reflected at different distances from the detectors, which results in different measured intensities at the detector positions.

Figure 4.31.: Schematic description of the single-source dual-detector design (illustration based on [184, Figure 2.2, p. 16]): Solid red arrows indicate light traveling through air, dashed red arrows indicate light traveling through tissue.

from four subjects, as well as reference data collected similarly to [185], except that both a frontal and a profile view were recorded using two cameras. The cameras were fixed in place relative to the speaker's head using a custom-made mounting system and the reference trajectories of both lip protrusion and opening were extracted using a custom image processing pipeline [186]. The recorded utterances in the study were of the pattern /VmV/, where V was replaced by the German tense vowels /aː, eː, iː, oː, uː, ɛː, ʌː, yː/ to cover the entire articulatory space along both dimensions (opening and protrusion) of the lips. Using these data, a correlation analysis was conducted to estimate the information gain by adding the second detector (see Table 4.3).

	$r_{p,o}$	r_{d_1,d_2}
subject 1	-0.28	0.87
subject 2	-0.59	0.75
subject 3	-0.35	0.79
subject 4	-0.15	0.72

Table 4.3.: Pearson correlation coefficient of the two detectors in the single-source, dual-detector lip sensor design (data taken from [184]): Even though the ground truth parameters lip opening and lip protrusion were generally not highly correlated with one another, the detector outputs were quite correlated, indicating redundancy in the sensor readings and thus a non-optimal setup.

For 3 out of the 4 analyzed subjects, the Peason correlation coefficient between the articulatory parameters lip opening and protrusion was fairly low ($r_{p,o} < 0.4$). The detector outputs, however, were quite correlated with one another (up to $r_{d_1,d_2} = 0.87$) , which means there is a high redundancy in the outputs, i.e., very little information gain by adding a second sensor. Because of the findings of this study, the single-source, dual-detector setup was once again revised and extended by a second light source.

4.3.3. Dual-source, dual-detector design

One major implicit assumption underlying the single-source designs was that the lip configuration could be derived from capturing data of the upper lip alone. However, as experiments in [184] and an unpublished diploma thesis [187] have shown, the lip opening is in fact only very weakly represented by the upper lip. So in order to capture it, a downward facing source-detector pair as proposed by [187] would be desirable. Therefore, the final sensor configuration developed as part of this dissertation was the dual-source, dual-detector design, where one source-detector pair was basically identical with the single-source, single-detector design, and a second source-detector pair was placed on a flap of flexible circuit board that was folded at an angle that would direct the sensor towards the lower lip (see Figure 4.32).

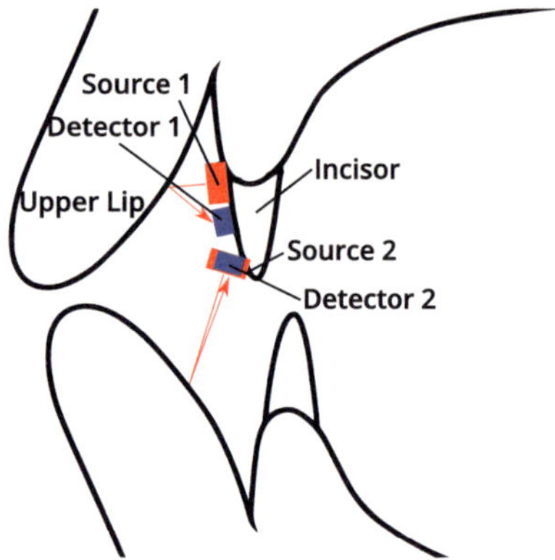

Figure 4.32.: Schematic description of the dual-source, dual-detector design (illustration based on [187, Figure 8.3, p. 55]): Each source-detector pair captures a different lip.

Intuitively, one might think that in this setup, the downward facing source-detector pair would measure the lip opening and the forward facing pair would measure the protrusion. However, both pairs capture a mix of both articulatory degrees of freedom, because the reasoning given above regarding the upper lip are analogously valid for the lower lip: the same measured "distance" can be caused by different combinations of lip opening and protrusion. However, it is to be expected that each pair's output is *dominated* by the respective degree of freedom and that by combining the outputs of both pairs, e.g., in a linear regression model, the actual articulatory dimensions lip opening and protrusion could be extracted, as was attempted in [187] for a similar setup. While the extraction would be of interest from a feature engineering standpoint since they appear to be approximately orthogonal features and thus maximize the discriminant information, it was beyond the scope of this work. For the machine learning models used in the ATT and ATS experiments of this dissertation, it was deemed sufficient to use the raw sensor output and let the downstream mapping from the feature vectors to the classification or regression output implicitly model the mapping from the detector outputs to the latent articulatory space, as well.

4.4. Sensor Unit

The electrical and optical sensors described in the previous sections need to be integrated into a probe of some kind (a *sensor unit*), that is then inserted into the subject's mouth to measure the speech movements. As a palatographic measurement technique (see section 3.9), EOS uses an intraoral sensor unit that is worn on the upper jaw (*maxilla*), similar to a dental brace or mouthguard (see Figure 4.1(a)). The design concept of the sensor unit emphasizes portability and low cost: it consists of a plastic base plate (made of polyethylene) that is individually thermoformed to fit a subject's maxilla and palate, and a flexible circuit board that carries the sensor electronics and is attached to the base plate with a light-curing, resin-based dental restorative material. While the previous sections described the sensors themselves, this section presents the sensor unit that encompasses a specific setup of the described sensors on a flexible circuit board fixed to a base plate and the manufacturing process that was developed to allow a quick and simple assembly of this sensor unit.

4.4.1. Concept of the multi-modal measurements

Before the sensor unit is described, a brief discussion of the reasoning behind combining two different kinds of sensing modalities on the device should be provided, because in theory, a sensor system could be conceived that exclusively uses optical sensors. Spread out across the entire hard palate, essentially forming a grid of OPG sensors instead of just a single row along the midsagittal line, it would look similar to the optopalate proposed in [166]. However, since the optical sensors can only be sampled one at a time to avoid optical crosstalk (as shown by [166]), the number of sensors directly impacts the possible sampling period and thus the rate at which the entire palate can be scanned (the frame rate). Using the optopalate in [166] as an example: Given the frame rate of 100 Hz and assuming no additional overhead due to switching times, transient behaviour or data transfer protocols, the sampling period T_n for each sensor is

$$T_n = \frac{1}{100\,\text{Hz} \cdot n} = \frac{10\,\text{ms}}{n}, \tag{4.26}$$

where n is the number of sensors in the setup. The optopalate and its 9 sensors could therefore achieve a sampling period of approximately 1.1 ms under ideal circumstances. Assuming a low-cost ADC and a reasonable analog-to-digital conversion rate of 10 kHz (as provided by, e.g., the ATmega328 [188], which powers the popular Arduino developer board), this would correspond to 11 samples per sensor, which are averaged to obtain the final sensor value. Oversampling the signal in this way and then averaging across all K samples greatly improves the Signal-to-Noise Ratio (SNR) by reducing the noise power by a factor of K (see section B.2). If only 4 sensors were used (e.g., the four midsagittal ones in the optopalate setup), the sampling period per sensor would increase to 2.5 ms and the number of samples accordingly to 25. In terms of the SNR, the additional 14 samples would reduce the noise power by an additional factor of 2.3. This simplified example demonstrates that while it is desirable to use a high number of sensors to obtain a good spatial resolution of the measurements, it is at the same time beneficial to maximize the sampling time for each sensor to improve the SNR of the sampled signal. The frame rate is the limiting factor here and forces a trade-off between these two requirements.

However, the entire predicament described above only comes about because of the single modality in the system and the inability to sample several sensors concurrently because of the optical crosstalk. Using electrical contact sensors alongside the optical sensors resolves this dilemma. With any microcontroller that supports Direct Memory Access (DMA) and interrupt-controlled programming (which are very common features), the sensing of the two modalities can be interleaved to greatly speed up the data acquisition (see Figure E.1). Using contact sensors in the lateral dimensions of course means the loss of some distance information. For an accurate 3D reconstruction of the mouth cavity, this would most likely pose a severe limitation. For the analysis of speech sounds, however, this is much less of an issue: As described in chapter 2, speech sounds are discriminated by their (midsagittal) tongue contour and the degree of lip rounding (in case of vocoids), or by their place of articulation and their articulator (in case of consonants). If those features can be reliably captured, then the speech movements are unambiguously identifiable. Because of these synergetic properties, the EOS system adopted this multimodal setup.

4.4.2. Combined sensor board

The sensors are mounted onto a flexible printed circuit board (PCB), made to fit onto the relatively small area of the hard palate. The upper boundaries for the geometrical dimensions of this flex PCB were taken from a study conducted for [189], who measured the palate dimensions of 191 subjects (85 male, 106 female, age 11-55) along the lines shown in Figure 4.33a. For the flex PCB dimensions, the lines marked as A1 through A4 (summing up to the palate length), as well as the line B1 (the maximum palate width) are of greatest importance. As shown in Figure 4.33b and Figure 4.33c, the distributions of these dimensions were approximately normal with a mean of 49.95 mm and a standard deviation of 4.19 mm for $A1+A2+A3+A4$, and a mean of 46.1 mm and a standard deviation of 4.45 mm for $B1$.

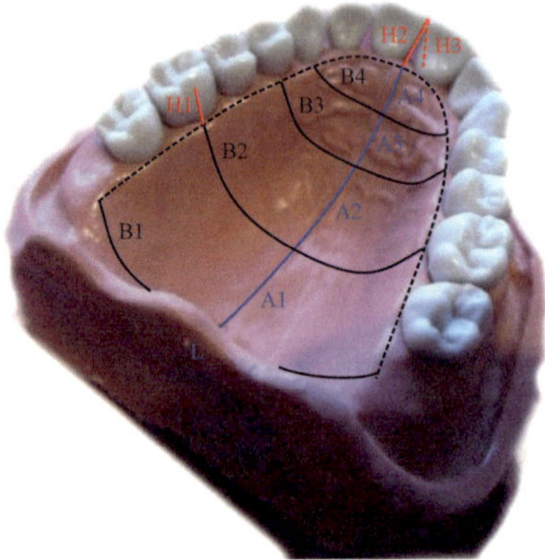

(a) Measured dimensions in the study. The length of the line B1 and the sum of the line segments A1 through A4 are of immediate interest to constrain the PCB dimensions for an intraoral measurement device like EOS.

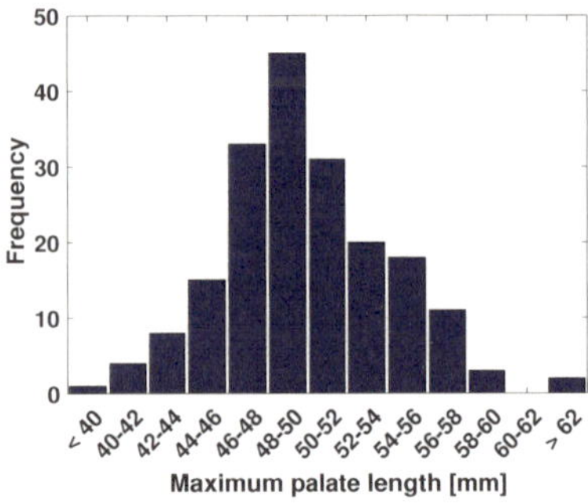

(b) Distribution of the palate length $A1 + A2 + A3 + A4$ across all 191 subjects ($\mu = 49.95$ mm, $\sigma = 4.19$ mm)

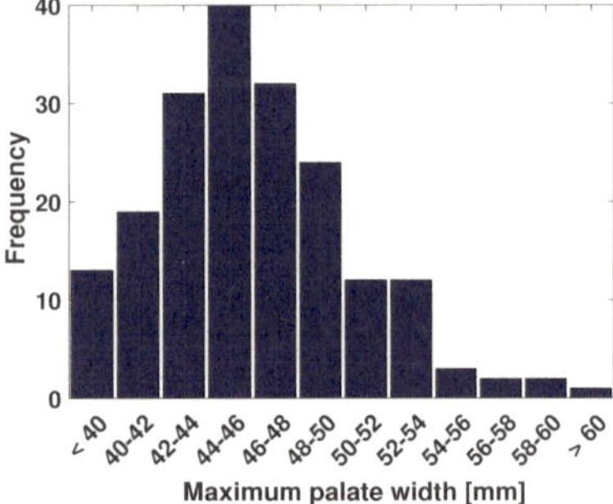

(c) Distribution of the palate width $B1$ across all 191 subjects ($\mu = 46.1$ mm, $\sigma = 4.45$ mm)

Figure 4.33.: Palate dimensions measured in a large-scale study performed in [189]

To design a sensor unit that fits on most palates, two lengths of flexible PCB were initially considered: one large sized PCB for a palate length of 53 mm (approximately one standard deviation above the mean) and one small sized PCB for a palate length of 46 mm (approximately one standard deviation below the mean). In contrast to the palate length, which should not be overshot to avoid a gag reflex of the user, the PCB width can be slightly larger than the actual palate width without causing any uncomfortable side effects. Therefore and in order to keep the total number of different sizes small, both the larger and the smaller size were designed with a maximum width of 46 mm, which was approximately the mean of the width distribution in the subject study. While PCBs were designed for both of these sizes for earlier iterations of the sensor unit, the final prototype currently only comes in the larger size (see section C.5), since no subjects encountered in the ATT and ATS experiments of this dissertation actually needed a small-sized palate. However, scaling the large sized palate down to the smaller size is a straight-forward procedure and can be done at a later time, if necessary.

The next step in the design of the sensor unit was to arrange the individual sensors. For the contact sensors, the pattern was already discussed in section 4.1. Since the optical tongue sensors had to be midsagittal by definition of the tongue contour measurement concept, the five sensors were regularly spaced after aligning the most anterior sensor with the base of the incisors. The different lip sensor designs also required different PCB designs. For both single-source designs, the sensor was placed on the face of the upper incisors facing the lip. For the dual-source design, the first source-detector pair was placed approximately at the same position as the single-detector sensor. The second source-detector pair was laterally displaced and put onto the bottom of a foldable flap of the PCB. After the component placement, the flap would then be folded at a roughly 90° degree angle and fixed in place using the same orthodontic agent used in the assembly of the entire sensor unit (see below).

After positioning all the sensors in the available space of the PCB, the wiring necessary to control and read the individual sensors using an external control unit (see section 4.5) had to be routed. If every contact sensor were routed to the outside control unit individually, the number of wires exiting the mouth would either mean (a) a very wide flexible PCB at the mouth opening, which would interfere strongly with the lip articulation, or (b) a flexible multi-layer PCB, which is several times more expensive than a two-layer one and would therefore go against the design premises of the system, or (c) a manual individual soldering of microwire to each contact sensor, as was done for previous EPG systems (see Figure 3.13) and is the main cause for their high cost per unit. So in order to avoid that, the EOS palate included an analog 1:32 multiplexer (Analog Devices ADG731 [190]) with a three-wire, Serial Peripheral Interface (SPI)-compatible serial interface. This reduced the number of wires from 32 (if each sensor was connected individually) to six (one wire for the serial clock, one for the serial data line, one chip-select line, one supply-voltage line, one ground connection, and one line for the multiplexer output). In earlier iterations of the sensor unit (e.g., the one shown in Figure 4.34a), two or even four of these multiplexers were used to connect 64 or 124 contact sensors, respectively (4 contact sensors had to be excluded because of the geometric constraints). However, these designs were abandoned because they failed to result in robust units. With four multiplexer Intergrated Circuits (ICs), there was not enough room to route all the necessary lines along the midline of the board, so the ICs had to be laterally displaced into areas where the palate tends to be much more curved. The ICs locally increased the stiffness of the flexible circuit board in that area which caused the flaps with the ICs on their back to stand up slightly, becoming noticable, obstructive protrusions in the mouth and creating a potential breaking point due to added mechanical stress from the tongue pushing against the circuits, bending the leads and connector pads. With only two multiplexers, the ICs could be squeezed onto the midsagittal line, but one of the ICs had to move to the back of the palate, where it was also prone to breaking because of mechanical stress during the assembly and the use of the sensor unit. Ultimately, the single-IC solution was preferred due to the increased robustness at the cost of a lower spatial resolution.

In order to register tongue contact at the contact sensors, a small reference voltage needs to be applied to the subject (see section 4.5 for details on the specification of this voltage). In earlier prototypes, this voltage was applied through a hand-held electrode (similar to the commercial WinEPG system by Articulate Instruments). For the final prototype, this hand-held electrode was replaced by a large foldable flap of the circuit board that carries an array of gold contacts and protrudes beyond the hard palate (see Figure 4.34b). When the flexible PCB is glued to the acrylic base plate (see below) during the assembly of the sensor unit, this flap is folded around the posterior edge of the base plate and then glued to the back of the unit, so that it ends up sandwiched between the sensor unit and the subject's hard palate when the unit is worn. The tight fit of the thermoformed base plate (see below) ensures a slight, constant pressure that keeps the contacts on the folded flap pressed against the hard palate.

The final part of the flexible circuit board was the connector. Earlier iterations used a non-standard connector layout based on the way slotted extension cards in personal computers are connected using edge connectors: A row of blank traces that plug into a matching socket. The socket itself was not available in the appropriate size, so a larger socket was sawed off to the right length. Since these sockets are made for solid PCBs, the much thinner flexible sensor circuit board had to be thickened using a piece of solid PCB material, sanded down to the right height so that the total thickness including the flexible PCB (glued on with a cyanoacrylate adhesive) would match the sockets opening. This process was unnecessarily labor-intensive and also prone to erros, since none of the parts conformed to established standards, which easily caused accidental misalignment or reversed polarity. Therefore, the final iteration used a standard 12x2 box header as a socket on the sensor circuit board, which received an Insulation-Displacement Connector (IDC) plug affixed to a ribbon cable and thus connected to the control board. An example of an now obsolete circuit board from earlier iterations developed as part of this dissertation is shown in Figure 4.34a, while the most recent design is shown in Figure 4.34b.

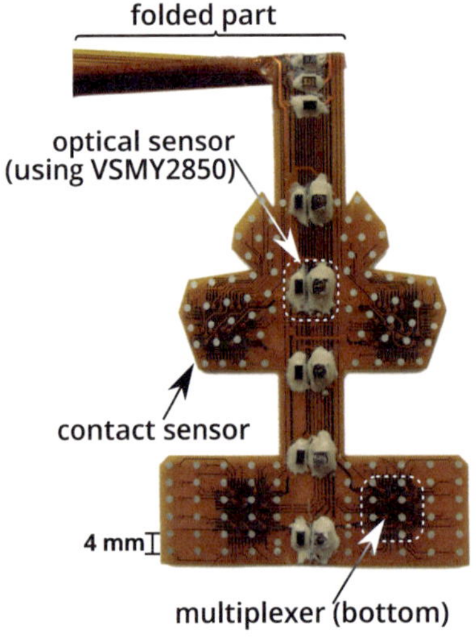

(a) Obsolete flexible circuit board using the VSMY2850 LED, four multiplexers to connect 124 contact sensors, the single-source, dual-detector lip sensor and an external voltage reference for the contact sensing.

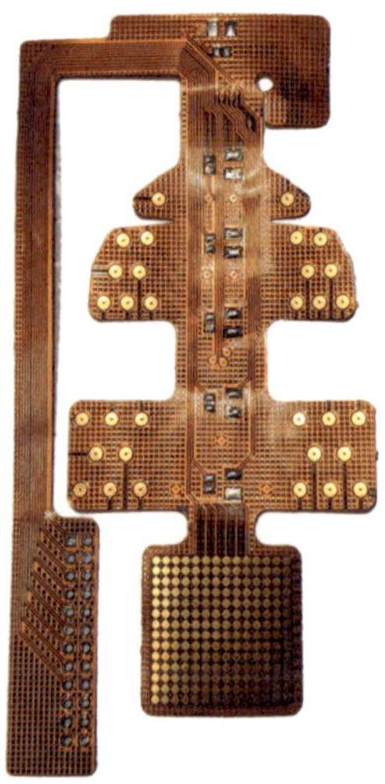

(b) Final iteration of the sensor circuit board using the OP280V, the dual-source, dual-detector lip sensor design (soldering pads for the downward facing source-detector pair is on the bottom of the lateral flap), a single multiplexer to connect 32 contact sensors, and the reference voltage contact matrix on the foldable posterior flap.

Figure 4.34.: Circuit boards carrying the sensors

As was already mentioned, the flexible PCB carrying the sensors was glued to an acrylic base plate. This base plate is thermoformed to perfectly fit each subject's maxilla using a plaster model of their upper jaw (see Figure 4.35).

The material used for the base plate was Erkodent Erkodur with a thickness of 0.5 mm before the thermoforming. This material was chosen because it is a commonly used orthodontic material and readily available and low cost. Affixing the flexible circuit board to the thermoformed base plate is a non-trivial task, because commonly used agents like superglue should not be used inside the mouth cavity. The first iterations used a vinylpolysiloxane relining material called GC Reline Soft, which is used for denture relining as a kind of artificial gingiva. The material was chosen because it was approved for intra-oral application and because of its adhesive qualities. However, its high viscosity eventually proved cumbersome when trying to seal the small structures on the sensor board, and the very short curing time made the process unecessarily slow. Instead, another set of orthodontic materials was ultimately chosen based on advice from orthodontic experts[3]: The

[3]A very cordial thank you to the very helpful team of Müller Dental, Dresden, and Peter Birkholz is in order here for their

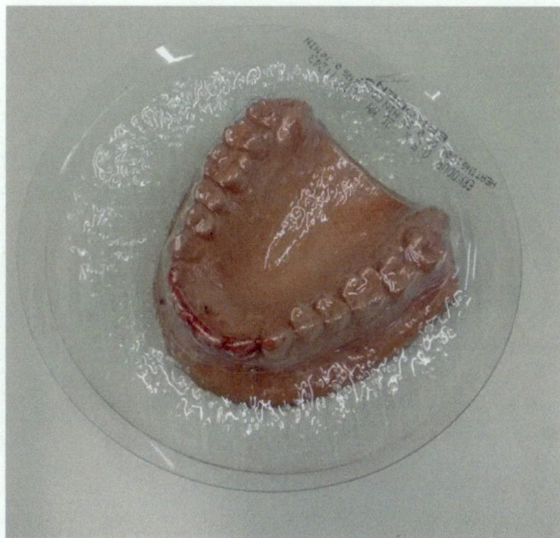

Figure 4.35.: Thermoformed base plate of the sensor unit fit to a plaster model of the subject's maxilla. The red color is from bits of wax that is used to fill-in the small gaps between the incisors to facilitate the removal of the thermoformed material from the plaster model.

flowable radiopaque composite Tertric EvoFlow, which is used as a linder and a restorative material for filling small cavities, and the light-curing bonder Primotec Primostick, which is used to prime the surface to ensure good adhesion. Using these materials and a thorough trial and error process, a workflow for the assembly of the base plate and the flexible PCB into a sensor unit was established that should allow even non-specialist to produce units at great speed and with little room for error. The process was documented in a step-by-step guide and can be found in Appendix D. Completely assembled sensor units are shown in Figure 4.36. The schematics for the final sensor unit design are shown in section C.4 and the layout for the corresponding flexible circuit board is shown in section C.5.

4.5. Control Unit

While the ideal system would incorporate all the hardware necessary to capture the articulatory data *and* the preprocessing on the sensor unit itself and then wirelessly transmit those to a pocket-sized device (e.g., a smartphone) that runs the recognition or synthesis software, the experimental state of this new technology did not make that approach seem advisable at the time. During the development of the EOS system presented in this dissertation, an attempt was made to have an external company design an integrated version of the sensor unit that combined the sensor and control unit on the pseudopalate, but no working prototype was produced. Still, future work should focus on integrating the hardware described here, which has finally reached a mature and stationary enough stage so that initiating the next steps of integration, miniaturization, and increasing usability is the logical next stage. For now, however, the EOS sensors are controlled and read by an extra-oral device connected to the sensor unit via a 24-wire ribbon cable. This control unit was developed alongside the various versions of the sensor unit and adapted to the requirements of the sensors. Therefore, earlier iterations of the control unit incorporated current sources based on operational amplifiers to drive the now obsolete VSMY2850 (see Figure 4.6a) and a different pinout to contact the various lip sensor designs. This section only presents the final prototype, which was given the revision number 3.2, and was designed to control the most advanced sensor unit shown

help in identifying the materials and refining the assembly workflow.

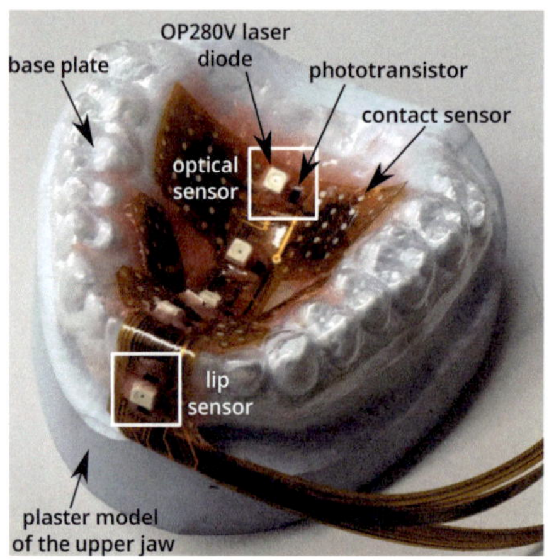

(a) Assembled, obsolete sensor unit from an earlier iteration using the OP280V VCSEL diode, the single-source, dual-detector lip sensor, 124 contact sensors, an external reference voltage for the contact sensing, and the GC Reline sealing material (red material in the picture).

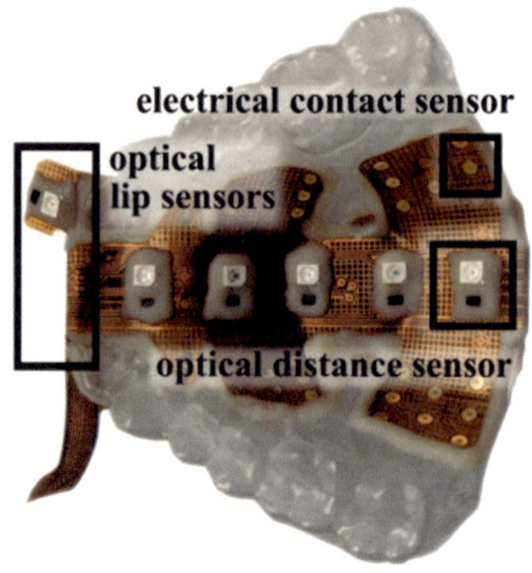

(b) Assembled final sensor unit using the OP280V VCSEL diode, the dual-source, dual-detector lip sensor, 32 contact sensors, the internal reference voltage (contact matrix is folded to the back of the base plate), and sealed using EvoFlow (the beige material).

Figure 4.36.: Assembled sensor units

in Figure 4.36b. The schematics of the control unit are shown in section C.1 and the board layout is given in section C.2.

The control unit measures 160 mm × 100 mm and thus fits on a standard Eurocard solid PCB. It acts as a bridge between the sensor unit, which captures the raw data, and a personal computer, which does the high-level processing of the captured data. To fulfill this purpose, the control unit needs to be able to control and read the sensors on the sensor unit and communicate the digitized, measured data to the computer. From the design of the sensor unit, the specifications of the control unit can therefore be directly derived. The control unit (and therefore the processor or controller powering the control unit) must offer:

- A current supply of 11.5 mA for the optical sensors.
- A fast ADC with a high number of quantization levels to measure the analog optical sensor output with high precision.
- An SPI to interface with the ADG731 32:1 multiplexer to connect the individual contact sensors.
- A Digital-to-Analog Converter (DAC) to generate the reference voltage signal for the contact sensor measurements (see below).
- Some way to allow concurrent processing of the multi-modal measurements for an improved frame rate.
- Sufficient processing power to perform fast low-level measurement data pre-processing.
- A widely supported communications interface to communicate with the connected personal computer for high-level processing.
- The option to be battery-powered, i.e., low supply voltage and current consumption.

A Microcontroller Unit (MCU) is perfectly suited for a portable device like this. While there are many options by various manufacturers on the market, the Atmel SAM3S4B was ultimately chosen. The SAM3S provides the folloing features that meet or exceed the requirements defined above:

- A maximum output current of 18 mA.
- An ADC with 12-bit resolution at a 1 MHz conversion rate and up to 16 input channels, making an additional external multiplexing of the optical sensor data unnecessary.
- A three-wire SPI matching the interface specification of the ADG731 multiplexer.
- A DAC with 12-bit resolution, up to 2 MHz conversion rate, and up to two output channels.
- A peripheral DMA controller which removes processor overhead by reducing its intervention during the transfer from peripherals (like the ADC and DAC) to memory and vice-versa and thus enables quasi-concurrent processing.
- A main clock of 64 MHz and 48 kB high-speed SRAM, making it more than capable to pre-process the sensor data stream.
- Various serial communication standards, including a two-wire universal asynchronous receiver-transmitter (UART) interface.
- A low supply voltage range of 1.62 V to 3.6 V and low-power "sleep" modes for all peripherals, allowing a long battery life.

The SAM3S4B was available in different versions differing in number of pins and the package. To allow easy manual soldering, the SAM3S4BA-AU was selected for the control unit because it offered a Low-Profile Quad Flat Package (LQFP) with 64 pins and a pitch of 0.5 mm, which was still manageable using manual soldering. As is evident by the list of features, choosing the SAM3S was not the most parsimonious approach. But given the low cost of the controller (about 4.33 €[4]), it was still considered an affordable component and left some design space to try different hardware approaches regarding the sensor.

Since the chosen MCU already included many of the necessary peripherals, only a small amount of additional circuitry was necessary. Besides some standard circuitry to power and program the MCU and connect the UART, four additional functional circuits were necessary: the current source and the detector circuit for the optical sensors, the generation of the reference voltage and the detector circuit for the contact sensors.

The current source for the optical sensors was implemented by simply adding a series resistor between one of the general purpose output pins of the MCU and the pin connecting to the respective light source on the sensor unit. Each light source was therefore controlled by an independent output. This approach made an external multiplexer unnecessary, but required careful timing of the switching so that only one light source was turned on at any given time. As was already shown by [166], the optical cross-talk between the different light sources otherwise becomes too large beyond 5 mm. While an external multiplexer could have enforced this switching rule, the added complexity in the circuitry and the additional switching overhead to control the muliplexer was not considered proportionate and instead it was left to the firmware to ensure the strictly sequential switching.

The detector circuit for the optical sensors was implemented as shown in Figure 4.6b using one circuit for each sensor. Again, the repetitive circuitry could have been simplified using a multiplexer, but since concurrent sampling of several phototransistors was also of interest (see subsection 4.2.3) and the detector circuit was quite simple, this parallel approach was chosen.

The reference voltage for the contact sensors was generated by the DAC controller of the MCU because an AC voltage was required to avoid cytolytic effects a unipolar voltage might have when continuously applied to human tissue. According to [152], the reference voltage in their EPG system

[4]Retrieved on June 06, 2020 from `https://www.mouser.de`

continuously applied to human tissue. According to [152], the reference voltage in their EPG system (which used the same basic measurement principle) was 300 mV at a frequency of 15 kHz. Since a higher frequency allows a faster registration of contacts (see below), the EOS system's reference voltage is generated at 40 kHz but at a lower amplitude of 200 mV, which was found to be sufficient in an exploratory, informal measurement. The control unit is generally designed with a unipolar supply voltage, and therefore the DAC can only generate a unipolar signal. Therefore, the reference voltage is first generated at an offset of 900 mV, shifting it well into the available positive voltage range, and then filtered using an analog first order *RC* low-pass filter to shift the voltage back to an offset of zero. The Bode plot of the filter is shown in Figure 4.37 and shows that the offset is well-suppressed, while the actual reference voltage signal at 40 kHz is unaffected by the filter.

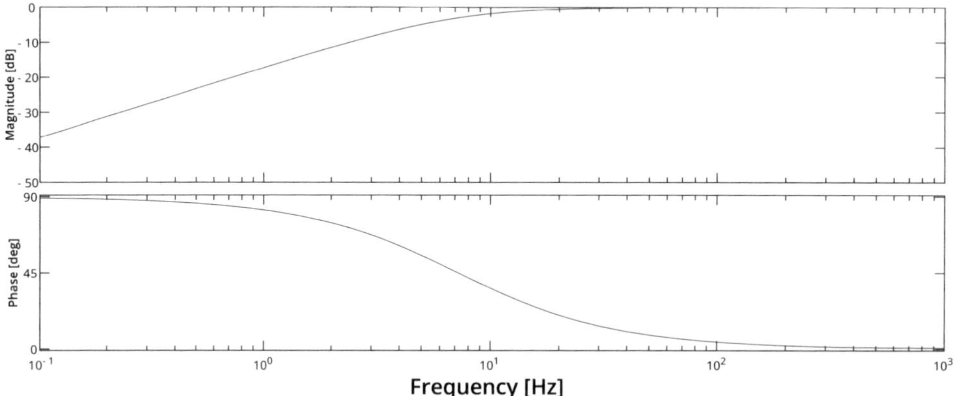

Figure 4.37.: Filter response of the reference voltage output filter for the contact sensor measurements

The detector circuit for the contact sensors was based on the simplified circuit shown in Figure 4.2. The goal of the detector circuit is to turn the analog, bipolar, noisy, low-amplitude sinusoidal voltage at the contact sensors into a unipolar, full-range rectangular voltage representing a 1-bit digital signal with the same frequency that can then be further processed by the digital input pins of the MCU. The first stage therefore shifts the measured voltage to the center of the supply voltage range at 1.65 V. Because the voltage at the contact sensors may have a spurious offset due to external influences, it is first filtered using another *RC* low-pass filter with the same filter response as the reference voltage output filter and then the offset is added. To turn the sinusoidal voltage into a 1-bit digital signal, it is then compared to 1.65 V by an LM339 opamp comparator, configured with a hysteresis of approximately 20 mV to avoid output oscillation for a small input signal delta. The output of the comparator is wired to a general purpose pin of the MCU configured as a digital input. Since the contact sensors are multiplexed on the sensor unit, only a single detector circuit is required. All schematics, layouts, and bills of material for both the sensor unit and the control unit are provided in Appendix C.

4.5.1. Firmware and measurement protocol

The firmware running on the MCU was written in the programming language C using Atmel Studio 7.0 (an Integrated Development Environment (IDE) provided by the MCU manufacturer), which included an extensive software framework to allow high-level programming access to the various hardware components of the MCU. The program flow was kept intentionally simple: when the device is powered on, several initialization and configuration routines are run. After initialization, the firmware enters an infinite loop. In each iteration of this infinite loop, the sensor unit is scanned once, sampling all sensors. The lower boundary for an acceptable frame rate (number of complete sensor unit scans per second) to properly capture each vocal tract configuration and the transitions in between can be derived from the assumption of quasi-stationary speech [191]: a commonly adopted window length in *acoustic* analyses is 20 ms to 40 ms assuming that the source for the signal does not change within that time window. Therefore, the vocal tract configuration does not change significantly. To be able to resolve changes on that time scale, the vocal tract configuration would have to be captured at a frame rate of more than $\frac{2}{40\,\text{ms}} = 50\,\text{Hz}$ (according to the Nyquist-Shannon sampling theorem [192]). The specified frame rate of the proposed EOS system was therefore set to 100 Hz to be well above the critical rate while still allowing for sufficient sampling periods for each sensor. Earlier versions of the EOS hardware (up to revision number 2.x) used a strictly sequential program flow for the measurements: Each sensor, starting with the optical sensors followed by the contact sensors, was sampled in sequence. This firmware version also supported the sampling of the two adjacent detectors for each sensor (see the angle correction technique derived in subsection 4.2.2). The sampling code could be switched from sampling only one detector to also sampling the adjacent ones through a control parameter received from the connected computer software EOS Workbench (see subsection 4.6.1). The measurement data frame format for this deprecated version of the firmware is shown in Table E.1, while the frame format for the incoming control parameters is shown in Table E.2.

To allow longer sampling times and thus more stable measurements (see section B.2), as well as to leave enough time for the serial communication to the downstream computer and the switching and settling times for all involved sensors, the sampling of the optical sensors and the sampling of the contact sensors were interleaved using hardware interrupts. This strategy enabled a certain degree of concurrency in the program flow and was used for the final hardware revision number 3.2. The program flow is visualized in Figure E.1. The measurement protocol was as follows: Before each optical measurement, the ambient light level was determined by sampling the detector while all the light sources were off. Then, an optical measurement was triggered: The light source of the respective optical sensor was switched on and a hardware timer of 100 µs was started. After the timer ran out, the ADC sampling of the detector circuit voltage was started and 40 digital samples were collected, corresponding to a signal length of 125 µs. Both the timer and the ADC were controlled by the peripheral DMA controller of the MCU. Therefore, during the collection of the sensor value of an optical sensor, some of the contact sensors were sampled concurrently. To sample a contact sensor, first the multiplexer on the sensor unit was switched to the corresponding input. Due to the measurement principle of the contact sensing (see section 4.1), the sampling required registering the presence or absence of the reference voltage at the selected sensor. Because the analog contact sensor signal was digitized by the external comparator circuitry (see above), the sampling was implemented by measuring the time between the first two rising and falling edges in the digital signal during a period of 60 µs. If this pulse width was half the reference voltage period of 25 µs (with a tolerance of ± 3 µs), the sensor was registered as contacted. Once all sensors were sampled, a data frame was built according to the frame format given in Table E.3. The data frame was then sent via UART (managed once again by the peripheral DMA controller in the background) and the remainder of the current measurement period was waited before another cycle began. A full scan of the palate was performed in a little less than 5 ms, theoretically allowing for a higher frame rate than 100 Hz. However, since future applications (e.g., the addition of the angle-correction mode or a velum state sensor) may require more measurement time, it was considered wise to leave some room so that the frame rate would not have to change between different versions of the sensor unit or different measurement modes. The timing of a single sensor unit scan is shown in Figure 4.38.

4.6. Software

Downstream of the data acquisition, the measurement data is further processed and visualized in a Graphical User Interface (GUI) by a consumer-grade personal computer. Since EOS can be used for many more applications than "just" the data acquisition frontend of an SSI, experiments regarding its other possible uses were carried out as well. In order to avoid a convoluted and complicated user interface, a specialized program was written for each use-case. Not all of the studies carried out

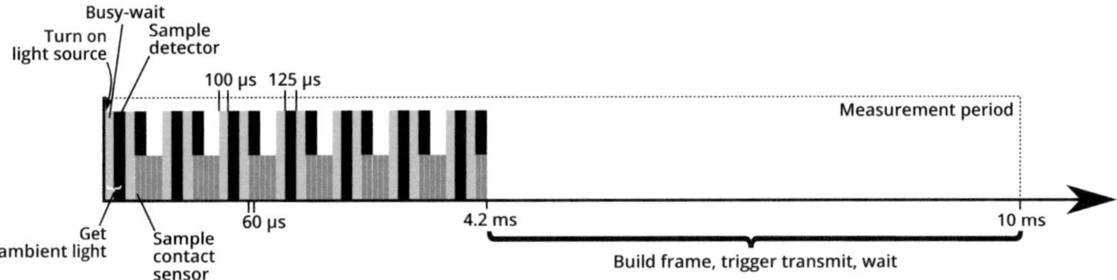

Figure 4.38.: Timing of a single complete sensor unit scan

using EOS were directly connected to the research goals of this dissertation and their methods and results are therefore not described in this work (the reader is directed towards the corresponding papers instead). However, to give a complete picture of the software suite surrounding EOS, the respective software is briefly described.

All EOS software was written in C++ for Windows 7 upwards using the wxWidgets cross-platform GUI toolkit, which should allow relatively easy portation to other operating systems. During the development of the earlier iterations of EOS, the software used to receive and display the sensor data streams was called EOS Workbench (see subsection 4.6.1). While the capabilities of EOS as an articulometric technique were being explored, a tool to visualize live-feedback of a user's articulation in a "talking head" fashion (the Vocal Tract Visualization Tool, see subsection 4.6.2), and a serious game that used EOS data to enable a tongue-controlled game of skill aimed at speech therapy and rehabilitation (the Biofeedback Game, see subsection 4.6.3), were also developed. The main software for EOS in its most advanced form was Second Voice PC (see subsection 4.6.4), which allowed both the collection of EOS data and the concurrent synthesis of speech based on those data in real-time.

4.6.1. EOS Workbench

The original purpose of the EOS Workbench was as a debugging and analysis tool for the raw data streams coming from the EOS control unit. A screenshot of its GUI is shown in Figure 4.39. It was written using wxWidgets 2.8.

Each optical sensor is shown as a function of time in an individual track and the resulting tongue-contour is displayed in a cross-sectional view near the top of the window. The contact pattern is also displayed in its own track (currently hidden in Figure 4.39) and in a contact pattern view next to the tongue contour. An audio track is also recorded during the measurements and displayed for reference.

The EOS Workbench can be set to three different modes using the radio buttons on the top left. In real-time feedback mode, the stream of sensor data is displayed in real-time on the screen and the views near the top of the window always show the current frame of measurement data. In recording analysis mode, no additional data is recorded and instead the current record can be scrolled through, with the top views showing the frame at the current cursor position in the audio and/or sensor tracks. The third mode is used for statistical analysis. In this mode, the beginning and end of a segment of data can be selected and averaged using a right-click context menu. The top views then display the averaged frame data.

To correctly map the raw ADC data of the tongue distance sensors to a distance in mm and to use a non-generic hard palate outline for the visualization, a user-dependent palate description file is used. This palate file has an XML-like structure and describes the geometry of the midsagittal palate outline and provides a set of pairs of ADC and mm values that are used to describe the distance sensing function and the coefficients necessary for the angle correction (see subsection 4.2.2). An example palate file is shown in Appendix F. The EOS Workbench currently exclusively uses the deprecated data frame format (see Table E.1) and is thus only compatible with EOS hardware up to revision 2.x.

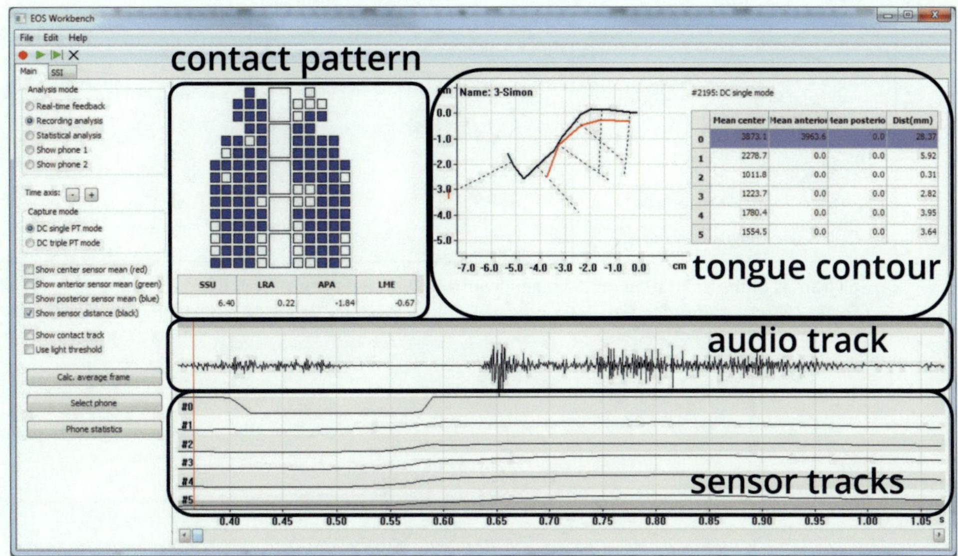

Figure 4.39.: Graphical User Interface of the EOS Workbench

4.6.2. Vocal Tract Visualization Tool

Using the same backend as EOS Workbench, the Vocal Tract Visualization Tool (written using wxWidgets 2.8) extended the tongue contour view from EOS Workbench to a full midsagittal view of a talking head. Since only five points on the tongue contour are measured, the contour is estimated using a linear regression approach and the measured distances as the predictors in a set of regression models (see [193] and [194] for details). Using this software, a pilot study was conducted to investigate whether the displayed tongue contour can be used in a biofeedback paradigm. Since the use-case of this software is not within the scope of this dissertation, the reader is directed to the description and discussion of the study in [195] instead. A few screenshots of the GUI are shown in Figure 4.40 to illustrate the animation model.

4.6.3. Biofeedback Game

Essentially an extension of the Vocal Tract Visualization Tool, the Biofeedback Game (written using wxWidgets 2.8) is a proof-of-principle of a biofeedback application using the optical sensor data from EOS. The game is entirely controlled by tongue movements. The objective of the game is to keep a boat level while it is being tossed back and forth by the waves. The player can counter the tipping movement of the boat by putting their tongue either on the most anterior sensor (to counter the boat tipping to the left) or the most posterior sensor (to counter the boat tipping to the right). The intention of the game is to improve oral motor skills by offering an accessible user interface and an entertaining task. A few screenshots illustrating the game interface and the basic control scheme are shown in Figure 4.41. Since the use-case for this software is outside the scope of this dissertation, the reader is referred to [196] for more details.

4.6.4. Second Voice PC

Starting with EOS hardware revision 3.0, a different, more specialized software called "Second Voice PC" was used to facilitate the recognition and synthesis experiments (see chapter 5 and chapter 6). A screenshot of the GUI is shown in Figure 4.42. Since the use case of Second Voice PC was its application in an SSI, the user interface contained the synthesis components alongside the sensor data

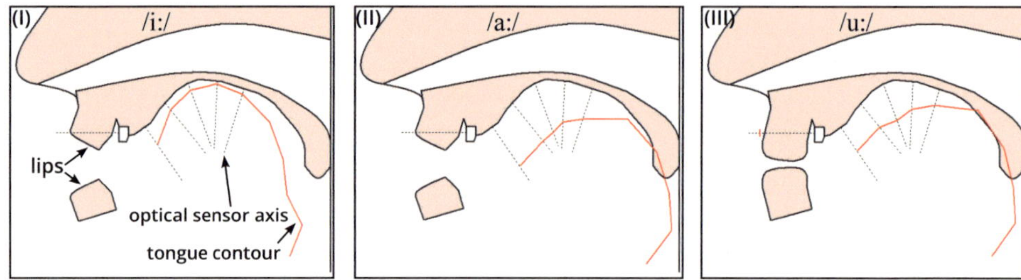

(a) Still frames of the animation model taken from a real-time measurement using the same speaker with the tongue contour painted in red: (I) Front vowel /iː/, (II) low back vowel /aː/, (III) high back vowel /uː/.

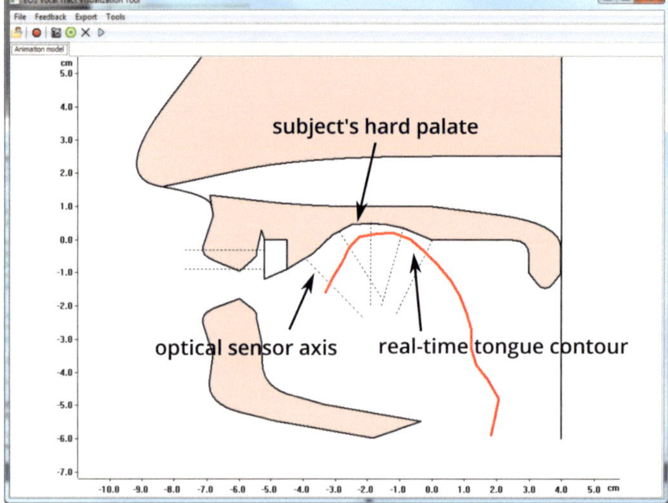

(b) Screenshot of the 2D animation model during articulation of /j/. The hard palate is loaded individually for each subject using a palate file. The solid red tongue contour is updated in real-time. The dotted lines mark the optical axes of the sensors.

Figure 4.40.: Screenshots of the Vocal Tract Visualization Tool

and control. The real-time tongue profile and the current contact pattern were removed from the interface because real-time articulatory feedback was no longer the major interest of this software. Instead, the focus was on building a transparent link between the EOS data and the articulatory synthesis model (see section 6.3). To that end, the *articulatory* feedback section of the EOS Workbench was replaced by a *synthesis* feedback section, which contains both the vocal tract model and the corresponding vocal tract transfer function. The vocal tract model's parameters can be manipulated manually by clicking and/or dragging the marked control points, selecting pre-defined vocal tract shapes from the dropdown menu in the control section, or by enabling the direct mapping from the EOS data to the vocal tract parameters using the pre-trained models presented in section 6.6. Two more tracks were added to the optical and contact sensor tracks to leave space for articulatory and phonatory information that may be captured by additional sensors in the future: one track for the fundamental frequency f_0 , voicing, breathiness, and lung pressure (see section 6.7) and one track for a prospective velum sensor (see, e.g., [197, 198]).

Second Voice PC is compatible with EOS hardware revision 3.0 and newer and uses the frame format according to Table E.3. A palate file is no longer required since the palate outline used for articulatory feedback is no longer needed.

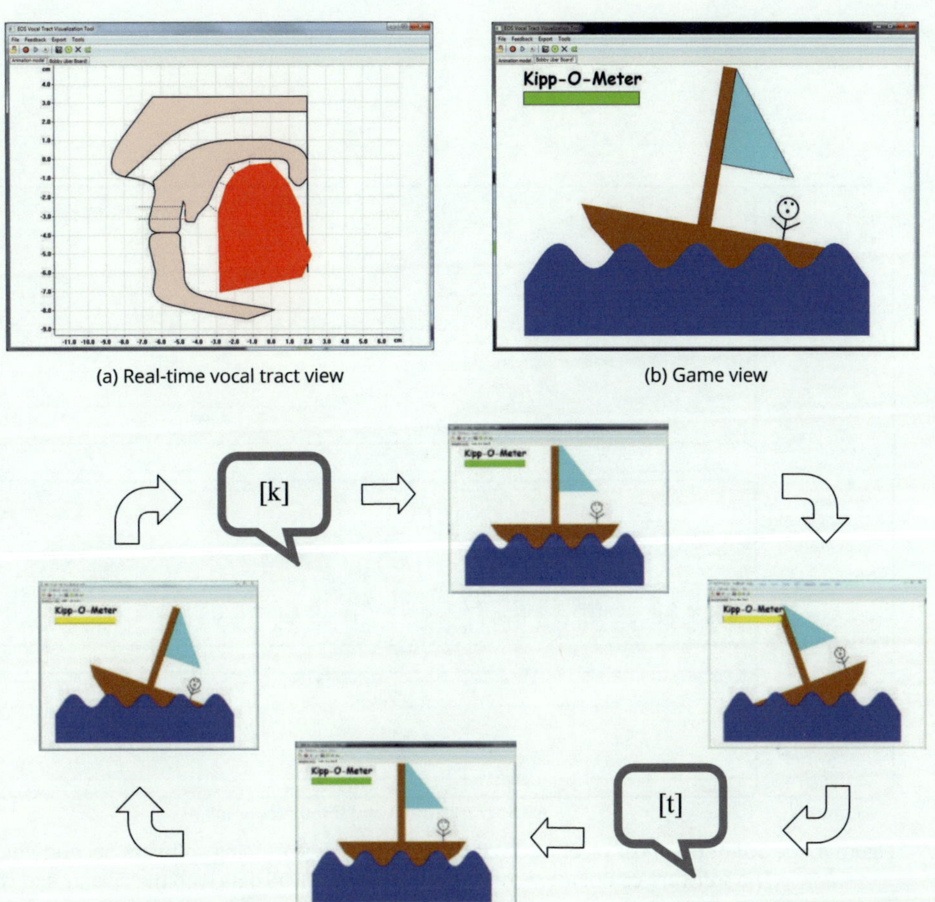

(a) Real-time vocal tract view

(b) Game view

(c) Basic concept of the game: The boat is about to capsize and must be kept from tipping over by specific tongue positions.

Figure 4.41.: The tongue-controlled Biofeedback Game

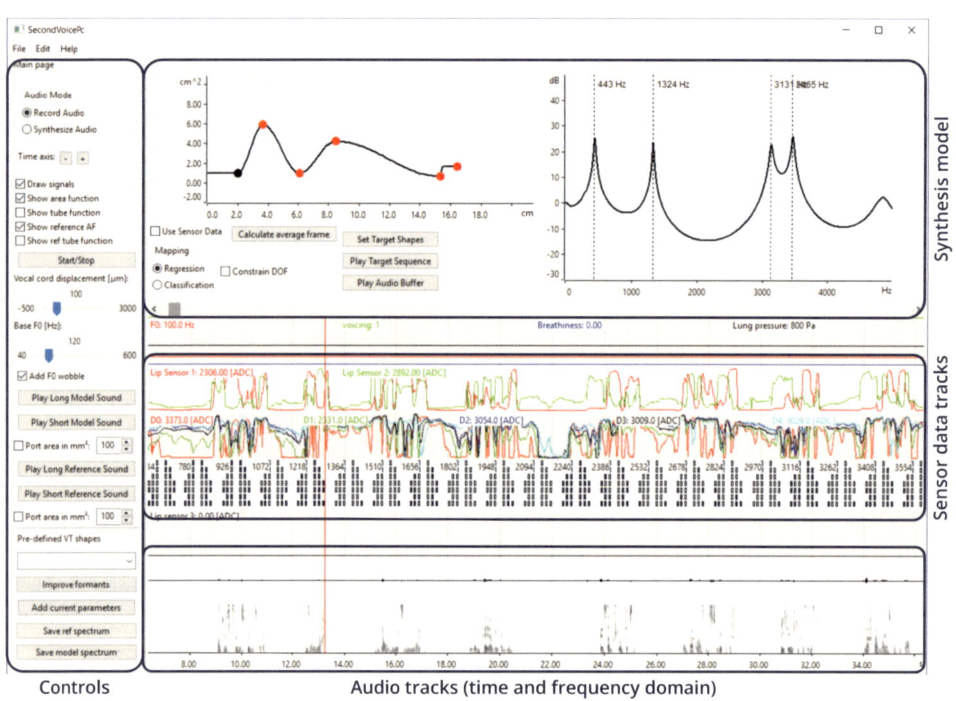

Figure 4.42.: GUI of the most recent EOS data analysis and processing software Second Voice PC. The software combines recording and dispaly of EOS data with the display and control of the speech synthesis model (see chapter 6).

5. Articulation-to-Text

5.1. Introduction

As described in the introduction to this dissertation in chapter 1, Articulation-to-Text (ATT) refers to the concept of classifying speech utterances without any acoustic data based entirely on articulatory information. As presented in chapter 3, numerous technologies have been employed for this task in the past to varying degrees of success. Using the novel articulometric measurement technique presented in chapter 4, two studies were conducted to assess the feasibility of an ATT system using EOS as the data acquisition frontend. The first study, published in [199] and presented in the following section 5.2, was a pilot study using an earlier prototype of the EOS device, a single user, and a basic classification model. Building on the promising results from this pilot, a larger-scale study using the most recent version of the EOS hardware was conducted with four speakers, a more sophisticated classification scheme, and an inter- and intra-speaker analysis of the results (see section 5.3). The result of that study were also published in [200].

5.2. Command word recognition pilot study

The goal of the pilot study was to deliver a proof-of-principle of ATT using EOS. The setup was therefore quite basic: EOS data of a single speaker articulating 30 common, isolated German words was recorded in two sets. One set was then used for training, while the other set was used for validation. The study used EOS hardware revision 1.2 (single-source, dual-detector lip sensor, and 124 contact sensors). An additional page was added to the interface of EOS Workbench (see subsection 4.6.1) that allowed the training and validation of the classifier inside the software. Figure 5.1 shows a screenshot of the interface.

5.2.1. Data

The words used in the pilot study were 30 of the most common German nouns, adjectives, and verbs (10 of each, see the first three columns in Table 5.1). Besides their relevance because of their high frequency in German, the words in the data set also cover a wide range of German phonemes (cf. chapter 2). EOS data of 5 repetitions of each of the 30 words was recorded using a single speaker (male, 31 years old). The words were randomized during the recording to avoid successive repetitions of the same word. Each word was produced in the normal, audible way, but only the articulatory information was used in the remainder of the study.

The measurement protocol was as follows:

1. The subject was shown a dialog box with the label of the word to be uttered.

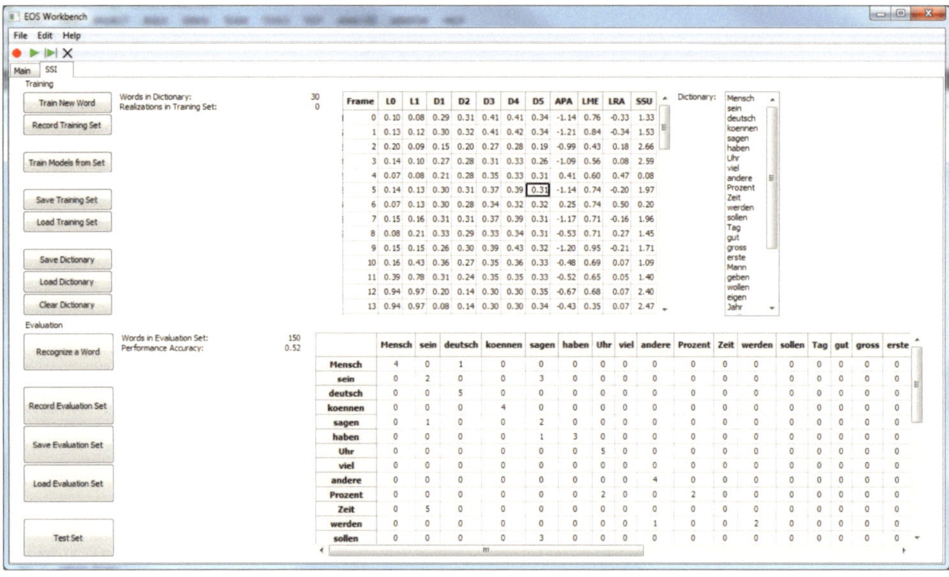

Figure 5.1.: Screenshot of the user interface for the command word recognizer in EOS Workbench. The SSI tab holds buttons for training and testing the word models.

2. The subject hit the enter key on a computer keyboard and the recording started.
3. The subject produced the utterance.
4. The subject hit enter and the recording stopped.
5. Repeat from step 1 until all recordings were made.

No further segmentation of the recordings was made, since the applied classification scheme can tolerate short initial and final periods of no articulatory activity (see subsection 5.2.2). Two complete sets were recorded independently with a short break between the recordings. During that break, the EOS sensor unit was removed from the subject's mouth and the subject rinsed his mouth to "reset" the intraoral conditions as much as possible. The first recorded set of EOS data of 150 utterances (5×30 words) was used as the training set, and the second set of the same size and composition was used for evaluation.

Noun		Adjective		Verb		Digit	
Jahr	jaːʁ	neu	nɔœ̯	werden	vˈeːɐ̯dn̩	Null	nʊl
Uhr	uːɐ̯	andere	ˈandəʁə	haben	hˈaːbm	Eins	aɛ̯ns
Prozent	pʁ̥otsˈɛnt	groß	gʁoːs	sein	zaɛ̯n	Zwei	tsv̥aɛ̯
Million	mɪli̯on	erste	ˈeːɐ̯stə	können	kˈœnən	Drei	dʁaɛ̯
Euro	ˈɔœ̯ʁoː	viel	fiːl	müssen	mˈʏsn̩	Vier	fiːɐ̯
Zeit	tsaɛ̯t	deutsch	dɔœ̯tʃ	sollen	zɔln	Fünf	fʏnf
Tag	taːk	gut	guːt	sagen	zˈaːgŋ̍	Sechs	zɛks
Frau	fʁ̥ao̯	weit	vaɛ̯t	geben	gˈeːbm̩	Sieben	zˈiːbm̩
Mensch	mɛnʃ	klein	klaɛ̯n	kommen	kˈɔmən	Acht	axt
Mann	man	eigen	ˈaɛ̯g ŋ̍	wollen	vɔln	Neun	nɔœ̯n

Table 5.1.: Standard pronunciation of the words used in the ATT studies (according to and following the transcription conventions of [201]). The pilot study used only the nouns, adjectives, and verbs, while the small-scale study additionally used the digits in a separate set.

The EOS data for training and evaluation of the ATT system consisted of five 12-bit ADC values from the optical distance sensors that were related to a distance in cm using the calibration scheme described in subsection 4.2.2. Each EOS data frame also contained the two 12-bit ADC values from the single-source, dual-detector lip sensor, and 124 binary values of the contact sensors representing the palatolingual contact pattern. The measured distances and the lip sensor values were directly used as features, but in order to reduce the dimensionality of the feature vectors, the coefficients proposed by [202] were used instead of the entire contact pattern. In summary, the articulatory feature vector therefore consisted of 11 features (2 lip, 5 tongue distance, 4 contact pattern). All features were transformed to the same range by maximum-absolute-value normalization.

5.2.2. Training

To obtain an articulatory word model for each of the 30 words, a standard Viterbi algorithm (using the Euclidean distance as the cost function) was used to find an average sequence of EOS feature vectors that optimally represented the five repetitions of each word. The Viterbi algorithm was implemented in the EOS Workbench and used the following conventions: The length of each word model was set to half the median length of all corresponding utterances in the training set. The initial model was found by linearly projecting the sequence of feature vectors from each utterance to the shorter model vector sequence and calculating each model vector as the average of all associated utterance vectors. Next, the initial model was improved by remapping the vectors from the utterance sequences to the model vectors using Dynamic Programming. There were no time distortion, skip, or loop penalties because the utterances were not manually segmented and penalizing skips would make the model less robust against initial and trailing articulatory silence. The squared Euclidean distance measure was used to calculate the distance between vectors. The mapping was updated using each training utterance until the change in the model vectors was below an ε of 0.01. All models converged after at most ten epochs, i.e, after ten iterations through the entire training set.

5.2.3. Evaluation

In the evaluation step, each repetition of each utterance was classified by finding the label of the most similar articulatory word model (Nearest Neighbor classification). The similarity was determined using Dynamic Programming and the Euclidean distance as a cost function. Once again there were no penalties for time distortion, node loops, or skips and the parameters of the Dynamic Programming itself were not optimized, since the goal of the pilot study was not to fine-tune an optimal recognition engine but to investigate the general suitability of EOS data for ATT.

5.2.4. Results

When using the entire feature vector, only very poor recognition accuracies of less than 15 % were achieved. Through successive feature elimination, the contact sensor data was identified as too noisy and therefore subsequently excluded from this study. The final results were achieved by using only the optical sensors and reached 92 % recognition accuracy on the evaluation set. The confusion matrix of the classification is shown in Figure 5.2.

5.2.5. Conclusion

The pilot study confirmed that EOS is in principle well-suited to perform silent-speech recognition, or ATT. Even with the implemented very basic training and matching algorithms, competitive performance accuracies could be achieved. The simplicity of the system allowed the quick training of a small vocabulary command word recognizer. However, the fact that high accuracies could only be achieved by exclusively using the optical distance sensors showed the limitations of the early prototype of the EOS hardware. This was the most important evidence for a major revision of the

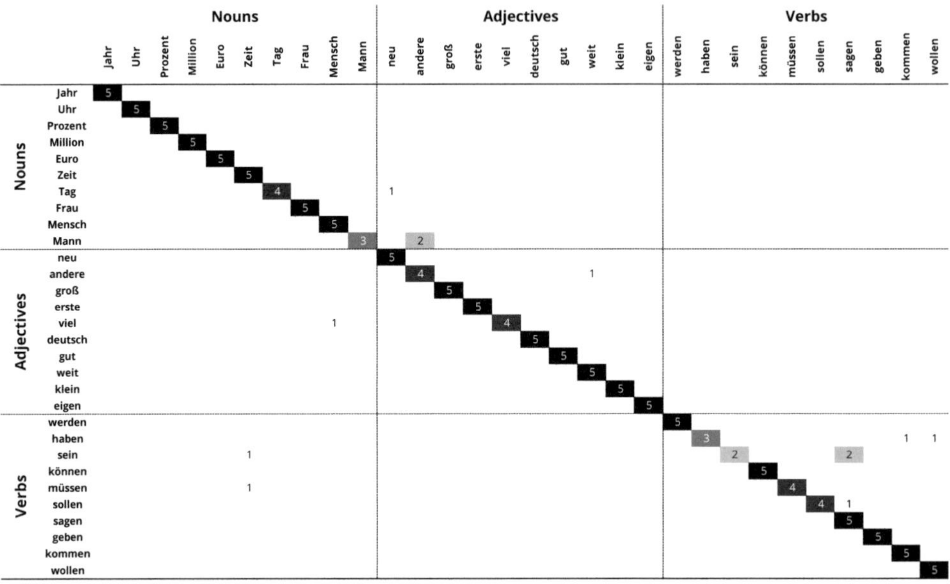

Figure 5.2.: Confusion matrix of the classification results on the evaluation set (which was entirely distinct from training set). Only the optical distance sensor data were used, resulting in an overall Performance Accuracy of 92 %.

contact sensor setup of the early iteration of the EOS hardware and led to the increase of the contact sensor size at the expense of a lower total number of contact sensors in later iterations (see chapter 4). Another limitation of the study was the single-speaker setup, which did not allow any robust estimates of the speaker-dependency of an EOS-driven ATT system. The second study was therefore designed differently to address these shortcomings of the pilot study.

5.3. Command word recognition small-scale study

The results of the pilot study, while encouraging, were obtained with a non-optimized hardware version of both the sensor board and the control unit and validated on a rather small number of repetitions. Most importantly, though, only one speaker was recorded, which excludes the analysis of inter-speaker differences. Another study was therefore designed in a similar fashion, but with more speakers and using further developed hardware. This small-scale study was also presented in [200].

5.3.1. The dataset

The study used four native German speakers (all male, age 30-41), the same 30 most common German words as in the pilot study and additionally the ten German digit words for the digits 0 to 9 (similar to the setup in [118], see Table 5.1). Each group of words was repeated 10 times for a total of 300 instances in the frequent words data set and 100 instances in the numbers data set for each speaker.

The data was collected using the software "Second Voice PC" (see subsection 4.6.4), a Plantronics Blackwire C720 M stereo headset (for reference audio) and an EOS device with the internal version number 3.2 using a sensor unit with 32 contact sensors, five optical tongue distance sensors, and the dual-source, dual-detector lip sensor design. The recordings were made in a quiet office environment. The speakers were prompted to read a carrier word (the German indefinite article "eine"

- /ˈaɡ̊nə/) followed by the word of interest. The schwa /ə/ at the end of the carrier word ensured a neutral vocal tract configuration at the beginning of the word of interest. The words were produced in a natural way, i.e., with phonation and at an unregulated speaking rate of each speaker's individual choice. The EOS data was recorded continuously and therefore needed to be segmented so that each training sequence only contained data from the actual articulation of the target word (and not from the carrier word or from the neutral vocal tract configuration between items). In terms of acoustic speech recognition, this would be done by VAD. But since articulation and the acoustic result are not entirely aligned in time, the individual words were manually segmented using both the EOS data and the reference audio and the following technique:

1. Set the beginning of the word to the center of the first sound in the word (which may be a glottal stop in case of an initial vowel) as identified in the audio.

2. Set the end of the word to the first turnaround point in the EOS tongue distance sensor data that occurs after the audio. If no such point can be easily identified, set it to the end of the audio.

An example segmentation is shown in Figure 5.3. For a fully automatic recognition system, this step would need to be automated as well to achieve an "Articulation Activity Detection", analogously to VAD. However, this poses its own problems that are beyond the scope of this work.

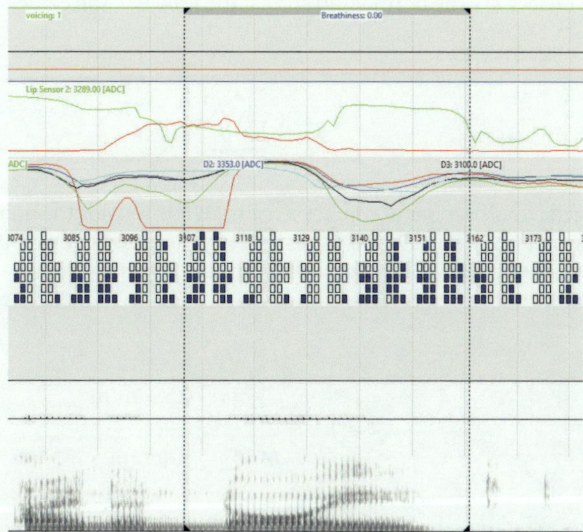

Figure 5.3.: An example of the manual segmentation of the words used for the recognition small scale study. Here: the word "neu" (/nɔœ̯/, engl.: "new").

A sequence of feature vectors was created from the segmented data. Each feature vector consisted of the ADC data of the 2 lip sensor detectors, 5 distance sensor values, and 3 factors describing the contact pattern for a total of 10 features per vector. The distance sensor values were (depending on the hyperparameter setting) either raw ADC values or converted to mm using the calibration scheme described in subsection 4.2.2, the latter potentially reducing the in-session variance of the measurements. The contact pattern factors were calculated to reduce the dimensionality of the feature vectors, as the raw contact pattern would introduce 32 binary features instead. The factors were inspired by the factors used in the Articulate Assistant software [203], which was the user interface for a discontinued commercial EPG system. To calculate the factors in a concise way, the non-rectangular contact sensor layout is considered as a rectangular matrix, where each cell represents a contact sensor and can either have the value 0 (no contact) or 1 (contact). Some of

Figure 5.4.: The non-rectangular contact sensor layout in rectangular matrix representation. Cells with solid lines correspond to physical contact sensors on the sensor board and can adopt the values 0 (no contact) or 1 (contact), while the dashed cells do not have physical correspondences and therefore are assumed to be always 0.

the cells in the regular grid do not have correspondences to physical sensors on the sensor board and are simply considered to be always 0 (see Figure 5.4).

The chosen factors are the normalized sum of the activity s, the center of gravity c, and the laterality measure l:

$$s = \frac{1}{K} \sum_{m=1}^{M} \sum_{n=1}^{N} x(m,n) \tag{5.1}$$

with K being the total number of contact sensors (32), M, N being the number of rows and columns of the contact pattern matrix (7 and 6, respectively) and $x(m,n)$ being the binary contact sensor value at the position (m,n) in the pattern. Using the same naming conventions, the center of gravity c calculation was:

$$c = 1 - \frac{\sum_{m=1}^{M} \sum_{n=1}^{N} (m - 0.5)\, x(m,n)}{M \cdot \sum_{m=1}^{M} \sum_{n=1}^{N} x(m,n)} \tag{5.2}$$

and finally, the laterality measure l was given by:

$$l = \frac{\sum_{m=1}^{M} \sum_{n=1}^{N} \left| n - \frac{N+1}{2} \right| \cdot x(m,n)}{\frac{N}{2} \sum_{m=1}^{M} \sum_{n=1}^{N} x(m,n)}. \tag{5.3}$$

These three measures represent normalized measures of the total palato-lingual contact area (given by s), of the ratio of contact in the front of the palate over contact in the back (given by c), and of the ratio of contact on the lateral edges of the palate as opposed to the contact near the midline of the palate (given by l). Other measures exist in the literature but are either motivated by capturing pathologies (e.g., the asymmetry measure) or by analyzing patterns over time (e.g., the standard deviation measure). Therefore, only the three factors described above seemed useful for the intended purpose of describing normal articulatory states.

5.3.2. Training

A Bidirectional Long Short-Term Memory (BLSTM) network was trained to recognize the command words and validated using Matlab 2018b. The network was trained for both data sets (numbers and frequent words) independently. Due to the large number of hyperparameters of BLSTM networks, some of the hyperparameters were set to reasonable, fixed values: the number of hidden layers was set to 1 because of the small number of training data. The gradient was clipped at 1, which is common practice to avoid the exploding gradient problem. The number of training epochs was set sufficiently large (300) but at the same time early stopping was used, so the training never actually timed out but was always stopped due to a diverging validation loss. The validation frequency for early stopping was 10 iterations and the validation patience was 5. These values were empirically determined by manual examination of the training progress with various settings. The learning rate was set to a constant value of 0.01 and the size of the mini-batches was aligned with the size of the respective vocabulary (i.e., 10 in the case of the numbers data set and 30 in the case of the frequent words data set). The number of neurons N in the hidden layer, the dropout ratio δ, and the choice of the data format (raw ADC values or converted to mm) were subject to Bayes optimization with 30 evaluations of the cost function. The search space for these was the integer interval between 100 and 256 for N and the continuous interval between 0.2 and 0.9 for δ. All other hyperparameters and options were set to the default values suggested by Matlab. Regardless of the considerations behind the choices for these parameters, the hyperparameters of a BLSTM network are largely without interactions, according to [204]. Therefore, they can be optimized independently, which means that the optimal values found for the examined parameters will likely hold even if future work varies some or all of the hyperparameters that were fixed in this study. A summary of the hyperparameter settings is shown in Table 5.2.

Hyperparameter	**Evaluated values/ranges**
Number of hidden layers	1
Number of neurons N	[100, 256]
Dropout δ	[0.2, 0.9]
Gradient threshold	1
Max. number of epochs	300
Validation frequency	10
Validation patience	5
Learn rate	0.01
Mini-batch size	10 (numbers), 30 (frequent words)
Data format	{ADC, mm}

Table 5.2.: Hyperparameter settings of the BLSTM networks used in the small-scale recognition study. The optimal hyperparameter combination was found using Bayes optimization with 30 evaluations of the cost function.

5.3.3. Results

Two different evaluation paradigms were used: a speaker-dependent evaluation and a cross-speaker evaluation.

Intra-speaker validation

In this paradigm, the data sets recorded with each of the four speakers were used independently to train the BLSTM network. Since both data sets contained 10 repetitions of each item, one instance of each item was excluded from training and used for evaluation while the other 9 instances were used for training the network. This strategy is a special kind of leave-one-out cross-validation or non-randomly partitioned 10-fold cross-validation and was chosen to keep the number of models to train low while at the same time giving a fair estimation of the accuracy of the prediction on unseen data. The accuracy on the evaluation set was measured by predicting the label for each instance and determining the percentage of correct predictions. This procedure was repeated until every instance was part of the evaluation set once. The results using the optimal hyperparameters (see previous section) are given in Table 5.3 and Table 5.4.

Subject	1	2	3	4	Average
Hyperparameters	$N=151, \delta=0.31$, [mm]	$N=132, \delta=0.14$, [ADC]	$N=133, \delta=0.88$, [ADC]	$N=123, \delta=0.34$, [mm]	
Fold 1	100 %	100 %	100 %	100 %	100 %
Fold 2	100 %	100 %	100 %	100 %	100 %
Fold 3	100 %	100 %	100 %	100 %	100 %
Fold 4	100 %	100 %	100 %	100 %	100 %
Fold 5	100 %	100 %	100 %	100 %	100 %
Fold 6	100 %	100 %	100 %	100 %	100 %
Fold 7	100 %	100 %	100 %	100 %	100 %
Fold 8	100 %	100 %	100 %	100 %	100 %
Fold 9	100 %	100 %	90 %	100 %	97.5 %
Fold 10	100 %	90 %	100 %	100 %	97.5 %
Average	100 %	99 %	99 %	100 %	99.5 %

Table 5.3.: Recognition accuracy in the intra-speaker evaluation on the numbers corpus. Each fold contained one instance of each of the ten digit words.

Subject	1	2	3	4	Average
Hyperparameters	$N=132, \delta=0.84$, [mm]	$N=215, \delta=0.39$, [mm]	$N=202, \delta=0.16$, [ADC]	$N=248, \delta=0.67$, [ADC]	
Fold 1	96.67 %	96.67 %	96.67 %	93.33 %	95.84 %
Fold 2	93.33 %	100 %	100 %	100 %	98.33 %
Fold 3	96.67 %	100 %	93.33 %	100 %	97.5 %
Fold 4	96.67 %	90 %	100 %	96.67 %	95.84 %
Fold 5	93.33 %	100 %	100 %	100 %	98.33 %
Fold 6	96.67 %	96.67 %	100 %	96.67 %	97.5 %
Fold 7	96.67 %	100 %	96.67 %	90 %	95.84 %
Fold 8	96.67 %	90 %	96.67 %	96.67 %	95 %
Fold 9	100 %	96.67 %	100 %	96.67 %	98 %
Fold 10	100 %	96.67 %	100 %	93.33 %	97.5 %
Average	96.67 %	96.67 %	98.33 %	96.33 %	97 %

Table 5.4.: Recognition accuracy in the intra-speaker evaluation on the frequent words corpus when using the raw ADC sensor values. Each fold consisted of 30 words containing one instance of each word from the dictionary.

Inter-speaker validation

Articulatory data is generally highly specific to each individual. In the EOS data, the main differences likely originate in the different sensor positions relative to each subject's anatomy of their anterior mouth cavity. While the sensors have the same relative positions to one another because they are mounted to flexible circuit boards of the same layout, the incisor geometry and curvature of the hard palate is different for every subject. Therefore, the optical axes of the optical sensors were at different angles for different subjects and the contact sensors ended up in different areas of the hard palate. An extreme example is shown in Figure 5.5: for subject 2, the optical axis of one of the light sources of the lip sensor is so skewed towards the base of the lip that it cannot capture any movement of the lip at all (as shown in Figure 5.6). This is an extreme example for similar problems across all sensors and subjects. To quantify the impact of this inter-speaker variability in the sensor data, another set of four BLSTM networks was trained using the data from three of the four subjects for training and the data of the fourth subject for validation so that every subject's data was used for validation once (leave-one-speaker-out cross-validation). The hyperparameter tuning followed the same procedure as described in subsubsection 5.3.3 and used the same search space. The results are shown in Table 5.5 for the numbers and in Table 5.6 for the frequent words dataset.

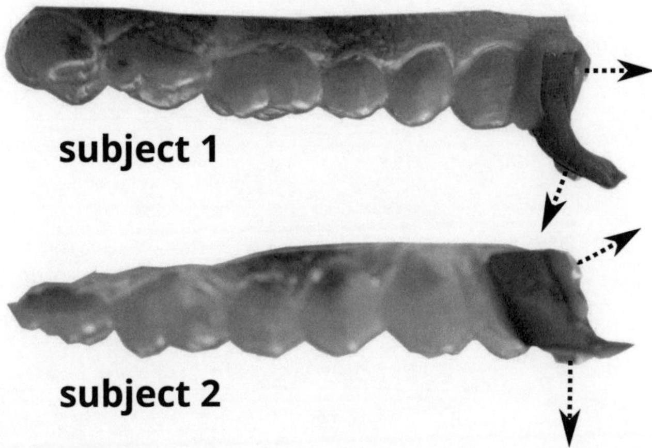

Figure 5.5.: Comparison of the lip sensor setup of subject 1 and subject 2: the arrows indicate the optical axes of the lip sensors. Similar differences are present across all subjects and can be observed for the other optical sensors as well.

Hyperparameters: $N = 117, \delta = 0.45$, [mm]					
Evaluation speaker	**1**	**2**	**3**	**4**	**Average**
Accuracy	33 %	52 %	80 %	82 %	61.75 %

Table 5.5.: Recognition accuracy in the inter-speaker evaluation on the numbers corpus. Four networks were trained to fit the data of three speakers and classify the data of the fourth speaker, using a different speaker for testing for each network (leave-one-speaker-out cross-validation).

5.3.4. Discussion

The results of the intra-speaker evaluation are comparable to the state-of-the-art in the field set by [118], who achieved an accuracy of 99 % on an English digits corpus for one male speaker and 82 % for a female speaker, as well as an accuracy of 95 % (male) and 76 % (female) on frequent words corpus using 47 English words in addition to the ten digit words. The reported errors are in-sample errors, however, and swing wildly between the two subjects. The results from this study were obtained in a more systematic fashion and are more consistent across the (admittedly all-male) speakers, while at the same time slightly surpassing the previous benchmarks. EOS therefore appears to capture the individual's articulation sufficiently well to discriminate between a limited set of words. It remains to be investigated if and how the accuracy decreases with increasing vocabulary size. It should also be investigated if the isolated evidence from [118] regarding a drop of the accuracy for a female subject can be reproduced systematically using EOS. Intuitively, there is no reason to assume that a female speaker's articulation should be harder to capture with EOS. The most salient difference between male and female anterior vocal tract geometry is the average size, which is not expected to adversely impact the measurement principles involved in EOS. Still, experimental evidence is needed to answer this question definitively.

The inter-speaker analysis identifies further room for improvement on the current system. The inter-individual differences of the speakers led to a precipitous drop in accuracy from an average of 99.5 % to an average of 61.75 % on the numbers corpus and from an average of 97 % to an average of 56.17 % on the frequent words corpus when training the system with other speakers. However, even for the worst evaluation speaker the accuracy was still way above chance level. Also, the

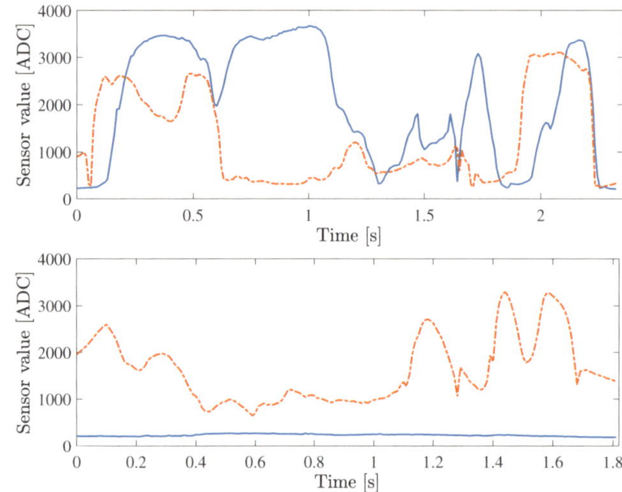

Figure 5.6.: Effect of the different sensor axes during the sentence "Heute ist schönes Frühlingswetter" (subject 1 above, subject 2 below): Dashed line is the downward facing light sensor, solid line is the sensor on the incisor.

Hyperparameters: $N = 119$, $\delta = 0.387$, [mm]

Evaluation speaker	1	2	3	4	Average
Accuracy	56 %	52.33 %	63.67 %	52.67 %	56.17 %

Table 5.6.: Recognition accuracy in the inter-speaker evaluation on the frequent words corpus. Four networks were trained to fit the data of three speakers and classify the data of the fourth speaker, using a different speaker for testing for each network (leave-one-speaker-out cross-validation).

variance of the accuracy across speakers is quite high: the achieved performance ranged from 33 % all the way to 82 %, depending on the evaluation speaker (see Table 5.5). When only considering the numbers data set, it appears that speaker 3 and 4 are more similar to one another than they are to the other speakers and than the other speakers are to one another, resulting in a higher cross-validation accuracy. However, as the vocabulary size increases to the frequent word data set, the variance across speakers diminishes and the individual performance is closer to the average. Nevertheless, a speaker adaptation of some sort is needed to achieve practically useful accuracy levels. This adaptation could be as simple as obtaining more training data from more speakers, or more elaborate and involve finding "alignment utterances" that map a speaker's articulatory space to a generic model speaker's space, in which the classification is subsequently performed. In both cases, more data needs to be acquired before further investigations can be pursued.

6. Articulation-to-Speech

6.1. Introduction

Articulation-to-Speech is the second major paradigm in the context of SSIs, as described in chapter 1, and summarily describes systems that convert articulatory data into audible speech. Despite the fact that *articulatory* data is obtained, the current state of the art in this field (see chapter 3) almost exclusively relies on speech signal generators that use statistical mappings to acoustic feature vectors to create speech (i.e., vocoders). One of the core ideas of this dissertation is to break away from the mainstream here and use the *articulatory* data (in this case EOS data) to drive an *articulatory* synthesizer. This chapter therefore describes the concept of articulatory synthesis in section 6.2, introduces a new vocal tract model suitable for the real-time synthesis of speech based on articulatory data in a closed-loop of capturing data and converting it to speech (see section 6.3, presents the evaluation of this model using both objective metrics (see section 6.4) and perceptual quality (see section 6.5), and includes a pilot study on using the new vocal tract model driven by EOS data for direct, real-time speech synthesis in an ATS system (see section 6.6). Finally, the chapter concludes with some additional analyses on important components of speech currently not captured by the articulatory data acquisition frontend (see section 6.7). The novel vocal tract model was also published in [205], while the results from the pilot study were published in [206].

6.2. Articulatory synthesis

To properly introduce and contextualize articulatory synthesis, it is necessary to give a brief overview of speech synthesis techniques in general. The techniques to perform speech synthesis, i.e., the artificial production of speech sounds, have historically been grouped in two distinct sets [207]: parametric synthesis (also called first generation techniques [208]) and concatenative synthesis. Given the recent advances of applying neural networks to directly generate a continuous speech signal waveform from text input (e.g., WaveNet [25], Tacotron [26] and Tacotron 2 [209]) and its dominance in the industrial applications of speech synthesis, these end-to-end techniques should be added to the list as a third set. But as important as these techniques are for the major consumer applications using speech synthesis, e.g., Google Assistant, their suitability for an ATS system is severely limited. Firstly, their focus is on text as an input and they are not easily adapted to a different kind of input space. Secondly, the amount of data needed to train such an end-to-end system is prohibitive for small-scale studies common in the academic field. Therefore, end-to-end systems were not considered for the synthesis backend in this dissertation.

Concatenative or unit-selection synthesis was the previous state-of-the-art in speech synthesis before the rise of end-to-end systems and is still deployed in many major consumer applications, e.g., Amazon Alexa or in-car assistants. Unit-selection synthesis relies on a large database of speech units of various lengths, ranging from individual phones, diphones, triphones, syllables, and words all the way to entire phrases in all kinds of different contexts. During synthesis, the system attempts to find the best-fitting unit, searching through its database from longest to shortest, trying to find a speech unit that was taken from the ideally exact same position in an utterance as the target utterance. The individual units are then concatenated to form the target utterance. Defining the cost function to identify the best-fitting unit is a complex task for any non-trivial system because it needs to incorporate the context of the utterance on many different levels, from neighboring phones up to the sentence or even paragraph level. Ill-fitting units can result in unnatural sounding speech, both in terms of intonation and articulation. To smooth out these shortcomings, a subsequent signal processing step can be applied that uses various techniques to manipulate the signal to achieve a more desirable outcome. Since the signal processing introduces artifacts and noise to the signal, the overall quality of the synthesis greatly depends on the size of the database and the number of speech units to choose from. However, larger databases also mean longer lookup times and the round-trip latency (the time from putting in the text to starting the audio playback) of a high-quality unit-selection synthesis system can be in the order of seconds. As described in section 1.1, a system could be conceived that maps the articulatory data to text first and then uses any TTS system to synthesize the speech, but that unnecessarily limits the possibilities of the ATS system to the possibilities of a TTS system. That is, specific articulation patterns, variations of the speech rate, and numerous other paralinguistic features would be irretrievably lost, which would greatly diminish the naturalness and individuality of the synthesized speech. It is therefore important to look at these synthesis techniques through the lens of *direct* synthesis, where the articulatory input data is mapped to the degrees of freedom of the synthesis. This formulation immediately disqualifies the concatenative techniques for a real-time ATS system, and a concatenative synthesis was therefore not considered for this dissertation.

Parametric synthesis, according to [208], encompasses all techniques based on parametric models derived from the theory of speech production as laid out in chapter 2. This comprises formant synthesis, classical linear prediction, and articulatory synthesis. The differences between formant synthesis and classical linear prediction are very minor here. Both are based on the source-filter model of speech production and use a vocal tract filter to filter an excitation source signal. In formant synthesis, this vocal tract filter is usually a parallel filter bank, while in linear prediction, a single all-pole filter is used. According to [208], formant synthesis can theoretically produce very natural sounding speech if the parameters of the filter bank are very accurately chosen but this is extremely hard to do without laborious manual trial-and-error. The parameters of the linear prediction filter, on the other hand, can be very easily estimated from natural speech samples and LPC-based speech coding is still a very relevant technique in speech transmission codecs (like the Adaptive Multi-Rate (AMR) codec) or in consumer technology like the "Speak and Spell" toys, an IEEE milestone in speech technology[1]. In the absence of reference speech samples for the parameter estimation, the synthesis quality is quite poor, however, and applications of linear prediction therefore mainly use it for speech signal compression and transmission instead of synthesis "from scratch".

The third major parametric synthesis technique, articulatory synthesis, is the most complex one. Articulatory synthesis computationally produces speech by simulating the air flow through the vocal tract during articulation using three basic components: a model of the vocal tract, a model of the articulatory control, and a model of the aerodynamic and/or acoustic processes to simulate the air flow. Depending on the level of detail to which these components are modeled, articulatory synthesis is in theory capable of simulating any given speech production system and can therefore potentially recreate any voice, any speaking style, and any vocal expression (e.g., emotional speech). In fact, its potential is so alluring that some consider it the way forward in speech synthesis in the long term [210]. Admittedly, that position paper was written well before the advent of end-to-end systems, and the commercial success of Big-Data-driven systems with less flexibility but very high

[1] https://ethw.org/Milestones:Speak_&_Spell,_the_First_Use_of_a_Digital_Signal_Processing_IC_for_Speech_Generation,_1978

naturalness have largely confined articulatory synthesis to the academic sector. But especially in the context of an SSI, articulatory synthesis offers a number of advantages unmatched by the other techniques:

- Low data requirements
- No signal processing artifacts or added noise (as opposed to, e.g., vocoder-based techniques)
- Explainable degrees of freedom
- Control parameters (often) have articulatory correlates, which match the measured articulatory input data

Especially the last point, the congruency of the input domain of an *articulatory* synthesizer and the nature of the measured *articulatory* data, strongly motivates an attempt to use it as the synthesizer in an ATS system.

A few modern articulatory synthesis systems exist, e.g., the Configurable Articulatory Synthesis (CASY) sytem [211], the ARTISYNTH project [212], or the VocalTractLab [213]. As pointed out in [214], the main challenge in the design of these systems is to successfully integrate models for all three components mentioned above: the vocal tract (e.g. [215–223]) and the vocal folds (e.g. [30, 224]), the articulatory control (e.g., [214, 225, 226]), and the aero-acoustic simulation (e.g., [227, 228]). Currently, the most advanced, feature-rich, and continuously developed articulatory synthesizer is arguably the VocalTractLab by Peter Birkholz [213]. On its website[2], it is described as "an interactive multimedial software tool to demonstrate the mechanism of speech production" meant to "facilitate an intuitive understanding of speech production for students of phonetics and related disciplines". It combines a powerful aero-acoustic simulation backend with a three-dimensional vocal tract model, a (geometric or physical) glottis model, and an articulatory model based on the Target Approximation Model [228, 229]. A GUI allows convenient and intuitive interaction with the various complex components of the very extensive program. While the naturalness and overall quality of speech synthesized with VocalTractLab is generally very high, there are a few obstacles that make it impossible to just "slot" the synthesizer into an ATS system as-is:

1. The three-dimensional vocal tract model has a large number of degrees of freedom, which makes the mapping from the articulatory data to the synthesizer very difficult.
2. The computational complexity involved in processing the three-dimensional vocal tract is very high.
3. The numerical solver used in the simulation backend has a real-time factor of more than 1 (as of version 2.1), which is too slow for a real-time application.

While the third point has been remedied by a different solver available since version 2.2 [230], the first two points are still a major issue. Both of them are, however, specific to the three-dimensional vocal tract model. If a simpler vocal tract model can be found that has a lower complexity with only negligible reduction in quality, a high quality, real-time articulatory synthesis controlled by measured articulatory data will be possible. Before a novel such model is presented in section 6.3, a brief discussion of various various forms of vocal tract models is required to properly motivate the approach taken.

6.2.1. Vocal tract models

As discussed in chapter 2, human speech is the result of acoustic wave propagation through the continuously reshaped "tube" of the vocal tract, i.e., the pharynx, the oral and nasal cavities. Thanks to modern imaging technologies, we have an accurate picture of what exactly these vocal tract shapes may look like. From the pioneer 2D X-ray images of vowels [231] and other articulations [232] to

[2] `www.vocaltractlab.de`

modern day MRI with high spatial resolution [233] and/or temporal dynamics [234–236], the understanding of the complex morphology and anatomy of the human vocal tract has grown rapidly. In order to simulate speech production, these complex volumetric shapes need to be described in some way by a vocal tract model. Defining such a model, however, is a daunting task due to the level of detail that may or may not be necessary to produce intelligible, natural sounding speech. Nevertheless, several approaches exist in the speech research community that can be grouped by their domain: modeling the entire 3D geometry of the vocal tract, reducing it to the 2D midsagittal plane, or reducing it even further by defining a 1D function that describes the cross-sectional area at any given position in the vocal tract (the *vocal tract area function*).

The approach using the fewest simplifications, the detailed reproduction of the 3D geometry, can be done in three different ways: explicitly modeling individual vocal tract shapes from imaging data (usually MRI) as a 3D mesh, e.g. [237–239], statistically modeling 3D vocal tract shapes as a mixture of the principal components found in a corpus of 3D scans of articulatory configurations [219,240], or simulating the biomechanics involved in the shaping of the vocal tract, e.g., [217,241]. Exploiting assumed symmetry of the vocal tract with respect to the midsagittal plane, many 2D vocal tract models discard the lateral dimension. The approaches here are similar to the 3D problem: direct geometric modeling, e.g., [215,242], or statistical modeling by superimposing differently weighted component shapes, e.g., [133,243,244]. The geometry of the vocal tract can be simplified even further if the assumption of planar sound wave propagation is made: In this case, the only relevant measure is the cross-sectional area along the vocal tract and thus its acoustic properties can be derived from the 1D vocal tract area function. Even though this assumption disregards higher modes [245], the differences are negligible in the perceptually relevant frequency range [246] and it has been known for a long time to work well for fast and high-quality synthesis. This kind of modeling also discards much of the anatomical detail present in 2D or 3D models but is comparatively fast and simple, which is a crucial factor when trying to perform direct ATS. In fact, even when used for any kind of speech synthesis, many of the 2D and 3D models are only used as intermediary steps to ultimately calculate the area function, which is then used for the actual synthesis (see, e.g., [133,213,217,237,238,241,242]). Therefore, it might be the most efficient approach to model the 1D area function directly. Simply specifying an array of cross-sectional area values and corresponding positions in the vocal tract for a set of sounds as in [247] could certainly work, but this brute-force approach to modeling the area function is not only wasteful (in terms of the number of model parameters) but also difficult to control when you want to move from one vocal tract shape to another, i.e., produce connected speech. Therefore, a lower-dimensional model (with regards to the parameter space) is desirable. Ideally, these parameters would also have some sort of physiological or articulatory correspondence, which would make the manual control of such a model more intuitive. A well-known model to attempt this is the Three Parameter Model by Fant [22,248,249]. Originally inspired by tube resonator models of the vocal tract, Fant refined the model in his later work to allow non-cylindrical segments and thus more natural area functions. The three parameters are the place of the constriction along the midsagittal section x_c, the area at the constriction A_c and the ratio of the overall tract length over the area of the lip opening $\frac{l_0}{A_0}$. These three parameters are used in three sets of equations, called prototypes, which break the possible area functions down into three cases: front, mid and back vowels. Depending on the class of vowel to be synthesized, a different set of equations is used. Each prototype uses a concatenation of linear and higher-order functions to model the corresponding sounds. While the parameterization and order of the interpolation functions change, all prototypes use the same larynx segment, itself a 2.5 cm long concatenation of constant segments of 0.5 cm length each and different cross-sectional areas. Consonants are modeled by decomposing the area function into an overall vocalic part (using parameters that yield the desired coarticulation) and a consonantal part, which then modifies or replaces the vocalic part [249,250]. This consonantal part is defined by four more parameters (bringing the total number of parameters up to seven): the place x_{cc} of the midsagittal constriction or closure, the area A_{cc} at the constriction, the width w of the local modification projected on the vocalic area function, and a tilt factor k_S, controlling the asymmetry of the constriction. The idea of mixing certain basic patterns or factors to form a final area function was also used concurrently by Fitch et al. [251] and Ru et al. [252], who both built on the factors found by Harshman et al. in [253]. Their models describe any vowel (but only vowel) area function as a linear combination of two sinusoidal base factors t_1 and t_2. The most sophisticated "statistical mixture model" is the model by Story ([254–258]). Conceptually combining Badin et al.'s guided PCA [240] and Öhman's notion of a vowel "substrate" with superimposed consonantal perturbations [243], he developed an extensive model that determines the area function as a composite of four perturbation "tiers" applied to a neutral area function (defined as an area function that produces equidistant formants). In each tier, time-invariant base structural components, derived by PCA of an MRI data corpus of vocal tract shapes, are mixed using time-varying control values to form intermediate outputs used in the next tier. These intermediate outputs are in order of tiers: the vowel substrate, the consonantal perturbation, vocal tract length changes, and nasalization. Finally, the intermediate outputs are mixed together to obtain the area function (the mixture of the vowel substrate and the consonantal perturbation), the warped location axis (length changes applied to the linear location axis), and the time-dependent area of the nasal port. The parameters of the model are therefore the weights applied to the base components in each tier, 14 in total.

Another 1D model by Ishizaka [259] discards the superpositional approach and instead models all possible area function shapes by concatenating a constant-area larynx tube section, two weighted cosine functions (one period of each), connected at the place of constriction x_c, and a constant area lip tube section. In total, the Ishizaka model uses six parameters: the total length L of the vocal tract, the maximum cross-sectional area A_b in the back (posterior) part of the mouth cavity, the location x_c of the constriction, the area A_c at the constriction, the area A_f in the front (anterior) part of the mouth cavity, and the area A_m of the mouth opening. In [260], Wei et al. devised a model that uses 9 distinct extremal points and interpolates between those points using a prototype function that depends on the distance of the glottis and the sound that is to be modeled.

Of all the models introduced above, Ishizaka's model uses the least parameters while still allowing high flexibility in terms of the area functions that may be produced. However, the assumption of symmetric cosine sections is a substantial simplification that accounts for most of the deviations from real area functions (as is evident in their own evaluation of their model in [259]). Wei somewhat eliminated those shortcomings by using different prototype functions in different sections, but in doing so greatly limited the variability of the possible shapes.

6.3. The six point vocal tract model

In this section, a new parametric one-dimensional vocal tract model is introduced that combines elements of Ishizaka's model and Wei's model, but overcomes their limitations by using half periods of cosine segments to interpolate between six control points that can additionally be shaped by a non-linear warping. The model uses a total of 16 parameters in the full configuration or 11 parameters in a reduced configuration, which achieves the lower dimensionality at a slightly reduced quality. The comparatively large number of parameters in the full configuration allows maximum variability of the vocal tract shapes that can be modeled without the inter-dependencies between different areas of the vocal tract inherent in factor-based models. The parameters also have anatomical correspondences, which makes their control potentially more intuitive than, e.g., the control of statistical weights. Through the introduction of *virtual targets*, similar to the concept introduced by [261], the model is furthermore capable to realistically model closures during stops, which Ishizaka and Wei did not discuss for their models. In contrast to Story's model, the parameters of the proposed model have a more direct anatomical correspondence to points in the vocal tract and can therefore be controlled according to observations of the geometrical features of the area function. These correspondences also allow the mapping of segments of the area function to articulators that dominantly shape that section, which is very important for the high-quality synthesis of consonants (see [262]). Finally, Story's statistical model needs to be recalculated with new speaker data to adapt it to a new speaker while the proposed model can be easily implemented using just a simple, piecewise function and manually fitted to any given area function by a simple, manual or automated, geometric fit.

In keeping with the Ishizaka and the Wei model, the proposed six point vocal tract model given by equation 6.1 defines the area function as a piece-wise concatenation of cosine functions and constant-area segments. An example of an area function created by the model is shown in Figure 6.1.

$$A(x) = \begin{cases} A_{\text{lar}} & \text{for } 0 \leq x \leq x_{\text{lar}} \\ \frac{A_{\text{p}}+A_{\text{lar}}}{2} + \frac{A_{\text{p}}-A_{\text{lar}}}{2} \cdot \cos\left(\pi\left(\frac{x_{\text{p}}-x}{x_{\text{p}}-x_{\text{lar}}}\right)^{n_{\text{lar,p}}}\right) & \text{for } x_{\text{lar}} < x \leq x_{\text{p}} \\ \frac{A_{\text{c}}+A_{\text{p}}}{2} + \frac{A_{\text{c}}-A_{\text{p}}}{2} \cdot \cos\left(\pi\left(\frac{x_{\text{c}}-x}{x_{\text{c}}-x_{\text{p}}}\right)^{n_{\text{p,c}}}\right) & \text{for } x_{\text{p}} < x \leq x_{\text{c}} \\ \frac{A_{\text{a}}+A_{\text{c}}}{2} + \frac{A_{\text{a}}-A_{\text{c}}}{2} \cdot \cos\left(\pi\left(\frac{x_{\text{a}}-x}{x_{\text{a}}-x_{\text{c}}}\right)^{n_{\text{c,a}}}\right) & \text{for } x_{\text{c}} < x \leq x_{\text{a}} \\ \frac{A_{\text{in}}+A_{\text{a}}}{2} + \frac{A_{\text{in}}-A_{\text{a}}}{2} \cdot \cos\left(\pi\left(\frac{x_{\text{in}}-x}{x_{\text{in}}-x_{\text{a}}}\right)^{n_{\text{a,in}}}\right) & \text{for } x_{\text{a}} < x \leq x_{\text{in}} \\ A_{\text{lip}} & \text{for } x_{\text{in}} < x \leq x_{\text{lip}} \end{cases} \tag{6.1}$$

where:

x: Position along the vocal tract center line in cm

$A(x)$: Cross-sectional area in cm^2 at the position x

x_{lar}: Length of the larynx tube in cm

A_{lar}: Cross-sectional area in cm^2 of the larynx tube

x_{p}: Position of the posterior control point in cm

A_{p}: Cross-sectional area in cm^2 at the posterior control point

$n_{\text{lar,p}}$: Warping exponent of segment between the larynx and the posterior control point

x_{c}: Position of the constriction in cm

A_{c}: Cross-sectional area in cm^2 at the constriction

$n_{\text{p,c}}$: Warping exponent of segment between the posterior control point and constriction

x_{a}: Position of the anterior control point in cm

A_{a}: Cross-sectional area in cm^2 at the anterior control point

$n_{\text{c,a}}$: Warping exponent of segment between the constriction and the anterior control point

x_{in}: Position of the incisors in cm

A_{in}: Cross-sectional area in cm^2 at the incisors

$n_{\text{a,in}}$: Warping exponent of segment between the anterior control point and the incisors

x_{lip}: Vocal tract length in cm

A_{lip}: Cross-sectional area in cm^2 at the lips

The vocal tract model uses six points (x_i, A_i), $i \in \{\text{lar, p, c, a, in, lip}\}$, as parameters: the length x_{lar} and the cross-sectional area A_{lar} of the larynx tube define the larynx control point, the position x_{p} and its corresponding area A_{p} the posterior control point, the position x_{c} and the area A_{c} the constriction control point, the position x_{a} and area A_{a} the anterior control point, the position x_{in} and area A_{in} the incisor control point, and finally the position x_{lip} (also the length of the vocal tract) and area A_{lip} of the lip control point. Except for the larynx tube and the segment between the incisor and

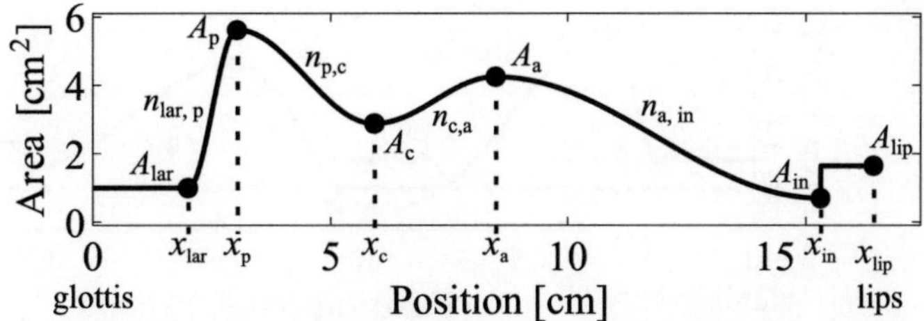

Figure 6.1.: Example (neutral, /ə/-like) area function created with the six point model

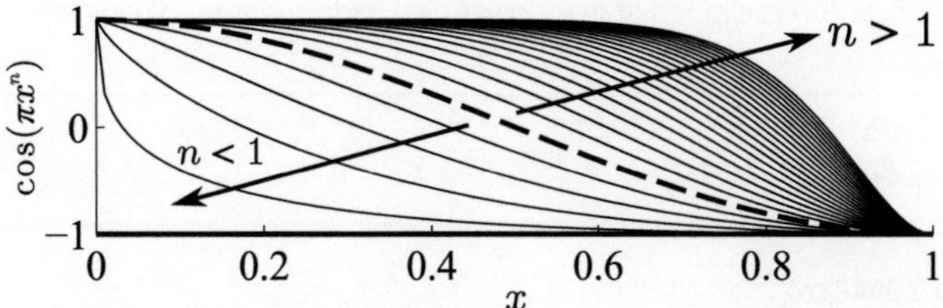

Figure 6.2.: Effect of the exponents n in the model equations (dashed line: $n = 1$): The argument of each cosine segment is normalized to the interval $[0, \pi]$ but non-linearly warped by the exponent n. When $n > 1$, the segment becomes more convex and could even approximate a right angle for very large n. When $n < 1$, the segment becomes more concave. To avoid discontinuities, only exponents $n > 0$ were used.

the lip control point, which are of constant cross-sectional area, the area function is calculated by interpolating between each two consecutive control points using half a period of a cosine function. In addition to the six control points, four warping parameters $n_{lar,p}$, $n_{p,c}$, $n_{c,a}$ and $n_{a,in}$ are used to independently warp the corresponding cosine segments (see Figure 6.2), bringing the total number of parameters up to 16.

Compared to the Ishizaka model, the use of half a period per cosine section allows asymmetric perturbations (with respect to the local maximum or minimum area) and the warping factors allow an even wider range of possible shapes, making the Ishizaka model essentially a special case of the six point model.

To model closures in the vocal tract, the domain of the area parameters is extended into the negative range. The codomain of the area function is, however, still constrained to the positive range: when a calculated $A(x)$ becomes less than zero, it is instead set to zero. This way, when a control point is moved into the negative area range (becoming a "virtual target" point), a wider segment of the area function can become zero (see Figure 6.3).

6.3.1. Parameter reduction

The six point model aims at maximum flexibility regarding the shape of the area function and therefore allows independent manipulation of all six control points. However, not all parameters of the model are necessarily degrees of freedom of the vocal tract shapes actually occurring in speech. Therefore, the 16 parameters were analyzed regarding simplifications by exploiting non-discriminatory variance or mutual dependencies in the evaluated vocal tract shapes discussed in section 6.4. Firstly, following the example of [259] and [215], the larynx tube length x_{lar} was set to 2 cm and its area A_{lar} to 1.5125 cm^2 (i.e., the average mean area across the first 1.5 cm of all reference area functions). Because the position x_p of the posterior control point anatomically corresponds to the piriform sinus and its morphological relationship to the larynx tube opening, a constant position of the larynx tube opening directly implies a constant position x_p and, by extension, a constant

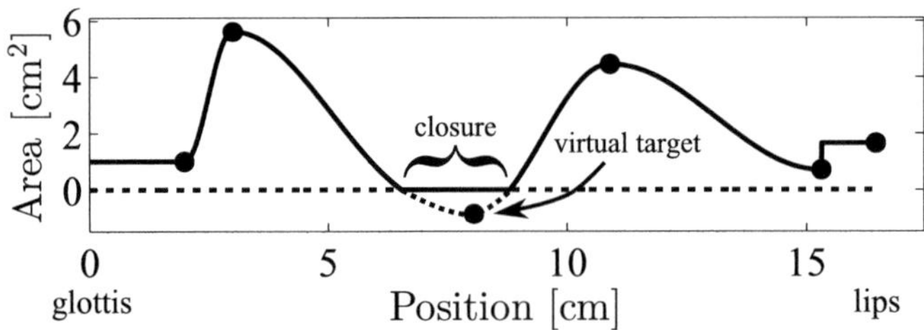

Figure 6.3.: Modeling closures (here, a velar closure): a control point is moved below the zero threshold to a "negative area" and thus becomes a *virtual target*. The calculated area function is clipped at zero, creating a wide segment of closure.

x_{lar}	$= 2\,\text{cm}$
A_{lar}	$= 1.5125\,\text{cm}^2$
$n_{lar,p}$	$= 1$
x_p	$= 3.0948\,\text{cm}$
x_a	$= -2.347 - 0.061 \cdot x_c - 2.052 \cdot n_{c,a} - 0.159 \cdot A_a$
	$+1.161 \cdot x_{in} + 0.143 \cdot x_c n_{c,a}$

Table 6.1.: Eliminated degrees of freedom of the model. Using these constraints, the six point model is fully determined by the remaining 11 free parameters (the reduced configuration).

transition (i.e., $n_{lar,p} = 1$) as well. To determine this position x_p, the model was geometrically fitted to the reference area functions as described below, but using the fixed larynx control point and only optimizing the posterior control point. The final position $x_p = 3.0948$ cm was then calculated as the average across all sounds. The possible mutual dependencies between the remaining parameters of the model were investigated with a leave-one-out paradigm using stepwise multiple linear regression: All but one parameter were predictors and the remaining parameter was the response variable. Starting with a simple constant model, the stepwise multiple linear regression algorithm (using Matlab's built-in *stepwiselm* function) then determined the optimal linear regression model including combinations of predictor variables and allowing up to quadratic terms. Because they were needed to form stops or constrictions, A_c, A_{in} and A_{lip} were excluded from the list of possible predictors and responses. Of the regression models found, only the one for x_a had an adjusted coefficient of determination $R^2_{adj} > 0.9$ and was thus above the commonly used threshold for a sufficiently precise model and therefore included in the area function model, eliminating another degree of freedom. Table 6.1 summarizes the eliminated 5 free parameters and their replacement values or function. The reduced number of parameters inherently comes at the cost of reduced flexibility because dependencies are introduced. To investigate if the reduction of complexity is worth the potential reduction in precision and quality, the model was evaluated in both the full 16 parameter configuration and the reduced 11 parameter configuration.

6.4. Objective evaluation of the vocal tract model

To objectively evaluate both the full and the reduced configuration of the six-point model, the model was fitted to a set of reference area functions derived from MRI data and both the geometric error and the acoustic error (in terms of formant deviation) were determined.

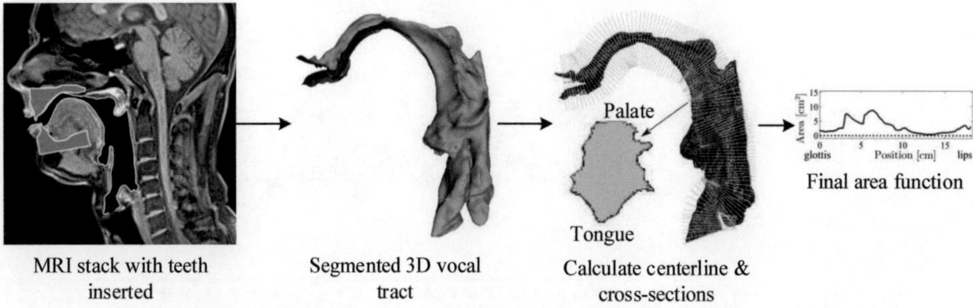

Figure 6.4.: Workflow to obtain the reference area functions: After the 3D scans of the plaster jaw models were inserted into the MRI stack, we segmented the vocal tract and converted it into a 3D mesh. The centerline was calculated in this mesh and the cross-sectional area sampled at 129 positions, yielding the final area function.

6.4.1. Reference vocal tract shapes

The reference vocal tract shapes were obtained from a corpus of MRI data consisting of 22 sounds produced by one male 38-year-old German native speaker: the German vowels /aː, a, eː, ɛː, ɛ, iː, ɪ, oː, ɔ, uː, ʊ, øː, œ, yː, ʏ, ə/ and the German consonants /l, f, s, ʃ, ç, x/. The MRI images were acquired on a Siemens 3T TIM Trio with a 12-channel head coil combined with additional neck elements. To image the throat, we used a sagittal 3D volume interpolated gradient echo sequence (VIBE - fl3d_vibe) with 1.2 mm × 1.2 mm × 1.8 mm resolution, 44 sequential slices, matrix size 192, field of view = $(230\,\text{mm})^2$, repetition time $TR = 5.53$ ms, echo time $TE = 2.01$ ms, flip angle 9°, Q-fatsat, 22 lines per shot, 7/8 phase partial Fourier, 6/8 slice partial Fourier, ipat factor 2 (PE only), 24 reference lines and a bandwidth of 220 Hz/pixel. The acquisition time for one volume was 14 s during which the speaker sustained the articulatory configuration and phonated the sounds. Because MRI cannot capture the teeth, which can have a significant impact on the radiated sound according to [263], plaster models of the subject's upper and lower jaw were scanned using a NextEngine 3D scanner and inserted into the MRI images by aligning anatomical landmarks present in both the MRI data and on the jaw models (e.g., the hard palate contour). For this purpose, we used the open-source software Meshlab [264] (for retouching of the 3D scanned models) and ITK-SNAP [265] (for the actual insertion and unification to obtain the final volume). The subsequent segmentation of the vocal tract in the combined volume was also done with ITK-SNAP. To calculate the vocal tract area function, we used a similar workflow and a custom software previously described in [266]: The segmented vocal tract was converted to a 3D mesh. The centerline was estimated according to [262], begins at the glottis and was terminated at the lips. More precisely, the acoustic termination at the lips was set halfway between the corners of the mouth and the connecting line between the upper and lower tips of the lips [267]. If the contour of the cross-section in that termination plane was not closed, we manually closed it using half-circle segments before calculating the lip opening area. The beginning and end of the segmented vocal tract was terminated with a straight cut perpendicular to the centerline using Meshlab. Between these first and last sections, 127 more, equally spaced sections were inserted. The cross-sectional area of the vocal tract was then determined for all sections, resulting in 129 samples of the reference area function per sound. The overall workflow is illustrated by Figure 6.4. The vocal tract data is included as subject 1 of the Dresden Vocal Tract Dataset (DVTD) [268].

6.4.2. Geometric evaluation

For each of the 22 reference area functions, we determined a set of 16 parameters for the full configuration of the vocal tract model that produces an optimal approximation of the respective reference. The parameters were initialized manually by moving the control points to appropriate

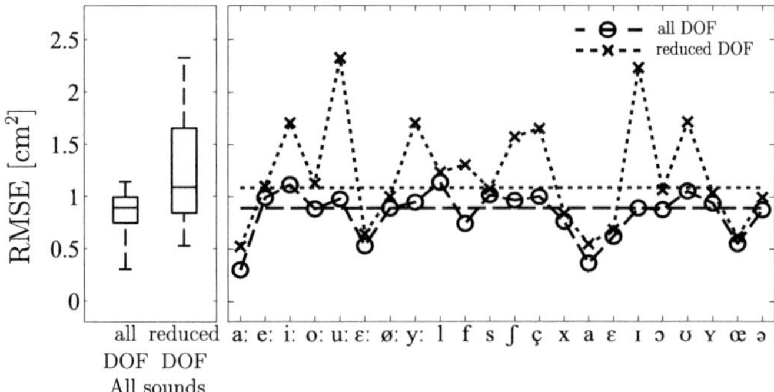

Figure 6.5.: Root-mean-square error (RMSE) in cm^2 for the area functions produced with the model with the full set of 16 degrees of freedom (DOF) and with the model and the reduced set of 11 DOF. The box plots to the left show the median error (horizontal line inside the box), the edges of the boxes show the 25th and 75th percentile and the whiskers extend to the outliers. To the right, the results are further broken down by sound.

starting positions using a graphical user interface (GUI) written in Matlab. The optimal solution was found using the Nelder-Mead algorithm [269] implemented in the built-in Matlab function *fminsearch*. The lip control point and the incisor control point were not subject to the optimization because they were landmark points that could be unambiguously identified in the reference functions. The remaining parameters were optimized so that the mean squared error between the logarithmized reference and the logarithmized model area function became minimal. The order of the control points was not allowed to change (meaning that their positions had to monotonously increase) to keep their anatomical correspondences intact. The warping factors had a lower limit of 0 because negative powers would turn the cosine sections into secant sections. The logarithm was taken of the area values to avoid a collapse of constrictions and emphasize the error at small constrictions as opposed to errors at sections of already large areas. After a set of optimal parameters was found, the root-mean-square error (RMSE) of the model area function was calculated for each reference. The results are shown in Figure 6.5: The error ranged from 0.302 cm^2 for /aː/ to 1.142 cm^2 for /l/ and the median error across all sounds was 0.891 cm^2 (produced by the model area functions for /oː/ and /ɪ/). All references and the geometrically fitted area functions using the full configuration of the model are shown in Figure 6.6. The largest deviations of the model area function from the reference occurred in the region of the epiglottis and the vallecula.

The same optimization was done for the reduced configuration using only 11 free parameters and the error results are also shown in Figure 6.5. Compared to 16 free parameters, the RMSE rose drastically for some sounds (e.g., by 137 % for /uː/) and only very little for others (e.g., by 6 % for /s/). Plots of the area functions in the reduced configuration are provided in Figure G.1.

6.4.3. Acoustic evaluation

An objective measure to compare the acoustic properties of the area functions generated with the proposed model that applies to all sounds is difficult to define. The relevant acoustic features for fricatives that are measured in acoustic realizations are heavily dependent on the noise source, which is in turn determined by the cross-sectional area of the critical constriction of the vocal tract. Since the spatial resolution of the MRI scanner (1.2 mm × 1.2 mm × 1.8 mm) was too low to capture these very fine constrictions reliably, an objective evaluation was not possible for these sounds and the subjective evaluation of the consonantal area functions only made sense after manual optimization of these critical constrictions (see subsection 6.5.1). For vowels, however, the objectively relevant acoustic properties are the first three formants $F1$, $F2$ and $F3$. To compare the formants of the vowel reference area functions obtained from the MRI data and of the corresponding model area

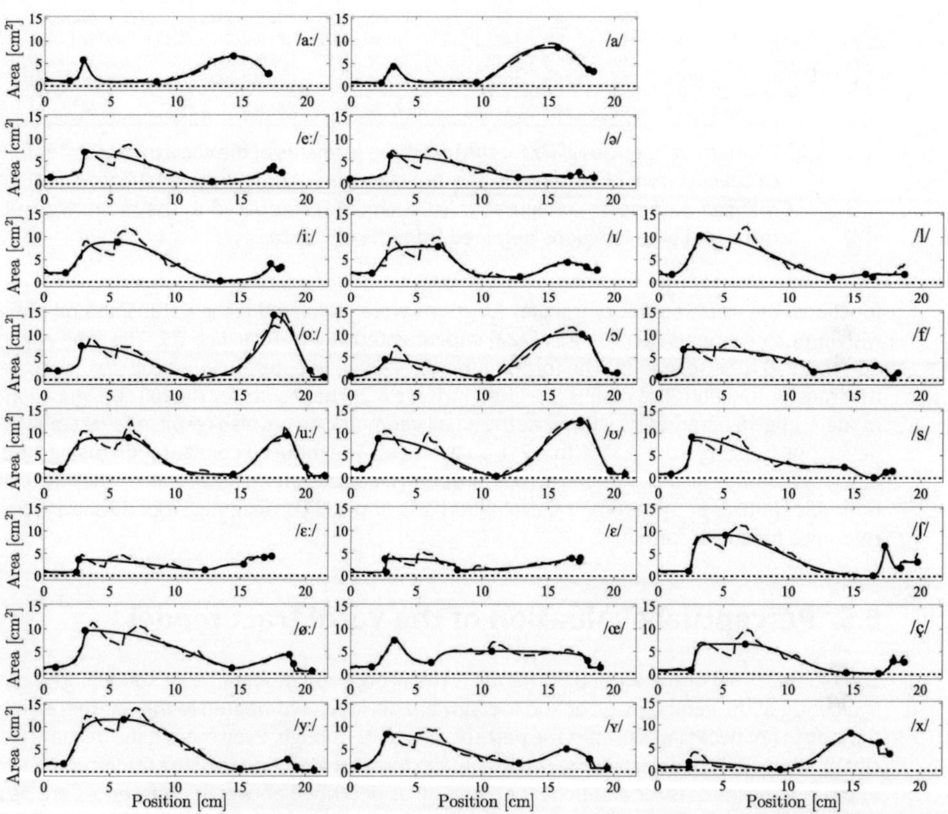

Figure 6.6.: Area functions of tense vowels (left column), lax and neutral vowels (center column), and consonants (right column). Dashed lines mark the references and solid lines the geometrically fitted model area functions in the full configuration. The black dots mark the six control points.

Sound	$F1_{ref}$	$F1_{16}$	$\Delta F1_{16}$	$F1_{11}$	$\Delta F1_{11}$	$F2_{ref}$	$F2_{16}$	$\Delta F2_{16}$	$F2_{11}$	$\Delta F2_{11}$	$F3_{ref}$	$F3_{16}$	$\Delta F3_{16}$	$F3_{11}$	$\Delta F3_{16}$
/aː/	611	645	5.56 %	589	3.6 %	1214	1219	0.41 %	1249	2.88 %	2478	2553	3.03 %	2510	1.29 %
/eː/	319	315	1.25 %	318	0.31 %	2080	2084	0.19 %	2065	0.72 %	2543	2633	3.54 %	2501	1.65 %
/iː/	245	246	0.41 %	260	6.12 %	2098	2098	0.43 %	2144	2.19 %	3002	3115	3.76 %	3342	11.36 %
/oː/	275	290	5.45 %	289	5.09 %	609	614	0.82 %	635	4.27 %	2293	2325	1.4 %	2368	3.27 %
/uː/	258	251	2.71 %	289	12.02 %	709	689	2.82 %	667	5.92 %	2131	2249	5.54 %	2180	2.3 %
/ɛː/	524	522	0.38 %	502	4.2 %	1822	1845	1.26 %	1802	1.1 %	2542	2579	1.46 %	2505	1.46 %
/øː/	291	281	3.44 %	280	3.78 %	1292	1297	0.39 %	1274	1.39 %	1981	2006	1.26 %	1992	0.56 %
/yː/	212	216	1.89 %	227	7.08 %	1336	1440	7.78 %	1396	4.49 %	1938	1973	1.81 %	2022	4.33 %
/a/	610	635	4.1 %	568	6.89 %	992	1015	2.32 %	984	0.81 %	2493	2616	4.93 %	2552	2.37 %
/ɛ/	516	525	1.74 %	496	3.88 %	1678	1707	1.73 %	1659	1.13 %	2564	2614	1.95 %	2565	0.04 %
/ɪ/	352	354	0.57 %	408	15.91 %	1568	1563	0.32 %	1480	5.61 %	2346	2498	6.48 %	2390	1.88 %
/ɔ/	396	420	6.06 %	418	5.56 %	698	743	6.45 %	739	5.87 %	2508	2674	6.62 %	2574	2.63 %
/ʊ/	276	284	2.9 %	294	6.52 %	591	596	0.85 %	603	2.03 %	2325	2455	5.59 %	2561	10.15 %
/œ/	444	441	0.68 %	441	0.68 %	1237	1227	0.81 %	1227	0.81 %	2100	2132	1.52 %	2124	1.14 %
/ʏ/	342	337	1.46 %	339	0.88 %	1173	1171	0.17 %	1195	1.88 %	2257	2237	0.89 %	2230	1.2 %
/ə/	386	380	1.55 %	374	3.11 %	1670	1674	0.24 %	1647	1.38 %	2415	2451	1.49 %	2399	0.66 %
all	-	-	2.51 %	-	5.35 %	-	-	1.69 %	-	2.66 %	-	-	3.2 %	-	2.89 %

Table 6.2.: Formant frequencies in Hz for the first three formants of the vocal tract transfer functions calculated from the model in the full parameter configuration (subscript 16) and the reduced parameter configuration (subscript 11) compared to the reference (subscript ref) vowel area functions obtained from the MRI data.

functions, the volume velocity transfer functions were calculated using a transmission-line model with lumped elements according to [227] implemented in VocalTractLab 2.2. The tube approximation used 40 tube segments. The formant frequencies were determined as the first three peaks in the transfer function. The results are given in Table 6.2. The results for the full configuration of the model using 16 parameters show that the small geometric errors also result in fairly small formant deviations (ranging from 2.51 % to 3.2 % on average). The reduced configuration (using 11 parameters) achieved similar deviations across all sounds, but the sounds /uː/ and /ɪ/ that were already noticable outliers in the geometric evaluation also showed consistently large deviations from the reference functions' formants.

6.5. Perceptual evaluation of the vocal tract model

The ultimate goal of the vocal tract model is the production of identifiable sounds. The objective evaluation of the geometric error and the formant deviations compared to the reference area functions does not necessarily predict the perceptual results, though. Even though the formant frequencies of the model are objectively fairly close to the formant frequencies of the references, the nature of the references calls for additional fine-tuning: as described above, the references are based on MRI recordings. During an MRI session, the speaker is in a horizontal (supine) position, which has been shown to influence articulation in a highly subject-dependent fashion [270]. Furthermore, each recorded sound had to be sustained for at least 14 s, which may be difficult to do correctly, especially for the lax vowels. Finally, the segmentation process is prone to small geometric errors that may add up to larger perceptual errors. To counter all of these potential errors, a perceptual optimization with respect to the best sound identification rate was conducted.

6.5.1. Perceptual optimization

To offset the errors described above, the parameters of the model area functions were optimized again, this time with respect to the formant frequencies following the algorithm described in [214]. Initially, target formant frequency values extracted from audio recordings of the speaker used in the MRI recording were considered. Due to the noisy environment in the MRI scanner, we recorded the audio of the speaker separately in a studio setting. However, even after careful selection of the analysis parameters, the formants calculated with Praat [176] did not lead to satisfying results in terms of the perceptual quality of sounds synthesized using those values. More references taken from Table 1 in [214], Table 1 in [271], and Table 2(b) in [34] were therefore included in the analysis. The optimization was performed repeatedly and the sound corresponding to the optimized area function synthesized after each passthrough until the achieved result was approved by a phonetics expert. The synthesis was performed using the time-domain aero-acoustic simulation backend of the articulatory synthesizer VocalTractLab 2.2 that is based on an acoustic tube system [213, 227, 272]. For the simulation, each continuous model area function was discretized into 40 tube segments of equal length and preceded by two tube segments representing the glottis (shaped according to the triangular glottis model by Birkholz et al. [273]) and a uniform tube of 14 cm representing the trachea. The final formant frequencies are given in Table G.5.

The critical constrictions of the fricative area functions were manually corrected as well to compensate the compound error of the MRI recording resolution, the precision of the plaster jaw models, the 3D scan resolution, and the precision of the manual insertion of the scanned jaw models. The control points governing the respective constrictions were slightly adjusted until each fricative was perceptually clearly identifiable by a phonetics expert. The synthesis was once again performed with the time-domain simulation backend of the VocalTractLab 2.2. As shown in [262], the synthesis of consonants is greatly improved by specifying the primary articulator forming a constriction for every tube segment. The area function was therefore divided into four regions and each region was assigned the respective articulator based on the model parameters: all tubes from the glottis to x_p were assigned an unspecified articulator, segments from x_p to the last full tube segment before x_{in} were associated with the tongue, the tube segment around x_{in} was marked as the lower incisors, and the segments from the first tube segment after x_{in} to x_{lip} were assigned the lower lip.

After the formant optimization of all vowels and the manual perceptual tuning of the consonants for both the full configuration and the reduced configuration (using 16 and 11 free parameters, respectively), their intelligibility was assessed in an identification test. The geometrically fitted area functions in the full configuration from section 6.4 were also included in this test as a baseline.

6.5.2. Selection and synthesis of stimuli

The stimuli were the isolated tense vowels /aː, eː, iː, oː, uː, ɛː, øː, yː/ (8 stimuli), the lax vowels /a, ɛ, ɪ, ɔ, ʊ, œ, ʏ/ embedded in the carrier pseudo-word /bVbə/ (7 stimuli), the consonants /b, d, g, l, f, s, ʃ, ç, x/ in CV syllables using /aː, iː, uː/ as context ($9 \cdot 3 = 27$ stimuli), each produced by the geometrically fitted full configuration, the perceptually optimized full configuration, and the perceptually optimized reduced configuration of the area functions for a total of $42 \cdot 3 = 126$ stimuli per trial. The neutral vowel /ə/ was excluded from the evaluation because it is difficult for non-experts to identify. Since there were no reference area functions available for the stops /b, d, g/, they were manually created by starting with the respective context vowel and inserting a closure at the corresponding place of articulation (using the lip, the anterior or the constriction control point, respectively) as described in Figure 6.3. The synthesis was once again performed as above, using the time-domain simulation backend of VocalTractLab 2.2. In order to keep as many synthesis variables as possible constant, all stimuli used the same settings for the triangular glottis model: Subglottal pressure 1000 Pa, lower and upper vocal cord rest displacement 0.1 mm, arytenoid area 0 cm, and an aspiration strength of −40 dB. These parameters result in modal phonation. Therefore, items generated with the area functions of originally unvoiced consonants now should sound voiced. However, the constrictions in the geometrically fitted area functions of /s/, /ʃ/ and /ç/ were so small, that the intra-oral pressure in the simulation became so large that it pushed the vocal folds open resulting in unvoiced sounds. These unrealistically small constrictions were corrected as part of the perceptual optimization (see subsection 6.5.1), so all of the stimuli generated with perceptually optimized area functions sounded voiced using the voiced excitation source. To avoid confusion and to stay consistent with the previous labeling, we will continue to identify all stimuli using their unvoiced transcription.

The synthesis was controlled by specifying the time variation of each of the free parameters of the model functions. Their temporal trajectories were calculated by specifying area functions for the target shapes in each stimulus (e.g., a stop in the closed phase and a context vowel for the CV syllables) and interpolating between those shapes using half a cosine period to insert smooth transitions. An example of a varying area function is given in Figure 6.7. The durations for the static and transient periods and the f_0 contour of the excitation in each stimulus were approximated to samples from natural speech and were kept constant across each group of stimuli (tense vowels, lax vowels, consonants). Finally, the amplitude of all stimuli was normalized.

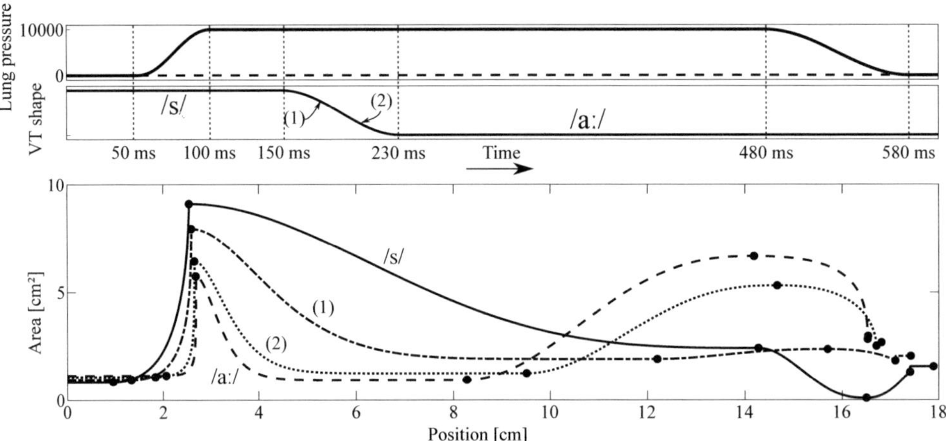

Figure 6.7.: Example of a time-varying area function: A connected utterance is created by defining the target shapes (in this case /s/ and /aː/) and their respective stationary durations, and the transition time between them. During this transition, the parameter values of the area function are interpolated between the initial and the final shape by using a cosine interpolation for each parameter. The transitional shapes marked are after (1) one third and (2) two thirds of the transition time.

6.5.3. Subjects and test setup

The 126 stimuli were presented to 18 subjects (German native speakers, 4 female, 14 male, age 23-64, median age 30, with backgrounds in education and engineering) using Praat [176]. Each group of stimuli (tense vowels, lax vowels, consonants) was presented in a separate trial. During each trial, the subjects were asked to identify the utterance in a forced choice setup with no time limit and five allowed repetitions. In the consonant trial, the buttons were labeled with both the voiced and unvoiced version of each sound because this discrimination was out of the scope of this test. The subjects were also provided with a printout of a table of all the occurring sounds and corresponding common examples in German words to avoid confusion.

6.5.4. Results and discussion

The perceptual results for the vowel area functions are shown in Figure 6.8.

It is evident that the area function model is generally capable to reproduce all reference vowel area functions sufficiently precise to preserve the intelligibility of the corresponding sounds in all tested configurations (full or reduced) and conditions (geometrically fitted or perceptually optimized). However, the geometrically fitted area functions of the lax vowels /ɪ/, /œ/ and /ʏ/ resulted in significantly lower recognition rates than the ones of the tense vowels. Their fairly average geometric errors (see Figure 6.5) and small formant errors (see Table 6.2) may contribute to the confusion, but it is also likely that the references were already not perfectly intelligible, especially since lax vowels are difficult to sustain for the entire 14 s of the recording. Unfortunately, no reference

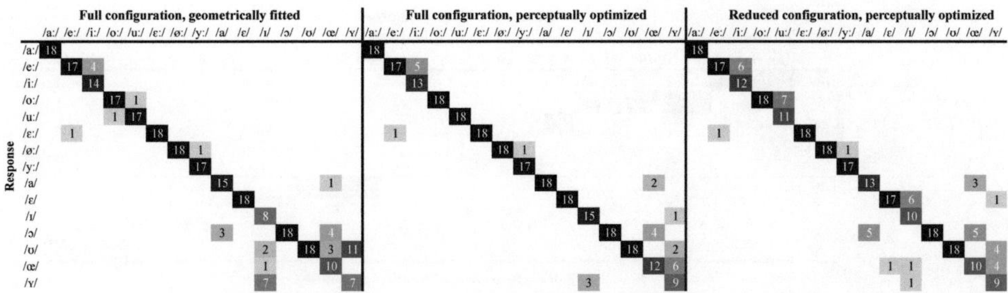

Figure 6.8.: Absolute number of responses for the tense and lax vowels out of $N = 18$ responses per sound. The recognition rate was improved by the perceptual optimization and deteriorated after the parameter reduction, especially for lax vowels.

audio recordings taken simultaneously with the MRI were available due to the noisy environment in the MRI scanner. After the perceptual optimization, the results were somewhat improved, but only for /ɪ/ was the increase in correct responses statistically significant ($p < 0.05$, calculated using Fisher's exact test). The simplifications made to reduce the number of parameters evidently caused a decrease of the intelligibility of several tense and lax vowels, which is in-line with the larger geometric errors shown in Figure 6.5. The global recognition rates were 85.2 % (geometrically fitted full configuration), 90.7 % (perceptually optimized full configuration), and 83 % (perceptually optimized reduced configuration). To put those numbers into perspective, the identification rates of 11 English vowels in a similar listening test using Story's model (see [257]) ranged from 79 % to 87 % depending on the modeled speaker. The comparison should however not be used as a true benchmark since both studies used different sounds (English vs. German vowels) and different modeled speakers. The consonant confusion matrices are shown in Figure 6.9.

The stops, which were modeled by starting with the area function of the context vowel and then inserting the closure, achieved some mixed results: the recognition rate ranged from 0 % to 100 %, depending on the place of articulation and the context vowel. Considering the large influence of coarticulation on stops and the importance of the closure duration and exact timing during the release of the closure and the transition to the vowel, this is probably largely due to the very basic temporal control of the synthesizer chosen here, which does not allow to influence these fine details directly. Also, the voice-onset time was not controlled here, which is another cue for the discrimination of different stops (see, e.g., [274, 275]) and may have adversely affected the recognition rate here. The further loss of control of the transitions caused by the parameter reductions appears to exacerbate these issues as well (with the notable exception of /b(i)/), to the degree that /g/ was hardly identifiable at all.

The lateral approximant /l/ was also rarely recognized in any context for the geometrically fitted area functions. The recognition rate was even worse after the perceptual optimization in the reduced configuration but slightly improved in the full configuration, at least for /l(a)/. However, this sound is generally difficult to synthesize using the acoustic tube model as implemented in VocalTractLab, because it assumes a central air stream with no turns, therefore the flow along the side(s) of the tongue is not accurately modeled. This conceptual shortcoming of the synthesis in general makes it difficult to interpret these results with respect to the capabilities of the area function model.

The labio-dental fricative synthesized using the geometrically fitted area function was only identified correctly in 14.8 % of the responses. It appears that this was caused by improperly placed teeth in the MR images, which are crucial for the correct production of this sound. After correcting the lip opening area during the perceptual optimization the recognition rate surged to 83.3 %. A similar correction improved the recognition rates of the palatal and velar fricatives from 66.7 % to 88.9 % and 55.6 % to 90.7 %, respectively. The alveolar and postalveolar fricatives remained largely unchanged, but it should be noted that the optimization removed the unrealistically small constric-

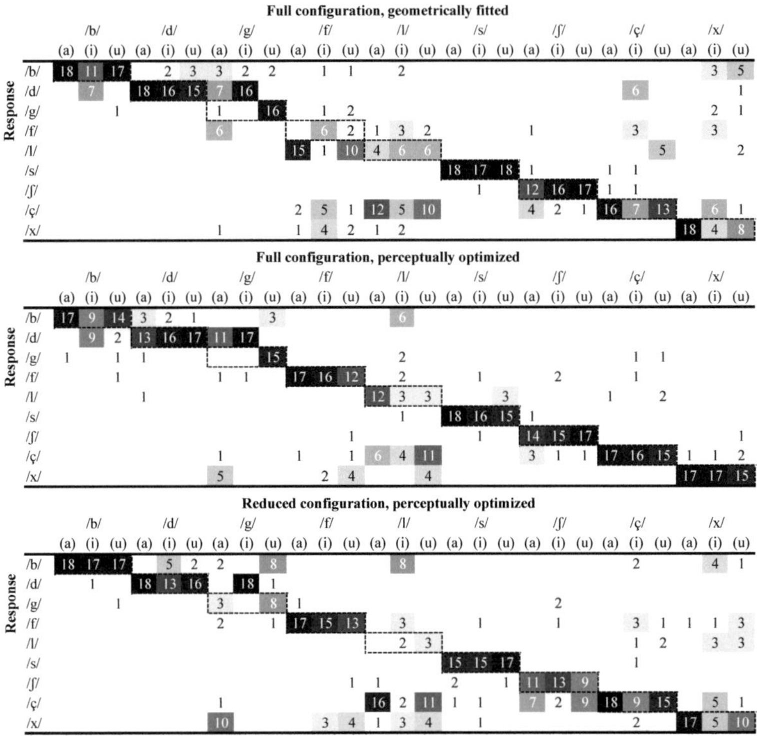

Figure 6.9.: Absolute number of responses for the consonants out of $N = 18$ responses per syllable. The subjects were not asked to identify the context vowel. The recognition rate was greatly improved by the perceptual optimization but deteriorated after the parameter reduction.

tions as described above. For most fricatives, the parameter reduction did not significantly improve and mostly worsened the recognition rate.

The total recognition rates across all consonants of the geometrically fitted full configuration, the perceptually optimized full configuration, and the perceptually optimized reduced configuration of the area functions were 61.2 %, 73.2 %, and 64.1 %, respectively.

6.5.5. Summary

A new 1D vocal tract model for articulatory synthesis of speech sounds was proposed that directly models an arbitrary area function using 16 parameters in a full configuration or 11 parameters in a reduced configuration. The model is conceptually and computationally simple, can be easily implemented with a single, piecewise function, and the control points have interpretable anatomical correspondences allowing manual adjustment of the model according to phonetic standard configurations, even in the absence of any reference data. The model was evaluated based on real vocal tract area functions from MRI image stacks of a male human speaker. After fitting the model to the references and tuning the parameters with respect to the perceptual result, the recognition rate of 15 different German vowel sounds was 90.7 % and of 9 German consonants in 3 different vowel contexts was 73.2 %. The median geometric error between the references and the model functions was 0.891 cm^2 and thus fairly low, while some sounds (especially stops) achieved a low perceptual recognition rate. This shows that the temporal control and coordination of the parameters is very important, especially for stops. The uncontrolled voice-onset time may have also been a major influence on the low recognition rates of the stops. Future work should investigate these relationships further and discard the simplistic cosine interpolation between static shapes used in this work for a more sophisticated control mechanism. The results of the identification tests also show the limitations of the MRI data used in this study: the consonantal shapes were not context-dependent and thus difficult to recognize in some cases. Future studies should therefore adopt a similar approach as in [214] and record consonants in different contexts as references. The parameter reduction should also be investigated further and the effect of each discarded degree of freedom analyzed individually to find the optimum number of free parameters for the model. The model currently does not include a parameter describing the velum. To complete it, further reference vocal tract shapes of nasals including the velo-pharyngeal opening area are needed. All optimal parameter values for each of the configurations (full and reduced) and conditions (geometrically fitted and perceptually optimized) described in this section are provided in Appendix G, and the stimuli used in the listening test are included in the digital supplemental material to this dissertation.

In spite of the open research questions, it has been successfully demonstrated that the proposed six point vocal tract model resolves the remaining issues regarding the use of the VocalTractLab synthesis backend in an ATS system as laid out in section 6.2: The one-dimensional model has only 16 parameters in the full configuration instead of the 23 parameters of the original three-dimensional model [214]. The computational complexity could also be greatly reduced, because no further processing of a three-dimensional model is necessary to eventually arrive at the vocal tract area function, but instead the area function is modeled directly, completely skipping the slow and complex calculations of the cross-sectional areas in 3D space. Finally, both of these simplifications could be achieved with a minimal impact on the intelligibility, as proven by the perception experiment. Therefore, the six point vocal tract model is used in the following section 6.6 as part of an ATS pilot study.

6.6. Direct synthesis using EOS to control the vocal tract model

6.6.1. The concept of direct synthesis

As discussed in section 1.1, an SSI can include a synthesis component that produces the corresponding acoustic result of a sequence of articulator movements. This form of an SSI is also called an ATS. While there is, of course, the possibility to implement an ATS as a two-step system, where an articulatory speech recognizer is followed by a traditional TTS system, the direct mapping of articulatory data to the corresponding acoustic result (i.e., *direct synthesis*) offers a number of advantages. Because all non-linguistic information (e.g., timing or articulatory precision) is part of the input data for the synthesis, all of this para-linguistic information, which can encode the speakers emotional or even physical state (e.g., hasty or slurred speech, or overly enunciated speech), can potentially be preserved by simply synthesizing the speech exactly as intended. However, this is only possible if the synthesizer can actually produce and manipulate such details, which essentially requires an articulatory synthesizer (see section 6.2). Again, a two-step solution could be imagined, e.g., where the first step is recognizing the speaker's emotional state and then using an emotionally expressive synthesis system to convey this state in the synthesized utterance. But research into what exactly encodes information in speech (let alone in articulation) is still on-going (see, e.g., [276] for a recent review) and even if the target emotions were determined, their synthesis is also not yet consistently and convincingly possible to a sufficient degree (see [277]). Direct synthesis using an articulatory synthesizer offers a critical advantage over these two-step solutions, which require both descriptive and generative models of emotion in speech: Speech can be produced from the articulatory movements *without* any knowledge about its contents, both linguistic and para-linguistic. Therefore, anything that is encoded in the articulation will be transferred to the acoustic speech, provided the synthesizer is sufficiently accurate. Without further proof, it can be assumed that the vocal tract model proposed in section 6.3 and the aero-acoustic simulation backend provided by VocalTractLab, is at least in theory able to deliver the necessary accuracy. It is beyond the scope of this dissertation to prove this claim, because VocalTractLab is in under continuous development and must be considered "on its way" to this level of expressiveness. But if it can be shown that the synthesizer can be controlled using the articulatory data, all future improvements of the synthesizer can directly benefit the direct synthesis.

In summary, the concept of direct synthesis as proposed in this dissertation is as follows: The idea is to control the parameters of the vocal tract model in real time using kinematic articulatory data. Since there is no one-to-one mapping from the EOS data to the degrees-of-freedom of the vocal tract model proposed in section 6.3, a more complicated mapping needs to be found. For this mapping, a number of approaches can be taken: the most straight-forward one would be a classification approach that selects a vocal tract model parametrization from a list of defined vocal tract shapes based on the EOS data. This would ensure that only valid shapes are adopted and thus be very robust to noisy measurement data. To synthesize connected speech, however, the database of vocal tract shapes would have to be very large to properly incorporate not only the static articulations but the transitions between sounds, as well. This approach would also be plagued by the same limitations that a two-step solution with a unit-selection synthesis would suffer from: the range of possible outputs would be limited to the samples from the training set and all the expressive potential of the articulatory synthesizer would be lost. So instead of mapping the continuous range of the EOS data to a discrete set of vocal tract shapes, the mapping should therefore be from the continuous range of the EOS data to the continuous range of the vocal tract model parameters, i.e., it should be performed by a regression model of some kind. To explore the feasibility of this approach, a small study was devised that trained four different families of regression models to map average frames of articulatory EOS data recorded during the stationary phase of the articulation of various speech sounds produced by four subjects to the corresponding vocal tract shapes. In an informal evaluation, the mapping was then applied to continuous EOS data from the same subjects to explore the ability of the models to generalize to transitional vocal tract states, as well. This pilot study was also published in [206].

6.6.2. Dataset

The training and evaluation data was recorded using the same subjects as in the small-scale recognition study: four native German speakers, all male, age 30-41. A more diverse and larger set of subjects would of course be desirable. But given the experimental stage, the necessity to produce costly and labor-intensive hardware, and the fact that, for now, only a subject-dependent system was trained, this limitation was deemed acceptable. The recorded dataset consisted of two parts: one subset of recordings to train the mapping from EOS sensor data frames to vocal tract shapes (the training set), and a second subset of recordings to evaluate the mapping on continuous sensor data (the evaluation set).

Training the mapping required example EOS sensor data frames recorded during the articulation of each of the target sounds (or vocal tract shapes), i.e., the German vowels /aː, eː, iː, oː, uː, ɛː, øː, yː, a, ɛ, ɪ, ɔ, ʊ, œ, ʏ/ and consonants /b, d, ɡ, j, ʁ, v, z, ʒ/. To account for the effect of coarticulation (see section 2.5), each target sound was produced in different articulatory contexts. To that end, the subjects were asked to produce a number of pseudowords: The vowel-specific pseudowords had the form /CV_tdə/, where V_t were the tense vowel of interest (i.e., /aː, eː, iː, oː, uː, ɛː, øː, yː/), or /CV_ltə/, where V_l were the lax vowels /a, ɛ, ɪ, ɔ, ʊ, œ, ʏ/. The consonant-specific pseudowords had the form /V_tCV_t/, where V_t were once again the tense vowels. Although lax vowels would also be of interest in the articulatory context, they are very difficult to produce in this manner for untrained subjects and were therefore excluded. Another limitation was the use of only symmetric contexts (same vowel before and after the sound of interest) for the consonants and asymmetric contexts (different consonants before and after the sound of interest) for the vowels. However, including all kinds of contexts would have greatly increased the number of items to record for each subject beyond a reasonable amount. Even with these limitations in place, the numer of recorded items for each subject was 165 vowel pseudowords (15 vowels × 11 context vowels) and 88 consonant pseudowords (11 consonants times 8 tense vowels) for a total 253 unique sound-context-combinations.

The evaluation set consisted of the words from the small-scale recognition study (see Table 5.1) and additionally of 20 sentences from the "Berlin sentences" [278, page 243], which are a set of phonetically balanced German sentences. The list of the sentences used in this study is given in Table 6.3.

	Sentence		Translation
1	Heute ist schönes Frühlingswetter.	hɔ̯ɪtə ɪst ʃøːnəs fʁyːlɪŋsvɛtɐ	It's a nice spring weather today.
2	Die Sonne lacht.	diː zɔnə laxt	The sun is smiling.
3	Am blauen Himmel ziehen die Wolken.	am bla̯ʊən hɪml̩ t͡siːn diː vɔlkn̩	Clouds are moving across a blue sky.
4	Über die Felder weht ein Wind.	yːbɐ diː fɛldɐ veːt a̯ɪn vɪnt	A wind is blowing through the fields.
5	Gestern stürmte es noch.	ɡɛstɐn ʃtyːʁmtə ɛs nɔx	It was still stormy just a day ago.
6	Montag war es uns zu regnerisch.	moːntaːk vaːɐ̯ ɛs ʊns t͡suː ʁeːɡnəʁɪʃ	Monday was too rainy for us.
7	Riecht ihr nicht die frische Luft?	ʁiːçt ɪɐ̯ nɪxt diː fʁɪʃə lʊft	Can't you smell the fresh air?
8	Die Nacht haben Maiers gut geschlafen.	diː naxt habm̩ ma̯ɪɐs guːt ɡəʃlaːfn̩	The Maiers slept well last night.
9	Jetzt sitzen sie beim Frühstück.	jɛt͡st zɪt͡sn̩ ziː ba̯ɪm fʁyːʃtʏk	Now they are having breakfast.
10	Es ist acht Uhr morgens.	ɛs ɪst axt uːɐ̯ mɔʁɡn̩s	It is eight o'clock in the morning.
11	Vater hat den Tisch gedeckt.	faːtɐ hat deːn tɪʃ ɡədɛkt	Father has set the table.
12	Mutter konnte länger schlafen.	mʊtɐ kɔntə lɛŋɐ ʃlaːfn̩	Mother could sleep in.
13	Der Kaffee dampft in den Tassen.	deːɐ̯ kafeː damp͡ft ɪn deːn tasn̩	The coffee is steaming in the cups.
14	Messer und Gabel liegen neben dem Teller.	mɛsɐ ʊnt ɡaːbl̩ lɪɡŋ̍ neːbm̩ deːm tɛlɐ	Knife and fork are sitting next to the plate.
15	In der Mitte steht ein Brötchenkorb.	ɪn deːɐ̯ mɪtə ʃteːt a̯ɪn brøːtçənkɔʁb	In the center, there is a bread basket.
16	Wer möchte keinen Kuchen?	veːɐ̯ mœçtə ka̯ɪnən kʊxn̩	Who does not want any cake?
17	Hans isst so gerne Wurst.	hans ɪst zoː ɡeːɐ̯nə vʊʁst	Hans really likes to eat sausage.
18	Gib mir bitte die Butter!	ɡɪp miːɐ̯ bɪte diː bʊtɐ	Please pass me the butter!
19	Bald ist der Hunger gestillt.	balt ɪst deːɐ̯ hʊŋɐ ɡəʃtɪlt	Soon the hunger is sated.
20	Wer möchte noch Milch?	veːɐ̯ mœçtə nɔx mɪlç	Who wants some milk?

Table 6.3.: Standard pronunciation of the sentences used in the ATS study (according to [49]).

Note that both words and sentences contained voiceless sounds, while the training utterances only included voiced sounds. Since EOS currently captures only supraglottal articulation, the distinction between voiced and voiceless sounds was not made in this study. So even in a best-case scenario, the utterances in the evaluation set would sound entirely voiced. As will be shown in section 6.7, this limitation is, however, not necessarily required even when capturing only supraglottal articulation, if the measured data are sufficiently precise. Still, it was imposed here to keep the setup as simple as possible.

The data was collected in the same session as the data for the small-scale recognition study and the measurement therefore followed the same protocol using the software "Second Voice PC" (see subsection 4.6.4), a Plantronics Blackwire C720 M stereo headset (for reference audio) and an EOS device with the internal version number 3.2 using a sensor unit with 32 contact sensors, five optical tongue distance sensors, and the dual-source, dual-detector lip sensor design. The recordings were made in a quiet office environment. The speakers were prompted to read a carrier word (the German indefinite article "eine" - /ˈa̯ɪnə/) followed by the (pseudo-) word of interest. The schwa /ə/ at the end of the carrier word ensured a neutral vocal tract configuration at the beginning of the word of interest. In case of the sentences, there was no carrier word and the prompts were shown at a slow-enough pace so that several seconds of (articulatory) silence clearly marked the space in-between the items. The words were produced in a natural way, i.e., with phonation and at an unregulated speaking rate of each speaker's individual choice. The words in the evaluation set were the same ones used in the small-scale command word recognition study and were segmented in the same way (see section 5.3). The sentences were cut out of the continuous recording starting at the time instant just before articulatory movements were visible in the EOS data stream up to the point of post-sentence silence in the audio stream. From the sound of interest in each training utterance, a segment of about 100 ms for the tense vowels and about 50 ms for the consonants and lax vowels was extracted, which was approximately stationary in terms of articulatory movements. If no stationary segment of this length was identifiable, the longest possible segment was extracted from the center of the sound of interest. From this segment, the median frame was extracted. The feature vector used as input for the mapping was also the same vector as used in the recognition study, consisting of the ADC data of the 2 lip sensor detectors, 5 distance sensor values, and 3 factors describing the contact pattern for a total of 10 features per vector. In contrast to the small-scale recognition study, the distance sensor value format (raw ADC values or converted to millimeter) was not treated as a hyperparameter because no cross-speaker training or evaluation took place and a calibration was thus considered unnecessary.

6.6.3. Regression models

To illustrate the approach in a loosely formalized way, let the desired mapping from the continuous sensor data $\vec{s}$ to the continuous vocal tract shape (described by its cross-sectional area function) $A(x)$ be a called g:

$$A(x) = g\left(\vec{s}\right). \tag{6.2}$$

Using the six point vocal tract model defined in section 6.3, we can also describe the area function $A(x)$ as a function f of the vocal tract model parameters and the location x along the vocal tract center line:

$$A(x) = f\left(x, x_{\text{lar}}, A_{\text{lar}}, \ldots, A_{\text{lip}}\right) = g\left(\vec{s}\right). \tag{6.3}$$

The function f is the six point vocal tract model. Therefore, mapping the sensor data to the vocal tract shape can be accomplished by finding a mapping from the sensor data $\vec{s}$ to the model parameters $\left(x_{\text{lar}}, A_{\text{lar}}, \ldots, A_{\text{lip}}\right)$:

$$h\left(\vec{s}\right) = \left(x_{\text{lar}}, A_{\text{lar}}, \ldots, A_{\text{lip}}\right). \tag{6.4}$$

Since the analysis of the vocal tract model parameters in section 6.3 has shown little inter-dependency of the parameters, this vector function h can be decomposed into its individual components, so that the 10-to-16 mapping becomes a set of 16 10-to-1 mappings, each using the sensor data as input and only one of the model parameters as output:

$$h_{x_{\text{lar}}}\left(\vec{s}\right) = x_{\text{lar}} \tag{6.5}$$

$$h_{A_{\text{lar}}}\left(\vec{s}\right) = A_{\text{lar}} \tag{6.6}$$

$$\vdots$$

$$h_{A_{\text{lip}}}\left(\vec{s}\right) = A_{\text{lip}}. \tag{6.7}$$

Each of these mappings could be provided by a different kind of regression model. For this study, four families of models were therefore investigated, for each mapping independently, using the Statistics and Machine Learning Toolbox in Matlab 2019b: linear models (linear regression using L^2 (ridge) and L^1 (LASSO) regularization, and a linear SVM), linear and non-linear SVMs, ensemble models of random trees (using both bagging and boosting as the ensemble meta-algorithm), and Gaussian Process Regression (GPR). Each model was trained on the training set and 5-fold cross-validated to optimize the respective hyperparameters using Bayes optimization and 100 iterations. The optimized hyperparameters are listed in Table 6.4. The 5-fold loss from this training step for the optimal hyperparameter combination was the objective measure for the prediction accuracy. To allow a subjective evaluation, each model was trained again using the previously identified optimal hyperparameters and a leave-one-out cross-validation (where “one” means one sound-context-combination) to produce predicted area function model parameters based on data unseen in the training. These predictions were then used to synthesize sounds, which could be acoustically evaluated. Finally, the best model was determined individually for each parameter (based solely on the objective measure of 5-fold loss), and used to predict the vocal tract shape trajectories based on the EOS data from the evaluation set (both words and sentences). These trajectories were then synthesized to allow acoustic, subjective evaluation, but because of the lack of known target trajectories, no objective error measure could be calculated.

Model	Hyperparameter	Evaluated values/range
Linear models	Learner	{least-squares, linear SVM}
	Lambda	log-scaled in $\left[4 \times 10^{-8}, 4 \times 10^{8}\right]$
	Regularization	{ridge, LASSO}
	Standardize predictors	yes
Non-linear SVMs	Box constraint C	log-scaled in $\left[1 \times 10^{-3}, 1 \times 10^{3}\right]$
	Slack variable ε	log-scaled in $\left[1 \times 10^{-3}, 1 \times 10^{2} \cdot \mathrm{IQR}\,(y)\right]$
	Kernel function	{linear, Gaussian, polynomial}
	Kernel scale γ	log-scaled in $\left[1 \times 10^{-3}, 1 \times 10^{2}\right]$
	Polynomial order	$\{2, 3, 4\}$
	Standardize predictors	{yes, no}
Ensemble trees	Ensemble meta-algorithm	{bagging, boosting}
	Number of learning cycles	integer in $[10, 500]$
	Learning rate	log-scaled in $\left[1 \times 10^{-3}, 1\right]$
	Minimum leaf size	log-scaled in $[1, 126]$
	Maximum number of splits	integers in $[1, 252]$
	Number of variables to sample	integers in $[1, 10]$
GPR	Basis function	{constant, none, linear, pure quadratic}
	Kernel function	{exponential, squared exponential, Matern kernel (3/2 and 5/2), rational quadratic} plus each kernel with separate length scale per predictor
	Kernel scale	$\left[1 \times 10^{-3} \cdot s_{\max}, s_{\max}\right]$ (where $s_{\max}$ is the maximum predictor range)
	Noise standard deviation σ	$\left[1 \times 10^{-4}, \max(1 \times 10^{-3}, 10 \cdot \sigma_y)\right]$ (where σ_y is the standard deviation of the predicted area function parameter)
	Standardize predictors	{yes, no}

Table 6.4.: Optimized hyperparameters of the investigated regression models

6.6.4. Results

All models were trained on the subset of data from each subject individually. The results of the hyperparameter optimization in terms of the 5-fold loss are shown in Table 6.5. The respective optimal hyperparameter values are given in Appendix H.

The subject-dependent results show that for all area function model parameters, non-linear models should generally be preferred over linear least-squares models. The differences across the non-linear models are, however, mostly fairly small. Nevertheless, GPR and ensemble models of regression trees were generally the best-performing ones (in that order), with SVMs a close second. The averaged best performance across the four subjects was $\mu_{\text{best}} = 0.7433$ with a standard deviation of $\sigma_{\text{best}} = 0.065$. The overall best performance with the lowest average 5-fold loss across all area function parameters was subject 4.

Since the loss as an objective metric is hard to relate to the perceived quality of the synthesis, a series of informal listening tests was performed. To realistically evaluate the synthesis quality, the identified optimal hyperparameters were used to train one more model from each evaluated family for each subject and area function parameter, and each sound-context combination in a leave-one-out paradigm. All parameter sets predicted in this way are provided as text files (file extension ".params") in the digital supplemental materials to this dissertation and can be loaded in the Second Voice PC software (see subsection 4.6.4) to synthesize the corresponding audio. To give an impression of the range of the quality, synthesized samples using optimal GPR models of each target sound for subject 1 (the worst average loss) and subject 4 (the best average loss) are also provided as WAVE files. Listening to these isolated sounds, which are based on data frames from the same recording session as the training data and whose only challenging property is the different context sound, it was immediately obvious that vowels would be fairly well identifiable,

Parameter	Subject 1 Linear models	Subject 1 Ensemble	Subject 1 SVMs	Subject 1 GPR	Subject 2 Linear models	Subject 2 Ensemble	Subject 2 SVMs	Subject 2 GPR	Subject 3 Linear models	Subject 3 Ensemble	Subject 3 SVMs	Subject 3 GPR	Subject 4 Linear models	Subject 4 Ensemble	Subject 4 SVMs	Subject 4 GPR
x_{lar}	0.3931	0.3823	0.3613	0.3697	0.4065	0.3588	0.3230	0.3034	0.3553	0.3052	0.3527	0.2677	0.3992	0.3300	0.3395	0.2529
A_{lar}	0.1663	0.1184	0.1541	0.1285	0.1605	0.1176	0.1269	0.1170	0.1531	0.1088	0.1373	0.1145	0.1616	0.1050	0.1240	0.1054
n_{lar}	0.9320	0.8263	0.7208	0.7327	0.9384	0.6212	0.7553	0.6493	0.8674	0.5814	0.5595	0.5735	0.9195	0.5200	0.7195	0.5026
x_p	0.9772	0.9035	0.9390	0.7966	0.9493	0.7878	0.8255	0.7569	0.9136	0.6379	0.7258	0.5824	0.9308	0.5992	0.7461	0.5622
A_p	1.4231	1.2905	1.2404	1.1237	1.3374	1.3130	1.3579	1.2022	1.3115	1.0387	1.2109	1.1414	1.2232	1.1949	1.0407	1.0265
n_p	1.3183	0.8847	0.9998	0.9301	1.2480	0.9872	0.9498	0.8643	1.2617	0.8528	1.0538	0.8942	1.2437	0.8446	0.7636	0.9604
x_c	1.5313	1.3173	1.3010	1.3058	1.4858	1.2369	1.3627	1.2067	1.4545	1.1806	1.2658	1.0381	1.2829	1.0878	1.2589	1.0166
A_c	0.2463	0.1983	0.2082	0.2010	0.3020	0.2721	0.2650	0.2546	0.2852	0.2142	0.1948	0.2165	0.3106	0.1760	0.2001	0.1768
n_c	0.7884	0.7904	0.6865	0.7462	0.8043	0.6947	0.7280	0.6468	0.8138	0.7860	0.7355	0.6623	0.8305	0.5831	0.4807	0.4538
x_a	1.2904	1.2404	1.1116	1.1932	1.2505	1.2417	1.2683	1.2363	1.2332	1.1396	1.2930	1.1092	1.2465	0.8597	0.8054	0.9035
A_a	2.1235	1.8832	2.0819	2.0255	2.0760	1.9899	2.0492	2.0454	2.1722	1.8650	2.0612	1.8420	2.1155	1.6210	1.6217	1.6266
n_a	1.6526	1.2585	1.3281	1.1708	1.6211	0.9492	1.3946	0.9928	1.5609	1.2044	1.1287	1.2086	1.6360	1.1817	1.2074	1.2339
x_{in}	0.7160	0.5545	0.6171	0.6057	0.6307	0.6125	0.6187	0.5810	0.6385	0.4961	0.6289	0.4937	0.5834	0.5082	0.4654	0.4969
A_{in}	0.6463	0.4487	0.4950	0.4304	0.6235	0.5454	0.6232	0.4803	0.6491	0.3778	0.4777	0.4850	0.5472	0.4220	0.4967	0.4707
x_{lip}	0.7717	0.5597	0.6635	0.6556	0.6045	0.5329	0.5915	0.5912	0.6615	0.4930	0.6511	0.5685	0.5855	0.4645	0.4298	0.4505
A_{lip}	0.6937	0.5055	0.5256	0.5083	0.5660	0.5163	0.5592	0.5283	0.5696	0.3603	0.3986	0.4322	0.5089	0.3556	0.3030	0.3234
Mean	0.9794	0.8226	0.8396	0.8077	0.9378	0.7986	0.8624	0.7785	0.9313	0.7276	0.8047	0.7269	0.9078	0.6783	0.6876	0.6602

Table 6.5.: Subject-dependent cross-validation results (in terms of the 5-fold loss) using the optimal hyperparameters for each model. The highlighted cells contain the subject-related minimum loss across the investigated models for this area function parameter.

but consonants would not be intelligible at all. Instead of identifying the place of articulation (as in normal consonant perception), only the context vowel was perceived. Given this poor quality, the evaluation on the words and sentences was limited to the objectively best-performing subject 4. Using all available data from this subject's training set, an optimal model was trained for each area function parameter (i.e., the highlighted models in Table 6.5 using their respective optimal hyperparameters from Appendix H). Then, using the recorded data of subject 4's evaluation set, the area function model parameters were predicted frame-by-frame and the audio signal was predicted in 10 ms increments using the function `vtlTubeSynthesisAdd` from the VocalTractLab 2.2 Application Programming Interface (API). The results (also provided in the digital supplemental materials) were also informally evaluated and confirmed the initial impressions from the leave-one-out evaluation on the training set: the synthesized result is almost entirely vocalic and hardly any consonants can be heard, with the notable exception of some occasional stops. Given the overall very poor quality of the synthesis, a formal listening test with a large number of naive participants was not conducted.

Despite the fairly low regression error averaged across all target sounds, the synthesis results for words and sentences were very poor, which was probably due to the poor intelligibility of consonants, which were not even reliably synthesized in the leave-one-out cross-validation using the training data. The most likely explanation for this is the coarticulatory effect of the context vowels (see section 2.5) on the adjacent consonant. This is very apparent in the low-dimensional projections of the EOS training data in Figure 6.10.

6.6.5. Discussion

The *t*-SNE projections show that the EOS frames containing a particular target consonant were more similar to EOS frames containing that consonant's context vowel than to EOS frames containing the same consonant (but with a different context vowel). The EOS frames containing vowels, on the other hand, were mostly similar to one another and not as strongly affected by their context consonants. This means that the vowel subset of the training data contained fairly compact (high-dimensional) clusters, one for each vowel, and the context consonants introduced only a modest amount of noise. For the consonants, however, the training data did not contain any clusters, which means that any consonant-context combination would need its own target area function shape, and that there was only a single instance of each co-articulated consonant for the models to learn from. To remedy these issues, co-articulated area function shapes for all target consonants and contexts would be required. Therefore a very large database of MRI images would have to be recorded to obtain the target area function parameters as described in section 6.4. Given the number of possible coarticulatory contexts (even if only considering symmetric contexts), this approach appears infeasible. As an alternative, coarticulated shapes of each consonant could be manually produced,

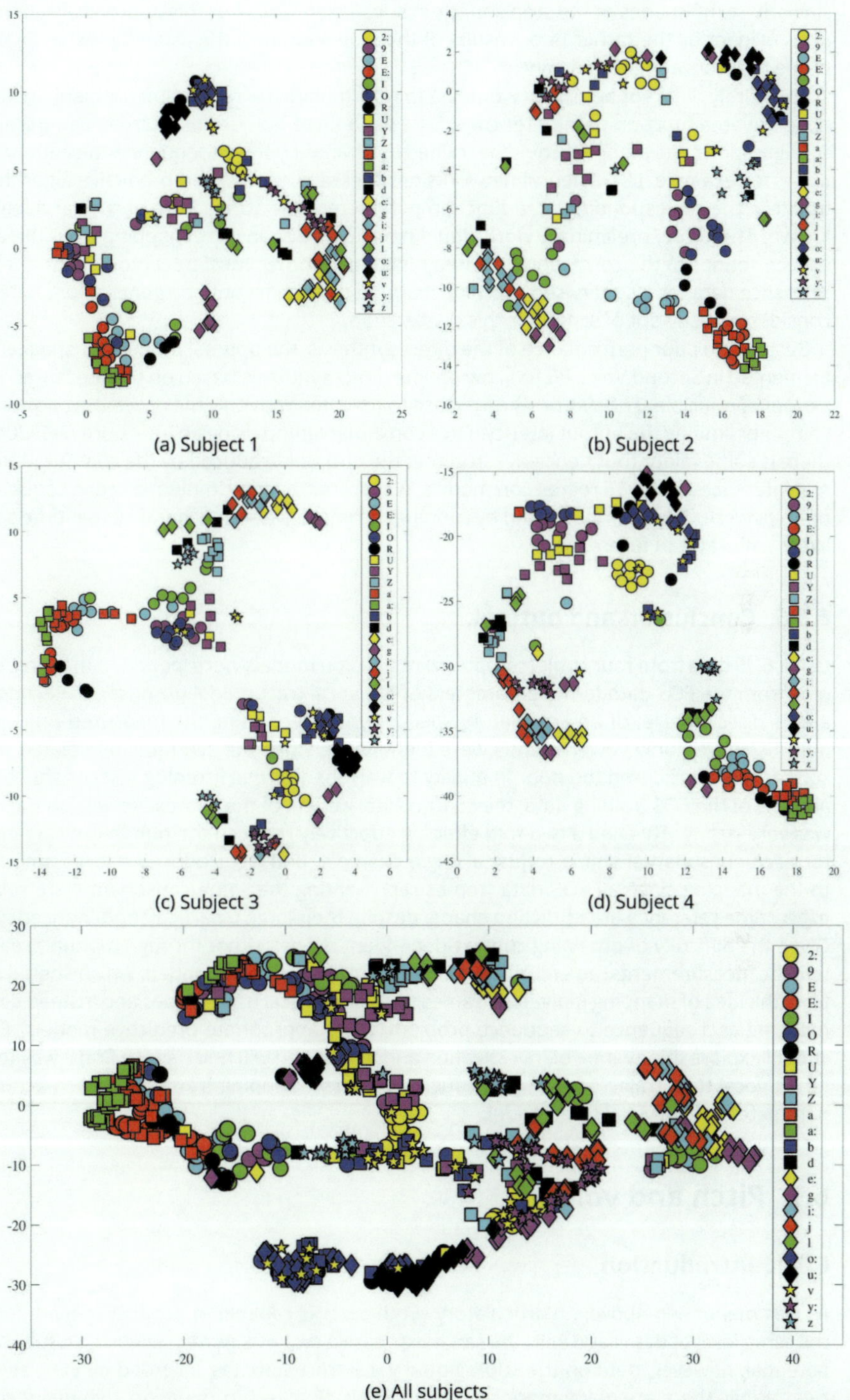

(a) Subject 1 (b) Subject 2

(c) Subject 3 (d) Subject 4

(e) All subjects

Figure 6.10.: Low-dimensional projection of the high-dimensional training data (using *t*-SNE) for the four subjects

similarly to the shapes of the stop sounds in subsection 6.5.2, but this approach is also challenging (as is evident by the rather poor results of the stop sounds in the listening test in Figure 6.9) and prone to errors and inconsistencies.

An entirely different approach would be to reformulate the regression problem: Instead of sampling the area function parameter trajectories at a finite number of discrete, canonical vocal tract configurations, the mapping could be trained in a frame-by-frame sequence-to-sequence paradigm using, for example, LSTM neural networks or other sequence-based predictive algorithms. Unfortunately, the corresponding area function parameter trajectories for a particular speaker are unknown. Therefore, preliminary work would have to find an inverse mapping from the acoustics of speech sounds to the corresponding area function (or other vocal tract model) parameters so that reference data for a supervised machine learning algorithm could be generated. This is, however, considered vastly out of scope for this dissertation.

Despite the poor performance of the direct synthesis, the optimal models for speaker 4 were implemented in Second Voice PC to allow on-line direct synthesis based on the measured EOS data as a proof of principle. The synthesis runs close to real-time with only the processing power of the host computer limiting the output latency. On a consumer laptop using an Intel Core i7-3520M (2.9 GHz), there is some minor (but noticable) stutter in the output introduced by the computationally expensive inferences of the 16 regression models, which are currently implemented in sequence. Using a more powerful host computer and by running the inference step in parallel, real-time speed is very likely achievable in future work.

6.6.6. Conclusion and outlook

Using EOS data from four subjects, optimal regression models were identified that provided a mapping from the EOS data to the parameters of the vocal tract model proposed in section 6.3, which allows direct control of an articulatory speech synthesizer using the measured articulatory input data. However, only vowel sounds were identifiable, while the synthesis of isolated consonantal sounds was considered too poor in quality to warrant a formal listening test. As shown by a *t*-SNE analysis of the EOS training data, the coarticulatory effect of the context vowels on the consonants was very strong. This had a two-fold effect: it effectively reduced the number of training instances for each consonantal shape to just a single example, and it introduced a large amount of noise to the mapping since all EOS data frames representing the same consonant were related to the exact same reference area function shape, despite their large (coarticulation-induced) differences. Given the difficulty of obtaining context-dependent shapes either through manual creation or systematic measurements, an entirely different approach is recommended, which should move away from the idea of mapping individual frames to discrete vocal tract shapes and instead considers the mapping as a sequence-to-sequence problem, using appropriate predictive models. Future work should explore this avenue of investigation and to that end will first have to find a way to obtain the target vocal tract trajectories, e.g., through an inverse mapping from the speech acoustics to the parameters of the vocal tract model.

6.7. Pitch and voicing

6.7.1. Introduction

As was mentioned above, an articulatory synthesizer is capable of producing synthetic speech at the same level of detail and with the same expressive range as human speech. To fully harness this potential, however, data on the supraglottal vocal tract state (as recorded by EOS) seems insufficient. While there are many more layers and levels of speech production, two major components shall be discussed in this section in greater detail: the f_0 contour of an utterance over time (i.e., the intonation), and the distinction between voiced and voiceless sounds (i.e., the voicing). Based on phonetic knowledge (see chapter 2), it should not be possible to derive either of these components from supraglottal articulation alone but would necessitate glottal, or at least laryngeal, information on the vocal tract excitation source, as well. However, in a truly silent system, there is no active excitation that could be measured. This leaves two options: a manual control of these features or a (somewhat phonetic theory-defying) prediction based on the trajectories of the supraglottal articulatory data, under the assumption that the temporal patterns of fluent speech may hold latent information that could be used for the prediction of voicing and intonation.

In the remainder of this section, both of these approaches are investigated in two proof-of-principle studies. The two respective research questions were as follows:

1. Can a human user learn to manually control the intonation of an utterance in a way that produces natural sounding speech?

2. Can intonation and voicing be predicted based on supraglottal articulatory information alone?

Both studies aimed at eliminating all factors not directly connected to these questions to investigate the feasibility of the respective approach on principle, not necessarily only when using EOS or the six point vocal tract model. Therefore, instead of using the ATS system proposed in section 6.6, generated intonation patterns were impressed on natural speech material to minimize perceived quality due to synthesis artifacts. To avoid a large impact of possible shortcomings of the precision or accuracy of EOS data, the gold-standard in articulometry, EMA (see section 3.7), was used to investigate the second question. Even though the results in both cases are therefore not immediately applicable outside of a lab setting, they set an upper limit for what seems feasible. The manual intonation control study was also published in [279] and the study on predicting intonation and voicing was published in [280]. Both studies were conducted in cooperation with two students as part of their respective theses, which are cited were applicable.

6.7.2. Manual intonation control

In human speech, numerous prosodic features encode diverse information ranging from the speaker's intention (e.g., [281,282]) to their emotional state (e.g., [283,284]). The absence of prosody in a synthesized utterance therefore immediately degrades the perceived naturalness and thus the quality of the synthesis. One major prosodic feature is the change of the fundamental frequency f_0 over time. Current text-to-speech systems (e.g., MARY TTS [285]) derive the intonation from a combination of prosody rules based on parts-of-speech tagging and punctuation information. While this technique yields satisfying results, it requires the use of a labeling system (e.g., the German Tones and Break Indices (GToBi) [286]) to mark up the text or phonetic representation of the desired utterance. However, in systems where the synthesis is directly driven by acoustic or articulatory features, this information is not available unless explicitly passed as an additional feature. Because our system does not use any text or linguistic representation of the articulated speech, rule-based or parts-of-speech approaches are immediately disqualified. Instead, the user of the system could provide the time-varying f_0 contour manually, on-line and in real-time. The direct approach to obtain the contour from the user would be to let them "direct" the speech like a director would lead a choir or orchestra, using finger and hand gestures corresponding to pitch accents or tone height. In fact, systems based on this approach exist in the context of the so-called "performative voice synthesis" (e.g., [287]). As the name of these systems suggest, they are however exclusively used in artistic performances and for educational or edutainment purposes. Because of the constant cognitive load of directly controlling the f_0 contour, a generative intonation model is required that only requires the user's attention at critical moments during an utterance or phrase.

Numerous f_0 models exist and among the most commonly used in speech synthesis are the Tilt Model by [288], the Target Approximation Model (TAM) by Xu [289, 290], and the Fujisaki Model [291]. The Tilt Model is purely mathematical, in the sense that there are no underlying motivations from physiological processes during speech production. It is essentially a concatenation of parameterized curve segments to obtain any desired intonation trajectory. The user sets the duration, amplitude and tilt of each segment sequentially. While this allows total freedom in the creation of the intonation, there is also no way to limit this technique to guarantee realistic or at least physiologically possible trajectories. In contrast, the TAM is physiologically motivated. In [289], the authors describe their model as the simulation of "the effects of the aggregated force of the laryngeal controls". It uses syllable-based pitch targets, set by the user, that can either be constant (a static f_0 level) or dynamic (a linearly rising or falling target f_0). The pitch targets of an utterance are concatenated and then passed to the model, which generates the intonation curve by asymptotically approximating the target using an exponential function. By imposing reasonable limitations onto the parameters, the model will therefore always generate realistic intonation curves and artifacts can mostly be avoided. However, both the Tilt and the Target Approximation Model are based on sequentially concatenating segments (of the f_0 curve directly or of the f_0 targets, respectively). In a real-time system, this demands a lot of planning and precise control by the user, since they have limited possibilities to correct themselves once the segment has been parameterized.

The Fujisaki model, on the other hand, is superpositional in nature. The motivation for this parallel approach, according to [292], is that the variation of the f_0 in speech is caused by the cricothyroid muscle moving the thyroid cartilage, which in turn changes the tension of the vocal folds that are attached to it and, consequently, the f_0. This movement has two degrees of freedom (translation and rotation) and thus can be described by two components that are independent of one another: a phrase component and an accent component. These components are the responses of critically-damped second-order low-pass filters to an impulse (the phrase command) as given by

$$G_p(t) = \begin{cases} \alpha^2 t e^{-\alpha t} & t \geq 0 \\ 0 & t < 0, \end{cases} \tag{6.8}$$

where α is the time constant of the phrase component, or to a step-wise function (the accent command) as given by

$$G_a(t) = \begin{cases} \min(1 - (1 + \beta t) e^{-\beta t}, \gamma) & t \geq 0 \\ 0 & t < 0, \end{cases} \tag{6.9}$$

where β is the time constant and γ is the ceiling level of the accent component. The generated components are summed up and then added to a logarithmic base frequency to calculate the final, logarithmic f_0. As the example in Figure 6.11 shows, even complex f_0 contours can be generated with just a few commands.

Table 6.6 summarizes the properties of the three models introduced above. Even for a simple contour, the curve segments in the Tilt Model are too complicated and unintuitive for the user to parameterize in real-time and the model's non-physiological background may lead to very unnatural sounding contours, when non-optimal parameters are chosen. The TAM should generally produce natural sounding contours and may be a good choice for simple contours (e.g., a continuously declining f_0), but becomes much more difficult to handle in real-time if used to generate more complex contours involving accents. The Fujisaki model, however, only needs a single parameter for a basic, declining contour and only two more for each accent. More detailed contours can easily be generated by superimposing simple contours. Therefore, it is the most suitable for the purpose of a real-time intonation generator with minimal cognitive overhead for the user.

	Tilt Model	**Target Approximation Model**	**Fujisaki Model**
Motivation	purely mathematical	physiological	physiological
Elements	pitch events	syllables	phrases and accents
Contour generation	sequential	sequential	superpositional
Parameters	3 (per element)	3 (per element)	2 per phrase, 3 per accent

Table 6.6.: Comparison of three intonation models commonly used in speech synthesis

To evaluate the feasibility of manipulating the intonation of an utterance in real-time, a soft-

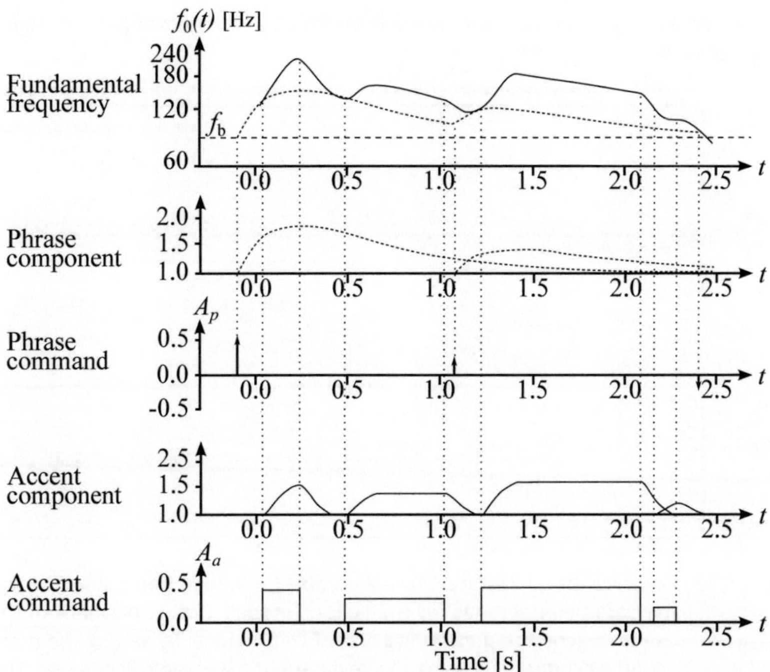

Figure 6.11.: The Fujisaki intonation model (figure recreated from [292]): The final f_0 contour is a superposition of a phrase component and an accent component. The phrase component is generated as the response of a critically-damped second-order lowpass filter to sequence of (weighted) impulses (the phrase commands A_p) and the accent component is the response of another critically-damped second-order low-pass to a step-wise function of varying height and width (the accent commands A_p). The components are summed up and added to a base frequency f_b in the logarithmic domain to obtain the final contour.

ware called Wearable Intonation Generator (WIG) was developed by Konrad Schulze as part of his student's thesis [293] using the C++ library wxWidgets (version 2.8.12, `www.wxwidgets.org`). The software consists of a graphical user interface (see Figure 6.12) that allows the user to load a wave file into the program buffer. After pressing the "Play Sound" button, the file is played back and the user can manipulate the intonation contour using the Fujisaki model, which is then impressed on the played-back utterance in real-time using a Time Domain Pitch-Synchronous Overlap and Add (TD-PSOLA) algorithm. The control of the Fujisaki model is further simplified by setting the parameters α, β and γ and the phrase and accent command magnitudes for the entire utterance using the settings tab. Because the Fujisaki model is superpositional, the user can reclaim some of the freedom that is lost due to the static parameters by "stacking" several commands, which is not possible with the other models. While this restricts the shape of the components that can be generated, it reduces the entire control of the intonation generation to setting the timing of the commands using only two buttons: one to trigger a phrase command (an impulse) and one to trigger an accent command (push to step up, hold, release to step down). The software supports two input modalities to use as these controls: the keyboard (Spacebar for phrase, Strg for accent commands) or the mouse (left button for phrase, right button for accent commands). Since the system is intended to be used as a component in a wearable speech synthesis system, WIG also supports the use of the wireless Mycestro 3D mouse (`www.mycestro.com`), which is a small device that is strapped to one of the user's index fingers and communicates with the PC via Bluetooth. The Mycestro mouse supports three buttons and a scroll wheel, of which only two buttons (left and right) are needed to control the WIG.

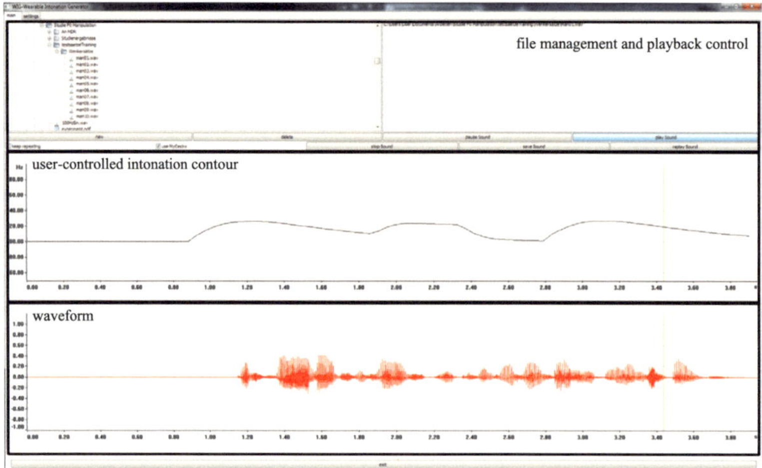

Figure 6.12.: Graphical user interface of the Wearable Intonation Generator. The settings tab hides the parameter settings for the Fujisaki model. During playback of the wave file, the user can generate phrase and accent components by setting the timing of the corresponding commands using the keyboard or a wearable 3D mouse. The f_0 of the wave file is manipulated on-line using a TD-PSOLA algorithm.

Even though only two buttons are needed to create even complex f_0 contours, the task to give the commands on-line and in real-time is unusual for the user and requires a usability test. A study was therefore designed with 16 subjects (native-level German speakers, age 21-30) who were asked to manipulate the f_0 contours of 10 German sentences (based on the Wenker sentences used in [294], see Table 6.7). The sentences were recorded with a professional male speaker and their intonation flattened to a constant f_0 of 100 Hz using the software Praat [176]. As mentioned above, this approach was chosen over a (unit selection or articulatory) synthesis of the sentences with a constant f_0 because the introduction of additional unnaturalness due to synthesis artifacts was to be avoided. It also provided a truly natural sample for reference during the rating part.

	German	English translation
1.	Das Feuer war zu heiß, die Kuchen sind ja unten ganz schwarz.	The fire was too hot, the cakes are all black on the bottom.
2.	Wem hat er denn die neue Geschichte erzählt?	Whom did he tell the new story?
3.	Ihr dürft nicht solche Kindereien treiben!	You should not horse around!
4.	Das war recht von Ihnen!	You did good!
5.	Ich bin mit den Leuten da hinten über die Wiese ins Korn gefahren.	I drove with the people over there across the meadow into the field.
6.	Wir sind müde und haben Durst.	We are tired and thirsty.
7.	Es hört gleich auf zu schneien, dann wird das Wetter wieder besser	It is going to stop snowing soon, then the weather will improve again.
8.	Wie viel Pfund Wurst und wie viel Brot wollt ihr haben?	How many pounds of sausage and how much bread do you want?
9.	Ich verstehe euch nicht, ihr müsst ein bisschen lauter sprechen.	I don't understand you, you have to speak a little louder.
10.	Er ist vor vier oder sechs Wochen gestorben.	He died four or six weeks ago.

Table 6.7.: List of German test sentences used in the usability study and their English translation for reference

In preparation of the experiment, each subject was asked to familiarize themselves with the controls of the software using it with a standard desktop mouse on their own computer and by manipulating a continuous 100 Hz sine tone. During the experiment, each subject used the lab computer and the Mycestro 3D mouse. In order to avoid mistakes due to the use of this unusual input device, each subject did a little exercise where they had to repeatedly click with the 3D mouse into a specific cell of a spreadsheet. Once they were comfortable with the handling of the device, each subject was presented with one of the 10 monotone sentences and was asked to manipulate the intonation in real-time during playback to make it sound more natural. If they were not satisfied with the result of a manipulation, they were allowed to try again with the same sentence. Once the subject was content with the result or after a maximum allowed manipulation time of three minutes, the last generated contour and the corresponding manipulated audio file were saved and the experiment continued with the next sentence. The order in which the sentences were presented was randomized for each subject. After all 160 manipulations (16 subjects times 10 sentences) had been made, the entire set of 160 manipulated audio files plus the 10 original recordings (with a natural intonation) and the 10 recordings with a flattened intonation was rated by each subject on a naturalness scale from 1 (totally unnatural) to 5 (totally natural).

For each subject, 10 manipulations were rated. Calculating the global mean across all 10 manipulations would potentially yield large standard deviations (SDs), since some of the sentences may have been easier to manipulate than others. So instead of the global mean and SD, the mean and SD of the ratings of each manipulation were calculated. Since every manipulation produced by a subject is a manifestation of that subject's ability to use the system efficiently, this proficiency could be regarded as a stochastic process and the manipulation as a realization from that process. To characterize each subject's ability to produce natural sounding contours, a naturalness score ν was calculated by combining the means and standard deviations across the manipulated samples from each subject by iteratively multiplying the corresponding (presumably) Gaussian density functions. The result of each multiplication of a distribution with a mean μ_i and an SD σ_i and a distribution with a mean μ_j and an SD σ_j is again a Gaussian density function with mean μ_{ij} and an SD σ_{ij} according to:

$$\mu_{ij} = \frac{\mu_i \sigma_j^2 + \mu_j \sigma_i^2}{\sigma_i^2 + \sigma_j^2} \qquad \text{and} \qquad \sigma_{ij} = \sqrt{\frac{\sigma_i^2 \sigma_j^2}{\sigma_i^2 + \sigma_j^2}}. \tag{6.10}$$

The results of the study are summarized in Figure 6.13. Compared to the sample with a flat intonation, only subject 14 was generally not able to improve the naturalness of the intonation with our system. While a distinct gap remains in the perceived naturalness between the original recording and even the manipulations made by the best subject, the majority of the subjects (10 out of 16) achieved a naturalness score of more than three, which is considered natural. As illustrated by Table 6.8, there is only a very weak positive correlation between the average time to settle on a contour and its naturalness, and a somewhat stronger, but still weak, negative correlation between the average number of attempts and the naturalness.

Subject	1	2	3	4	5	6	7	8	9	10	11	12	13	14	15	16
Mean manipulation time [min:s]	n/a	n/a	1:14	1:28	0:39	1:06	1:28	0:47	1:00	1:00	1:11	1:19	0:55	1:16	1:11	0:57
Mean number of attempts	n/a	n/a	11	9.1	5.1	9.8	12.4	7.7	10.7	10.7	16.2	19.9	13.9	21.6	17.3	5.8
Naturalness score	3.03	3.59	3	3.34	3.6	3.2	3.6	2.7	3.5	2.5	3.1	3.75	3.14	1.56	2.6	3.1

Table 6.8.: Average amount of time and mean number of attempts each subject needed to settle on a contour. The time and number of attempts was not tracked for the first two subjects. The correlation coefficient between the average manipulation time and the naturalness score is $\rho_t = 0.012$ and the correlation coefficient between the number of attempts and the naturalness score is $\rho_n = -0.38$.

Summary and conclusion

Intonation is a major component of natural speech but cannot be directly measured from supraglottal articulation. A manual control of the intonation is conceivable, but the usability of such a system needed to be investigated. To that end, the presented system used a wearable input device

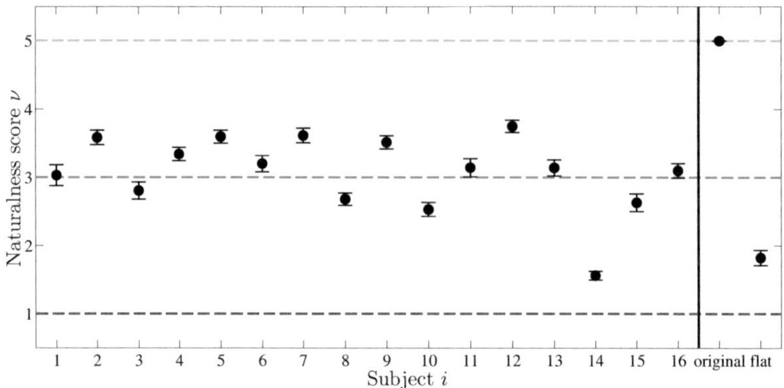

Figure 6.13.: Mean (dots) and variance (whiskers) of the perceived naturalness ν (rated by all subjects) of the 10 samples generated by the respective subject i. The original sample was a natural recording, the flat sample was the same recording manipulated to a flat 100 Hz intonation.

(Mycestro 3D mouse) and a PC software to allow the real-time on-line manipulation of the intonation of pre-recorded sentences with flat intonation. The system's usability was evaluated by a small-scale user study and the results showed that the majority of the users were generally able to produce natural sounding f_0 contours. However, the users were given an indefinite number of retries and a rather long time period to manipulate the short sentences. Future studies should therefore examine, how the naturalness is affected by stricter limitations, since the final application is supposed to be in a wearable speech synthesis system, where usually only a single attempt for each sentences is possible. Another future study should also examine, how subjects improve over time as they train on one set of sentences with an indefinite number of attempts and are then tested on a different second set with only one attempt per sentence. It is also of interest to see if the users' proficiency can be improved by teaching them the theory behind the Fujisaki model. In the presented study, the users were not told anything about the underlying concept of distinct phrase and accent components to avoid bias in how they use the system. As illustrated by Figure 6.14, a basic understanding of this concept may lead to better results.

Another possible improvement could be to use a declining base f_0 or even a phrase component as a base. This would further reduce the user's workload to triggering the accents only, which may be easier to accomplish because of the more immediate response to a command (as opposed to the comparatively slowly rising response to a phrase command). This is especially advantageous for the target audience of a speech prosthesis, among which cognitive impairments are likely to occur. Lastly, because the present study did only consider the general naturalness (a fairly abstract measure), another experiment should examine to what extent the subjects are able to intentionally convey information using the artificial intonation (e.g., stressing specific words or syllables to resolve ambiguities).

6.7.3. Predicting voicing and intonation from supraglottal articulatory trajectories

As discussed above, voicing and intonation are components of speech that originate in the excitation source of the vocal tract, which is not included in supraglottal articulatory data as captured by, e.g., EOS. However, recent studies have shown that the f_0 contour can nevertheless be derived from the articulatory data directly (e.g., [135,295–298]), from respiration [299], or by predicting the parameters of an intonation model [300]. While those studies showed promising results, they used different data sets, classifiers, regression models, different strategies for dealing with unvoiced seg-

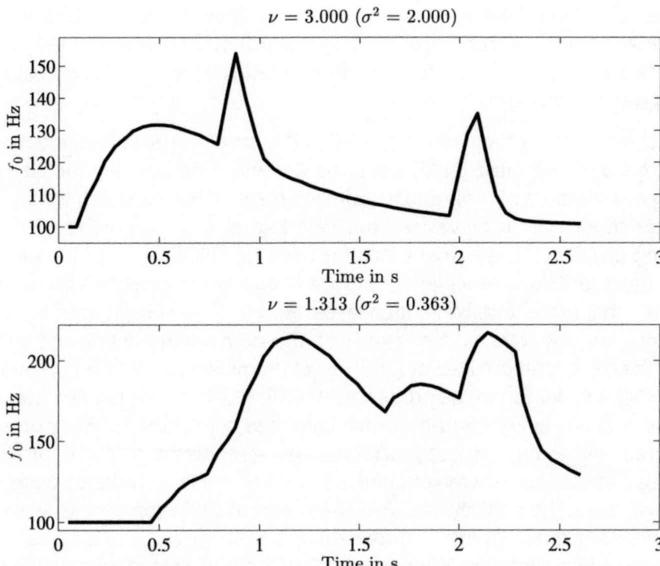

Figure 6.14.: Example f_0 contours generated by the highest-scoring subject (above) versus the lowest-scoring subject (below). Apparently, both subjects had a similar target contour in mind (one phrase with two accents) but subject 14 seemingly had some difficulties with both timing and choice of the commands.

ments and non-speech segments, and performed several predictions at the same time (e.g., a full articulation-to-speech mapping), which makes a reproduction and comparison of their results difficult. Given the focus on deep neural networks in most current studies, it was also of interest if a simpler model architecture that is less complex to train and has fewer hyperparameters to tune may be a good alternative in case of limited resources. Especially in the context of ATS systems, which are currently exclusively developed in academic research contexts and thus lack the access to large-scale data from many different speakears, this is an important advantage. The presented study therefore systematically explores the performance of a set of commonly used models on the freely available `mngu0` corpus [301] containing synchronous speech audio and EMA data. Both the ternary classification of silent, voiced and unvoiced segments as well as the prediction of the f_0 contour were performed and evaluated. EMA data was chosen over EOS data because of its superior and well-proven accuracy in recordings with many speakers. While this helps eliminate the error introduced by a possibly imprecise articulometric technique, it unfortunately also makes the results from this study inapplicable to real-world ATS systems, since EMA data can only be recorded in a lab setting (see section 3.7). But since the research question of this investigation was concerned with the general feasibility of such predictions, it was considered the best option to establish an upper limit for such an approach.

In a setup described above, where only the supraglottal articulation is measured and used to drive a speech synthesizer, no information on the voicing or even the voice activity is available. This poses two problems: when should the synthesizer be started and stopped and when should the synthesizer produce the voiced or the unvoiced instance of the same supraglottal articulation (e.g., when should it output a /g/ vs /k/)? These two distinct problems call for two separate, binary classifiers: one to classify speech from non-speech and one to classify voiced from unvoiced speech. These classifiers can be cascaded, so that the speech/non-speech classifier only passes frames containing speech to the voiced/unvoiced classifier, or run in parallel and then superimposed (where results from the voiced/unvoiced classifier are gated by the decision of the speech/non-speech classifier). While speech activity and voicing is a ternary classification problem, the prediction of the f_0

at any given point in time is a regression problem, since the pitch can take on any value in a continuous range between certain physiological constraints. Therefore, the f_0 contour was predicted using the same methods as for the voiced/unvoiced/silence classification but modified to be used for the regression problem.

The machine learning techniques applied in this study were all implemented by Philipp Schmidt as part of his diploma thesis [302] using the C++ machine learning toolkit "dlib" [303]. While the toolkit offers a plethora of tools and algorithms, three of the most commonly used families of algorithms were chosen for this investigation: SVM, Kernel Ridge Regression (KRR), and DNN. For both investigated problems, the kernel functions used for the SVM and KRR were a linear kernel (LK), the radial basis function kernel (RBK), and the histogram intersection kernel (HIK). The DNNs were trained with one, three and five hidden layers with 512 neurons in each layer (to study the impact of the depth), and with two hidden layers with 512 neurons in the first and 1024 in the second layer (to mirror the configuration used by [296]), all of them using a Rectified Linear Unit (ReLU) activation function [304]. In addition to the properties described above, the hidden layers of these DNNs were fully connected, i.e., every neuron in each layer was connected to every other neuron in the next layer. To train and evaluate these machine learning models, a corpus of articulatory data with corresponding pitch contours was required, since all of these techniques were supervised methods. One such corpus is the publicly available `mngu0` corpus [301] containing synchronous speech audio and, among other forms of articulatory data, electromagnetic articulography data of one speaker from two recording sessions. We used the Day 1 set of EMA data along with the corresponding audio data and extended Speech Assessment Methods Phonetic Alphabet (SAMPA) annotation for training and evaluation of the classification and regression models. The Day 1 set contains 1354 utterances by one male British professional speaker amounting to 67 min of speech data, which were randomly split (without breaking up utterances) into a training set (80 % of the total data frames) and a test set (the remaining 20 % of the data). The sentence lengths ranged from 1 to 48 words and included questions, statements and exclamations (and therefore a variety of intonation contours). In total, the set contained approximately 1715 unique diphones and 12 322 unique triphones. The EMA data was sampled using the Carstens AG500 articulograph, which is capable of tracking 12 EMA sensor coils in 3D space with two angles of rotation for a total of 5 measurements per sensor coil. The study used only the x- and y-coordinates of six coils (placed on the upper lip, the lower lip, the lower incisor, the tongue tip, the tongue body, and the tongue dorsum) in the midsagittal plane for a total of 2 x 6 = 12 channels (number of dimensions times number of coils). This limitation was imposed to remain within the subset of data that the authors of the corpus had already evaluated and processed themselves: The `mngu0` corpus contains processed EMA data of these 12 channels. Due to possible overlap of some of the corresponding audio files (according to the dataset's readme file), the raw data were used and then standardized channel-wise so that each channel (containing data representing one spatial dimension of one coil) exhibited a mean of 0 and a standard deviation of 1. The corpus contains two sets of audio recordings: one recorded using a Sennheiser MKH50 hypercardioid, which picked up background noise from the AG500 starting at about 7.5 kHz, and a PHON-OR noise-canceling optical microphone, which had a smaller bandwidth and did not pick up low frequencies very well. Because this study was interested in the fundamental frequency, the Sennheiser MKH50 audio recordings were used for training and evaluating the f_0 prediction as the noise interference was well above the expected frequency range of interest. The data were presented to the machine learning algorithms as a series of feature vectors, each of which represented one frame of EMA data sampled every 5 ms. The feature vectors consisted of the 12 channel data in that frame (x- and y- coordinates of the six sensor coils as described above), the element-wise, normalized difference of the current 12 channel data to the previous 12 channel data (i.e., delta features), and the element-wise, normalized difference of the current difference to the previous difference (i.e., delta-delta features). In total, each feature vector therefore had a length of 36. To include an articulatory context for each feature vector, several consecutive feature vectors were stacked. Two different kinds of context were studied: using only previous feature vectors and additionally using subsequent feature vectors, as well. The former case is feasible in a real-time ATS synthesis system as described above, while the latter setting was expected to improve the results at the cost of a small delay. Context lengths of 25 ms, 50 ms, and 75 ms were studied, but for the sake of conciseness, only the best results are reported here, which were achieved with a context of 50 ms corresponding to 10 frames for both look-back and look-ahead.

To train the supervised machine learning models used in this study, each training frame was assigned a label for unvoiced/voiced/silence classification and an f_0 value for regression. The silence label could be directly extracted from the extended SAMPA annotation of the `mngu0` corpus. But since no narrow transcription of the utterances was available, we based the voiced/unvoiced label on the results of the f_0 extraction: if no f_0 could be determined, the frame was labeled "unvoiced", otherwise it was considered "voiced". The f_0 of each non-silent frame was determined using Praat's [176] autocorrelation-based *To Pitch...* function with a pitch floor of 50 Hz and a pitch ceiling of 200 Hz. As illustrated by the histogram in Figure 6.15, these parameters accurately captured the f_0 range present in the data while at the same time avoiding octave errors by constraining the search space.

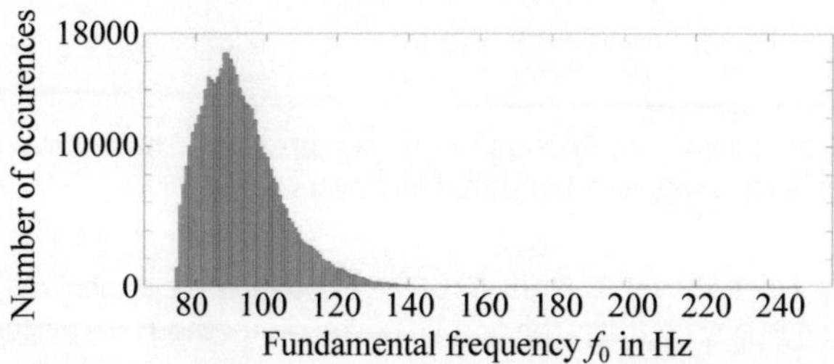

Figure 6.15.: Histogram of the pitch values included in the analyzed subset of the `mngu0` dataset

If the Praat algorithm could not find a sufficiently clear peak in the autocorrelation-function, it returned the value "undefined" for that frame. This was replaced by the numeric value -1 and used as the unvoiced-flag so that for the voiced-unvoiced classification all positive values were interpreted as a "voiced" label. In total, 363 502 voiced samples and 368 021 unvoiced samples were used for training, and 126 651 voiced frames and 121 965 unvoiced and silent frames for testing the classifiers. The regression models were trained and tested with the voiced frames only, although unvoiced or silent frames were included in the articulatory feature vectors if they appeared in the context of a voiced frame.

Even though the `mngu0` corpus proposes a standard split for training, validation and testing, a new split was made following a practice suggested by [305]. As described above, 80 % of the feature vectors and their corresponding labels were used for the training of all investigated classifiers and regression models and 20 % of the data was kept separately for testing. The validation set for hyperparameter tuning (as a subset of the training set) was determined differently for each class of models: The neural networks were trained using a mini-batch paradigm with a batch size of 512. The learning rate was the only hyperparameter that was tuned. Its optimum was found by successively shrinking the learning rate from 0.1 by a factor of 10 after every training epoch and evaluation on the test set. The hyperparameters of the SVMs were optimized using a grid search of the parameter space and a two-fold cross-validation on the training set. Due to the large training set, a higher number of folds was too computationally expensive. The hyperparameter λ for the KRR was found using leave-one-out cross-validation since training was much faster and thus allowed a more thorough cross-validation. The final hyperparameter values for all models are summarized in Table 6.9 and Table 6.10.

After training the models on the training sets using these optimal hyperparameters, the trained models were then evaluated on the respective test sets. The evaluation was performed using both objective measures (the classification score and the regression error) and a subjective listening test using human listeners. The classification score was calculated by dividing the number of correctly classified voiced and unvoiced frames by the total number of frames in the test set. The regression error was determined in terms of the RMSE between the predicted f_0 and the reference f_0 deter-

	SVM				KRR				DNN
	LK	RBK		HIK	LK	RBK		HIK	all
Context (before | after) in ms	C	C	γ	C	λ	λ	γ	λ	LR
50 | 0	2e+06	9.842e+05	0.0045	3e+05	0.0001	0.01	0.0081	0.01	0.0001
50 | 50	2e+06	2e+06	0.0015	3e+05	0.0001	0.001	0.0009	1	0.0001

Table 6.9.: Optimal hyperparameters for the silence/voiced/unvoiced classifiers. The optimal learning rate (LR) was the same for every number of hidden layers of the DNN.

	SVR	KRR				DNN
	LK	LK	RBK		HIK	all
Context (before | after) in ms	C	λ	λ	γ	λ	LR
50 | 0	1.968e+05	1e-05	0.01	0.0009	0.01	1e-07
50 | 50	5e+05	1e-05	0.1	0.0009	0.01	1e-07

Table 6.10.: Optimal hyperparameters for the f_0 regression. The optimal learning rate (LR) was the same for every number of hidden layers of the DNN.

mined with Praat (see above). The results of the evaluation are shown in Figure 6.16 and Figure 6.17. It is evident that in both settings the non-linear kernel methods outperformed the linear methods.

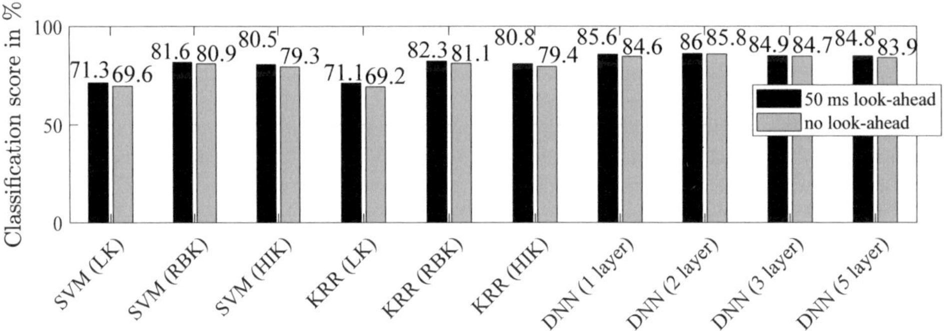

Figure 6.16.: Voiced/unvoiced/silence classification score in percent of correctly classified frames

The DNNs also generally slightly outperformed SVM and KRR models for classification. For the regression task, the DNNs are generally on par with the Support Vector Regression (SVR) or KRR models with a KRR using a radial basis kernel achieving the overall best result of an RMSE of 10.3 Hz. This is somewhat surprising, given the dominance of deep networks in almost every field. An explanation could be the vast number of possible network topologies and hyperparameter settings of a DNN. Even with the careful approach taken here, there is no guarantee that the true global optimum was found. Compared to the previous benchmark set by [296], which was an RMSE of 12.6 Hz achieved on the same corpus using an LSTM network, the results from this study are an improvement of approximately 17 %. However, another study using an LSTM [298] performed slightly better with a reported RMSE of 10.162 Hz when using the same input data as in this study, most likely due to using a (well-tuned) LSTM instead of a simple feed-forward DNN. While adding a look-ahead for the articulatory context improved the results marginally, the proposed techniques are still sufficiently precise for a real-time application in an ATS synthesis system even when no "future" context is used.

While the RMSE is a commonly used objective measure to evaluate a regression model and a good index to compare different algorithms, it is not intuitively clear how it relates to perceived quality or

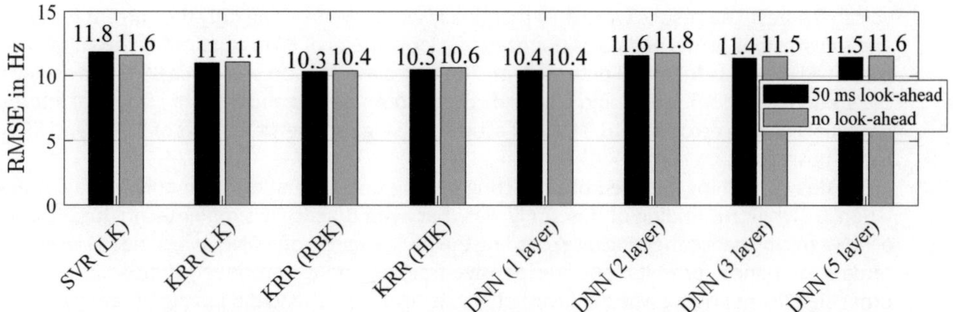

Figure 6.17.: RMSE of predicted f_0 contour with respect to the reference f_0

naturalness of the produced contours. Therefore, a listening test was conducted, where a subset of the results was rated by 20 human listeners (8 female, 12 male, age 22-56, average age 30.4). To limit the number of the stimuli to a reasonable amount, the utterances from the test set were grouped into tertiles using the RMSE: the best (lowest RMSE) third (T1), the median third (T2), and worst (highest RMSE) third (T3). Then, one short, one long and one medium long utterance were randomly selected from each third. For each of these nine utterances, the f_0 contour in the original audio recordings was manipulated to match the f_0 contour predicted by the best regression model with look-ahead and without look-ahead using Praat. A sample of each utterance with a completely flattened intonation (setting it to its mean f_0) and the unmodified recordings of each sample were also added to the set[3]. The resulting 9 utterances $\times$ 4 versions = 36 utterances were presented to the subjects three times in a randomized fashion for a total of 108 items per test. The items were presented to the listeners in a quiet room using a Focusrite Saffire Pro 40 audio interface and a pair of Beyerdynamic T70p headphones. The raters were asked to grade each item on a scale from 1 (unnatural) to 4 (very natural). The results of the test are shown in Figure 6.18. The original f_0 contours and the flattened f_0 contours scored highest and lowest, as could be expected. The ratings of the predicted f_0 contours were also consistent with the objective evaluation. The selected sentences are provided in the digital supplemental material accompanying this dissertation.

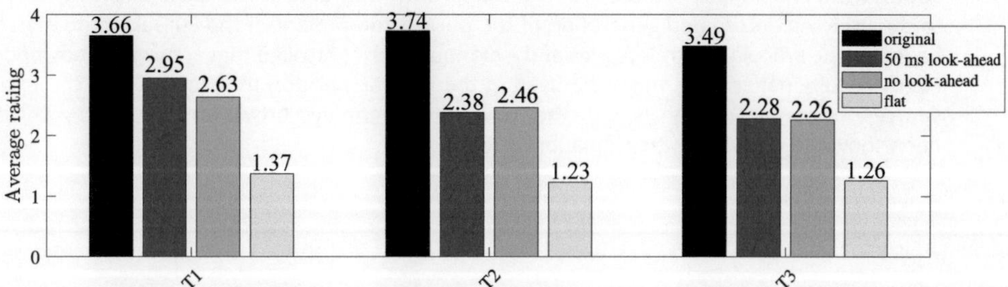

Figure 6.18.: Average naturalness rating in the listening test of the resynthesized utterances using the orignal, predicted, and flattened f_0 contours.

Summary and conclusion

A systematic comparison of a number of machine learning algorithms' (SVM, KRR, and DNN) performances for f_0 prediction from articulatory data was presented. The results show that DNNs are generally a good option for both classification of voiced/unvoiced frames and predicting the f_0 in

[3]"Unmodified" means that we passed it through Praat's pitch manipulation algorithm once without changing anything. This seemingly redundant step was necessary because the pitch manipulation algorithm introduces a small amount of noise that would otherwise unfairly skew the comparison.

voiced frames. The results were only marginally worse when using only the current feature vector and the previous 50 ms of data as opposed to a look-ahead of 50 ms, indicating the suitability of the proposed methods for a real-time system. The best classification score was 86 % and achieved by a DNN with two hidden layers and 50 ms of context both before and after the frame of interest. The lowest prediction error was 10.3 Hz and achieved using symmetric context of 50 ms and KRR with a radial-basis function kernel.

Besides confirming the idea of predicting voicing and intonation from only supraglottal articulation, a significant finding of this study was that even drastically simpler techniques like KRR can achieve performance meeting or exceeding the performance of a DNN, which needs large amounts of data, demands computationally expensive training and is notoriously difficult to optimize. Another significant finding was the fact that not using a look-ahead did not significantly decrease the performance of both unvoiced/voiced/silence classification and f_0 regression. This is an important fact for the design of real-time ATS systems. The results from the listening test suggest that the RMSE is a valid error measure even if ultimately perceptual quality is of importance, since the tested items were rated in the same relative ranked order than their respective RMSE.

6.7.4. Conclusion and Outlook

As shown by each study and discussed in the respective section, both the manual control of the intonation and an automated approach based on machine learning are generally feasible. For the voicing decision, a manual control seems inadvisable because it would require immensely precise timing to trigger the correct voicing that seems superhuman to achieve. Here, a purely machine learning based approach as described above could be a solution, given the very good performance of approximately 85 % correctly classified frames on the EMA data. A possible explanation for this might be that the classifiers implicitly learn a language model: since articulatory context is provided, the probability of certain sequences of articulations factors into the decision. For the intonation, however, an entirely automatic approach with no user input on the f_0 contour may be frustrating to the user. It is likely that the reason for the fairly low errors is the limited range and variety of intonation contours in the analyzed dataset. In real-world scenarios, the user will probably want to stress certain words to emphasize and broadcast intend. It remains to be investigatted if pitch accents could also be derived from the timing and the pattern in the supraglottal articulatory data. Future work should also explore if a hybrid approach may deliver the most satisfying experience to the user: An automated generation of the phrase component of the Fujisaki intonation model based on the articulatory trajectories and a manual, user-controlled trigger for accent components. Finally, additional sensors might be used in the data acquisition that capture not the excitation source, but correlated signals, e.g. the movement of the eye brows during speech, which have been shown to correlate with intonation [306].

7. Summary and outlook

7.1. Summary of the contributions

This dissertation made three major contributions to the field of silent-speech interfaces:

1. A novel measurement technique to measure articulatory movements in the anterior oral cavity called Electro-Optical Stomatography (EOS).
2. A low-dimensional, parametric vocal tract model for high-quality, natural-sounding articulatory synthesis in real-time.
3. A new Articulation-to-Text (ATT) system performing at a state-of-the-art level.

Furthermore, it explored the possibility of using EOS in an ATS system, which was not able to reach state-of-the-art performance, yet. However, it succeded in pinpointing major obstacles in the development of such a system and made specific recommendations on how to proceed in future work.

The articulatory measurement technique EOS was developed with its application in portable silent-speech systems in mind. The measurement hardware is therefore compact (the control unit measures only) 160 mm × 100 mm) and battery powered. EOS uses a pseudopalate, which the user wears on their upper jaw like a retainer. On the pseudopalate, two kinds of sensors measure the movement of the lips and the tongue: electrical contact sensors register the palato-lingual contact pattern, and optical sensors measure the midsagittal tongue contour and the lip opening and protrusion. The distance measurements can be calibrated using a newly developed calibration model. The model predicts a set of calibration points (pairs of digital values and distances in millimeters) for each optical distance sensor based on a single digital sensor value measured during direct contact between the user's tongue and the sensor. A calibration characteristic is then generated by interpolating between these calibration points. Since distance values obtained with this characteristic may still be subject to an error caused by angular displacement of the tongue towards the optical axis of the sensor, a second, additional calibration model was developed that compensates this error. Beyond the use in silent-speech interfaces, EOS can be used in any context where tracking the intraoral articulation is of interest and several possible applications were pointed out (and explored in studies considered out-of-scope for this dissertation).

The six point vocal tract model proposed in this dissertation is an improvement on previous parametric 1D vocal tract models because it can model all kinds of sounds with the same set of parameters (as opposed to, .e.g., the Three Parameter Model by Fant [249]) using intuitively meaningful degrees of freedom with phonetic/articulatory correspondences (as opposed to, e.g., the statistical mixture model by Story [258]). It extends the Ishizaka model [259] in numerous ways to allow the modeling of sounds with much greater flexibility. The intelligibility of sounds synthesized with the six point models was proven in a listening experiment and approaches the levels of natural speech for most analyzed sounds. The availability of a flexible, low-dimensional parametric vocal tract model that can produce intelligible speech on par with more complex models (e.g., 3D vocal tract models as in [214]) is a great boon to any silent-speech system that wants to include low-latency, real-time articulatory synthesis. Thoroughly evaluated parameter sets for most German speech sounds were provided.

The presented ATT system achieved state-of-the-art performance of more than 90 % in a speaker-dependent command word recognition task. In addition to that, the inter-speaker performance was also evaluated and shown to be still within the range of some speaker-dependent ATT systems based on other articulometric frontends, even without any explicit speaker adaptation strategy.

The ATS study, unfortunately, did not match the high performance of the other contributions of this dissertation. The chosen approach of finding a mapping from EOS sensor data frames to their corresponding discrete area function shapes proved to be too naive. Despite thorough evaluation and in-depth optimizations of a suite of regression models, no model could overcome the strong coarticulatory influence on the consonants in the data and the lack of properly coarticulated target area function shapes. However, the realization that this approach was too simplistic could in itself be considered a (minor) contribution to the field of ATS research.

7.2. Outlook

In addition to the contributions outlined in the previous section, each component of this dissertation could of course be further improved in future work.

For EOS, some short-term work will have to deal with the unfortunate fact that the OP280V VCSEL diode is no longer available on the market at the time this is written. A possible replacement is the VC850M-SMD infrared VCSEL by Roithner LaserTechnik GmbH, which has similar specifications and even comes in a much smaller 0603 package of only 1.60 mm × 0.8 mm. Given the slightly different electrical and optical characteristics, though, it is unclear if it can serve as a simple drop-in replacement or if recalculation of the calibration models are necessary, which would require the re-recording of the data used in subsection 4.2.2 according to the specifications outlined in that chapter.

It should also be investigated if a more phonetically motivated arrangement of the contact sensors (similar to the EPG Reading palate in Figure 3.13) on an EOS sensor unit can improve the results: A more densely spaced group of contact sensors in the alveolar and postalveolar region might help discriminate better between sounds with those places of articulation. Furthermore, the contact sensor detection circuit should be optimized. While the current input filter circuit has a very well-suited frequency response, the step response (as shown in Figure 7.1) is too slow.

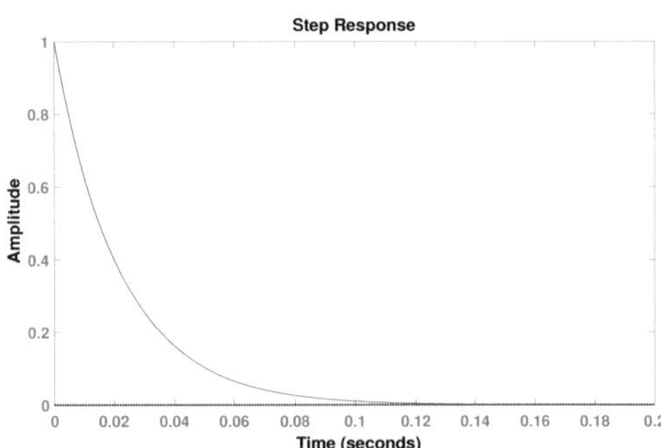

Figure 7.1.: (Down)step response of the contact sensor input filter

This means that the fast multiplexing of the contact sensors causes a rather "muddled" signal, where the various contact sensor signals partially overlap in time. Tuning the components in the detector circuit to achieve a better (faster) step response may therefore greatly increase the time resolution of the contact sensor data.

While some attempts were made to relate the raw lip sensor data to the phonetic dimensions lip opening and protrusion (mostly in parallel to this dissertation in [187]), none were satisfyingly precise so far. Especially the issue illustrated by Figure 5.5 shows the necessity for some kind of lip sensor calibration for the EOS data to become less speaker-dependent.

The EOS control unit could be further miniaturized to improve portability. Also, a wireless data transfer from the control unit to the measurement computer would be desirable. This could be comparatively easily accomplished by adding a Bluetooth transceiver. Much more complicated, but even more beneficial to the usability and user-friendliness of the EOS system would be a wireless sensor unit. Since the EOS sensors are active sensors (requiring power to work), this involves finding an embeddable power source (a battery, most likely) in addition to developing a board layout that squeezes the necessary circuitry for the power management and the wireless communication into the small space available on the hard palate.

The six point vocal tract model could also be further improved. In addition to finding optimal parameter sets for speech sounds from other languages than German, especially a better dynamic control would be of great interest to improve the synthesis of stops. Also, a model for coarticulation similar to the one proposed in [214] would most likely greatly improve the quality and intelligibility of synthesized consonants.

The promising results from the ATT studies should be repeated with a larger vocabulary and for more speakers, eventually developing the system into a large vocabulary continuous articulatory speech recognizer, leveraging articulatory sound and language models to further boost the performance. Along these lines, possible improvements of the inter-speaker performance, e.g., by using alignment utterances to normalize the articulatory spaces of the speakers, should also be explored.

Finally, the biggest room for improvement remains for the ATS system. As discussed in subsection 6.6.6, the approach taken in this work appears to be a dead-end, because of the strong influence of coarticulation. Future work should therefore reformulate the problem of mapping individual EOS data frames to sounds into a sequence-to-sequence mapping between continuous EOS data and continuous vocal tract trajectories. To that end, the unknown vocal tract trajectories necessary to train a supervised sequence-to-sequence model (e.g., an LSTM network), first need to be estimated in an inverse mapping from acoustic speech data to the vocal tract model parameters. This mapping could be learned by minimizing the perceptual difference between synthesized speech using the vocal tract model and the input acoustic speech signal as a function of the vocal tract model parameters. This would be of great interest to articulatory synthesis in general and could benefit all kinds of ATS systems (not just the one presented in this dissertation using EOS) but is obviously a challenging task for multiple future works.

Beyond EOS, more articulometric technologies are constantly being proposed and developed, and even the field of BCIs, which was entirely excluded from the review in chapter 3, may experience rapid acceleration in the near future with increased industrial interest partly generated by Elon Musk's company Neuralink. But to paraphrase the final words from the landmark SSI review paper by Denby et al. [50], which is as true at the time of this writing as it was in 2010: The last word on silent-speech interfaces has not been spoken!

Appendix

A. Overview of the International Phonetic Alphabet

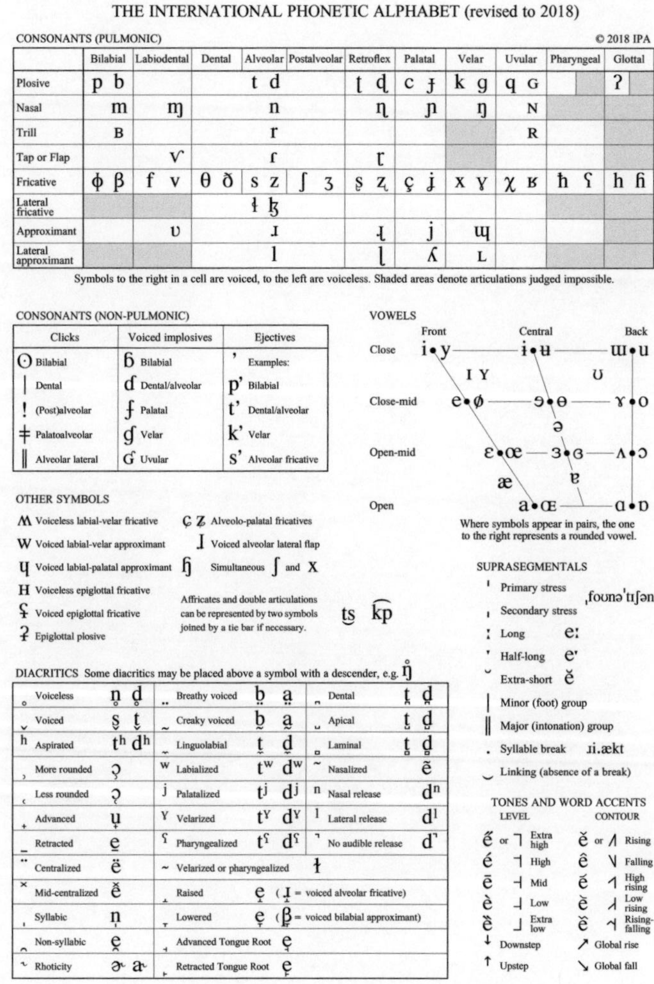

THE INTERNATIONAL PHONETIC ALPHABET (revised to 2018)

CONSONANTS (PULMONIC)

	Bilabial	Labiodental	Dental	Alveolar	Postalveolar	Retroflex	Palatal	Velar	Uvular	Pharyngeal	Glottal
Plosive	p b			t d		ʈ ɖ	c ɟ	k ɡ	q ɢ		ʔ
Nasal	m	ɱ		n		ɳ	ɲ	ŋ	ɴ		
Trill	ʙ			r					ʀ		
Tap or Flap		ⱱ		ɾ		ɽ					
Fricative	ɸ β	f v	θ ð	s z	ʃ ʒ	ʂ ʐ	ç ʝ	x ɣ	χ ʁ	ħ ʕ	h ɦ
Lateral fricative				ɬ ɮ							
Approximant		ʋ		ɹ		ɻ	j	ɰ			
Lateral approximant				l		ɭ	ʎ	ʟ			

Symbols to the right in a cell are voiced, to the left are voiceless. Shaded areas denote articulations judged impossible.

CONSONANTS (NON-PULMONIC)

Clicks	Voiced implosives	Ejectives
ʘ Bilabial	ɓ Bilabial	ʼ Examples:
ǀ Dental	ɗ Dental/alveolar	pʼ Bilabial
ǃ (Post)alveolar	ʄ Palatal	tʼ Dental/alveolar
ǂ Palatoalveolar	ɠ Velar	kʼ Velar
ǁ Alveolar lateral	ʛ Uvular	sʼ Alveolar fricative

VOWELS

Where symbols appear in pairs, the one to the right represents a rounded vowel.

OTHER SYMBOLS

ʍ Voiceless labial-velar fricative

w Voiced labial-velar approximant

ɥ Voiced labial-palatal approximant

ʜ Voiceless epiglottal fricative

ʢ Voiced epiglottal fricative

ʡ Epiglottal plosive

ɕ ʑ Alveolo-palatal fricatives

ɺ Voiced alveolar lateral flap

ɧ Simultaneous ʃ and x

Affricates and double articulations can be represented by two symbols joined by a tie bar if necessary. t͡s k͡p

SUPRASEGMENTALS

ˈ Primary stress ˌfoʊnəˈtɪʃən

ˌ Secondary stress

ː Long eː

ˑ Half-long eˑ

˘ Extra-short ĕ

| Minor (foot) group

‖ Major (intonation) group

. Syllable break ɹi.ækt

‿ Linking (absence of a break)

DIACRITICS Some diacritics may be placed above a symbol with a descender, e.g. ŋ̊

̥ Voiceless	n̥ d̥	̤ Breathy voiced	b̤ a̤	̪ Dental	t̪ d̪
̬ Voiced	s̬ t̬	̰ Creaky voiced	b̰ a̰	̺ Apical	t̺ d̺
ʰ Aspirated	tʰ dʰ	̼ Linguolabial	t̼ d̼	̻ Laminal	t̻ d̻
̹ More rounded	ɔ̹	ʷ Labialized	tʷ dʷ	̃ Nasalized	ẽ
̜ Less rounded	ɔ̜	ʲ Palatalized	tʲ dʲ	ⁿ Nasal release	dⁿ
̟ Advanced	u̟	ˠ Velarized	tˠ dˠ	ˡ Lateral release	dˡ
̠ Retracted	e̠	ˤ Pharyngealized	tˤ dˤ	̚ No audible release	d̚
̈ Centralized	ë	̴ Velarized or pharyngealized	ɫ		
̽ Mid-centralized	e̽	̝ Raised	e̝ (ɹ̝ = voiced alveolar fricative)		
̩ Syllabic	n̩	̞ Lowered	e̞ (β̞ = voiced bilabial approximant)		
̯ Non-syllabic	e̯	̘ Advanced Tongue Root	e̘		
˞ Rhoticity	ɚ ɑ˞	̙ Retracted Tongue Root	e̙		

TONES AND WORD ACCENTS

LEVEL		CONTOUR	
e̋ or ˥	Extra high	ě or ˩˥	Rising
é ˦	High	ê ˥˩	Falling
ē ˧	Mid	e᷄ ˦˥	High rising
è ˨	Low	e᷅ ˩˨	Low rising
ȅ ˩	Extra low	e᷈ ˧˦˧	Rising-falling
↓	Downstep	↗	Global rise
↑	Upstep	↘	Global fall

Figure A.1.: IPA Chart, `http://www.internationalphoneticassociation.org/content/ipa-chart`, available under a Creative Commons Attribution-Sharealike 3.0 Unported License. Copyright © 2015 International Phonetic Association.

B. Mathematical proofs and derivations

B.1. Combinatoric calculations illustrating the reduction of possible syllables using phonotactics

The following calculations are in support of the example in section 2.6. The syllable structure in English (according to [46]) is zero to three consonants in the syllable onset, one obligatory vowel (or syllabic consonant) in the nucleus, and zero to four consonants in the coda:

$$\underbrace{(C)(C)(C)}_{\text{onset}}\ \overbrace{V}^{\text{nucleus}}\ \underbrace{(C)(C)(C)(C)}_{\text{coda}} \tag{B.1}$$

In chapter 2, I introduced 24 consonants and 15 vowel sounds in English. If no constraints are imposed, the number of possible syllables N would be:

$$\begin{aligned}
N = (\ & \underbrace{24\cdot 24\cdot 24}_{\substack{\text{all 3 positions}\\ \text{in onset are filled}\\ \text{with one of 24 consonants}}} + \underbrace{24\cdot 24}_{\substack{\text{only 2 positions}\\ \text{in onset are filled}}} + \underbrace{25}_{\substack{\text{one or none positions}\\ \text{in onset are filled}}}\ ) && \text{(B.2)}\\
& \cdot \underbrace{15}_{\text{one of 15 vowels in coda}} && \text{(B.3)}\\
& \cdot \underbrace{(24\cdot 24\cdot 24\cdot 24 + 24\cdot 24\cdot 24 + 24\cdot 24 + 25)}_{\substack{\text{zero to four positions}\\ \text{in coda are filled}\\ \text{with one of 24 consonants}}} && \text{(B.4)}\\
& = 14425\cdot 15\cdot 346201 && \text{(B.5)}\\
& = 74\,909\,241\,375 && \text{(B.6)}
\end{aligned}$$

If no consecutively repeated consonats are allowed in onset and coda, the possible combinations are:

$$\begin{aligned}
N &= (24\cdot 23\cdot 23 + 24\cdot 23 + 25)\cdot 15\cdot (24\cdot 23\cdot 23\cdot 23 + 24\cdot 23\cdot 23 + 24\cdot 23 + 25) && \text{(B.7)}\\
&= 13273\cdot 15\cdot 305281 && \text{(B.8)}\\
&= 60\,779\,920\,695 && \text{(B.9)}
\end{aligned}$$

Removing the velar nasal /ŋ/ as an option in the onset and the glottal fricative /h/ from the coda leads to:

$$\begin{aligned}
N &= (23\cdot 22\cdot 22 + 23\cdot 22 + 24)\cdot 15\cdot (23\cdot 22\cdot 22\cdot 22 + 23\cdot 22\cdot 22 + 23\cdot 22 + 24) && \text{(B.10)}\\
&= 11662\cdot 15\cdot 256566 && \text{(B.11)}\\
&= 44\,881\,090\,380 && \text{(B.12)}
\end{aligned}$$

Excluding the affricates $/\widehat{\text{tʃ}}/$ and $/\widehat{\text{dʒ}}/$ and the glottal fricative /h/ from complex onsets, means that there are only 20 possible options to choose from in the onset if there is more than one consonant:

$$N = (20 \cdot 19 \cdot 19 + 20 \cdot 19 + 24) \cdot 15 \cdot (23 \cdot 22 \cdot 22 \cdot 22 + 23 \cdot 22 \cdot 22 + 23 \cdot 22 + 24) \tag{B.13}$$
$$= 7624 \cdot 15 \cdot 256566 \tag{B.14}$$
$$= 29\,340\,887\,760 \tag{B.15}$$

Excluding the six remaining sonorant consonants as options for the first consonant in the onset and the seven remaining voiced obstruents as options for the second consonant, when there are exactly two consonants, leads to:

$$N = (20 \cdot 19 \cdot 19 + 14 \cdot 13 + 24) \cdot 15 \cdot (23 \cdot 22 \cdot 22 \cdot 22 + 23 \cdot 22 \cdot 22 + 23 \cdot 22 + 24) \tag{B.16}$$
$$= 7426 \cdot 15 \cdot 256566 \tag{B.17}$$
$$= 28\,578\,886\,740 \tag{B.18}$$

If the first consonant in a two-consonant onset is an /s/, the second consonant cannot be /ʃ/. If the first consonant is not an /s/, the second consonant must be /l/, /ɹ/, /w/, or /j/:

$$N = (20 \cdot 19 \cdot 19 + \underbrace{1 \cdot 11}_{\substack{\text{first consonant}\\ \text{is an /s/}}} + \underbrace{13 \cdot 4}_{\substack{\text{first consonant}\\ \text{is not an /s/}}} + 24) \cdot 15 \cdot (23 \cdot 22 \cdot 22 \cdot 22 + 23 \cdot 22 \cdot 22 + 23 \cdot 22 + 24) \tag{B.19}$$
$$= 7307 \cdot 15 \cdot 256566 \tag{B.20}$$
$$= 28\,117\,067\,940 \tag{B.21}$$

Applying the rules for two-consonant onsets to both substrings of a three-consonant onset and considering that there is no /w/ or /j/ in syllable codas, leads to the following:

$$N = (\underbrace{1}_{\substack{\text{only /s/}\\ \text{is possible}}} \cdot \underbrace{5}_{\substack{\text{only /p, t, k, f, θ/}\\ \text{are possible}}} \cdot \underbrace{4}_{\substack{\text{only /l, ɹ, w, j/}\\ \text{are possible}}} \tag{B.22}$$
$$+ 1 \cdot 11 + 13 \cdot 4 + 24) \cdot 15 \cdot (21 \cdot 20 \cdot 20 \cdot 20 + 21 \cdot 20 \cdot 20 + 21 \cdot 20 + 22) \tag{B.23}$$
$$= 107 \cdot 15 \cdot 176842 \tag{B.24}$$
$$= 283\,831\,410 \tag{B.25}$$

Removing /ŋ/, /θ/, /ɹ/, and /ʒ/ as options for second to fourth coda consonants leads to:

$$N = (1 \cdot 5 \cdot 4 + 1 \cdot 10 + 13 \cdot 4 + 24) \cdot 15 \cdot (21 \cdot 16 \cdot 16 \cdot 16 + 21 \cdot 16 \cdot 16 + 21 \cdot 16 + 22) \tag{B.26}$$
$$= 107 \cdot 15 \cdot 91750 \tag{B.27}$$
$$= 147\,258\,750 \tag{B.28}$$

In German, the syllable structure is the same but there are 18 vowels and 24 consonants. Therefore the theoretical maximum number of syllables is:

$$N = (24 \cdot 24 \cdot 24 + 24 \cdot 24 + 25) \cdot 18 \cdot (24 \cdot 24 \cdot 24 \cdot 24 + 24 \cdot 24 \cdot 24 + 24 \cdot 24 + 25) \tag{B.29}$$
$$= 14425 \cdot 18 \cdot 346201 \tag{B.30}$$
$$= 89\,891\,089\,650 \tag{B.31}$$

Limiting the combinations to the sequences according to [47], the number is reduced to:

$$N = 50 \cdot 18 \cdot 160 \tag{B.32}$$
$$= 136\,000 \tag{B.33}$$

B.2. Signal Averaging

In 4.4.1, I postulated that averaging over K samples reduces the noise power by a factor of K. The following proof of this statement closely follows the argument layed out in [307].

- Let $s(t)$ be a signal of constant power, which is corrupted by uncorrelated noise $n(t)$.
- Let $n(t)$ be a realization of the process N with a mean $\mu = 0$ and constant variance σ^2.
- Let the SNR be defined as $\mathrm{SNR} = \frac{P_{\mathrm{signal}}}{P_{\mathrm{noise}}} = \frac{E[s^2]}{E[n^2]}$.

When several frames of the noisy signal are averaged, the signal power remains the same (because it is constant). However, when averaging K realizations n_i of the random process N, we get:

$$\mathrm{Var}\left(\frac{1}{K}\sum_{i=1}^{K} n_i\right) = \frac{1}{K^2}\mathrm{Var}\left(\sum_{i=1}^{K} n_i\right) = \frac{1}{K^2}\sum_{i=1}^{K}\mathrm{Var}\left(n_i\right) \tag{B.34}$$

Since the noise variance $\mathrm{Var}(n) = \sigma^2$ is constant and thus the same for each realization, we may write the above equation as:

$$\frac{1}{K^2}\sum_{i=1}^{K}\mathrm{Var}\left(n_i\right) = \frac{1}{K^2}K\sigma^2 = \frac{1}{K}\sigma^2 \tag{B.35}$$

This demonstrates that the variance of the *averaged* noise realizations, and by extension the SNR, is inversely proportional to the number of averaged realizations K. Or in other terms: averaging K realizations of the same, uncorrelated noise reduces the noise power by a factor of K.

B.3. Effect of the contact sensor area on the conductance

Section 4.1 mentions an proportional relationship between the area of a contact sensor and its conductance. A high electrical conductance means that current can more easily flow into the contact, improving the coupling between the tongue and the sensor and lessening any voltage drops due to resistance at the interface. The conductance G is the reciprocal of the resistance R and can be calculated by [308]:

$$G = \frac{1}{R} = \frac{A}{\rho l}, \tag{B.36}$$

where ρ is the resistivity of the conducting material. As equation B.36 shows, the conductance is directly proportional to the conductor area and large contact sensor areas are therefore advantageous for the signal coupling.

B.4. Calculation of the forward current for the OP280V diode

The OP280V VCSEL diode is rated at a forward current of 7 mA. Since the MCU used in the EOS control unit (Atmel SAM3S, see section 4.5) can supply up to 9 mA continuously according to the data sheet, the light source can be controlled directly by the MCU using a general purpose digital output pin without any additional circuitry except for a current-limiting series resistor. The value of the series resistor R_{vcsel} determines the forward current through the diode, since the output pins of the MCU are digital and can only switch back and forth between Low (corresponding to a voltage of 0 V) and High (corresponding to 3.3 V). When the output voltage at the MCU pin becomes High, the OP280V turns on and the voltage drop across the diode typically becomes 1.95 V (according to the data sheet). The remaining 3.3 V – 1.95 V = 1.35 V drop across R_{vcsel}. The current through R_{vcsel} and consequently the forward current I_F through the VCSEL therefore can be calculated by the following simple formula:

$$I_F = \frac{1.35\,\text{V}}{R_{\text{vcsel}}} \tag{B.37}$$

The value of the series resistor necessary to set a required forward current can be obtained by simply rearranging this equation:

$$R_{\text{vcsel}} = \frac{1.35\,\text{V}}{I_F} \tag{B.38}$$

In practice however, the value for R_{vcsel} is usally rounded towards the next value available as a single physical component. Resistor components come at values of so called *preferred numbers* for inventory simplification and more flexible supply chains. These preferred numbers are defined in a couple of normed series (DIN IEC 60063), one of which is the commonly used E12 series. This series, which was also used for this dissertation, defines 12 different values per decade (hence the name): 1.0, 1.2, 1.5, 1.8, 2.2, 2.7, 3.3, 3.9, 4.7, 5.6, 6.8 and 8.2. Multiplying any of these values by the desired power of ten then results in a resistor value in Ohm that should be readily available on the market as a single physical component.

With these constraints in mind, a desired forward current of $I'_F = 7\,\text{mA}$ in equation B.37 leads to:

$$R'_{\text{vcsel}} = \frac{1.35\,\text{V}}{0.007\,\text{A}} \tag{B.39}$$

$$= 192.86\,\Omega \tag{B.40}$$

The next resistor in the E12 series has a value of 180 Ω. Using that component, the actual forward current I_F becomes:

$$I_F = \frac{1.35\,\text{V}}{180\,\Omega} \tag{B.41}$$

$$= 7.5\,\text{mA} \tag{B.42}$$

The maximum rated forward current for the OP280V is $I_{F,max} \approx 12\,\text{mA}$. Using a resistor value of 120 Ω sets the forward current to 11.25 mA, while 100 Ω (the next smaller E12 value) would overshoot it at 13.5 mA. Finally, measurements using about 3.5 mA (half the rated forward current) may deliver interersting data points as well, which can be achieved using a series resistor of 390 Ω.

These theoretical values assume that the forward voltage of the VCSEL is always 1.95 V, indepedently of the forward current, that there is no additional series resistance in the pin connection and the VCSEL itself, and that the digital output level High ideally reaches the full supply voltage rail of 3.3 V. All of these assumptions are simplifications, however, and therefore, the actual forward currents for each of these resistor values were verified by measuring the voltage drop across R_{vcsel} and their exact values as used in the comparison between the VSMY2850 and the OP280V were thusly determined as 3 mA, 7 mA and 11.5 mA for resistor values of 390 Ω, 180 Ω and 120 Ω, respectively (see subsection 4.2.1).

C. Schematics and layouts

C.1. Schematics of the control unit.

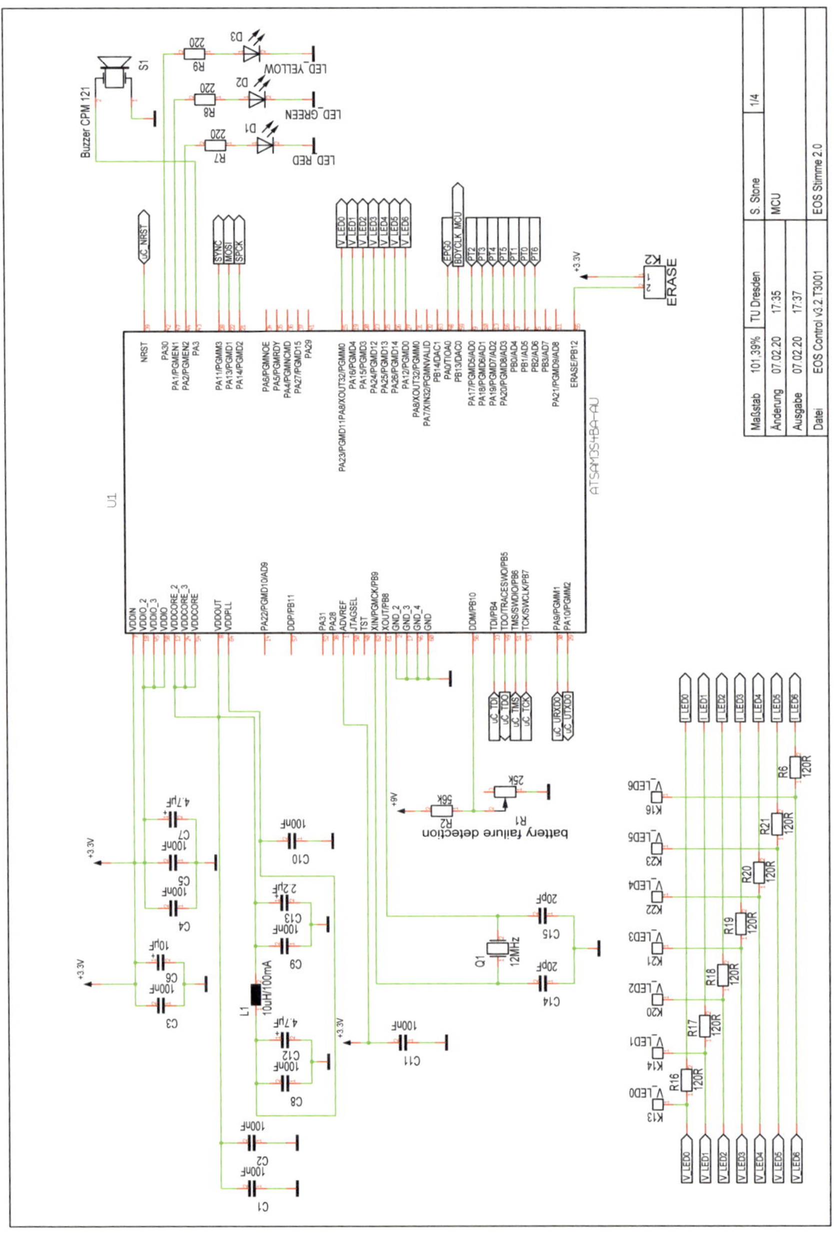

Figure C.1.: Connections to and from the ATSAM3S4B microcontroller.

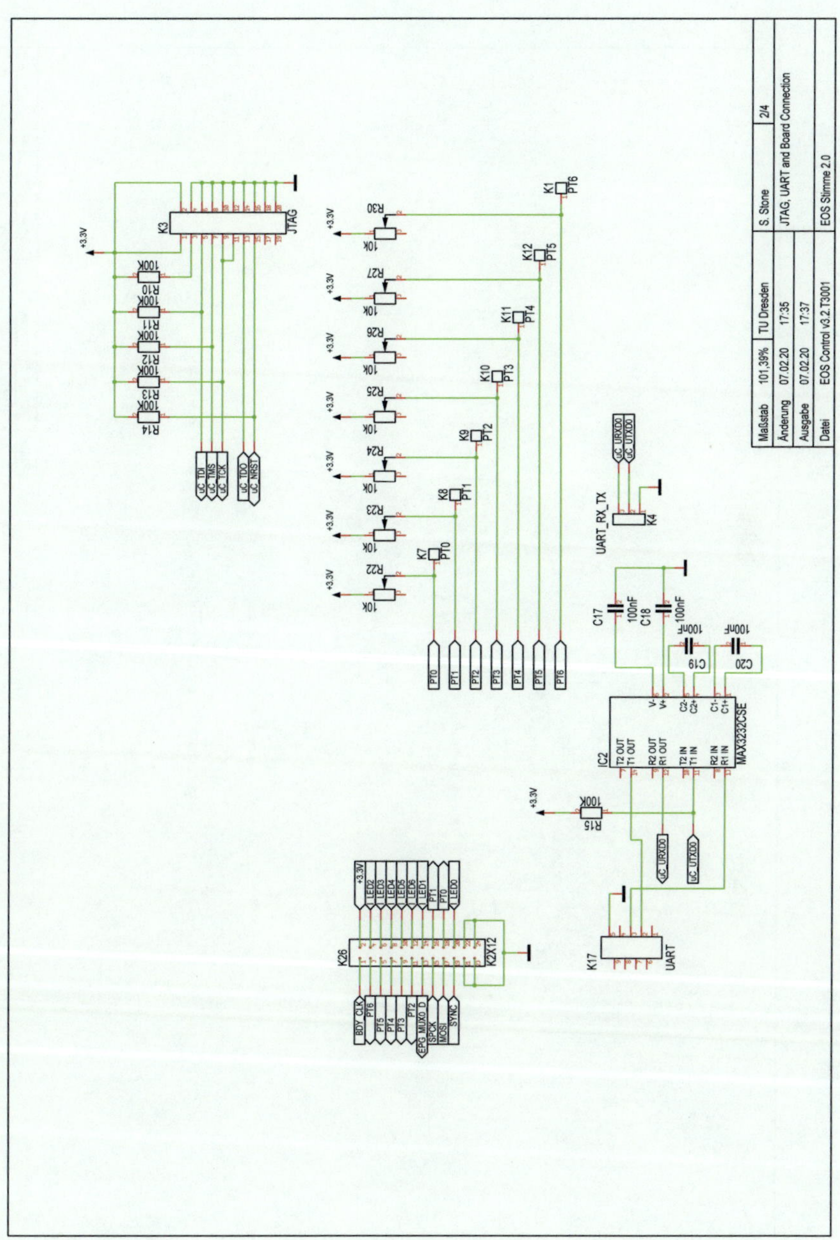

Figure C.2.: Incoming and outgoing board connections (Joint Test Action Group (JTAG) for debugging, UART for communication with the computer software, and a custom connector to connect the sensor unit) and optical sensor detector circuitry.

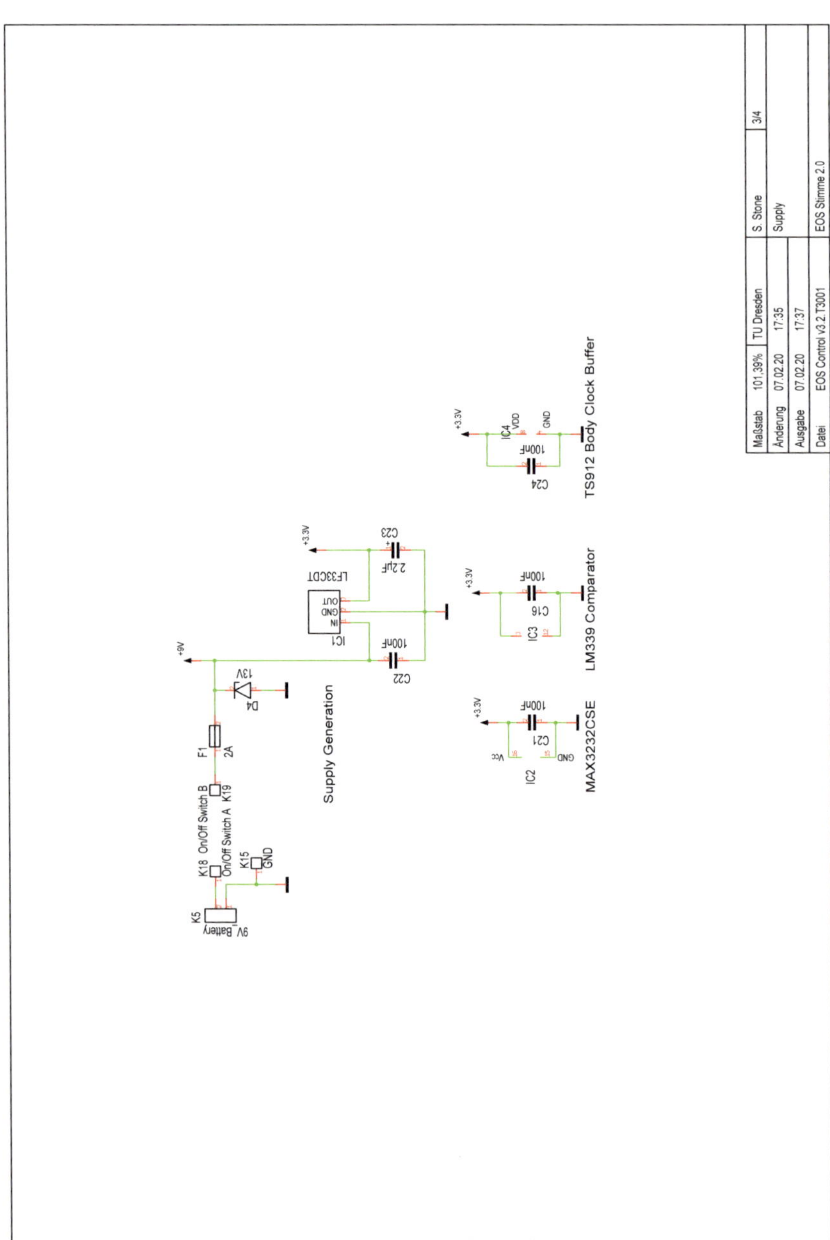

Figure C.3.: Supply voltage generation.

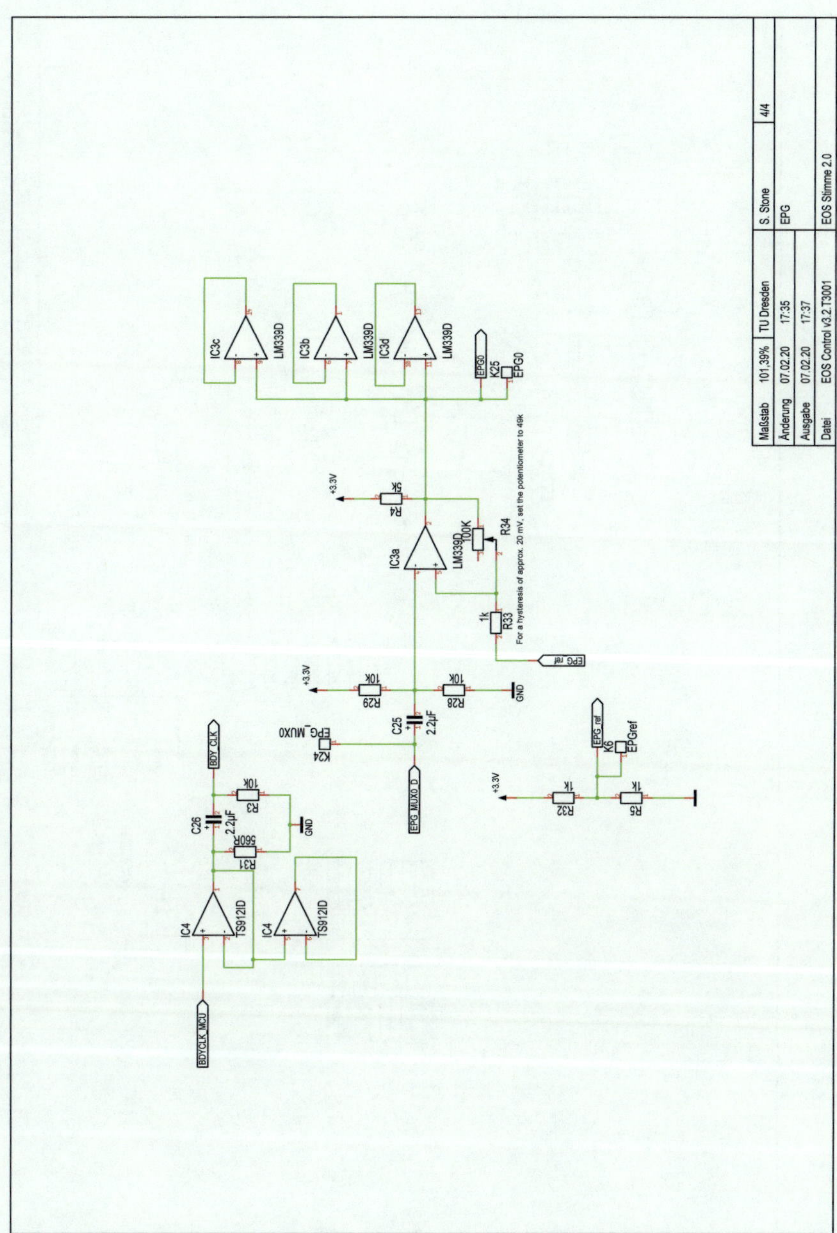

Figure C.4.: Analog contact sensor circuitry: Reference voltage generation, incoming contact sensor signal registration, and analog filtering.

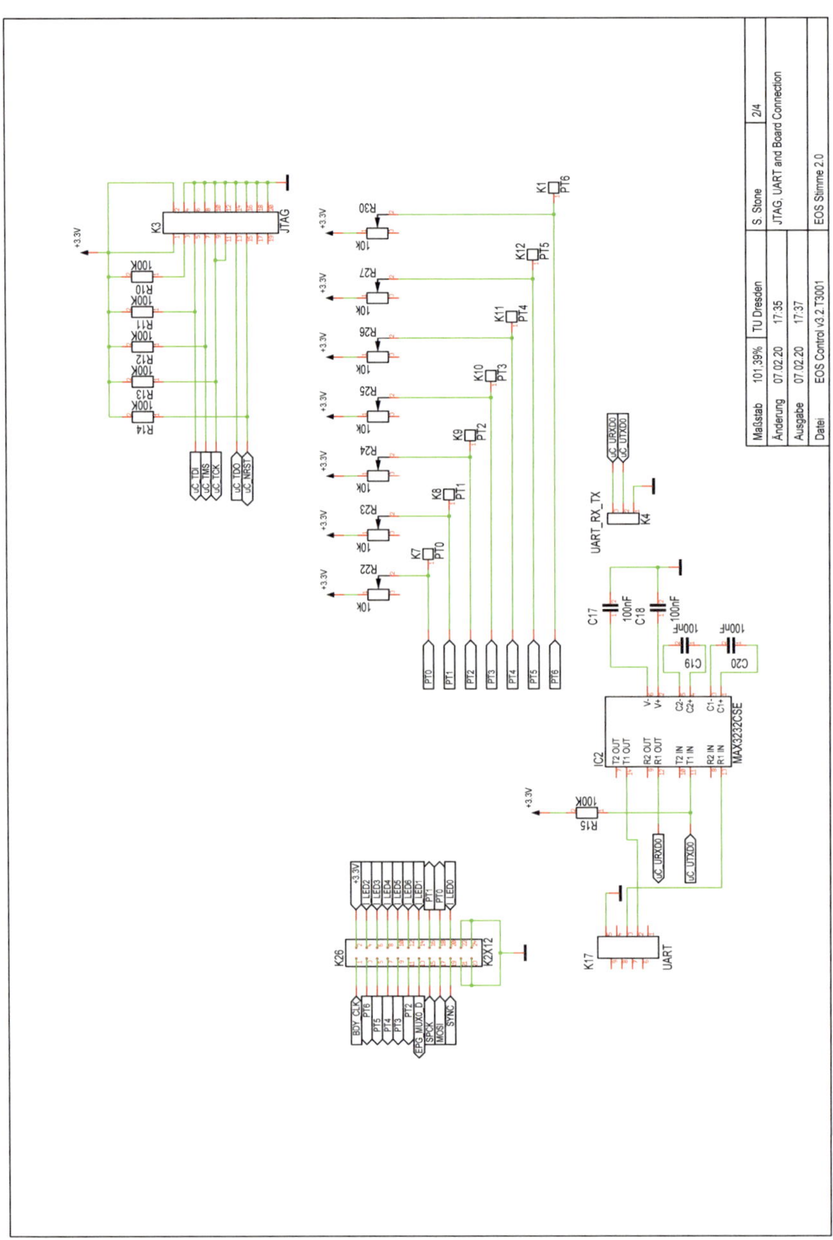

Figure C.5.: Incoming and outgoing board connections: JTAG for debugging, UART for communication with the computer software, and a custom connector to connect the sensor unit.

C.2. Layout of the control unit

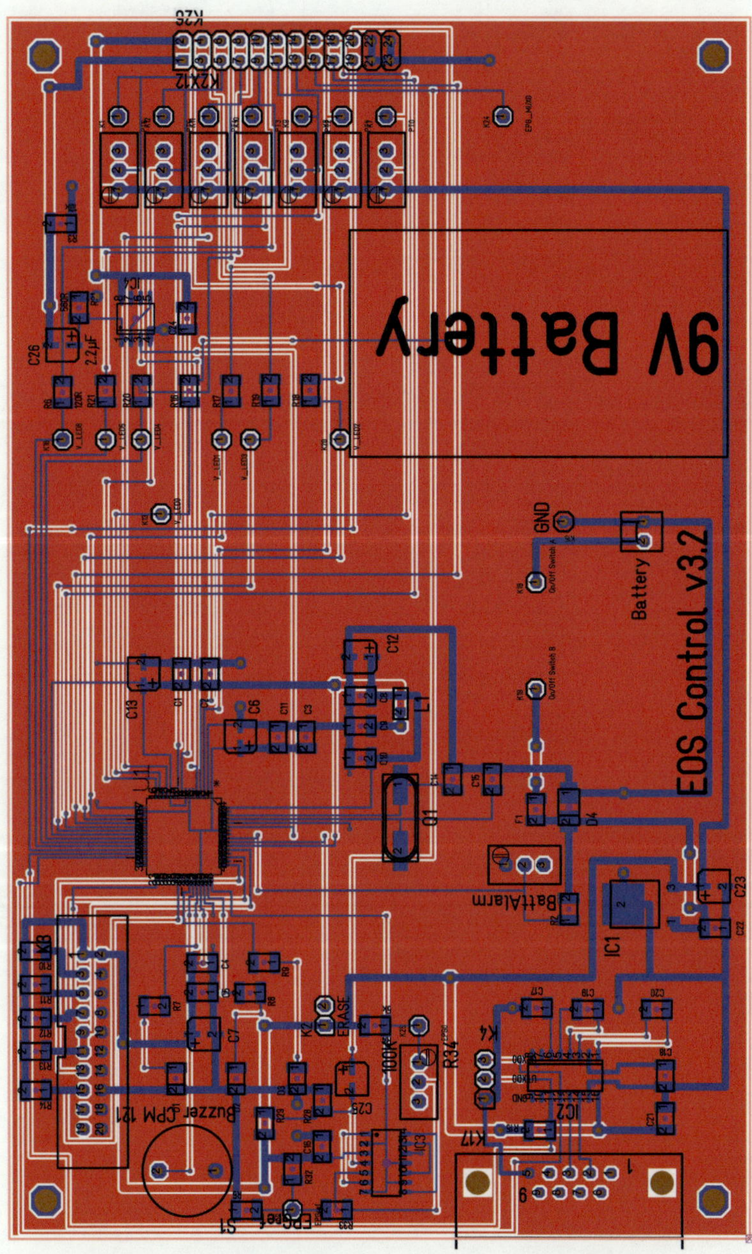

Figure C.6.: Layout of the control unit for a double-sided PCB.

C.3. Bill of materials of the control unit

Pos	Name	Value	Package
1	C1	100 nF	1206
2	C2	100 nF	1206
3	C3	100 nF	1206
4	C4	100 nF	1206
5	C5	100 nF	1206
6	C6	10 µF	SMD R4X6 e-cap
7	C7	4.7 µF	SMD R4X6 e-cap
8	C8	100 nF	1206
9	C9	100 nF	1206
10	C10	100 nF	1206
11	C11	100 nF	1206
12	C12	4.7 µF	SMD R4X6 e-cap
13	C13	2.2 µF	SMD R4X6 e-cap
14	C14	20 pF	1206
15	C15	20 pF	1206
16	C16	100 nF	1206
17	C17	100 nF	1206
18	C18	100 nF	1206
19	C19	100 nF	1206
20	C20	100 nF	1206
21	C21	100 nF	1206
22	C22	100 nF	1206
23	C23	2.2 µF	SMD R4X6 e-cap
24	C24	100 nF	1206
25	C25	2.2 µF	SMD R4X6 e-cap
26	C26	2.2 µF	SMD R4X6 e-cap
27	D1	LED_RED	1206-D
28	D2	LED_GREEN	1206-D
29	D3	LED_YELLOW	1206-D
30	D4	13 V	SMA
31	F1	2 A	1206
32	IC1	LF33CDT	TO252
33	IC2	MAX3232CSE	SO16
34	IC3	LM339D	SO14
35	IC4	TS912ID	SO8
36	K1	PT6	1X01
37	K2	ERASE	Pin header 1x02 pitch 2.54 mm
38	K3	JTAG	Box socket 2 rows 20 pins
39	K4	UART_RX_TX	Pin header 1x02 pitch 2.54 mm
40	K5	9V_Battery	SL-MTA 2 pins pitch 2.54 mm
41	K6	EPGref	1X01
42	K7	PT0	1X01
43	K8	PT1	1X01
44	K9	PT2	1X01
45	K10	PT3	1X01
46	K11	PT4	1X01
47	K12	PT5	1X01
48	K13	V_LED0	1X01
49	K14	V_LED1	1X01

Pos	Name	Value	Package
50	K15	GND	1X01
51	K16	V_LED6	1X01
52	K17	UART	DE09 socket
53	K18	On/Off Switch A	1X01
54	K19	On/Off Switch B	1X01
55	K20	V_LED2	1X01
56	K21	V_LED3	1X01
57	K22	V_LED4	1X01
58	K23	V_LED5	1X01
59	K24	EPG_MUX0	1X01
60	K25	EPG0	1X01
61	K26	K2X12	2X12
62	L1	10 µH/100 mA	0805
63	Q1	12 MHz	HC49 SMD
64	R1	25 kΩ potentiometer	VISHAY_64W
65	R2	56 kΩ	1206
66	R3	10 kΩ potentiometer	1206
67	R4	5 kΩ potentiometer	1206
68	R5	1 kΩ potentiometer	1206
69	R6	120 Ω	1206
70	R7	220 Ω	1206
71	R8	220 Ω	1206
72	R9	220 Ω	1206
73	R10	100 kΩ	1206
74	R11	100 kΩ	1206
75	R12	100 kΩ	1206
76	R13	100 kΩ	1206
77	R14	100 kΩ	1206
78	R15	100 kΩ	1206
79	R16	120 Ω	1206
80	R17	120 Ω	1206
81	R18	120 Ω	1206
82	R19	120 Ω	1206
83	R20	120 Ω	1206
84	R21	120 Ω	1206
85	R22	10 kΩ	VISHAY_64W
86	R23	10 kΩ	VISHAY_64W
87	R24	10 kΩ	VISHAY_64W
88	R25	10 kΩ	VISHAY_64W
89	R26	10 kΩ	VISHAY_64W
90	R27	10 kΩ	VISHAY_64W
91	R28	10 kΩ	1206
92	R29	10 kΩ	
93	R30	10 kΩ	VISHAY_64W
94	R31	560 Ω	1206
95	R32	1 kΩ	1206
96	R33	1 kΩ	
97	S1	Buzzer CPM 121	Pitch 7.62
98	U1	ATSAM3S4BA-AU	QFP50P1200X1200X160-64N

C.4. Schematics of the sensor unit

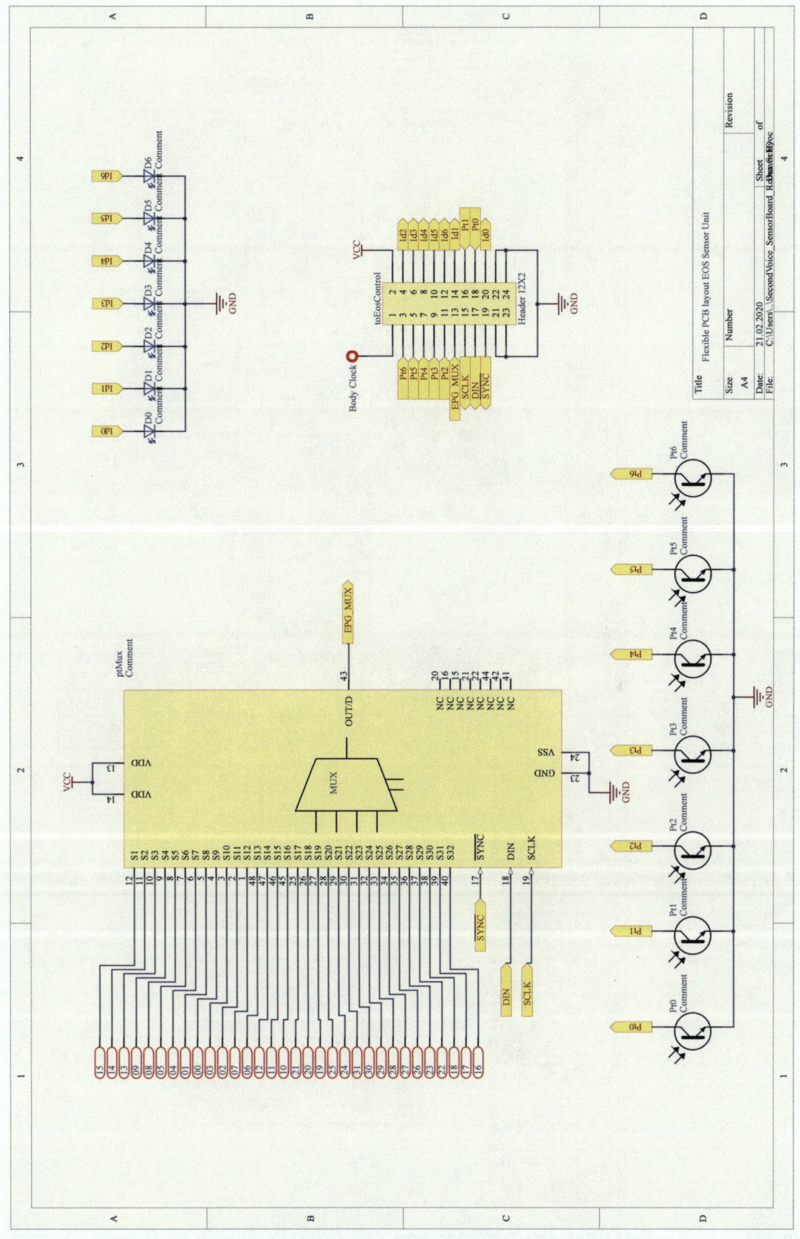

Figure C.7.: Schematics of the sensor unit.

C.5. Layout of the sensor unit

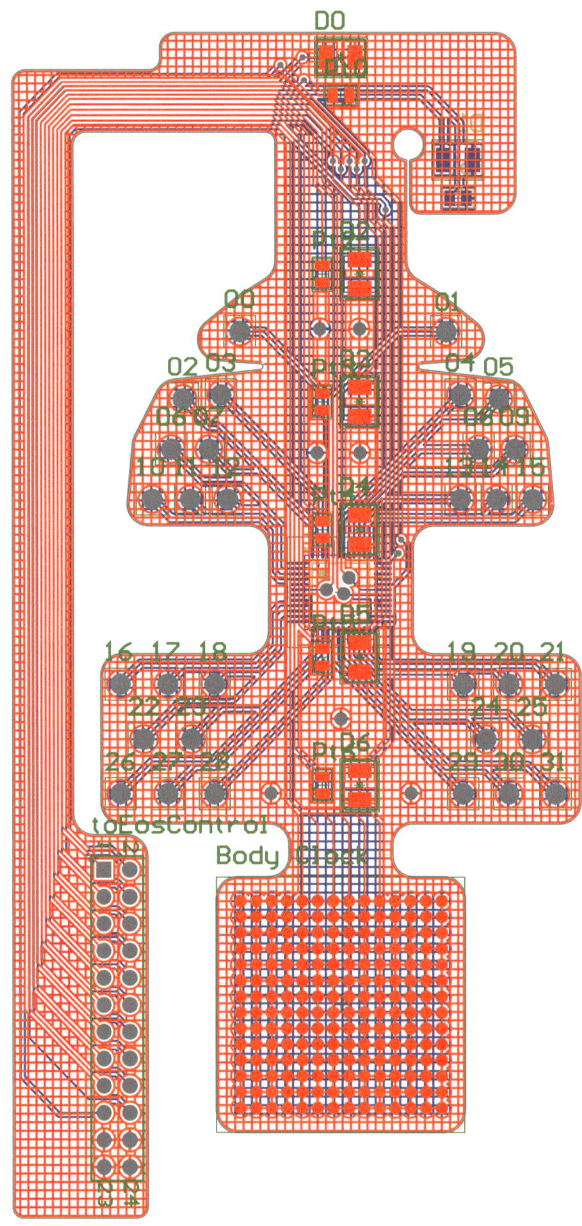

Figure C.8.: Layout of the sensor unit for a double-sided flexible PCB. The area around the connector socket should be stiffened with a thicker polyamide layer.

C.6. Bill of materials of the sensor unit

Pos	Name	Value	Package
01	00 to 31	Tongue contact sensor	Blank hard gold plated pad
02	Body Clock	Reference voltage contact	Matrix of hard gold plated pads
03	D0, D1, D2, D3, D4, D5, D6	OP280V	PLCC-2
04	Pt0, Pt1, Pt2, Pt3, Pt4, Pt5, Pt6	Phototransistor	TEMT7100
05	ptMux	ADG731	TQFP
06	toEosControl	Pin header	2 rows times 12 pins

D. Sensor unit assembly

Workflow for the assembly of an EOS sensor unit

1. Thermoform the Erkodur 0.5 mm base plate; remove protective foil

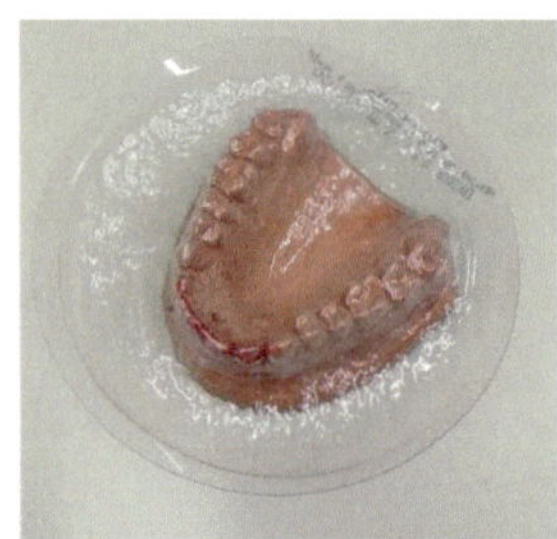

2. Trim the base plate to perfectly fit the plaster model and check the fit of the flexible sensor circuit board, especially if the contact array flap can be folded to the back side of the base plate

3. Mark the edge of the flexible circuit board on both top and bottom of the base plate

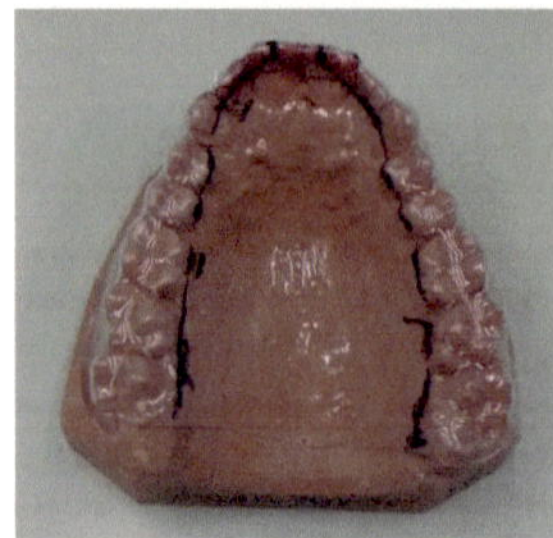

4. Mask all contacts (sensors and pads) with masking tape. Try to mask only the blank areas and cover as little of the area around it
   Mask dimensions:
   Optical sensors (7x) 6 mm x 6 mm
   Multiplexer (1x): 12 mm x 12 mm
   Connector (1x): 40 mm x 20 mm
   Contact sensors (2x): 60 mm x 30 mm)
   Contact array (1x): 21 mm x 21 mm

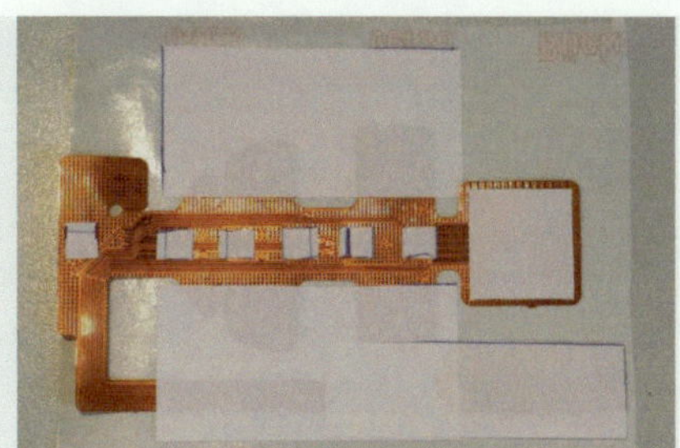

5. Using a sandblaster, roughen the base plate (2 bar, 50 µm): Base plate top (sensor side) and bottom (contact array side) and front (lip sensor side)

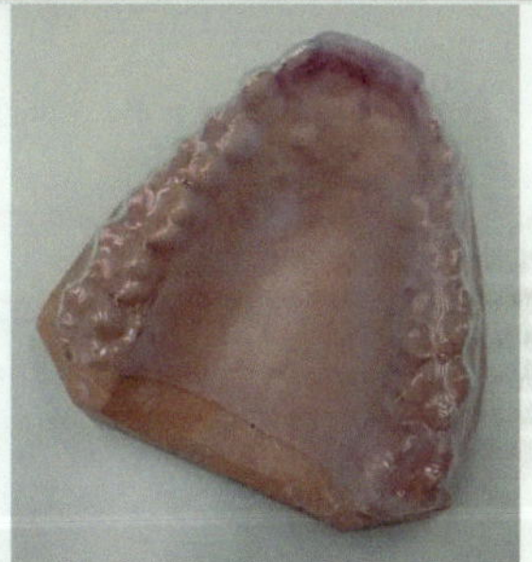

6. Using a sandblaster, roughen the unmasked area of the cover layer oft he circuit board (2 bar, 50 µm).

7. Remove contact sensor masking tape and mask the contact array and the connector on the bottom side of the board

8. **Sandblast the bottom of the flexible circuit board (2 bar, 50 µm)**

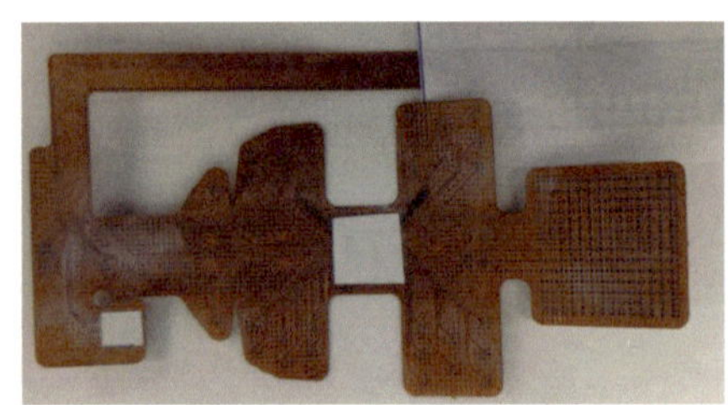

9. **Remove all masking tape**

10. **Clean base plate and circuit board using an alcohol wipe**

11. **Mount all electronic components on the circuit board**

12. **Apply Dentona Primostick Primer to the roughened areas of the base plate (top, front, and bottom)**

13. **Apply Dentona Primostick to the roughened area of the circuit board bottom**

14. **Harden the primer in UV oven (4 minutes per side)**

15. Seal the multiplexer on the bototm of the circuit board using Tetric EvoFlow

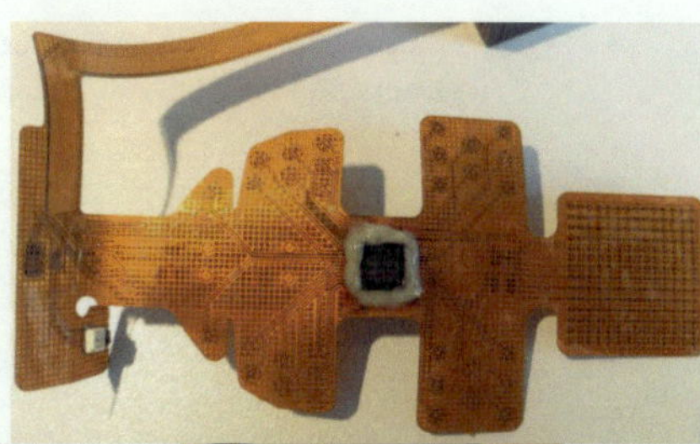

16. Harden the EvoFlow using a blue light lamp.

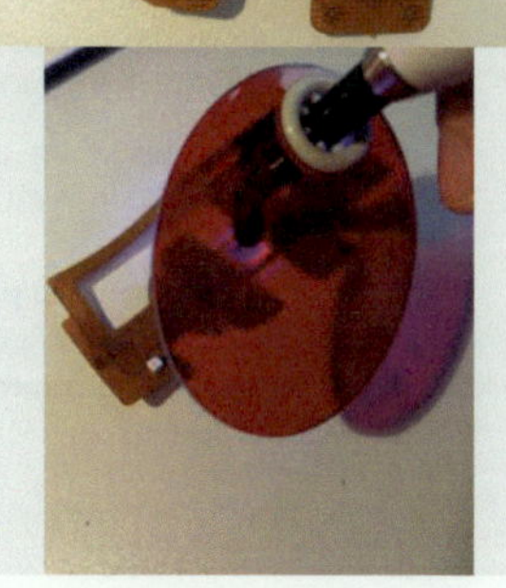

The following step is ideally performed by two people:

17. Affix the circuit board to the base plate using EvoFlow. Apply the glue in the order according to SecondVoice_SensorBoard_glueAreas.pdf and hard it with the blue light lamp after every step.
18. Fold the downward facing source-detector pair of the lip sensor, apply primer and let it harden in the UV oven.
19. Fix the folded flap in place using EvoFlow. Harden with blue light lamp.

20. **Apply primer around all the optical sensors and let it harden in the UV oven.**

21. **Seal all optical sensors using EvoFlow. Harden with the blue light lamp.**
22. **Seal the edges of the circuit board with EvoFlow. Harden with the blue light lamp.**
23. **Fix the circuit board part that exits the mouth in place using EvoFlow. Harden with the blue light lamp.**

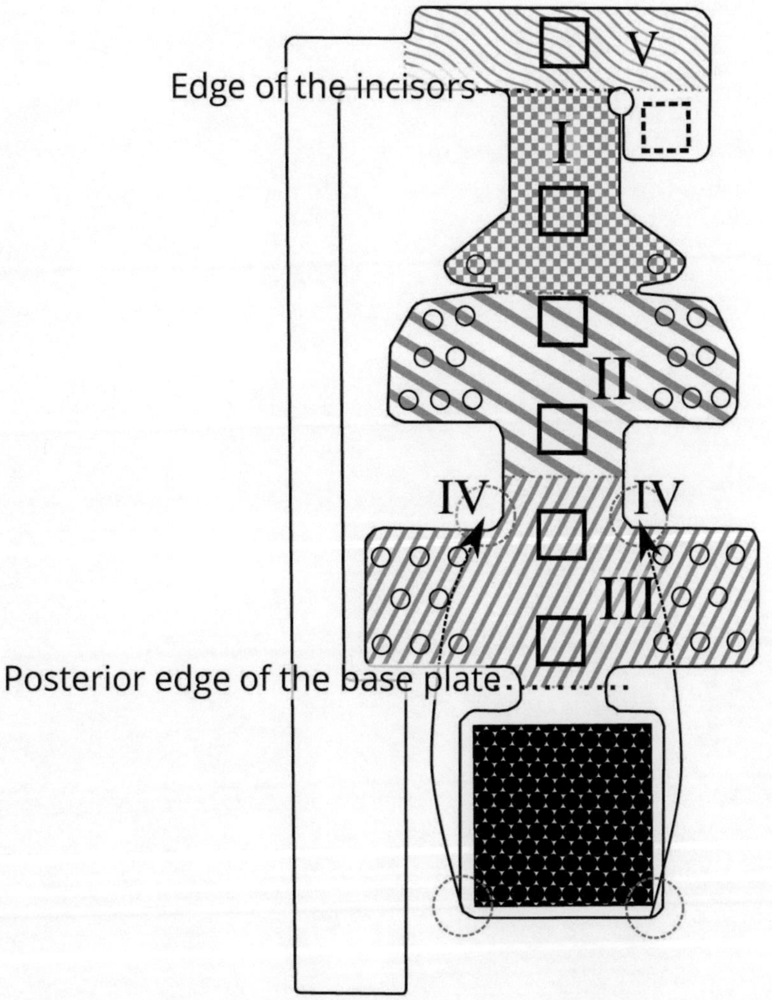

Figure D.1.: Instructions given in SecondVoice_SensorBoard_glueAreas.pdf regarding the order of glueing the flexible PCB to the base plate

E. Firmware flow and data protocol

Block meaning	Header		Mode	Frame index		Lip sensor						Optical sensor 1						Optical sensor 2-5	Contact sensors	Checksum
						Mean top		Mean bottom		Not used		Mean center		Mean anterior		Mean posterior			1 bit per sensor	Sum of all bytes except header bytes (overflow possible
Byte value	0xA5	0x5A	0x00	L	U	L	U	L	U	0x00	0x00	L	U	L	U	L	U	…		

Table E.1.: Deprecated frame format of the data sent from the control unit up to revision number 2.3 to the computer. All multi-byte data are sent with the lower byte (L) before the upper byte (U), i.e., in ittle-endian format.

Block meaning	Header bytes		Mode	Checksum
Byte value	0xA5	0x5A	0x00 or 0x01	Equals the Mode byte

Table E.2.: Frame format of the control parameter frame sent from the computer to the MCU. The Mode parameter could be "0" to sample only one detector per sensor, or "1" to sample the adjacent detectors, as well.

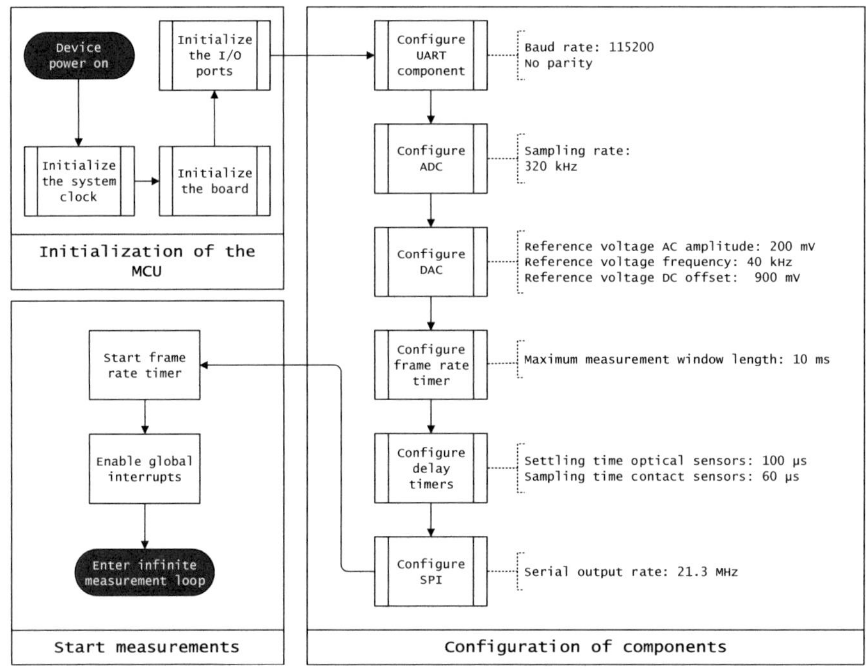

(a) Initialization and start of measurement loop

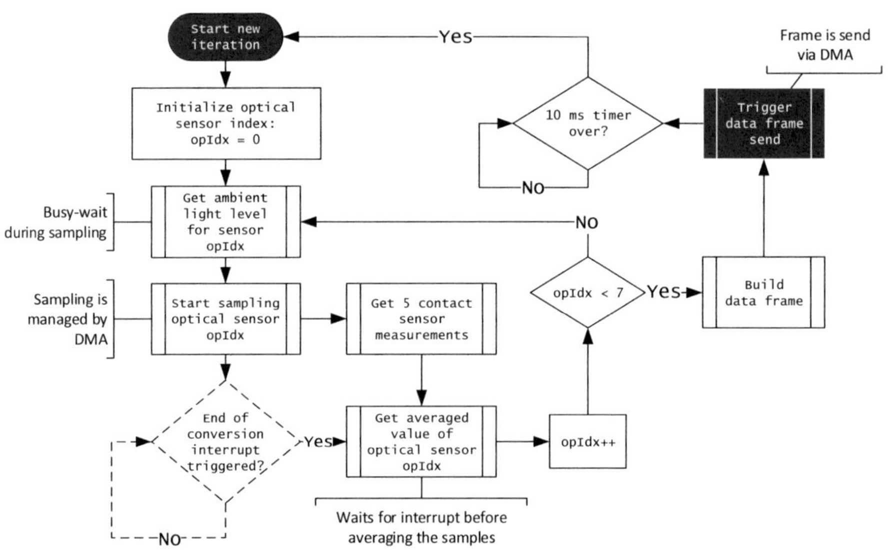

(b) Flow of the (infinite) measurement loop

Figure E.1.: Program flow of the firmware

Block meaning	Header	Frame index	Lip sensor (front-facing detector)	Lip sensor (down-facing detector)	Placeholder (velum)	Tongue distance sensors (front to back)	Contact sensors (1 bit per sensor)	Placeholder (additional contact sensors)	Placeholder (f_0 in Hz $\times 10$))	Placeholder (voicing)	Placeholder (breathiness)	Placeholder (lung pressure)	Checksum
Byte value	0x5A 0xA5	L U	L U	L U	L U	L U L U L U L U L U	see contact mapping	0x00 0x00 0x00 0x00	0xE8 0x03	0x01	0x00	0x40 0x1F	Sum of all bytes except header bytes (overflow possible)

Table E.3.: Frame format of the data sent from the control unit to the computer. The placeholders reserve space for future additional information. All multi-byte data are sent with the lower byte (L) before the upper byte (U), i.e., in ittle-endian format.

F. Palate file format

The palate files used to describe the palate outline and the sensor unit configuration have an XML-like structure. The following shows an example file:

```
<palate name="4-Simon">
<shape_2d points_x_y_cm ="␣-0.102000␣0.010000␣-0.669000␣0.065000␣-1.184000␣0.127000
-1.937000␣0.158000␣-2.354000␣-0.052000␣-2.783000␣-0.571000
-3.103000␣-0.936000␣-3.451000␣-1.446000␣-3.869000␣-1.833000
-4.366000␣-2.303000␣-4.683000␣-2.576000␣-5.073000␣-2.100000
-5.323000␣-1.594000"/>
<contact_sensors quantity = "64">
</contact_sensors>
<light_sensors quantity = "6">
<light_sensor index ="0"
x_cm = "-5.170000"
y_cm = "-1.900000"
angle_deg = "-153.700000"
calibration_dc_mm_adc = "0.000000␣0.000000␣30.000000␣4095.000000"
coefficients_triplePT = "1.000000␣0.000000␣0.000000␣0.000000"/>
<light_sensor index ="1"
x_cm = "-4.140000"
y_cm = "-2.090000"
angle_deg = "-46.600000"
calibration_dc_mm_adc = "0.000000␣439.465494␣5.000000␣2159.479062
10.000000␣3308.020694␣15.000000␣3670.415668
20.000000␣3831.927234␣25.000000␣3923.939653
30.000000␣3972.534454"
coefficients_triplePT = "1.000000␣0.000000␣0.000000␣0.000000"/>
<light_sensor index ="2"
x_cm = "-3.300000"
y_cm = "-1.230000"
angle_deg = "-34.300000"
calibration_dc_mm_adc = "0.000000␣1000.360965␣5.000000␣2447.305798
10.000000␣3388.112120␣15.000000␣3704.338295
20.000000␣3850.458449␣25.000000␣3934.754741
30.000000␣3975.982471"
coefficients_triplePT = "1.000000␣0.000000␣0.000000␣0.000000"/>
<light_sensor index ="3"
x_cm = "-2.550000"
y_cm = "-0.290000"
angle_deg = "-39.600000"
calibration_dc_mm_adc = "0.000000␣1528.228752␣5.000000␣2506.601168
10.000000␣3460.317472␣15.000000␣3736.252028
20.000000␣3868.718543␣25.000000␣3947.935527
30.000000␣3987.481818"
coefficients_triplePT = "1.000000␣0.000000␣0.000000␣0.000000"/>
<light_sensor index ="4"
x_cm = "-1.540000"
y_cm = "0.140000"
angle_deg = "-92.600000"
calibration_dc_mm_adc = "0.000000␣418.100000␣5.000000␣2143.920000
```

```
10.000000␣3304.840000␣15.000000␣3669.090000
20.000000␣3831.210000␣25.000000␣3923.650000
30.000000␣3970.040000"
coefficients_triplePT = "1.000000␣0.000000␣0.000000␣0.000000"/>
<light_sensor index ="5"
x_cm = "-0.360000"
y_cm = "0.040000"
angle_deg = "-95.500000"
calibration_dc_mm_adc = "0.000000␣276.100000␣5.000000␣2032.080000
10.000000␣3283.990000␣15.000000␣3660.500000
20.000000␣3826.670000␣25.000000␣3921.460000
30.000000␣3972.100000"
coefficients_triplePT = "1.000000␣0.000000␣0.000000␣0.000000"/>
</light_sensors>
</palate>
```

The individual tags have the following meaning:

palate: The *palate* tag encapsulates the entire palate file. Its only attribute is *name*, which holds the name of the palate file to be displayed in the GUI.

shape_2d: This self-closing tag has only one attribute *points_x_y_cm*, which is a list of x- and y-coordinates of the mid-sagittal cross-section of the sensor unit. The origin for these coordinates may be chosen arbitrarily, but using the most posterior point of the sensor unit profile is recommended.

contact_sensors: This tag has only one attribute *quantity* stating the number of contact sensors on the palate.

light_sensors: This tag has one attribute *quantity*, which holds the number of optical sensors (lip and tongue) on the sensor unit. Its content is a series of *light_sensor* tags.

light_sensor: This self-closing tag has the following attributes:

- **index:** Index of the optical sensor (usually from front to back)
- **x_cm:** x- coordinate in cm of the sensor along the palate profile using the same origin as *shape_2d*.
- **y_cm:** y- coordinate in cm of the sensor along the palate profile using the same origin as *shape_2d*.
- **angle_deg:** Angle in degree of the optical axis of the sensor
- **calibration_dc_mm_adc:** Pairs of distances in mm and the corresponding sensor output in ADC for the distance sensing function (see subsection 4.2.2).
- **coefficients_triplePT:** Coefficients used for the angle-correction (see subsection 4.2.2).

G. Supplemental material regarding the vocal tract model

Sound	x_{lar}	A_{lar}	$n_{lar,p}$	x_p	A_p	$n_{p,c}$	x_c	A_c	n_c	x_a	A_a	$n_{c,a}$	x_{in}	A_{in}	x_{lip}	A_{lip}
/aː/	1.866	1.153	0.418	2.893	5.755	7.363	8.477	0.951	0.852	14.385	6.655	0.543	17.028	2.706	17.099	2.787
/eː/	0.458	1.474	0.208	3.043	7.055	0.833	12.78	0.478	0.473	17.236	3.199	0.586	17.499	3.859	18.142	2.485
/iː/	1.644	2.046	2.391	5.625	8.834	0.955	13.45	0.275	0.298	17.323	4.055	1.408	17.936	2.929	18.136	3.298
/oː/	1.059	1.983	0.217	2.839	7.53	0.722	11.405	0.421	0.4	17.574	14.351	0.736	20.3451	2.087	21.425	0.638
/uː/	1.278	1.904	4.252	6.448	8.881	2.13	14.457	0.782	1.043	18.572	9.436	1.019	20.002	2.288	21.519	0.423
/ɛː/	2.477	0.772	1.066	2.647	3.614	0.773	12.300	1.316	1.635	15.279	2.632	8.927	16.851	4.133	17.422	4.392
/øː/	0.895	1.460	0.324	3.122	9.609	0.653	14.390	1.305	0.873	18.767	4.274	1.583	19.101	2.221	20.538	0.62
/yː/	1.510	1.776	3.013	6.103	11.572	0.935	15.014	0.597	0.592	18.637	2.741	0.918	19.313	1.044	20.688	0.342
/a/	2.319	0.685	1.268	3.247	4.311	6.154	9.551	0.776	1.593	15.677	8.536	0.725	18.042	3.637	18.421	3.216
/ɛ/	2.756	0.772	1.276	2.643	3.818	0.275	8.136	1.325	0.508	16.795	3.951	0.594	17.38	3.283	17.474	4.015
/ɪ/	1.606	1.958	3.7	6.628	7.822	2.747	12.842	1.155	1.082	16.456	4.364	0.629	17.894	3.368	18.712	2.681
/ɔ/	0.0	0.817	0.428	2.625	4.504	0.941	10.556	0.506	1.798	17.55	10.108	0.808	19.366	2.08	20.241	1.563
/ʊ/	0.863	1.978	0.515	2.098	8.708	0.792	11.086	0.347	0.925	17.442	12.732	0.852	19.684	1.584	20.848	0.816
/œ/	1.634	1.526	0.791	3.369	7.445	1.928	6.158	2.493	5.605	10.767	5.019	0.225	18.042	2.929	19.012	1.405
/ʏ/	0.594	1.167	0.464	2.773	8.247	0.905	12.8	1.894	0.761	16.428	5.053	0.581	18.201	2.858	19.541	0.816
/ə/	0.0	1.077	0.208	3.074	6.256	0.726	12.783	1.456	2.679	16.725	1.773	0.896	17.407	2.575	18.56	1.405
/f/	0.021	0.753	0.18	1.922	6.776	0.367	11.861	1.804	1.319	16.584	3.22	0.743	17.894	0.548	18.302	1.622
/l/	1.013	1.726	0.618	3.139	10.243	0.817	13.349	1.085	0.703	15.843	1.807	1.388	16.374	1.201	18.767	1.796
/s/	0.968	0.855	0.301	2.554	9.109	1.525	14.274	2.416	1.222	16.495	0.092	0.586	17.407	1.301	17.892	1.561
/ʃ/	2.35	1.079	5.222	5.154	9.078	1.301	16.442	0.127	0.438	17.329	6.732	1.77	18.519	1.867	19.765	3.172
/ç/	2.545	0.875	9.361	6.716	6.61	1.002	14.464	0.311	1.5	16.9	0.16	0.57	17.982	2.877	18.812	2.681
/x/	2.406	0.718	0.074	2.406	1.822	0.806	9.412	0.2	0.741	14.815	8.271	1.392	16.93	6.115	17.745	3.708

Table G.1.: Parameter values for the geometrically fitted full configuration of the six point model. All positions x_i, $i \in \{\text{lar, p, c, a, in, lip}\}$, are in cm, all areas A_i in cm^2 and all warping exponents n_i are dimensionless.

Sound	A_p	$n_{p,c}$	x_c	A_c	n_c	A_a	$n_{c,a}$	x_{in}	A_{in}	x_{lip}	A_{lip}
/aː/	5.755	7.363	8.477	0.951	0.852	6.655	0.543	17.028	2.706	17.099	2.787
/eː/	7.055	0.833	12.78	0.478	0.473	3.199	0.586	17.499	3.859	18.142	2.485
/iː/	8.834	0.955	13.45	0.275	0.298	4.055	1.408	17.936	2.929	18.136	3.298
/oː/	7.53	0.722	11.405	0.421	0.4	14.35	0.736	20.345	2.087	21.425	0.638
/uː/	8.881	2.13	14.457	0.782	1.043	9.436	1.019	20.002	2.288	21.519	0.423
/ɛː/	3.614	0.773	12.3	1.316	1.636	2.632	8.927	16.851	4.133	17.422	4.392
/øː/	9.609	0.653	14.39	1.305	0.873	4.274	1.583	19.101	2.221	20.538	0.62
/yː/	11.572	0.935	15.014	0.597	0.592	2.741	0.918	19.312	1.044	20.688	0.342
/a/	4.311	6.154	9.551	0.776	1.593	8.537	0.725	18.042	3.637	18.421	3.216
/ɛ/	3.818	0.275	8.136	1.325	0.508	3.951	0.594	17.38	3.283	17.474	4.015
/ɪ/	7.822	2.747	12.842	1.155	1.082	4.364	0.629	17.894	3.368	18.712	2.68
/ɔ/	4.504	0.941	10.556	0.506	1.798	10.108	0.808	19.366	2.08	20.241	1.563
/ʊ/	8.708	0.792	11.086	0.347	0.925	12.732	0.852	19.684	1.584	20.848	0.816
/œ/	7.445	1.928	6.158	2.493	5.605	5.019	0.225	18.042	2.929	19.012	1.405
/ʏ/	8.247	0.905	12.8	1.894	0.761	5.053	0.581	18.201	2.858	19.541	0.816
/ə/	6.256	0.726	12.783	1.456	2.679	1.773	0.896	17.407	2.575	18.56	1.405
/f/	6.776	0.367	11.861	1.804	1.319	3.22	0.743	17.894	0.548	18.302	1.622
/l/	10.243	0.817	13.349	1.085	0.703	1.807	1.388	16.374	1.201	18.767	1.797
/s/	9.109	1.525	14.274	2.416	1.222	0.092	0.586	17.407	1.301	17.892	1.561
/ʃ/	9.078	1.301	16.442	0.127	0.438	6.732	1.77	18.519	1.867	19.765	3.172
/ç/	6.61	1.002	14.464	0.311	1.5	0.16	0.57	17.982	2.877	18.812	2.681
/x/	1.822	0.806	9.412	0.2	0.741	8.271	1.392	16.930	6.115	17.745	3.708

Table G.2.: Parameter values for the geometrically fitted reduced configuration of the six point model. All positions x_i, $i \in \{\text{lar, p, c, a, in, lip}\}$, are in cm, all areas A_i in cm^2 and all warping exponents n_i are dimensionless.

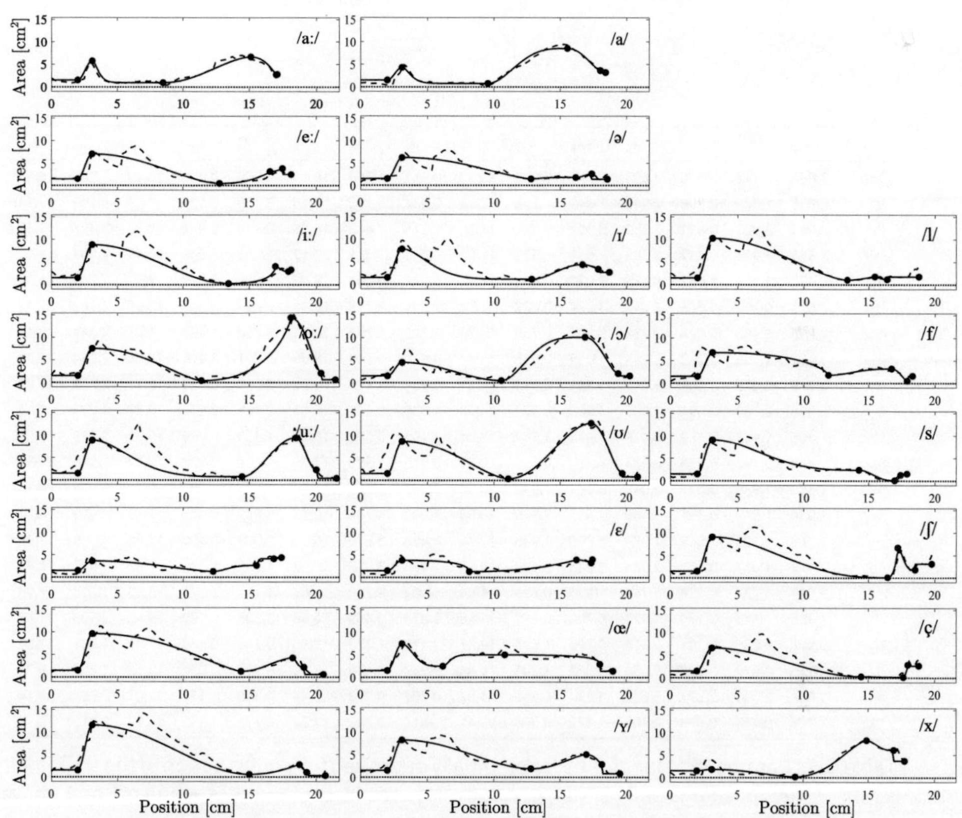

Figure G.1.: Area functions of tense vowels (left column), lax and neutral vowels (center column), and consonants (right column). Dashed lines mark the references and solid lines the geometrically fitted reduced configuration of the six point model. The black dots mark the six control points.

Sound	x_{lar}	A_{lar}	$n_{lar,p}$	x_p	A_p	$n_{p,c}$	x_c	A_c	n_c	x_a	A_a	$n_{c,a}$	x_{in}	A_{in}	x_{lip}	A_{lip}
/aː/	2.066	1.143	0.118	2.693	5.745	6.963	8.277	0.941	1.252	14.19	6.665	0.243	16.52	2.83	16.53	2.969
/eː/	0.658	1.464	0.208	2.943	7.045	1.233	12.98	0.488	0.473	17.14	3.189	0.586	17.5	3.859	17.94	2.495
/iː/	2.044	2.026	0.891	3.352	8.991	0.8	13.39	0.216	2.413	16.06	0.714	0.814	17.32	3.421	17.63	2.925
/oː/	1.359	1.963	0.217	2.789	7.51	1.522	11.01	0.441	0.6	17.17	14.33	1.536	20.45	2.107	21.02	0.658
/uː/	1.477	1.894	3.852	6.138	9.035	1.33	14.31	0.628	0.843	18.26	11.42	0.919	20.2	2.545	21.52	0.762
/ɛː/	2.627	0.762	0.666	2.847	3.624	0.673	12.4	1.306	1.235	15.38	2.622	9.327	16.65	4.143	17.27	4.402
/øː/	1.295	1.463	0.024	3.122	9.589	0.753	14.74	1.325	1.273	18.82	4.284	1.583	19.1	2.221	20.19	0.64
/yː/	1.91	1.756	2.213	6.103	11.55	0.935	15.41	0.617	0.392	18.69	2.761	0.618	19.46	1.054	20.29	0.362
/a/	2.519	0.675	0.868	3.047	4.301	6.554	9.751	0.786	1.193	15.88	8.527	0.325	18.17	3.647	18.22	3.226
/ɛ/	2.556	0.762	0.876	3.987	3.808	0.375	8.336	1.335	0.308	16.59	3.961	0.194	17.38	3.293	17.4	4.015
/ɪ/	1.806	1.948	3.3	6.428	7.812	2.347	13.04	1.165	0.682	16.66	4.354	0.229	18.09	3.378	18.51	2.691
/ɔ/	0.4	0.797	0.028	2.525	4.484	0.641	10.51	0.526	1.398	17.95	10.09	0.008	19.37	2.06	19.84	1.583
/ʊ/	1.663	1.938	0.015	2.048	8.668	1.992	10.54	0.387	0.325	17.74	12.73	1.052	20.14	1.308	20.14	1.291
/œ/	1.834	1.517	0.391	3.569	7.435	2.328	6.358	2.503	5.205	10.97	5.009	0.625	17.89	2.919	18.81	1.415
/ʏ/	-0.2	1.107	1.508	2.074	6.206	1.926	12.18	1.486	3.879	16.13	1.808	0.496	17.86	1.9	18.76	1.395
/ə/	0.2	1.067	0.108	2.874	6.246	1.126	12.58	1.466	3.079	16.52	1.783	1.296	17.46	2.585	18.36	1.415
/l/	1.017	1.727	0.624	3.149	10.26	0.826	13.4	1.07	0.719	15.67	1.732	1.177	16.33	1.298	18.09	1.721
/f/	0.0	0.75	0.179	1.922	6.799	0.379	11.88	1.878	0.456	14.68	3.321	0.582	17.43	2.504	18.3	0.259
/s/	0.968	0.855	0.301	2.554	9.109	1.525	14.27	2.416	1.222	16.5	0.149	0.586	17.41	1.301	17.89	1.561
/ʃ/	2.35	1.079	5.222	5.154	9.078	1.301	16.44	0.212	0.438	17.33	6.732	1.77	18.52	1.867	19.77	3.172
/ç/	1.644	2.046	2.391	5.625	8.834	0.955	14.02	0.202	0.313	15.44	0.569	1.114	17.61	3.255	18.14	3.298
/x/	2.406	0.718	0.074	2.406	1.822	0.806	9.441	0.14	0.741	14.82	8.271	1.392	16.93	6.115	17.75	3.708

Table G.3.: Parameter values for the perceptually optimized full configuration of the six point model. All positions x_i, $i \in$ {lar, p, c, a, in, lip}, are in cm, all areas A_i in cm^2 and all warping exponents n_i are dimensionless.

Sound	A_p	$n_{p,c}$	x_c	A_c	n_c	A_a	$n_{c,a}$	x_{in}	A_{in}	x_{lip}	A_{lip}
/aː/	5.735	8.163	8.077	0.971	1.452	6.655	0.543	17.03	2.726	17.05	2.787
/eː/	7.045	1.233	12.58	0.488	0.373	3.189	0.986	17.55	3.869	17.94	2.495
/iː/	8.824	1.055	13.5	0.285	0.198	4.065	1.008	17.74	2.939	17.94	3.298
/oː/	7.52	1.122	11.21	0.431	0.6	14.36	0.736	20.3	2.097	21.23	0.648
/uː/	8.858	1.43	14.41	0.795	0.643	9.421	1.619	19.55	2.273	21.09	0.515
/ɛː/	3.604	0.873	12.35	1.306	1.435	2.642	9.327	16.65	4.143	17.22	4.402
/øː/	9.599	0.753	14.59	1.315	1.073	4.264	1.483	19.3	2.211	20.34	0.63
/yː/	11.56	0.935	15.11	0.607	0.192	2.751	0.818	19.16	1.044	20.49	0.352
/a/	4.301	6.554	9.701	0.786	1.193	8.527	0.325	18.17	3.647	18.22	3.226
/ɛ/	3.808	0.375	8.336	1.335	0.408	3.961	0.194	17.38	3.293	17.4	4.015
/ɪ/	7.812	2.347	13.04	1.145	0.682	4.354	0.229	18.09	3.378	18.51	2.691
/ɔ/	4.474	0.641	10.21	0.536	1.698	10.08	0.108	19.69	2.344	19.87	1.622
/ʊ/	8.698	0.592	11.19	0.357	0.525	12.72	1.252	19.88	1.594	20.65	0.826
/œ/	7.425	2.728	6.158	2.513	5.105	4.999	0.925	18.19	2.917	18.61	1.425
/ʏ/	8.217	2.105	12.2	1.924	0.261	5.06	0.981	18.35	2.868	18.94	0.846
/ə/	6.246	1.126	12.58	1.466	3.079	1.783	1.296	17.46	2.585	18.36	1.415
/f/	6.776	0.367	11.86	1.804	1.319	3.22	0.743	17.89	0.272	18.41	0.277
/l/	10.24	0.817	13.35	1.085	0.703	1.807	1.388	16.37	1.201	18.77	1.796
/s/	9.109	1.525	10.71	2.416	1.222	0.134	0.586	17.41	1.301	17.89	1.561
/ʃ/	9.078	1.301	16.11	0.156	0.438	6.622	1.77	18.65	1.895	19.77	3.172
/ç/	6.61	1.002	14.52	0.247	1.5	0.192	0.57	17.98	2.877	18.81	2.681
/x/	1.822	0.806	9.412	0.182	0.741	8.271	1.392	16.93	6.115	17.75	3.708

Table G.4.: Parameter values for the perceptually optimized reduced configuration of the six point model. All positions x_i are in cm, all areas A_i in cm^2 and all warping exponents n_i are dimensionless.

Sound	$F1_{16}$	$F1_{11}$	$F2_{16}$	$F2_{11}$	$F3_{16}$	$F3_{11}$
/aː/	702	622	1246	1123	2679	2676
/eː/	323	319	2132	2141	2709	2679
/iː/	257	258	2066	2174	3038	3124
/oː/	325	311	601	602	2646	2583
/uː/	265	286	751	848	2122	2161
/ɛː/	528	504	1905	1832	2591	2550
/øː/	298	286	1300	1269	2025	2014
/yː/	228	225	1657	1614	2056	2119
/a/	671	569	1130	1106	2487	2432
/ɛ/	523	493	1805	1717	2566	2591
/ɪ/	355	394	1756	1652	2470	2480
/ɔ/	463	453	890	844	2522	2477
/ʊ/	327	287	997	750	2402	2391
/œ/	464	473	1313	1301	2224	2252
/ʏ/	372	380	1366	1290	2380	2316
/ə/	406	390	1626	1607	2520	2477

Table G.5.: Formant frequencies in Hz for the first three formants of the vocal tract transfer functions calculated from the the perceptually optimized full configuration (subscript 16) and the perceptually optimized reduced configuration (subscript 11) of the six point model.

H. Articulation-to-Speech: Optimal hyperparameters

This appendix lists the optimal hyperparameters for the best-performing regression models in the ATS study (see chapter 6) for each subject. The names of the various basis and kernel functions are given in Matlab terminology (e.g., "pureQuadratic") for ease of reference. Complete logs of the entire parameter optimizations (including all evaluated hyperparameter combinations and the optimal values for the other, not best-performing models) are given in the digital supplemental materials accompanying this dissertation.

		Subject 1
Parameter	**Best model**	**Optimal Hyperparameters**
x_{lar}	SVM	linear, $C = 3.2689$, $\varepsilon = 0.10424$, standardized
A_{lar}	Ensemble	bagging, 497 cycles, min. leaf size 1, max. splits 200, variables 10
n_{lar}	SVM	Gaussian, $C = 70.427$, $\gamma = 0.87274$, $\varepsilon = 0.0053359$, standardized
x_p	GPR	basis constant, kernel ardexponential, $\sigma = 0.23552$, not standardized
A_p	GPR	basis linear, kernel ardmatern32, $\sigma = 0.0060051$, standardized
n_p	Ensemble	boosting, 439 cycles, learn rate 0.011384, min. leaf size 16, max. splits 6, variables 10
x_c	SVM	polynomial order 2, $C = 0.018994$, $\varepsilon = 0.032298$, standardized
A_c	Ensemble	bagging, 45 cycles, min. leaf size 1, max. splits 96, variables 10
n_c	SVM	Gaussian, $C = 927.34$, $\gamma = 0.86081$, $\varepsilon = 0.001962$, standardized
x_a	SVM	Gaussian, $C = 28.632$, $\gamma = 0.73133$, $\varepsilon = 0.0031091$, standardized
A_a	Ensemble	bagging, 107 cycles, min. leaf size 2, max. splits 135, variables 6
n_a	GPR	basis constant, kernel ardexponential, $\sigma = 0.1947$, not standardized
x_{in}	Ensemble	boosting, 499 cycles, learn rate 0.042238, min. leaf size 1, max. splits 170, variables 4
A_{in}	GPR	basis none, kernel matern32, $\sigma = 0.00037503$, kernel scale 3.9826, standardized
x_{lip}	Ensemble	bagging, 249 cycles, min. leaf size 1, max. splits 203, variables 6
A_{lip}	Ensemble	boosting, 499 cycles, learn rate 0.013175, min. leaf size 2, max. splits 177, variables 3

Table H.1.: Optimal hyperparameters for the best-performing regression models of subject 1

		Subject 2
Parameter	Best model	Optimal Hyperparameters
x_{lar}	GPR	basis linear, kernel ardmatern52, $\sigma = 0.45901$, standardized
A_{lar}	GPR	basis constant, kernel exponential, $\sigma = 0.0021071$, kernel scale 3.8253, standardized
n_{lar}	Ensemble	boosting, 328 cycles, learn rate 0.049207, min. leaf size 8, max. splits 20, variables 1
x_p	GPR	basis constant, kernel exponential, $\sigma = 0.0078458$, kernel scale 3.8239, standardized
A_p	GPR	basis constant, kernel exponential, $\sigma = 0.00010236$, kernel scale 3.9581, standardized
n_p	GPR	basis none, kernel ardexponential, $\sigma = 0.71897$, not standardized
x_c	GPR	basis constant, kernel ardexponential, $\sigma = 0.00015348$, standardized
A_c	GPR	basis none, kernel exponential, $\sigma = 0.1859$, kernel scale 3.7686, standardized
n_c	GPR	basis pureQuadratic, kernel rationalquadratic, $\sigma = 0.003132$, kernel scale 142.39, standardized
x_a	GPR	basis none, kernel rationalquadratic, $\sigma = 0.021129$, kernel scale 39.396, not standardized
A_a	Ensemble	bagging, 425 cycles, min. leaf size 2, max. splits 70, variables 7
n_a	Ensemble	boosting, 143 cycles, learn rate 0.088615, min. leaf size 3, max. splits 23, variables 10
x_{in}	GPR	basis linear, kernel exponential, $\sigma = 0.42712$, kernel scale 3711.6, standardized
A_{in}	GPR	basis none, kernel exponential, $\sigma = 0.00069188$, kernel scale 3700, standardized
x_{lip}	Ensemble	bagging, 38 cycles, min. leaf size 4, max. splits 43, variables 8
A_{lip}	Ensemble	bagging, 44 cycles, min. leaf size 4, max. splits 204, variables 5

Table H.2.: Optimal hyperparameters for the best-performing regression models of subject 2

		Subject 3
Parameter	Best model	Optimal Hyperparameters
x_{lar}	GPR	basis constant, kernel exponential, $\sigma = 0.32651$, kernel scale 3849.9, not standardized
A_{lar}	Ensemble	boosting, 460 cycles, learn rate 0.059927, min. leaf size 8, max. splits 88, variables 8
n_{lar}	SVM	Gaussian, $C = 11.92$, $\gamma = 988.21$, $\varepsilon = 0.0013191$, not standardized
x_p	GPR	basis linear, kernel rationalquadratic, $\sigma = 0.013517$, kernel scale 3854.6, not standardized
A_p	Ensemble	boosting, 418 cycles, learn rate 0.17623, min. leaf size 1, max. splits 6, variables 9
n_p	Ensemble	boosting, 394 cycles, learn rate 0.0076947, min. leaf size 9, max. splits 106, variables 9
x_c	GPR	basis linear, kernel ardexponential, $\sigma = 0.00010261$, kernel scale 3854.6, not standardized
A_c	SVM	Gaussian, $C = 48.198$, $\gamma = 4.2594$, $\varepsilon = 0.029579$, standardized
n_c	GPR	basis constant, kernel ardrationalquadratic, $\sigma = 0.83801$, standardized
x_a	GPR	basis pureQuadratic, kernel ardexponential, $\sigma = 1.06$, standardized
A_a	GPR	basis none, kernel exponential, $\sigma = 0.20942$, kernel scale 3329.2, standardized
n_a	SVM	Gaussian, $C = 50.643$, $\gamma = 0.82798$, $\varepsilon = 0.0043948$, standardized
x_{in}	GPR	basis none, kernel exponential, $\sigma = 0.00010338$, kernel scale 2839.8, standardized
A_{in}	Ensemble	boosting, 256 cycles, learn rate 0.052565, min. leaf size 4, max. splits 187, variables 3
x_{lip}	Ensemble	boosting, 365 cycles, learn rate 0.14381, min. leaf size 2, max. splits 104, variables 1
A_{lip}	Ensemble	boosting, 194 cycles, learn rate 0.062969, min. leaf size 1, max. splits 167, variables 4

Table H.3.: Optimal hyperparameters for the best-performing regression models of subject 3

		Subject 4
Parameter	Best model	Optimal Hyperparameters
x_{lar}	GPR	basis constant, kernel ardexponential, $\sigma = 0.00026394$, not standardized
A_{lar}	Ensemble	bagging, 136 cycles, min. leaf size 1, max. splits 202, variables 7
n_{lar}	GPR	basis constant, kernel exponential, $\sigma = 0.00012277$, kernel scale 11.942, standardized
x_p	GPR	basis linear, kernel exponential, $\sigma = 0.00011001$, kernel scale 3609.2, not standardized
A_p	GPR	basis constant, kernel exponential, $\sigma = 0.00125$, kernel scale 71.779, standardized
n_p	SVM	Gaussian, $C = 1.6301$, $\gamma = 844.01$, $\varepsilon = 0.0008347$, not standardized
x_c	GPR	basis none, kernel rationalquadratic, $\sigma = 0.39846$, kernel scale 1568.1, not standardized
A_c	Ensemble	boosting, 486 cycles, learn rate 0.023963, min. leaf size 1, max. splits 15, variables 2
n_c	GPR	basis constant, kernel ardmatern32, $\sigma = 0.00028977$, standardized
x_a	SVM	Gaussian, $C = 7.3972$, $\gamma = 994.47$, $\varepsilon = 0.015899$, not standardized
A_a	Ensemble	boosting, 434 cycles, learn rate 0.13478, min. leaf size 1, max. splits 80, variables 1
n_a	Ensemble	boosting, 334 cycles, learn rate 0.014869, min. leaf size 4, max. splits 180, variables 2
x_{in}	SVM	polynomial order 2, $C = 0.079779$, $\varepsilon = 0.2974$, standardized
A_{in}	Ensemble	boosting, 405 cycles, learn rate 0.16239, min. leaf size 8, max. splits 5, variables 3
x_{lip}	SVM	polynomial order 3, $C = 0.048712$, $\varepsilon = 0.048712$, standardized
A_{lip}	SVM	Gaussian, $C = 4.289$, $\gamma = 3.6078$, $\varepsilon = 0.016092$, standardized

Table H.4.: Optimal hyperparameters for the best-performing regression models of subject 4

Bibliography

[1] K. H. Davis, R. Biddulph, and S. Balashek, "Automatic recognition of spoken digits," *The Journal of the Acoustical Society of America*, vol. 24, no. 6, pp. 637–642, 1952.

[2] J. Gertner, *The Idea Factory: Bell Labs and the Great Age of American Innovation*. New York, NY, USA: Penguin Books, 2012.

[3] International Business Machines Corporation, "IBM Shoebox." [Online]. Available: https://www-03.ibm.com/ibm/history/exhibits/specialprod1/specialprod1_7.html

[4] T. Sakai, "The Phonetic Typewriter: Its Fundamentals and Mechanism," *Studia Phonologica*, vol. 1, pp. 140–152, 1961.

[5] P. Denes, "The Design and Operation of the Mechanical Speech Recognizer at University College London," *Journal of the British Institution of Radio Engineers*, vol. 19, no. 4, pp. 219–229, April 1959.

[6] T. K. Vintsyuk, "Speech discrimination by dynamic programming," *Cybernetics and Systems Analysis*, vol. 4, no. 1, pp. 52–57, 1968.

[7] A. J. Viterbi, "Error bounds for convolutional codes and an asymptotically optimum decoding algorithm," *IEEE Transactions on Information Theory*, vol. 13, no. 2, pp. 260–269, 1967.

[8] H. Sakoe and S. Chiba, "Dynamic programming algorithm optimization for spoken word recognition," *IEEE Transactions on Acoustics, Speech, and Signal Processing*, vol. 26, no. 1, pp. 43–49, 1978.

[9] S. E. Levinson, L. R. Rabiner, and M. M. Sondhi, "An introduction to the application of the theory of probabilistic functions of a Markov process to automatic speech recognition," *The Bell System Technical Journal*, vol. 62, no. 4, pp. 1035–1074, 1983.

[10] B.-H. Juang, "On the hidden Markov model and dynamic time warping for speech recognition—A unified view," *AT&T Bell Laboratories Technical Journal*, vol. 63, no. 7, pp. 1213–1243, 1984.

[11] B.-H. Juang and L. R. Rabiner, "Automatic Speech Recognition – A Brief History of the Technology Development," in *Encyclopedia of Language & Linguistics*, 2nd ed., K. Brown, Ed. Oxford, UK: Elsevier, 2006, pp. 806 – 819.

[12] R. Pieraccini, *The Voice in the Machine: building computers that understand speech*. Cambridge, MA, USA: MIT Press, 2012.

[13] Tractica, "Prognose zum Umsatz im Bereich Spracherkennung weltweit von 2015 bis 2024 (in Millionen US-Dollar)," https://de.statista.com/statistik/daten/studie/621155/umfrage/prognose-zum-umsatz-im-bereich-spracherkennung-weltweit/, chart. [Online; accessed July 23, 2019].

[14] P. V. Pawar, S. I. Sayed, R. Kazi, M. V. Jagade *et al.*, "Current status and future prospects in prosthetic voice rehabilitation following laryngectomy," *Journal of cancer research and therapeutics*, vol. 4, no. 4, p. 186, 2008.

[15] R. Kaye, C. G. Tang, and C. F. Sinclair, "The electrolarynx: voice restoration after total laryngectomy," *Medical Devices (Auckland, NZ)*, vol. 10, p. 133, 2017.

[16] A. K. Fuchs, M. Hagmüller, and G. Kubin, "The new bionic electro-larynx speech system," *IEEE Journal of Selected Topics in Signal Processing*, vol. 10, no. 5, pp. 952–961, 2016.

[17] C. G. Kratzenstein, "Sur la naissance de la formation des voyelles," *Journal de Physique*, vol. 21, pp. 358–380, 1782.

[18] H. Dudley and T. H. Tarnoczy, "The Speaking Machine of Wolfgang von Kempelen," *The Journal of the Acoustical Society of America*, vol. 22, no. 2, pp. 151–166, 1950.

[19] Mehnert, D., *Historische phonetische Geräte*. Dresden, Germany: TUDPress, 2012.

[20] J. L. Kelly and C. C. Lochbaum, "Speech synthesis," in *Proc. of the Fourth International Congress on Acoustics*, Copenhagen, Denmark, 1962, pp. 1–4, reprinted in [309], pp. 127–130.

[21] D. Klatt, "The Klattalk text-to-speech conversion system," in *IEEE International Conference on Acoustics, Speech, and Signal Processing (ICASSP)*, vol. 7. Paris, France: IEEE, 1982, pp. 1589–1592.

[22] G. Fant, *Acoustic Theory of Speech Production*. The Hague, Netherlands: Mouton, 1960.

[23] K. N. Stevens, *Acoustic Phonetics*. Cambridge, Massachusetts, USA: The MIT Press, 1998.

[24] J. P. Olive and M. Y. Liberman, "Text to speech—an overview," *The Journal of the Acoustical Society of America*, vol. 78, no. S1, pp. S6–S6, 1985.

[25] A. van den Oord, S. Dieleman, H. Zen, K. Simonyan, O. Vinyals, A. Graves, N. Kalchbrenner, A. Senior, and K. Kavukcuoglu, "WaveNet: A generative model for raw audio," *arXiv:1609.03499*, 2016.

[26] Y. Wang, R. Skerry-Ryan, D. Stanton, Y. Wu, R. J. Weiss, N. Jaitly, Z. Yang, Y. Xiao, Z. Chen, S. Bengio, Q. Le, Y. Agiomyrgiannakis, R. Clark, and R. A. Saurous, "Tacotron: Towards end-to-end speech synthesis," *arXiv:1703.10135*, 2017.

[27] P. N. Ladefoged, "Phonetics," https://www.britannica.com/science/phonetics#/media/1/457255/3597, 8 2014, accessed: 2020-02-18.

[28] J. Forchhammer, *Die Sprachlaute in Wort und Bild*, ser. Indogermanische Bibliothek, H. Güntert, Ed. Heidelberg, Germany: Carl Winter's Universitätsbuchhandlung, 1942, vol. 18.

[29] I. R. Titze, *Principles of Voice Production*. Englewood Cliffs, NJ, USA: Prentice Hall, 1994.

[30] P. Birkholz, "A survey of self-oscillating lumped-element models of the vocal folds," in *Studientexte zur Sprachkommunikation: Elektronische Sprachsignalverarbeitung 2011*, B. J. Kröger and P. Birkholz, Eds. Aachen, Germany: TUDPress, Dresden, 2011, pp. 47–58.

[31] P. Birkholz, S. Drechsel, and S. Stone, "Perceptual optimization of an enhanced geometric vocal fold model for articulatory speech synthesis," Graz, Austria, 2019, pp. 3765–3769.

[32] I. P. Association, *Handbook of the International Phonetic Association: A Guide to the Use of the International Phonetic Alphabet*, ser. A Regents publication. Cambridge University Press, 1999. [Online]. Available: https://books.google.de/books?id=33BSkFV_8PEC

[33] J. C. Catford, *A Practical Introduction to Phonetics*. Clarendon Press, 1988.

[34] M. Pätzold and A. P. Simpson, "Acoustic analysis of German vowels in the Kiel Corpus of Read Speech," *Arbeitsberichte des Instituts für Phonetik und digitale Sprachverarbeitung Universität Kiel*, vol. 32, pp. 215–247, 1997.

[35] J. Clark, C. Yallop, and J. Fletcher, *An Introduction to Phonetics and Phonology*, 3rd ed. Malden, MA, USA: Blackwell Publishing, 2007.

[36] K. Kohler, "German," in *Handbook of the International Phonetic Association: A guide to the use of the International Phonetic Alphabet*, International Phonetic Association, Ed. Cambridge, UK: Cambridge University Press, 1999, pp. 86–89.

[37] I. R. Titze, R. J. Baken, K. W. Bozeman, S. Granqvist, N. Henrich, C. T. Herbst, D. M. Howard, E. J. Hunter, D. Kaelin, R. D. Kent *et al.*, "Toward a consensus on symbolic notation of harmonics, resonances, and formants in vocalization," *The Journal of the Acoustical Society of America*, vol. 137, no. 5, pp. 3005–3007, 2015.

[38] C. H. Shadle, H. Nam, and D. Whalen, "Comparing measurement errors for formants in synthetic and natural vowels," *The Journal of the Acoustical Society of America*, vol. 139, no. 2, pp. 713–727, 2016.

[39] P. Birkholz, F. Gabriel, S. Kürbis, and M. Echternach, "How the peak glottal area affects linear predictive coding-based formant estimates of vowels," *The Journal of the Acoustical Society of America*, vol. 146, no. 1, pp. 223–232, 2019.

[40] T. Cho and P. Ladefoged, "Variation and universals in VOT: evidence from 18 languages," *Journal of Phonetics*, vol. 27, no. 2, pp. 207–229, 1999.

[41] J. Ryalls, M. Simon, and J. Thomason, "Voice onset time production in older Caucasian- and African-Americans," *Journal of Multilingual Communication Disorders*, vol. 2, no. 1, pp. 61–67, 2004.

[42] W. Barry, "Phoneme," in *Encyclopedia of Language & Linguistics (Second Edition)*, second edition ed., K. Brown, Ed. Oxford: Elsevier, 2006, pp. 345–350. [Online]. Available: https://www.sciencedirect.com/science/article/pii/B0080448542000092

[43] B. Kühnert and F. Nolan, "The origin of coarticulation," in *Coarticulation: Theory, Data and Techniques*, W. J. Hardcastle and N. Hewlett, Eds. Cambridge University Press, 1999, pp. 1–30.

[44] J. E. Flege, "Anticipatory and carry-over nasal coarticulation in the speech of children and adults," *Journal of Speech, Language, and Hearing Research*, vol. 31, no. 4, pp. 525–536, 1988.

[45] E. Farnetani and D. Recasens, "Coarticulation and connected speech processes," in *The Handbook of Phonetic Sciences*, 2nd ed., W. J. Hardcastle, J. Laver, and F. E. Gibbon, Eds. Oxford, UK: Blackwell Publishing Ltd, 2010, pp. 371–404.

[46] H. Harley, *English Words - A Linguistic Introduction*, ser. The Language Library, D. Crystal, Ed. Malden, MA, USA: Blackwell Publishing, 2006.

[47] G. Ruske and T. Schotola, "An approach to speech recognition using syllabic decision units," in *IEEE International Conference on Acoustics, Speech and Signal Processing (ICASSP)*, vol. 3. Tulsa, OK, USA: IEEE, 1978, pp. 722–725.

[48] J. C. Wells, *Beyond the British Isles*, ser. Accents of English. Cambridge, UK: Cambridge University Press, 1982, vol. 3.

[49] S. Kleiner, R. Knöbl, and M. Mangold, *Duden - Das Aussprachewörterbuch*, 7th ed., ser. Duden - Deutsche Sprache in 12 Bänden, Bibliographisches Institut GmbH, Ed. Berlin, Germany: Dudenverlag, 2015, vol. 6.

[50] B. Denby, T. Schultz, K. Honda, T. Hueber, J. M. Gilbert, and J. S. Brumberg, "Silent speech interfaces," *Speech Communication*, vol. 52, no. 4, pp. 270–287, 2010.

[51] T. Schultz, M. Wand, T. Hueber, D. J. Krusienski, C. Herff, and J. S. Brumberg, "Biosignal-based spoken communication: A survey," *IEEE/ACM Transactions on Audio, Speech, and Language Processing*, vol. 25, no. 12, pp. 2257–2271, 2017.

[52] T. Hueber, E.-L. Benaroya, G. Chollet, B. Denby, G. Dreyfus, and M. Stone, "Development of a silent speech interface driven by ultrasound and optical images of the tongue and lips," *Speech Communication*, vol. 52, no. 4, pp. 288–300, 2010.

[53] M. Janke, M. Wand, K. Nakamura, and T. Schultz, "Further investigations on EMG-to-speech conversion," in *IEEE International Conference on Acoustics, Speech and Signal Processing (ICASSP)*. Kyoto, Japan: IEEE, 2012, pp. 365–368.

[54] É. Lombard, "Le signe de l'élévation de la voix," *Annales des Maladies de l'Oreille et du Larynx*, vol. XXXVII, no. 2, pp. 101–119, 1911.

[55] J. S. Brumberg, A. Nieto-Castanon, P. R. Kennedy, and F. H. Guenther, "Brain–computer interfaces for speech communication," *Speech Communication*, vol. 52, no. 4, pp. 367–379, 2010.

[56] E. D. Petajan, "Automatic lipreading to enhance speech recognition (speech reading)," Ph.D. dissertation, Champaign, IL, USA, 1984, aAI8502266.

[57] E. D. Petajan, B. Bischoff, D. Bodoff, and N. M. Brooke, "An improved automatic lipreading system to enhance speech recognition," in *Proc. of the SIGCHI Conference on Human Factors in Computing Systems*. ACM, 1988, pp. 19–25.

[58] H. McGurk and J. MacDonald, "Hearing lips and seeing voices," *Nature*, vol. 264, no. 5588, p. 746, 1976.

[59] C. G. Fisher, "Confusions among visually perceived consonants," *Journal of Speech and Hearing Research*, vol. 11, no. 4, pp. 796–804, 1968.

[60] G. Potamianos, C. Neti, J. Luettin, and I. Matthews, "Audio-visual automatic speech recognition: An overview," *Issues in Visual and Audio-Visual Speech Processing*, vol. 22, p. 23, 2004.

[61] Z. Zhou, G. Zhao, X. Hong, and M. Pietikäinen, "A review of recent advances in visual speech decoding," *Image and Vision Computing*, vol. 32, no. 9, pp. 590–605, 2014.

[62] Z. Zhou, X. Hong, G. Zhao, and M. Pietikäinen, "A compact representation of visual speech data using latent variables," *IEEE Transactions on Pattern Analysis and Machine Intelligence*, vol. 36, no. 1, pp. 181–187, 2013.

[63] J. S. Chung and A. Zisserman, "Lip reading in the wild," in *Asian Conference on Computer Vision*. Springer, 2016, pp. 87–103.

[64] T. Stafylakis and G. Tzimiropoulos, "Combining Residual Networks with LSTMs for Lipreading," in *Proc. of the Interspeech*, Stockholm, Sweden, 2017, pp. 3652–3656.

[65] N. Shrivastava, A. Saxena, Y. Kumar, R. R. Shah, D. Mahata, and A. Stent, "MobiVSR: A Visual Speech Recognition Solution for Mobile Devices," *arXiv:1905.03968*, 2019.

[66] I. McGraw, R. Prabhavalkar, R. Alvarez, M. G. Arenas, K. Rao, D. Rybach, O. Alsharif, H. Sak, A. Gruenstein, F. Beaufays, and C. Parada, "Personalized speech recognition on mobile devices," in *IEEE International Conference on Acoustics, Speech and Signal Processing (ICASSP)*. Shanghai, China: IEEE, 2016, pp. 5955–5959.

[67] I. Wilson, "Using ultrasound for teaching and researching articulation," *Acoustical Science and Technology*, vol. 35, no. 6, pp. 285–289, 2014.

[68] B. Denby and M. Stone, "Speech synthesis from real time ultrasound images of the tongue," in *IEEE International Conference on Acoustics, Speech, and Signal Processing (ICASSP)*, vol. 1. Montreal, Quebec, Canada: IEEE, 2004, pp. I–685.

[69] M. Stone and E. P. Davis, "A head and transducer support system for making ultrasound images of tongue/jaw movement," *The Journal of The Acoustical Society of America*, vol. 98, no. 6, pp. 3107–3112, 1995.

[70] Ouisper, "Oral Ultrasound synthetIc SpEech SouRce," National Research Agency (ANR), France, 2006-2009, contract No. ANR-06-BLAN-0166.

[71] T. Hueber and G. Bailly, "Statistical conversion of silent articulation into audible speech using full-covariance HMM," *Computer Speech & Language*, vol. 36, pp. 274–293, 2016.

[72] T. Hueber, G. Aversano, G. Cholle, B. Denby, G. Dreyfus, Y. Oussar, P. Roussel, and M. Stone, "Eigentongue feature extraction for an ultrasound-based silent speech interface," in *IEEE International Conference on Acoustics, Speech and Signal Processing (ICASSP)*, vol. 1. Honolulu, HI, USA: IEEE, 2007, pp. I–1245.

[73] T. Hueber, G. Chollet, B. Denby, and M. Stone, "Acquisition of ultrasound, video and acoustic speech data for a silent-speech interface application," in *8th International Seminar on Speech Production (ISSP)*, Strasbourg, France, 2008, pp. 365–369.

[74] T. Hueber, G. Chollet, B. Denby, G. Dreyfus, and M. Stone, "Phone recognition from ultrasound and optical video sequences for a silent speech interface," in *Proc. of the Interspeech*, Brisbane, Australia, 2008, pp. 2032–2035.

[75] ——, "Towards a segmental vocoder driven by ultrasound and optical images of the tongue and lips," in *Proc. of the Interspeech*, Brisbane, Australia, 2008, pp. 2028–2031.

[76] T. G. Csapó, M. S. Al-Radhi, G. Németh, G. Gosztolya, T. Grósz, L. Tóth, and A. Markó, "Ultrasound-Based Silent Speech Interface Built on a Continuous Vocoder," in *Proc. of the Interspeech*, Graz, Austria, 2019, pp. 894–898. [Online]. Available: http://dx.doi.org/10.21437/Interspeech.2019-2046

[77] E. Tatulli and T. Hueber, "Feature extraction using multimodal convolutional neural networks for visual speech recognition," in *IEEE International Conference on Acoustics, Speech and Signal Processing (ICASSP)*. New Orleans, LA, USA: IEEE, 2017, pp. 2971–2975.

[78] T. G. Csapó, T. Grósz, G. Gosztolya, L. Tóth, and A. Markó, "DNN-based ultrasound-to-speech conversion for a silent speech interface," in *Proc. of the Interspeech*, Stockholm, Sweden, 2017, pp. 3672–3676.

[79] G. Gosztolya, Á. Pintér, L. Tóth, T. Grósz, A. Markó, and T. G. Csapó, "Autoencoder-based articulatory-to-acoustic mapping for ultrasound silent speech interfaces," *arXiv:1904.05259*, 2019.

[80] Y. Ji, L. Liu, H. Wang, Z. Liu, Z. Niu, and B. Denby, "Updating the silent speech challenge benchmark with deep learning," *Speech Communication*, vol. 98, pp. 42–50, 2018.

[81] J. Cai, B. Denby, P. Roussel, G. Dreyfus, and L. Crevier-Buchman, "Recognition and real time performances of a lightweight ultrasound based silent speech interface employing a language model," in *Proc. of the Interspeech*, Florence, Italy, 2011, pp. 1005–1007.

[82] M. Kazamel and P. P. Warren, "History of electromyography and nerve conduction studies: A tribute to the founding fathers," *Journal of Clinical Neuroscience*, vol. 43, pp. 54–60, 2017.

[83] M. Piccolino, "Luigi Galvani and animal electricity: two centuries after the foundation of electrophysiology," *Trends in Neurosciences*, vol. 20, no. 10, pp. 443 – 448, 1997.

[84] "Nobel lectures," in *Physiology or Medicine 1922-1941*. Amsterdam, NL: Elsevier Publishing Company, 1965.

[85] A. C. Guyton and J. E. Hall, *Physiology*, 11th ed. Philadelphia, PA, USA: Elsevier Saunders, 2006.

[86] J. R. Daube and D. I. Rubin, "Needle electromyography," *Muscle & Nerve: Official Journal of the American Association of Electrodiagnostic Medicine*, vol. 39, no. 2, pp. 244–270, 2009.

[87] M. C. Garcia and T. Vieira, "Surface electromyography: Why, when and how to use it," *Revista Andaluza de Medicina del Deporte*, vol. 4, no. 1, pp. 17–28, 2011.

[88] S. Pullman, D. Goodin, A. Marquinez, S. Tabbal, and M. Rubin, "Clinical utility of surface EMG," *Neurology*, vol. 55, no. 2, pp. 171–177, 2000.

[89] J. Petrofsky and M. Laymon, "The relationship between muscle temperature, MUAP conduction velocity and the amplitude and frequency components of the surface EMG during isometric contractions," *Basic and Applied Myology*, vol. 15, no. 2, pp. 61–74, 2005.

[90] H. J. Hermens, B. Freriks, C. Disselhorst-Klug, and G. Rau, "Development of recommendations for SEMG sensors and sensor placement procedures," *Journal of Electromyography and Kinesiology*, vol. 10, no. 5, pp. 361 – 374, 2000. [Online]. Available: http://www.sciencedirect.com/science/article/pii/S1050641100000274

[91] P. Pluschinski, Y. Zaretsky, R. Sader, P. Birkholz, R. Mumtaz, C. Neuschaefer-Rube, and C. Hey, "Oberflächenmyographie als Biofeedback-Verfahren für Dysphagiepatienten: Bestimmung der optimalen Elektrodenpositionen und -anzahl," in *30. Wissenschaftliche Jahrestagung der DGPP*, Bochum, Germany.

[92] H. Ghapanchizadeh, S. A. Ahmad, A. J. Ishak, and M. S. Al-quraishi, "Review of surface electrode placement for recording electromyography signals." *Biomedical Research (0970-938X)*, vol. 28, pp. S1–S7, 2017.

[93] N. Sugie and K. Tsunoda, "A speech prosthesis employing a speech synthesizer-vowel discrimination from perioral muscle activities and vowel production," *IEEE Transactions on Biomedical Engineering*, no. 7, pp. 485–490, 1985.

[94] M. S. Morse and E. M. O'Brien, "Research summary of a scheme to ascertain the availability of speech information in the myoelectric signals of neck and head muscles using surface electrodes," *Computers in Biology and Medicine*, vol. 16, no. 6, pp. 399–410, 1986.

[95] J. Ladegaard, "Story of electromyography equipment," *Muscle & Nerve: Official Journal of the American Association of Electrodiagnostic Medicine*, vol. 25, no. S11, pp. S128–S133, 2002.

[96] D. C. Kozen, *Automata and computability*. New York, NY, USA: Springer Science & Business Media, 2012.

[97] S. Hartzog, M. S. Morse, B. Trull, C. Alegre, and P. Harris, "Recognition of speech from signals secondary to speech," in *Proc. of the Annual International Conference of the IEEE Engineering in Medicine and Biology Society*. IEEE, 1988, pp. 1188–1189.

[98] M. S. Morse, S. H. Day, B. Trull, and H. Morse, "Use of myoelectric signals to recognize speech," in *Proc. of the Annual International Engineering in Medicine and Biology Society,*, Nov 1989, pp. 1793–1794 vol.6.

[99] M. S. Morse, S. H. Day, and J. May, "Time domain analysis of the myoelectric signal secondary to speech," in *Proc. of the Annual International Conference of the IEEE Engineering in Medicine and Biology Society*, Nov 1990, pp. 1318–1319.

[100] J. Schmidhuber, "Deep learning in neural networks: An overview," *Neural networks*, vol. 61, pp. 85–117, 2015.

[101] M. S. Morse, Y. N. Gopalan, and M. Wright, "Speech recognition using myoelectric signals with neural networks," in *Proc. of the Annual International Conference of the IEEE Engineering in Medicine and Biology Society Volume 13: 1991*, Oct 1991, pp. 1877–1878.

[102] S. H. Day, M. S. Morse, and R. A. Day, "A proposed control scheme for a vocal prosthesis," in *IEEE Proceedings on Southeastcon*, April 1990, pp. 511–514 vol.2.

[103] L. Maier-Hein, F. Metze, T. Schultz, and A. Waibel, "Session independent non-audible speech recognition using surface electromyography," in *IEEE Workshop on Automatic Speech Recognition and Understanding*. IEEE, 2005, pp. 331–336.

[104] M. Wand, A. Himmelsbach, T. Heistermann, M. Janke, and T. Schultz, "Artifact removal algorithm for an EMG-based Silent Speech Interface," in *Proc. of the Annual International Conference of the IEEE Engineering in Medicine and Biology Society (EMBC)*. IEEE, 2013, pp. 5750–5753.

[105] G. S. Meltzner, G. Colby, Y. Deng, and J. T. Heaton, "Signal acquisition and processing techniques for sEMG based silent speech recognition," in *Proc. of the Annual International Conference of the IEEE Engineering in Medicine and Biology Society*. IEEE, 2011, pp. 4848–4851.

[106] Y. Deng, J. Heaton, and G. Meltzner, "Towards a practical silent speech recognition system," in *Proc. of the Interspeech*, Singapore, 2014, pp. 1164–1168.

[107] G. S. Meltzner, J. T. Heaton, Y. Deng, G. De Luca, S. H. Roy, and J. C. Kline, "Silent speech recognition as an alternative communication device for persons with laryngectomy," *IEEE/ACM Transactions on Audio, Speech, and Language Processing*, vol. 25, no. 12, pp. 2386–2398, Dec 2017.

[108] M. Wand and T. Schultz, "Session-independent EMG-based speech recognition." in *Biosignals*, 2011, pp. 295–300.

[109] ——, "Towards real-life application of EMG-based speech recognition by using unsupervised adaptation," in *Proc. of the Interspeech*, Singapore, 2014, pp. 1189–1193.

[110] M. Wand, T. Schultz, and J. Schmidhuber, "Domain-adversarial training for session independent EMG-based speech recognition." in *Proc. of the Interspeech*, Hyderabad, India, 2018, pp. 3167–3171.

[111] G. S. Meltzner, J. T. Heaton, Y. Deng, G. De Luca, S. H. Roy, and J. C. Kline, "Development of sEMG sensors and algorithms for silent speech recognition," *Journal of Neural Engineering*, vol. 15, no. 4, p. 046031, 2018.

[112] M. Wand and J. Schmidhuber, "Deep Neural Network Frontend for Continuous EMG-Based Speech Recognition." in *Proc. of the Interspeeech*, San Francisco, CA, USA, 2016, pp. 3032–3036.

[113] A. R. Toth, M. Wand, and T. Schultz, "Synthesizing speech from electromyography using voice transformation techniques," in *Proc. of the Interspeech*, Brighton, UK, 2009, pp. 652–655.

[114] M. Janke and L. Diener, "Emg-to-speech: Direct generation of speech from facial electromyographic signals," *IEEE/ACM Transactions on Audio, Speech and Language Processing (TASLP)*, vol. 25, no. 12, pp. 2375–2385, 2017.

[115] M. J. Fagan, P. Chapman, J. M. Gilbert, and S. R. Ell, "Generation of data from speech or voiceless mouthed speech," United Kingdom Patent GB2 422 238, 2005.

[116] M. J. Fagan, S. R. Ell, J. M. Gilbert, E. Sarrazin, and P. M. Chapman, "Development of a (silent) speech recognition system for patients following laryngectomy," *Medical Engineering & Physics*, vol. 30, no. 4, pp. 419–425, 2008.

[117] J. A. Gonzalez, L. A. Cheah, A. M. Gomez, P. D. Green, J. M. Gilbert, S. R. Ell, R. K. Moore, and E. Holdsworth, "Direct speech reconstruction from articulatory sensor data by machine learning," *IEEE/ACM Transactions on Audio, Speech, and Language Processing*, vol. 25, no. 12, pp. 2362–2374, Dec 2017.

[118] J. M. Gilbert, S. I. Rybchenko, R. Hofe, S. R. Ell, M. J. Fagan, R. K. Moore, and P. Green, "Isolated word recognition of silent speech using magnetic implants and sensors," *Medical Engineering & Physics*, vol. 32, no. 10, pp. 1189–1197, 2010.

[119] J. Gonzalez Lopez, L. A. Cheah, P. D. Green, J. M. Gilbert, S. R. Ell, R. K. Moore, and E. Holdsworth, "Evaluation of a silent speech interface based on magnetic sensing and deep learning for a phonetically rich vocabulary," in *Proc. of the Interspeech*, Stockholm, Sweden, 2017, pp. 3986–3990.

[120] L. A. Cheah, J. M. Gilbert, J. A. González, P. D. Green, S. R. Ell, R. K. Moore, and E. Holdsworth, "A wearable silent speech interface based on magnetic sensors with motion-artefact removal." in *Proc. of the BIOSTEC 2018*, Funchal, Madeira, Portugal, 2018, pp. 56–62.

[121] R. Hofe, S. R. Ell, M. J. Fagan, J. M. Gilbert, P. D. Green, R. K. Moore, and S. I. Rybchenko, "Evaluation of a silent speech interface based on magnetic sensing," in *Proc. of the Interspeech*, Makuhari, Chiba, Japan, 2010, pp. 246–249.

[122] ——, "Small-vocabulary speech recognition using a silent speech interface based on magnetic sensing," *Speech Communication*, vol. 55, no. 1, pp. 22–32, 2013.

[123] R. Hofe, J. Bai, L. A. Cheah, S. R. Ell, J. M. Gilbert, R. K. Moore, and P. D. Green, "Performance of the MVOCA silent speech interface across multiple speakers," in *Proc. of the Interspeech*, Lyon, France, 2013, pp. 1140–1143.

[124] H. Sahni, A. Bedri, G. Reyes, P. Thukral, Z. Guo, T. Starner, and M. Ghovanloo, "The tongue and ear interface: a wearable system for silent speech recognition," in *Proc. of the 2014 ACM International Symposium on Wearable Computers*. ACM, 2014, pp. 47–54.

[125] J. A. Gonzalez, L. A. Cheah, J. M. Gilbert, J. Bai, S. R. Ell, P. D. Green, and R. K. Moore, "A silent speech system based on permanent magnet articulography and direct synthesis," *Computer Speech & Language*, vol. 39, pp. 67–87, 2016.

[126] J. M. Gilbert, J. A. Gonzalez, L. A. Cheah, S. R. Ell, P. Green, R. K. Moore, and E. Holdsworth, "Restoring speech following total removal of the larynx by a learned transformation from sensor data to acoustics," *The Journal of the Acoustical Society of America*, vol. 141, no. 3, pp. EL307–EL313, 2017.

[127] J. A. Gonzalez, L. A. Cheah, J. M. Gilbert, J. Bai, S. R. Ell, P. D. Green, and R. K. Moore, "Voice restoration after laryngectomy based on magnetic sensing of articulator movement and statistical articulation-to-speech conversion," in *International Joint Conference on Biomedical Engineering Systems and Technologies*. Springer, 2016, pp. 295–316.

[128] J. J. Berry, "Accuracy of the NDI wave speech research system," *Journal of Speech, Language, and Hearing Research*, vol. 54, no. 5, pp. 1295–1301, 2011.

[129] P. Heracleous and N. Hagita, "Automatic recognition of speech without any audio information," in *IEEE International Conference on Acoustics, Speech and Signal Processing (ICASSP)*. Prague, Czech Republic: IEEE, 2011, pp. 2392–2395.

[130] S. Hahm and J. Wang, "Silent speech recognition from articulatory movements using deep neural network," in *Proc. of the 18th International Congress of Phonetic Sciences*, Glasgow, Scotland, UK, 2015.

[131] B. Cao, M. Kim, T. Mau, and J. Wang, "Recognizing whispered speech produced by an individual with surgically reconstructed larynx using articulatory movement data," in *Proc. of the Workshop on Speech and Language Processing for Assistive Technologies*, vol. 2016. NIH Public Access, 2016, p. 80.

[132] M. Kim, B. Cao, T. Mau, and J. Wang, "Speaker-independent silent speech recognition from flesh-point articulatory movements using an LSTM neural network," *IEEE/ACM Transactions on Audio, Speech and Language Processing (TASLP)*, vol. 25, no. 12, pp. 2323–2336, 2017.

[133] A. Toutios, S. Ouni, and Y. Laprie, "Estimating the control parameters of an articulatory model from electromagnetic articulograph data," *The Journal of the Acoustical Society of America*, vol. 129, no. 5, pp. 3245–3257, 2011.

[134] F. Bocquelet, T. Hueber, L. Girin, C. Savariaux, and B. Yvert, "Real-time control of an articulatory-based speech synthesizer for brain computer interfaces," *PLOS Computational Biology*, vol. 12, no. 11, p. e1005119, 2016.

[135] Z.-C. Liu, Z.-H. Ling, and L.-R. Dai, "Articulatory-to-acoustic conversion with cascaded prediction of spectral and excitation features using neural networks," in *Proc. of the Interspeech*, San Francisco, CA, USA, 2016, pp. 1502–1506.

[136] B. Cao, B. Y. Tsang, and J. Wang, "Comparing the performance of individual articulatory flesh points for articulation-to-speech synthesis," in *Proc. the 19th International Congress of Phonetic Sciences*, Melbourne, Australia, 2019, pp. 3041–3045.

[137] J. F. Holzrichter and L. C. Ng, "Speech coding, reconstruction and recognition using acoustics and electromagnetic waves," Mar. 17 1998, uS Patent 5,729,694.

[138] J. Holzrichter, G. Burnett, L. Ng, and W. Lea, "Speech articulator measurements using low power EM-wave sensors," *The Journal of the Acoustical Society of America*, vol. 103, no. 1, pp. 622–625, 1998.

[139] J. F. Holzrichter, "Characterizing silent and pseudo-silent speech using radar-like sensors," in *Proc. of the Interspeech*, Brighton, UK, 2009.

[140] A. M. Eid and J. W. Wallace, "Ultrawideband speech sensing," *IEEE Antennas and Wireless Propagation Letters*, vol. 8, pp. 1414–1417, 2009.

[141] A. M. Eid, "Ultrawideband circular patch antenna with guided ground plane for speech sensing applications," in *2013 Saudi International Electronics, Communications and Photonics Conference*. Riyadh, Saudi Arabia: IEEE, 2013, pp. 1–3.

[142] ——, "Ultrawideband speech sensing: Flat-face circular waveguide model," in *2013 Saudi International Electronics, Communications and Photonics Conference*. Riyadh, Saudi Arabia: IEEE, 2013, pp. 1–4.

[143] Y. Shin and J. Seo, "Towards contactless silent speech recognition based on detection of active and visible articulators using IR-UWB radar," *Sensors*, vol. 16, no. 11, p. 1812, 2016.

[144] P. Birkholz, S. Stone, K. Wolf, and D. Plettemeier, "Non-invasive silent phoneme recognition using microwave signals," *IEEE/ACM Transactions on Audio, Speech and Language Processing (TASLP)*, vol. 26, no. 12, pp. 2404–2411, 2018.

[145] E. R. Moses Jr., "A brief history of palatography," *Quarterly Journal of Speech*, vol. 26, no. 4, pp. 615–625, 1940.

[146] O. Coles, "On the production of articulate sound (speech)," *British Medical Journal*, vol. 1, no. 581, p. 181, 1872.

[147] D. Abercrombie, "Direct palatography," *STUF-Language Typology and Universals*, vol. 10, no. 1-4, pp. 21–25, 1957.

[148] G. Chi-Fishman and M. Stone, "A new application for electropalatography: Swallowing," *Dysphagia*, vol. 11, no. 4, pp. 239–247, Sep 1996.

[149] W. J. Hardcastle, "The use of electropalatography in phonetic research," *Phonetica*, vol. 25, no. 4, pp. 197–215, 1972.

[150] S. G. Fletcher and M. J. McCutcheon, "Pseudo palate useful for diagnosis and treatment of speech impairment," Patent, 09 1978, US 4112596.

[151] A. A. Wrench, "Advances in EPG palate design," *International Journal of Speech-Language Pathology*, vol. 9, no. 1, pp. 3–12, 2007.

[152] W. Hardcastle, W. Jones, C. Knight, A. Trudgeon, and G. Calder, "New developments in electropalatography: A state-of-the-art report," *Clinical Linguistics & Phonetics*, vol. 3, no. 1, pp. 1–38, 1989.

[153] W. J. Hardcastle, F. E. Gibbon, and W. Jones, "Visual display of tongue-palate contact: Electropalatography in the assessment and remediation of speech disorders," *International Journal of Language & Communication Disorders*, vol. 26, no. 1, pp. 41–74, 1991.

[154] K. Takinishi and J. Hattori, "Artificial palate for use in dynamic palatographical speech researches and improvements and method of fabricating the same," Patent, 11 1979, US 4175338.

[155] F. Gibbon, "Bibliography of electropalatographic (EPG) studies in english (1957–2013)," *Dept. Speech Hear. Sci., Univ. College Cork, Ireland, Rep. Staeno*, pp. 05–21, 2013.

[156] S. G. Fletcher, "Recognition of words from palatometric displays," *Clinical Linguistics & Phonetics*, vol. 4, no. 1, pp. 9–24, 1990.

[157] R. R. Riesz and L. Schott, "Visible speech cathode-ray translator," *The Journal of the Acoustical Society of America*, vol. 18, no. 1, pp. 50–61, 1946.

[158] A. Wrench and K. Richmond, "Continuous speech recognition using articulatory data," in *Proc. of the 6th International Conference on Spoken Language Processing (ICSLP)*, vol. 4, Beijing, China, 2000, pp. 145–148.

[159] E. Uraga and T. Hain, "Automatic speech recognition experiments with articulatory data," in *Proc. of the Interspeech*, Pittsburgh, PA, USA, 2006, pp. 353–356.

[160] M. Russell, "Towards speech recognition using palato-lingual contact patterns for voice restoration," Ph.D. dissertation, Faculty of Engineering, University of the Witwatersrand, 2011.

[161] R. Li, J. Wu, and T. Starner, "Tongueboard: An oral interface for subtle input," in *Proc. of the 10th Augmented Human International Conference 2019*. Reims, France: ACM, 2019, pp. 1–9.

[162] C.-K. Chuang and W. S. Wang, "Use of optical distance sensing to track tongue motion," *Journal of Speech and Hearing Research*, vol. 21, pp. 482–496, 1978.

[163] R. Masuda, S. Sasa, and K. Hasegawa, "Optical proximity sensor by using phase information," *Trans. SICE*, vol. 17, no. 9, pp. 945–950, 1981.

[164] J. E. Flege, S. G. Fletcher, M. J. McCutcheon, and S. C. Smith, "The physiological specification of American English vowels," *Language and Speech*, vol. 29, no. 4, pp. 361–388, 1986.

[165] S. G. Fletcher, M. J. McCutcheon, S. C. Smith, and W. H. Smith, "Glossometric measurement in vowel production and modification," *Clinical Linguistics & Phonetics*, vol. 3, no. 4, pp. 359–375, 1989.

[166] A. A. Wrench, A. D. McIntosh, and W. J. Hardcastle, "Optopalatograph: Development of a device for measuring tongue movement in 3D," in *Proc. of the Eurospeech*, Rhodes, Greece, 1997, pp. 1055–1058.

[167] ——, "Optopalatograph (OPG): A new apparatus for speech production analysis," in *Proc. of the 4th International Conference on Spoken Language (ICSLP)*, vol. 3, Philadelphia, PA, USA, 1996, pp. 1589–1592.

[168] A. A. Wrench, A. D. McIntosh, C. Watson, and W. J. Hardcastle, "Optopalatograph: Real-time feedback of tongue movement in 3D," in *Proc. of the 5th International Conference on Spoken Language Processing (ICSLP)*, Sydney, Australia, 1998.

[169] P. Birkholz and C. Neuschaefer-Rube, "Combined optical distance sensing and electropalatography to measure articulation," in *Proc. of Interspeech*, Florence, Italy, 2011, pp. 285–288.

[170] ——, "A new artificial palate design for the optical measurement of tongue and lip movements," M. Wolff, Ed. Dresden, Germany: TUDPress, 2012, pp. 89–95.

[171] P. Birkholz, P. Dächert, and C. Neuschaefer-Rube, "Advances in combined electro-optical palatography," in *Proc. of the Interspeech*, Portland, OR, USA, 2012, pp. 703–706.

[172] J. U. Sommer, R. Birk, K. Hörmann, and B. A. Stuck, "Evaluation of the maximum isometric tongue force of healthy volunteers," *European Archives of Oto-Rhino-Laryngology*, vol. 271, no. 11, pp. 3077–3084, 2014.

[173] K. Yamada, "Cobalt: Its role in health and disease," in *Interrelations between Essential Metal Ions and Human Diseases*, A. Sigel, H. Sigel, and R. K. Sigel, Eds. Dordrecht: Springer Netherlands, 2013, pp. 295–320.

[174] S. Preuß and P. Birkholz, "Fortschritte in der elektro-optischen Stomatographie," G. Wirsching, Ed. TUDPress, 2015, pp. 248–255.

[175] ——, "Optical sensor calibration for Electro-Optical Stomatography," in *Proc. of Interspeech*, Dresden, Germany, 2015, pp. 618–622.

[176] P. Boersma, "Praat, a system for doing phonetics by computer." *Glot International*, vol. 5, no. 9/10, pp. 341–345, 2001.

[177] S. Stone and P. Birkholz, "Angle correction in optopalatographic tongue distance measurements," *IEEE Sensors Journal*, vol. 17, no. 2, pp. 459–468, Jan 2017.

[178] C. M. Goral, K. E. Torrance, D. P. Greenberg, and B. Battaile, "Modeling the interaction of light between diffuse surfaces," *SIGGRAPH Comput. Graph.*, vol. 18, no. 3, pp. 213–222, Jan. 1984.

[179] B. T. Phong, "Illumination for computer generated pictures," *Commun. ACM*, vol. 18, no. 6, pp. 311–317, Jun. 1975.

[180] R. W. Boyd, *Nonlinear optics*. Amsterdam, Boston (Mass.), London: Academic Press, 2003.

[181] J. Stam, "Multiple scattering as a diffusion process," in *Rendering Techniques 95*. Springer, 1995, pp. 41–50.

[182] Y. Yunusova, J. R. Green, and A. Mefferd, "Accuracy assessment for AG500, electromagnetic articulograph," *Journal of Speech, Language, and Hearing Research*, vol. 52, no. 2, pp. 547–555, 2009.

[183] J. Gartner, "Automatische Lagebestimmung von Abstands- und Kontaktsensoren auf Gaumenplatten für die Messung von Zungen- und Lippenbewegungen," Institute of Acoustics and Speech Communication, Technische Universität Dresden, Germany, February 2016, unpublished student's thesis.

[184] F. Klause, "Messung der Lippenposition während des Sprechens mittels optischer Sensoren," Institute of Acoustics and Speech Communication, Technische Universität Dresden, Germany, August 2016, unpublished student's thesis.

[185] K. Kumar, T. Chen, and R. M. Stern, "Profile view lip reading," in *IEEE International Conference on Acoustics, Speech, and Signal Processing (ICASSP)*, vol. 4. Honolulu, HI, USA: IEEE, 2007, pp. IV–429.

[186] F. Klause, S. Stone, and P. Birkholz, "A head-mounted camera system for the measurement of lip protrusion and opening during speech production," in *Studientexte zur Sprachkommunikation: Elektronische Sprachsignalverarbeitung 2017*, J. Trouvain, I. Steiner, and B. Möbius, Eds. TUDpress, Dresden, 2017, pp. 145–151.

[187] F. Klause, "Entwicklung, Aufbau und Evaluation von optischen Sensoren zur Erfassung der Lippenposition während des Sprechens," Institute of Acoustics and Speech Communication, Technische Universität Dresden, Germany, Juni 2017, unpublished diploma thesis.

[188] M. T. Inc., *megaAVR Data Sheet*, 2018 (accessed January 19, 2020). [Online]. Available: https://www.microchip.com/wwwproducts/en/ATmega328

[189] P. Dächert, "Neuartige Artikulationsmessung mittels Elektropalatographie (EPG) und optischer Distanzmessung," Ph.D. dissertation, RTWH Aachen University, Aachen, 2014.

[190] I. Analog Devices, *ADG725/ADG731 Analog Multiplexers Data Sheet (Rev. B)*, 2015 (accessed January 26, 2020). [Online]. Available: https://www.analog.com/en/products/adg731.html#product-overview

[191] P. Vary and R. Martin, *Digital speech transmission: Enhancement, coding and error concealment*. Chichester, UK: Wiley, 2006.

[192] S. W. Smith, *The Scientist and Engineer's Guide to Digital Signal Processing*. San Diego, CA, USA: California Technical Publishing, 1997.

[193] S. Preuß, C. Neuschaefer-Rube, and P. Birkholz, "Real-time control of a 2d animation model of the vocal tract using optopalatography," in *Proc. of the Interspeech*, Lyon, France, 2013, pp. 997–1001.

[194] R. Mumtaz, S. Preuß, C. Neuschaefer-Rube, C. Hey, R. Sader, and P. Birkholz, "Tongue contour reconstruction from optical and electrical palatography," *Signal Processing Letters, IEEE*, vol. 21, no. 6, pp. 658–662, June 2014.

[195] S. Preuß, C. Neuschaefer-Rube, and P. Birkholz, "Evaluation of an OPG-controlled animated vocal tract model as a biofeedback system," in *10th International Seminar on Speech Production (ISSP)*, Cologne, Germany, 2014, pp. 340–343.

[196] S. Preuß, C. Eckers, P. Birkholz, and C. Neuschaefer-Rube, "Ein OPG-gesteuertes Serious Game zur Unterstützung mundmotorischer Übungen," *Studientexte zur Sprachkommunikation: Elektronische Sprachsignalverarbeitung 2014*, pp. 134–141, 2014.

[197] P. Birkholz, M. Schutte, S. Preuß, and C. Neuschaefer-Rube, "Towards non-invasive velum state detection during speaking using high-frequency acoustic chirps." TUDPress, Dresden, 2014, pp. 126–133.

[198] P. Birkholz, P. Bakardjiev, S. Kürbis, and R. Petrick, "Towards minimally invasive velar state detection in normal and silent speech," in *Proc. of the Interspeech*, San Francisco, CA, USA, 2016, pp. 1780–1784.

[199] S. Stone and P. Birkholz, "Silent-speech command word recognition using electro-optical stomatography," in *Proc. of the Interspeech*, San Francisco, CA, USA, 2016, pp. 2350–2351.

[200] ——, "Cross-speaker silent-speech command word recognition using electro-optical stomatography," in *IEEE International Conference on Acoustics, Speech and Signal Processing (ICASSP)*. IEEE, 2020, pp. 7849–7853.

[201] E. Krech, E. Stock, U. Hirschfeld, L. Anders, P. Wiesinger, W. Haas, and I. Hove, *Deutsches Aussprachewörterbuch*. De Gruyter, 2009.

[202] N. Nguyen, "EPG bidimensional data reduction," *European Journal of Disorders of Communication*, vol. 30, no. 2, pp. 175–182, 1995.

[203] *Articulate Assistant Advanced User Guide*, Version 2.14 ed., Articulate Instruments Ltd, Edinburgh, UK, 2012.

[204] K. Greff, R. K. Srivastava, J. Koutník, B. R. Steunebrink, and J. Schmidhuber, "LSTM: A search space odyssey," *IEEE Transactions on Neural Networks and Learning Systems*, vol. 28, no. 10, pp. 2222–2232, 2016.

[205] S. Stone, M. Marxen, and P. Birkholz, "Construction and evaluation of a parametric one-dimensional vocal tract model," *IEEE/ACM Transactions on Audio, Speech, and Language Processing*, vol. 26, no. 8, pp. 1381–1392, 2018.

[206] S. Stone and P. Birkholz, "Articulation-to-speech using electro-optical stomatography and articulatory synthesis," in *12th International Seminar on Speech Production (ISSP)*, Providence, RI, USA, accepted.

[207] P. Vary, U. Heute, and W. Hess, *Digitale Sprachsignalverarbeitung*, ser. Informationstechnik Series. Stuttgart, Germany: Vieweg+Teubner Verlag, 1998.

[208] P. Taylor, *Text-to-Speech Synthesis*, 1st ed. New York, NY, USA: Cambridge University Press, 2009.

[209] J. Shen, R. Pang, R. J. Weiss, M. Schuster, N. Jaitly, Z. Yang, Z. Chen, Y. Zhang, Y. Wang, R. Skerry-Ryan, R. A. Saurous, Y. Agiomyrgiannakis, and Y. Wu, "Natural TTS Synthesis by Conditioning WaveNet on Mel Spectrogram Predictions," 2017.

[210] C. H. Shadle and R. I. Damper, "Prospects for articulatory synthesis: A position paper," in *Fourth ISCA ITRW on Speech Synthesis (SSW-4)*, Perthshire, Scotland, 2001, pp. 121–126.

[211] P. Rubin, E. Saltzman, L. Goldstein, R. McGowan, M. Tiede, and C. Browman, "CASY and extensions to the task-dynamic model," in *1st ETRW on Speech Production Modeling: From Control Strategies to Acoustics; 4th Speech Production Seminar: Models and Data*, Autrans, France, 1996, pp. 125–128.

[212] J. E. Lloyd, I. Stavness, and S. Fels, "Artisynth: A fast interactive biomechanical modeling toolkit combining multibody and finite element simulation," in *Soft tissue biomechanical modeling for computer assisted surgery*. Springer, 2012, pp. 355–394.

[213] P. Birkholz, "3D-Artikulatorische Sprachsynthese (3D Articulatory Speech Synthesis)," Ph.D. dissertation, Universität Rostock, Berlin, 2005.

[214] ——, "Modeling consonant-vowel coarticulation for articulatory speech synthesis," *PLoS ONE*, vol. 8, no. 4, p. e60603, 2013.

[215] P. Mermelstein, "Articulatory model for the study of speech production," *Journal of the Acoustical Society of America*, vol. 53, no. 4, pp. 1070–1082, 1973.

[216] S. Maeda, "Compensatory articulation during speech: Evidence from the analysis and synthesis of vocal tract shapes using an articulatory model," in *Speech production and speech modelling*, W. J. Hardcastle and A. Marchal, Eds. Kluwer Academic Publishers, Boston, 1990, pp. 131–149.

[217] Y. Payan and P. Perrier, "Synthesis of V-V sequences with a 2d biomechanical tongue model controlled by the equilibrium point hypothesis," *Speech Communication*, vol. 22, pp. 185–205, 1997.

[218] J. Stark, C. Ericsdotter, P. Branderud, J. Sundberg, H.-J. Lundberg, and J. Lander, "The APEX model as a tool in the specification of speaker-specific articulatory behavior," in *Proc. of the 14th International Congress of Phonetic Sciences*, San Francisco, CA, USA, 1999, pp. 2279–2282.

[219] P. Badin, G. Bailly, L. Revéret, M. Baciu, C. Segebarth, and C. Savariaux, "Three-dimensional linear articulatory modeling of tongue, lips and face, based on MRI and video images," *Journal of Phonetics*, vol. 30, pp. 533–553, 2002.

[220] O. Engwall, “Combining MRI, EMA and EPG measurements in a three-dimensional tongue model,” *Speech Communication*, vol. 41, pp. 303–329, 2003.

[221] J. Dang and K. Honda, “Construction and control of a physiological articulatory model,” *Journal of the Acoustical Society of America*, vol. 115, no. 2, pp. 853–870, 2004.

[222] K. van den Doel, F. Vogt, R. E. English, and S. Fels, “Towards articulatory speech synthesis with a dynamic 3d finite element tongue model,” in *7th International Seminar on Speech Production (ISSP)*, Ubatuba, Brazil, 2006.

[223] P. Birkholz, D. Jackèl, and B. J. Kröger, “Construction and control of a three-dimensional vocal tract model,” in *IEEE International Conference on Acoustics Speech and Signal Processing Proceedings (ICASSP)*, vol. I. Toulouse, France: IEEE, 2006, pp. 873–876.

[224] P. Birkholz and D. Pape, “How modeling entrance loss and flow separation in a two-mass model affects the oscillation and synthesis quality,” *Speech Communication*, vol. 110, pp. 108–116, 2019.

[225] S. E. G. Öhman, “Numerical model of coarticulation,” *Journal of the Acoustical Society of America*, vol. 41, no. 2, pp. 310–320, 1967.

[226] P. Birkholz and B. J. Kröger, “Vocal tract model adaptation using magnetic resonance imaging,” in *7th International Seminar on Speech Production (ISSP)*, Ubatuba, Brazil, 2006, pp. 493–500.

[227] P. Birkholz and D. Jackel, “Influence of temporal discretization schemes on formant frequencies and bandwidths in time domain simulations of the vocal tract system.” in *Proc. of the Interspeech*, Jeju, Korea, 2004, pp. 1125–1128.

[228] P. Birkholz, “Control of an articulatory speech synthesizer based on dynamic approximation of spatial articulatory targets,” in *Proc. of the Eurospeech*, Antwerp, Belgium, 2007, pp. 2865–2868.

[229] S. Prom-on, Y. Xu, and B. Thipakorn, “Modeling tone and intonation in Mandarin and English as a process of target approximation,” *Journal of the Acoustical Society of America*, vol. 125, no. 1, pp. 405–424, 2009.

[230] J. A. Marwitz, S. Stone, and P. Birkholz, “Optimierung der Numerik eines linearen Gleichungssystems für die Simulation des Schallfeldes im Vokaltrakt,” *Studientexte zur Sprachkommunikation: Elektronische Sprachsignalverarbeitung 2018*, pp. 359–366, 2018.

[231] T. Chiba and M. Kajiyama, *The vowel: Its nature and structure*. Setagaya, Tokyo: Phonetic Society of Japan, 1958.

[232] G. Fant, *Acoustic theory of speech production: with calculations based on X-ray studies of Russian articulations*. Walter de Gruyter, 1971, vol. 2.

[233] J. Woo, J. Lee, E. Z. Murano, F. Xing, M. Al-Talib, M. Stone, and J. L. Prince, “A high-resolution atlas and statistical model of the vocal tract from structural MRI,” *Computer Methods in Biomechanics and Biomedical Engineering: Imaging & Visualization*, vol. 3, no. 1, pp. 47–60, 2015.

[234] S. Narayanan, K. Nayak, S. Lee, A. Sethy, and D. Byrd, “An approach to real-time magnetic resonance imaging for speech production,” *The Journal of the Acoustical Society of America*, vol. 115, no. 4, pp. 1771–1776, 2004.

[235] A. Niebergall, S. Zhang, E. Kunay, G. Keydana, M. Job, M. Uecker, and J. Frahm, “Real-time MRI of speaking at a resolution of 33 ms: Undersampled radial FLASH with nonlinear inverse reconstruction,” *Magnetic Resonance in Medicine*, vol. 69, no. 2, pp. 477–485, 2013.

[236] M. Fu, B. Zhao, C. Carignan, R. K. Shosted, J. L. Perry, D. P. Kuehn, Z.-P. Liang, and B. P. Sutton, “High-resolution dynamic speech imaging with joint low-rank and sparsity constraints,” *Magnetic Resonance in Medicine*, vol. 73, no. 5, pp. 1820–1832, 2015.

[237] O. Engwall, "Vocal tract modeling in 3D," *TMH-QPSR*, vol. 1, pp. 1–8, 1999.

[238] ——, "Synthesizing static vowels and dynamic sounds using a 3d vocal tract model," in *4th ISCA Tutorial and Research Workshop (ITRW) on Speech Synthesis*, 2001.

[239] D. Aalto, O. Aaltonen, R.-P. Happonen, P. Jääsaari, A. Kivelä, J. Kuortti, J.-M. Luukinen, J. Malinen, T. Murtola, R. Parkkola, J. Saunavaara, T. Soukka, and M. Vainio, "Large scale data acquisition of simultaneous MRI and speech," *Applied Acoustics*, vol. 83, pp. 64–75, 2014.

[240] P. Badin, G. Bailly, M. Raybaudi, and C. Segebarth, "A three-dimensional linear articulatory model based on MRI data," in *The Third ESCA/COCOSDA Workshop (ETRW) on Speech Synthesis*, 1998.

[241] S. Fels, F. Vogt, K. Van Den Doel, J. Lloyd, I. Stavness, and E. Vatikiotis-Bateson, "Artisynth: A biomechanical simulation platform for the vocal tract and upper airway," in *Proc. of the 7th International Seminar on Speech Production*, Ubatuba, Brazil, 2006.

[242] A. J. Teixeira, R. Martinez, L. N. Silva, L. M. Jesus, J. C. Príncipe, and F. A. Vaz, "Simulation of human speech production applied to the study and synthesis of European Portuguese," *EURASIP Journal on Applied Signal Processing*, vol. 2005, pp. 1435–1448, 2005.

[243] S. E. Öhman, "Coarticulation in VCV utterances: Spectrographic measurements," *The Journal of the Acoustical Society of America*, vol. 39, no. 1, pp. 151–168, 1966.

[244] ——, "Numerical model of coarticulation," *The Journal of the Acoustical Society of America*, vol. 41, no. 2, pp. 310–320, 1967.

[245] R. Blandin, M. Arnela, R. Laboissière, X. Pelorson, O. Guasch, A. V. Hirtum, and X. Laval, "Effects of higher order propagation modes in vocal tract like geometries," *The Journal of the Acoustical Society of America*, vol. 137, no. 2, pp. 832–843, 2015.

[246] M. Arnela, S. Dabbaghchian, R. Blandin, O. Guasch, O. Engwall, A. Van Hirtum, and X. Pelorson, "Influence of vocal tract geometry simplifications on the numerical simulation of vowel sounds," *The Journal of the Acoustical Society of America*, vol. 140, no. 3, pp. 1707–1718, 2016.

[247] P. Meyer, R. Wilhelms, and H. W. Strube, "A quasiarticulatory speech synthesizer for German language running in real time," *The Journal of the Acoustical Society of America*, vol. 86, no. 2, pp. 523–539, 1989.

[248] G. Fant, "Vocal tract area functions of Swedish vowels and a new three-parameter model," in *Second International Conference on Spoken Language Processing*, 1992.

[249] G. Fant and M. Båvegård, "Parametric model of VT area functions: vowels and consonants," *Speech Music Hearing*, vol. 38, no. 1, pp. 1–20, 1997.

[250] M. Båvegård, "Introducing a parametric consonantal model to the articulatory speech synthesizer," in *Proc. of the Eurospeech*, Madrid, Spain, 1995, pp. 1857–1860.

[251] H. L. Fitch, J. J. Kupin, I. J. Kessler, and J. DeLucia, "Relating articulation and acoustics through a sinusoidal description of vocal tract shape," *Speech Communication*, vol. 39, no. 3-4, pp. 243–268, 2003.

[252] P. Ru, T. Chi, and S. Shamma, "The synergy between speech production and perception," *The Journal of the Acoustical Society of America*, vol. 113, no. 1, pp. 498–515, 2003.

[253] R. Harshman, P. Ladefoged, and L. Goldstein, "Factor analysis of tongue shapes," *The Journal of the Acoustical Society of America*, vol. 62, no. 3, pp. 693–707, 1977.

[254] B. H. Story and I. R. Titze, "Parameterization of vocal tract area functions by empirical orthogonal modes," *Journal of Phonetics*, vol. 26, no. 3, pp. 223–260, 1998.

[255] B. H. Story, "A parametric model of the vocal tract area function for vowel and consonant simulation," *The Journal of the Acoustical Society of America*, vol. 117, no. 5, pp. 3231–3254, 2005.

[256] K. Bunton and B. H. Story, "Identification of synthetic vowels based on selected vocal tract area functions," *The Journal of the Acoustical Society of America*, vol. 125, no. 1, pp. 19–22, 2009.

[257] ——, "Identification of synthetic vowels based on a time-varying model of the vocal tract area function," *The Journal of the Acoustical Society of America*, vol. 127, no. 4, pp. EL146–EL152, 2010.

[258] B. H. Story and K. Bunton, "Relation of vocal tract shape, formant transitions, and stop consonant identification," *Journal of Speech, Language, and Hearing Research*, vol. 53, no. 6, pp. 1514–1528, 2010.

[259] J. L. Flanagan, K. Ishizaka, and K. Shipley, "Signal models for low bit-rate coding of speech," *The Journal of the Acoustical Society of America*, vol. 68, no. 3, pp. 780–791, 1980.

[260] D. Wei, J. Devaney, and C. C. Goodyear, "Voiced diphone synthesis using a parametric model and formant based mapping," in *Proc. of the Eurospeech*, 1995, pp. 1841–1844.

[261] P. Birkholz, B. J. Kröger, and C. Neuschaefer-Rube, "Model-based reproduction of articulatory trajectories for consonant-vowel sequences," *IEEE Transactions on Audio, Speech and Language Processing*, vol. 19, no. 5, pp. 1422–1433, 2011.

[262] P. Birkholz, "Enhanced area functions for noise source modeling in the vocal tract," in *Proc. of the 10th International Seminar on Speech Production (ISSP)*, Cologne, Germany, 2014, pp. 32–40.

[263] L. Traser, P. Birkholz, T. V. Flügge, R. Kamberger, M. Burdumy, B. Richter, J. G. Korvink, and M. Echternach, "Relevance of the implementation of teeth in three-dimensional vocal tract models," *Journal of Speech, Language, and Hearing Research*, vol. 60, no. 9, pp. 2379–2393, 2017.

[264] P. Cignoni, M. Callieri, M. Corsini, M. Dellepiane, F. Ganovelli, and G. Ranzuglia, "MeshLab: an Open-Source Mesh Processing Tool," in *Eurographics Italian Chapter Conference*, V. Scarano, R. D. Chiara, and U. Erra, Eds. The Eurographics Association, 2008.

[265] P. A. Yushkevich, J. Piven, H. Cody Hazlett, R. Gimpel Smith, S. Ho, J. C. Gee, and G. Gerig, "User-guided 3D active contour segmentation of anatomical structures: Significantly improved efficiency and reliability," *Neuroimage*, vol. 31, no. 3, pp. 1116–1128, 2006.

[266] M. Echternach, P. Birkholz, L. Traser, T. V. Flügge, R. Kamberger, F. Burk, M. Burdumy, and B. Richter, "Articulation and vocal tract acoustics at soprano subject's high fundamental frequencies," *The Journal of the Acoustical Society of America*, vol. 137, no. 5, pp. 2586–2595, 2015.

[267] P. Birkholz and E. Venus, "Considering lip geometry in one-dimensional tube models of the vocal tract," in *Proc. of the 11th International Seminar on Speech Production*, Tianjin, China, 2017, pp. 78–86.

[268] P. Birkholz, S. Kürbis, S. Stone, P. Häsner, R. Blandin, and M. Fleischer, "Printable 3D vocal tract shapes from MRI data and their acoustic and aerodynamic properties," *Scientific Data*, vol. 7, no. 1, pp. 1–16, 2020.

[269] J. A. Nelder and R. A. Mead, "A simplex method for function minimization," *Computer Journal*, vol. 7, pp. 308–313, 1965.

[270] M. Stone, G. Stock, K. Bunin, K. Kumar, M. Epstein, C. Kambhamettu, M. Li, V. Parthasarathy, and J. Prince, "Comparison of speech production in upright and supine position," *The Journal of the Acoustical Society of America*, vol. 122, no. 1, pp. 532–541, 2007.

[271] W. F. Sendlmeier and J. Seebode, "Formantkarten des deutschen Vokalsystems," https://www.kw.tu-berlin.de/fileadmin/a01311100/Formantkarten_des_deutschen_Vokalsystems_01.pdf, 2006, [Online; accessed Aug 8, 2017].

[272] P. Birkholz, D. Jackèl, and B. J. Kröger, "Simulation of losses due to turbulence in the time-varying vocal system," *IEEE Transactions on Audio, Speech, and Language Processing*, vol. 15, no. 4, pp. 1218–1226, 2007.

[273] P. Birkholz, B. J. Kröger, and C. Neuschaefer-Rube, "Synthesis of breathy, normal, and pressed phonation using a two-mass model with a triangular glottis," in *Proc. of the Interspeech*, Florence, Italy, 2011, pp. 2681–2684.

[274] L. Lisker and A. S. Abramson, "A cross-language study of voicing in initial stops: Acoustical measurements," *Word*, vol. 20, no. 3, pp. 384–422, 1964.

[275] D. H. Klatt, "Voice onset time, frication, and aspiration in word-initial consonant clusters," *Journal of Speech, Language, and Hearing Research*, vol. 18, no. 4, pp. 686–706, 1975.

[276] B. W. Schuller, "Speech emotion recognition: Two decades in a nutshell, benchmarks, and ongoing trends," *Communications of the ACM*, vol. 61, no. 5, pp. 90–99, 2018.

[277] M. Schröder, "Expressive speech synthesis: Past, present, and possible futures," in *Affective information processing*. Springer, 2009, pp. 111–126.

[278] "Arbeitsberichte (AIPUK)," K. Kohler, Ed. Kiel, Germany: Institut für Phonetik und digitale Sprachverarbeitung, Universität Kiel, 1996.

[279] S. Stone, K. Schulze, P. Steiner, and P. Birkholz, "Real-time manipulation of the F0-contour in synthetic speech using the Fujisaki model," *Studientexte zur Sprachkommunikation: Elektronische Sprachsignalverarbeitung 2017*, pp. 278–285, 2017.

[280] S. Stone, P. Schmidt, and P. Birkholz, "Prediction of voicing and the F0 contour from electromagnetic articulography data for Articulation-to-Speech synthesis," in *IEEE International Conference on Acoustics, Speech and Signal Processing (ICASSP)*. IEEE, 2020, pp. 7329–7333.

[281] J. Snedeker and J. Trueswell, "Using prosody to avoid ambiguity: Effects of speaker awareness and referential context," *Journal of Memory and Language*, vol. 48, no. 1, pp. 103–130, 2003.

[282] A. Cutler, D. Dahan, and W. Van Donselaar, "Prosody in the comprehension of spoken language: A literature review," *Language and Speech*, vol. 40, no. 2, pp. 141–201, 1997.

[283] K. R. Scherer, R. Banse, H. G. Wallbott, and T. Goldbeck, "Vocal cues in emotion encoding and decoding," *Motivation and emotion*, vol. 15, no. 2, pp. 123–148, 1991.

[284] M. D. Pell, "Influence of emotion and focus location on prosody in matched statements and questions," *The Journal of the Acoustical Society of America*, vol. 109, no. 4, pp. 1668–1680, 2001.

[285] M. Schröder and J. Trouvain, "The German text-to-speech synthesis system MARY: A tool for research, development and teaching," *International Journal of Speech Technology*, vol. 6, no. 4, pp. 365–377, 2003.

[286] M. Grice, S. Baumann, and R. Benzmüller, "German Intonation in Autosegmental-Metrical Phonology," *Prosodic typology: The phonology of intonation and phrasing*, vol. 1, p. 55, 2006.

[287] L. Feugère, S. Le Beux, and C. d'Alessandro, "Chorus digitalis: polyphonic gestural singing," in *1st International Workshop on Performative Speech and Singing Synthesis (P3S 2011), Vancouver (Canada)*, vol. 14, no. 03, 2011.

[288] P. Taylor, "The Tilt intonation model," in *Proc. of the 5th International Conference on Spoken Language Processing (ICSLP)*. International Speech Communication Association, 1998, p. 0827.

[289] C. X. Xu, Y. Xu, and L.-S. Luo, "A pitch target approximation model for F0 contours in Mandarin," in *Proc. of the 14th International congress of Phonetic Sciences*, 1999, pp. 2359–2362.

[290] Y. Xu and Q. E. Wang, "Pitch targets and their realization: Evidence from Mandarin Chinese," *Speech communication*, vol. 33, no. 4, pp. 319–337, 2001.

[291] H. Fujisaki, "A model for synthesis of pitch contours of connected speech," *Annual Report, Engineering Research Institute, University of Tokyo*, vol. 28, pp. 53–60, 1969.

[292] ——, "Information, Prosody, and Modeling - with Emphasis on Tonal Features of Speech," in *Speech Prosody*. International Speech Communication Association, 2004, pp. 1–10.

[293] K. Schulze, "Der Stimmdirigent - Hand- und Armgestengesteuerte F0-Manipulation," Institute of Acoustics and Speech Communication, Technische Universität Dresden, Germany, Juni 2016, unpublished student's thesis.

[294] D. Bock, B. Ganswindt, H. Girnth, S. Kasper, R. Kehrein, A. Lameli, S. Messner, C. Purschke, and A. Wolanska, *Regionalsprache.de (REDE). Forschungsplattform zu den modernen Regionalsprachen des Deutschen*, J. E. Schmidt, J. Herrgen, and R. Kehrein, Eds. Marburg: Forschungszentrum Deutscher Sprachatlas, 2008 ff.

[295] K. Nakamura, M. Janke, M. Wand, and T. Schultz, "Estimation of fundamental frequency from surface electromyographic data: EMG-to-F0," in *IEEE International Conference on Acoustics, Speech and Signal Processing (ICASSP)*, Prague, Czech Republic, 2011, pp. 573–576.

[296] C. Zhao, L. Wang, J. Dang, and R. Yu, "Prediction of F0 based on articulatory features using DNN," in *11th International Seminar on Speech Production (ISSP)*, Tianjin, China, 2017, pp. 58–67.

[297] T. Grósz, G. Gosztolya, L. Tóth, T. G. Csapó, and A. Markó, "F0 estimation for DNN-based ultrasound silent speech interfaces," in *IEEE International Conference on Acoustics, Speech and Signal Processing (ICASSP)*. IEEE, 2018, pp. 291–295.

[298] B. Cao, M. Kim, J. R. Wang, J. van Santen, T. Mau, and J. Wang, "Articulation-to-speech synthesis using articulatory flesh point sensors' orientation information," in *Proc. of the Interspeech*, Hyderabad, India, 2018, pp. 3152–3156.

[299] F. Ahmadi and T. Toda, "Designing a pneumatic bionic voice prosthesis - a statistical approach for source excitation generation," in *Proc. of the Interspeech*, 2018, pp. 3142–3146.

[300] B. Schnell and P. N. Garner, "A neural model to predict parameters for a generalized command response model of intonation," in *Proc. of the Interspeech*, Hyderabad, India, 2018, pp. 3147–3151.

[301] K. Richmond, P. Hoole, and S. King, "Announcing the electromagnetic articulography (day 1) subset of the mngu0 articulatory corpus," in *Proc. of the Interspeech*, Florence, Italy, 2011, pp. 1505–1508.

[302] P. Schmidt, "Vorhersage der Grundfrequenz aus artikulatorischen Daten für die direkte Sprachsynthese," Institute of Acoustics and Speech Communication, Technische Universität Dresden, Germany, August 2018, unpublished diploma thesis.

[303] D. E. King, "Dlib-ml: A machine learning toolkit," *Journal of Machine Learning Research*, vol. 10, pp. 1755–1758, 2009.

[304] V. Nair and G. E. Hinton, "Rectified linear units improve Restricted Boltzmann Machines," in *Proc. of the 27th International Conference on Machine Learning (ICML-10)*, Haifa, Israel, 2010, pp. 807–814.

[305] K. Gorman and S. Bedrick, "We need to talk about standard splits," in *Proc. of the 57th Annual Meeting of the Association for Computational Linguistics*. Florence, Italy: Association for Computational Linguistics, July 2019, pp. 2786–2791.

[306] C. Cavé, I. Guaïtella, R. Bertrand, S. Santi, F. Harlay, and R. Espesser, "About the relationship between eyebrow movements and fo variations," in *Proc. of the 4th International Conference on Spoken Language Processing (ICSLP 1996)*, vol. 4. IEEE, 1996, pp. 2175–2178.

[307] W. van Drongelen, "4 - Signal Averaging," in *Signal Processing for Neuroscientists*, W. van Drongelen, Ed. London, UK: Academic Press, 2007, pp. 55 – 70.

[308] W.-E. Büttner, *Grundlagen der Elektrotechnik 1*. Munich, Germany: Oldenbourg Wissenschaftsverlag GmbH, 2011, p. 23.

[309] J. L. Flanagan and L. R. Rabiner, Eds., *Speech Synthesis*. Stroudsberg, PA: Dowden, Hutchinson and Ross, 1973.